Historical Abuse
Systemic Review

ISBN 978-0-7559-5613-5

The Scottish Government
St Andrew's House
Edinburgh
EH1 3DG

Produced for the Scottish Government by RR Donnelley B53270 11-07

Published by the Scottish Government, November, 2007

Further copies are available from
Blackwell's Bookshop
53 South Bridge
Edinburgh
EH1 1YS

The text pages of this document are printed on recycled paper and are 100% recyclable

Contents

Foreword

Children are the most valuable and yet the most vulnerable group in society.

It is our responsibility to respect them, to care for them, to protect them, to acknowledge and respond to their needs and rights.

Abuse of children – however it is defined, whenever it occurs, whoever is responsible – must not be tolerated. It is self-indulgence in its ugliest form. When it occurs where children are placed for protection, it is even more despicable.

Those who experienced abuse in the past need to be heard; they need to know that society supports them in speaking out and that their experiences, however distressing, are recognised and addressed.

We all have a need and a right to know about our past, our childhood, our family circumstances, our home – wherever or whatever that was for each of us. Our sense of identity is based on this knowledge.

There are many challenges to finding out about our past and the process is even more daunting when those past experiences were bad. The reaction to our search can be cynical rather than constructive; the need to know can be viewed with insensitivity rather than with respect. The past is sometimes dismissed as over and done with: yet another unacceptable response.

As a society we need to learn from the past, to recognise the good and to understand how to prevent the bad. Learning from our mistakes is a sign of maturity, an indication that we want to do better and, in the context of this review, to do so for all who were or are children in the care of the state.

Abuse of children occurs throughout the world; it is a concern in many countries. It is a focus of the work of the United Nations. We can learn much from the experiences of other countries about how to identify abuse, how to respond to those who have been abused and how to prevent abuse. And we should do so now.

An apology, an essential part of any response to mistakes or failure, is but the beginning, not the end, of the process of addressing wrongs. The process needs to involve us all as we strive to meet the needs and entitlements of those whose cries for help were ignored in the past.

There can be no guarantee that abuse will never happen again – but we have a responsibility to do everything in our power to prevent it. This review is a contribution to meeting that objective.

Summary

This report is the direct outcome of a debate in the Scottish Parliament on 1st December 2004. The debate was on a motion on behalf of the Public Petitions Committee, seeking an inquiry into past institutional child abuse. It was the first time the Committee had secured such a debate.

The then Minister for Education and Young People, Peter Peacock, announced his intention to appoint someone with experience to analyse independently the laws, rules and regulations that governed children's residential establishments, how these were monitored and how they worked in practice.

This summary has the following sections:

1. Who carried out the review
2. What the review is – and isn't – about
3. What the review was asked to do
4. What we did
5. What the review found
6. What the review recommends

1. Who carried out the review

The Scottish Parliament appointed me, Tom Shaw, as Independent Expert to lead the review. I am the former Chief Inspector of Education and Training in Northern Ireland. I was assisted by researcher Nancy Bell and legal researcher Roddy Hart.

2. What the review is – and isn't – about

This is a systemic review: it's about systems – the systems of laws, rules and regulations (the regulatory framework) that governed residential schools and children's homes. It's about how these schools and homes complied with the regulatory framework, and about the systems for monitoring and inspecting the schools and homes.

It's **not** about individuals, individual institutions or organisations. I established a confidentiality policy from the outset. The report does not name individuals or organisations with whom I've had contact as part of the review.

And, as my remit specified, I am not reporting on the facts or circumstances of individual cases of abuse.

3. What the review was asked to do

The remit was to carry out an investigation against the background of abuse suffered by children in residential schools and children's homes in Scotland between 1950 and 1995. I could, if necessary, consider materials from outwith these periods if I felt these would be relevant.

I was to consider:
- the laws, rules, regulations and powers that governed how these schools were run, regulated and inspected;
- what systems were in place to make sure these laws, rules, regulations and powers were followed; and
- how these systems worked in practice.

To do this I would:
- have access to government records; and
- be expected to seek the co-operation of local authorities and other organisations that ran children's residential schools and homes.

I was not permitted to:
- report on the facts or circumstances of any individual cases of abuse; or
- take submissions from individuals.

I felt it was essential to talk to the people who had lived and worked in children's residential schools and homes. So I later sought, and received, permission to meet and receive information from individuals.

4. What the review did

The review used questionnaires and a survey to seek information from organisations – including local authorities and religious and voluntary organisations – and archivists.

The review received information from former residents, in interviews, telephone calls, emails, correspondence and from cuttings, video tapes and DVDs that former residents sent to us.

My researcher and I interviewed people who had worked in services involved with child care services.

My researcher and I reviewed files held in the National Archives of Scotland and the Scottish Executive Education Department and my researcher reviewed files in other archives held in various locations in Scotland and England.

I sought expert advice on aspects of the legal framework and commissioned two specialist reviews. My researcher and I focused on abuse in children's residential establishments and the other considered how society's attitudes to children and social policies have changed during the period of my review.

I established an advisory group of people drawn from backgrounds relevant to the review. My researcher and I examined previous reviews and inquiries.

5. What the review found

Looking back over a long period of time poses difficulties, not least the risk of imposing 21st century perspectives on what people did in the past. Research material about children's lives in Scotland and about

their experiences in residential childcare is scarce. Attitudes to children have changed gradually but only in the last 10 years or so in Scotland has there been full acknowledgement in law of children's rights.

Attitudes to punishment have been inconsistent. Although evidence indicates that abuse of children was known about throughout the review period, public awareness didn't develop until the 1980s.

Throughout the period there was a lack of qualified care staff, perhaps a symptom of the low status given to residential child care.

The law didn't provide adequately for talking and listening to children and taking their views into account until the end of the review period.

The law in place during the first half of the review period didn't ensure that children's residential care services responded sufficiently to the needs of the children requiring the services..

The law responded slowly to growing awareness of the abuse of children across the review period and to strengthening the protection of children in residential establishments and children's homes. Corporal punishment was permitted in residential establishments into the 1980s despite concerns expressed about abuse in residential child care. And the law did not require inter-agency working and sharing information as an aid to protecting children until after the review period.

Accountability for children's welfare and safety were weakened by the law's lack of insistence that children's residential care staff should be suitably qualified, by the lack of a national vetting system for residential care staff and by the lack of national care standards.

Monitoring and inspection requirements were subject to a considerable degree of interpretation across much of the review period. In the absence of national standards of care, consistency in the expectations and assessment of residential schools and children's homes could not be assured.

The law specified in varying degrees of detail what should be monitored and inspected in residential schools and children's homes to ensure the children's welfare and safety. Visits by various people, professional and lay, and records were the main approaches for monitoring and inspection mentioned in the legislation and some visits were to take place at specified intervals. However, the law did not provide for independence in monitoring and inspection, nor did it require public accountability for inspection until late in the 1980s. As there were no national standards for care, assessments of the welfare and safety of the children by visitors and inspectors could be inconsistent. And the vagueness of requirements for children to have the opportunity to talk to visitors could have limited the possibility of children expressing concerns about their safety. Although there is evidence in files in NAS of government inspectors talking to children during their visits, the action taken was at the inspectors' initiative and may not have been seen by the children as an opportunity for them to speak about any concerns. The lack of requirement for co-operation and sharing of information amongst professionals, may have inhibited valuable exchanges and limited the potential of the information for protecting children.

Identifying how residential schools and children's homes were monitored and inspected in practice – as opposed to what the laws said **should** be done – has proved very difficult. The search for information was affected by people's knowledge of what records existed, where they were located and what they contained. When people left or retired from organisations, they often took with them significant knowledge about records and past practices. Records were scattered across organisations, archives and even countries. Some records are now being examined; others sit in boxes on shelves with little or no hint of what they contain; others were destroyed.

Potentially important information about practice in inspection was lost because, as practice changed and new guidance issued, previous guidance papers were destroyed.

Finding even basic information often proved challenging

and time-consuming. No central government databases exist of children's residential establishments in Scotland between 1950-1995 or which organisations were involved in providing these services – let alone what records are associated with which services and where these might be. Hundreds of children's residential services existed in Scotland and across the review period they changed function, location, management or closed down.

The review met a number of obstacles in its search for information:
■ Some potentially significant records in archives were closed
■ There was no legal requirement for local authorities and organisations to help by giving access to information. Some were helpful; some were less so.
■ Local authorities, organisations and government departments were to provide the review with "relevant" records, but determining what was "relevant" proved difficult, confusing and time-consuming.

In general, the review's experience in seeking information reflected some of the difficulties that former residents described in their search for information about their experiences in residential schools and children's homes. Indeed many of them had found little of significance – or nothing at all – after years of trying.

And yet, many valuable records exist and could add significantly to our understanding of practices in residential child care in the past. These records need to be assembled, catalogued and made available for research and investigation.

Former residents have a key role in contributing to our understanding of past residential child care. The experiences of those I met deepened my understanding of the importance of listening to, respecting and treating children with dignity.

The lessons learned from this review focus on **former residents**, who have many needs arising from their experience in residential child care. These include:

- support services such as counselling;
- easy access to records can provide them with information about their childhood lives; and
- having a say in the services provided to meet their needs.

There is extensive experience in other countries of responding to and meeting the needs of those who have been abused when in children's residential establishments. There is much to learn from that experience in planning the way forward in Scotland, not least in finding ways of accommodating and meeting needs that are not adversarial or disrespectful.

This review's lessons also focus on **children today,** specifically on what are now termed looked-after children and accommodated children. All the former residents who contributed to the review wanted to do all they could to ensure that children in residential establishments today don't experience the kind of abuse that they endured and survived.

Having investigated the regulatory provisions for residential schools and children's homes in the past, it's clear to me that, despite extensive and complex regulation, the requirements weren't wholly effective in ensuring children's welfare and safety. Twelve years on from 1995 new legislation and new approaches to safeguarding children in residential establishments are in place. Monitoring and inspection have been developed to give greater attention to child welfare and safety. In some respects you could say that everything that was identified as needing to be done in 1995 is now in place. And yet, the same problems are occurring, the same needs exist and the concerns that motivated government to legislate in 1995 still exist.

6. What the review recommends

I have grouped recommendations into three areas:

a) Current provision to ensure the welfare and safety of looked-after and accommodated children

b) Former residents' needs

c) Records

a) Current provision to ensure the welfare and safety of looked-after and accommodated children

I believe there is a need to:

- develop a culture in residential child care founded on children's rights;
- raise respect for children in the care of the state;
- raise the status of residential childcare;
- raise the status of those working in residential child care;
- evaluate the fitness for purpose of new policy, new legislation, new structures, new ways of working and new ways of monitoring and inspecting the services provided for children in residential care of all kinds; and
- keep the services provided to children, and practice in these services, under continuous review.

1. I therefore recommend that a National Task Group should be established with oversight of services provided for looked-after and accommodated children. The Task Group should report to the Education, Lifelong Learning and Culture Committee of the Scottish Parliament. The Task Group should be asked to:

i.   audit annually the outcomes (those agreed through the Government's Vision for Children and Young People) for looked-after and accommodated children and report on the findings;

ii. audit the recommendations of previous reviews and inquiries to determine what action is outstanding and why;

iii. review the adequacy and effectiveness of the arrangements, including advocacy support, in place for children who wish to complain about the services they receive;

iv. monitor the progress in meeting the target of a fully qualified complement of staff in residential child care services, including the identification of barriers to reaching this target, and ways of overcoming them;

v.   audit the quality and appropriateness of training

and development for those employed in residential childcare;

vi. identify ways of making employment in residential child care a desirable career option;

vii. identify and disseminate best practice in recruitment and selection of staff in residential child care;

viii. ensure that monitoring and inspection focus on those aspects of provision and practice that will help to keep children safe and enable them to achieve their potential;

ix. monitor the extent to which self-evaluation is becoming established practice in residential schools and children's homes;

x. identify the most effective ways, through research and inspection findings and drawing on Scottish and international experience, of ensuring children's welfare and safety in residential establishments;

xi. review the quality and standards of accommodation for residential establishments and recommend improvements as necessary; and

xii. make recommendations for research and development.

b) Former residents' needs

2. The government in partnership with local and voluntary authorities should establish a centre, based on an existing agency if appropriate, with a role that might include:

- supporting former residents in accessing advocacy, mediation and counselling services.
- conducting research into children's residential services, including oral histories;
- maintaining a resource centre with information about historical children's residential services in general;
- maintaining a database of all past and present children's residential establishments in Scotland
- developing and maintaining an index for locations where children's residential services records are held

c) Records

The lessons of this review point to an urgent need to take action to preserve historical records, ensure that residents can get access to records and information about their location.

3. The government should commission a review of public records legislation which should lead to new legislation being drafted to meet records and information needs in Scotland. This should also make certain that no legislation impedes people's lawful access to records. This review's objectives should address the need for permanent preservation of significant records held by private, non-statutory agencies that provide publicly funded services to children.

4. All local authorities and publicly funded organisations with responsibility for past and present children's services should undertake to use the Section 61 Code of Practice on Records Management issued on behalf of Scottish Ministers and in consultation with the Scottish Information Commissioner and the Keeper of the Records of Scotland under the terms of the Freedom of Information Scotland Act 2002[1].

5. Training in professional records management practice and procedures should be available to all organisations and local authorities providing children's services. This might be provided by NAS or the Scottish Information Commissioner.

6. The government should invite NAS to establish a national records working group to address issues specific to children's historical residential services records. Appendix 4 of my report contains suggested representation and terms of reference.

7. Voluntary organisations, religious organisations and local authorities, working in partnership, should commission guidance to ensure that their children's residential services records are adequately catalogued to make records readily accessible.

8. Record management practices should be evaluated regularly where records associated with children's residential establishments are held, particularly records associated with monitoring children's welfare and safety. I recommend that the Care Commission should consider taking responsibility for this.

Introduction

This introduction has the following sections:

1. The background to this review
2. Who carried out the review
3. What the review is – and isn't – about
4. What the review was asked to do
5. How I interpreted the remit
6. The extent of the task
7. How we researched the review
8. Contributions to the review

1. The background to this review

This report is the direct outcome of a debate held in the Scottish Parliament on 1st December 2004. The debate was on a motion on behalf of the Public Petitions Committee, seeking an inquiry into past institutional child abuse. It was the first time the Committee had secured such a debate.

Preceding the debate, the then First Minister Jack McConnell stated:

> "Children suffered physical, emotional and sexual abuse in the very places in which they hoped to find love, care and protection... Such abuse of vulnerable young people – whenever or wherever it took place – is deplorable, unacceptable and inexcusable"

During the debate the then Minister for Education and Young People, Peter Peacock, said that the "Executive's policy is not about closing the book, but about opening a new chapter". Recognising that one issue for survivors was why the abuse "was – as they would put it – allowed to happen", and noting that "understanding why is not reasonable only for survivors, but for the wider society", he promised to take the issue forward.

His pledge, then, was the genesis of this report:

> "I intend to appoint someone with experience to analyse independently the regulatory requirements of the time, the systems that were in place to monitor operation of those requirements and, in general, to analyse how that monitoring was carried out in practice."

2. Who carried out the review

The Scottish Parliament appointed me, Tom Shaw, as Independent Expert to lead the review. I am the former Chief Inspector of Education and Training in Northern Ireland. I was assisted by researcher Nancy Bell and legal researcher Roddy Hart.

3. What the review is – and isn't – about

This is a systemic review: it's about systems – the systems of laws, rules and regulations (the regulatory framework) that governed residential schools and children's homes. It's about how these schools and homes complied with the regulatory framework, and about the systems for monitoring and inspecting the schools and homes.

From the outset there have been high expectations of what the review could deliver and strong views about what it should focus on. I've received some expressions of dissatisfaction from former residents about the terms of the remit. I and my researcher have had to explain many times to people inquiring about the review that our work is determined by the remit and that the focus is on systems, not on individuals or on individual institutions or organisations.

Many of those who contributed to the review felt that tracing appropriate information that would help to describe and evaluate practice in monitoring and inspection in the past would be an extremely difficult, if not impossible task, especially for the first half of the period spanned by the review. As chapter 5 indicates, there are many obstacles to be overcome in identifying potentially relevant sources of information, and in locating and accessing them. It also became clear as the review progressed that information about previous practice was generally not retained once changes in practice were introduced. There was, it would seem, a general concern to avoid the risk of confusing new and former practice, so papers relating to what had gone before were disposed of. For example, national inspectorates appear not to have had a policy for retaining this kind of information at any time during the period spanned by the review. In these circumstances, the process of assessing the effectiveness of past practice is problematic. Adding to the challenge is the lack of research into methods and the effectiveness of monitoring and inspection throughout the 45 years of the review period.

I established a confidentiality policy from the outset. Respecting this, I will not be naming in my report individuals or organisations with whom I've had contact as part of the review. Where the report draws from an individual's memories, an initial has been used, not a name. The report does occasionally name an individual where it refers – for example to set the context for the review – to reports of inquiries or reviews that focus on individuals outwith Scotland. This is a means of providing a time-line for events and developments.

As specified in my remit, I am not reporting on the facts or circumstances of individual cases of abuse.

4. What the review was asked to do

I was given the following remit:
1. "Against the background of the abuse suffered by children up to the age of 16 in residential schools and children's homes in Scotland over the period from 1950 to 1995 the Independent Expert is instructed to carry out an investigation and, as soon as may be practicable, to present a report for consideration and for publication by Scottish Ministers with the following objectives:

    i. to identify what regulatory requirements and powers were in place from time to time over that period and which provided for the provision, regulation and inspection of such schools and homes and for the welfare and protection from abuse of children resident in them;

    ii. to identify, and review the adequacy of any systems, whether at national, local or organisational levels, intended to ensure compliance with those requirements and with any prescribed procedures and standards from time to time including systems of monitoring and inspection;

    iii. to review the practical operation and effectiveness of such systems.

2. While the remit is primarily concerned with the period 1950 to 1995 the Independent Expert should not regard himself as precluded from considering material from outwith that period which he considers to be of relevance.

3. So as not to prejudice either any possible criminal proceedings or any litigation at the instance of the survivors of abuse the Independent Expert is not to report on the facts or circumstances of any individual cases of abuse.

4. For the purposes of his investigation the Independent Expert will, in addition to information that is publicly available:

    i. have access to all documentary records of the former Scottish Office in so far as in the possession of Scottish Ministers from the period under consideration and in so far as relating to residential schools and children's homes which will be subject to redaction to ensure that no individual can be identified ;

ii. be expected to seek the cooperation of local authorities and other organisations with responsibility for the management and administration of residential schools and children's homes in making available to him such documentary records and explanation of such records as he considers to be necessary for his purposes.

5. Except in so far as provided above the Independent Expert is not expected to consider material or submissions from individuals or from local authorities or such organisations except to the extent that he may consider it necessary for the purposes of his investigation to obtain information from organisations representing the interests of the survivors of abuse."

5. How I interpreted the remit

At the outset I considered that, to undertake a review of this kind, I'd need to be able to talk to and receive information from people who had lived in residential schools and children's homes in the past. I also considered it essential to talk to those who had worked in the residential childcare sector. The remit appeared to rule out making these contacts, and this was a major concern for the former residents who contacted the review asking about its work. I later sought and obtained the Minister's agreement to my meeting and receiving information from individuals. That agreement was confirmed in September 2006.

6. The extent of the task

The work that would be necessary to fulfil my remit is much greater than had been anticipated by those who drew it up. The research into the legislation covering such a long period of time has proved to be very demanding and time-consuming. The extent of

relevant legislation is vast. There are large numbers of potential sources of information about how residential schools and children's homes in Scotland were provided, monitored and inspected. These sources are in archives and storage facilities across Scotland, with some in England. The state of archived records added to the complexity and challenge of the work.

As Chapter 5 shows, many of the records that may be relevant have yet to be appropriately catalogued. Until this has been done, it is not possible to confirm what they contain and the extent to which their contents may be relevant to the review.

In some respects, the review's experience in searching for records has paralleled the difficulties of former residents as they search for information about the past.

7. How we researched the review

I employed a researcher and a legal researcher to assist me. I was fortunate enough to employ Nancy Bell as my researcher. Nancy had worked in the Ministry of Attorney General in Canada and subsequently in the British Columbia Children's Commission before coming to Scotland to study at the University of Glasgow. My legal researcher, Roddy Hart, who had read Law at the University of Glasgow was asked to undertake research into the relevant legislation relating to residential schools and children's homes across the review period.

We took forward the work of the review in various ways:

■ We sent a questionnaire to every local and voluntary authority, including churches and religious orders, in Scotland to establish whether they had provided residential schools and children's homes at any stage during the review period. I also asked for information about their policies and practice in residential child care in the past. Details of the questionnaire survey are in Appendix 3.

■ We conducted a survey with the help of local authority archivists to find out what children's residential services records and related information might be held in their archives.

■ Former residents told us about their experiences of living in residential establishments; some information was provided in meetings, some in telephone conversations and some in letters, emails, newspaper cuttings and papers that residents sent us, and some in VHS and DVD formats.

■ We interviewed people who had worked in organisations involved in providing, monitoring and inspecting services for children in residential establishments during the review period

■ My researcher reviewed files held in the National Archives of Scotland (NAS), SEED, and in other archives in various locations in Scotland and England. I also reviewed files in NAS and SEED.

■ I sought expert advice from Alan Finlayson and Professor Alan Miller on aspects of the legislative framework.

■ I commissioned a literature review focused on abuse in children's residential establishments from Dr Andrew Kendrick

■ I commissioned a paper on society's attitudes to children and social policy changes across the review period from Susan Elsley, consultant

■ My researcher and I examined the recommendations of reports of previous reviews and inquiries to identify which related to matters pertinent to my review

■ I established an advisory group whose members' expertise included inspecting social work services and education, children's hearings, archives and record-keeping, the oversight of residential child care, training and development for the care sector, the health service, academic research into residential child care and the police.

It surprised me that there was no government national database of children's residential establishments. My researcher had to build a database for this review but I couldn't justify the time and effort to take this to a level of inclusiveness to warrant its being regarded as a national database. Hopefully that work can be taken forward in the future, building on what the review has begun. I make a recommendation to that effect later in the report.

8. Contributions to the review

The range and number of people and organisations who have contributed to this review have been impressive. Without their generous contribution of time and expertise and their support and encouragement, the work and progress achieved by the review would not have been possible. I'm deeply grateful for the help, knowledge and support given to my researcher and me. I'm particularly grateful to former residents for their patience and forbearance in waiting for the work of the review to reach its conclusions, not least given the length of time some of them have waited for a public response to their legitimate needs.

Acknowledgements

I acknowledge with deep gratitude the invaluable contribution made to the work of the review by my researcher, Nancy Bell, and my legal researcher, Roddy Hart. Their work was essential to the progress of the review. The review's administrative support was provided ably and patiently by Jeff Sinton and Andy Goring. I also wish to acknowledge the invaluable advice and support of Robert McAllister, for plain language editing and my advisory group's generosity with their expertise and encouragement:

Ian Baillie	Former Director of Social Work (Church of Scotland)
Margery Browning	Former HM Assistant Chief Inspector – Education
Brigid Daniel	Professor of Social Work, University of Stirling
Canon Tom Gibbons	Former Administrator of Catholic Child Care Committee
Bruno Longmore	Head of Court and Legal Records Branch of National Archives of Scotland
Alan Miller	Principal Reporter, Scottish Children's Reporter Administration
Angus Skinner	Visiting Professor at the University of Strathclyde
Helen Zealley	Former Director of Public Health with NHS Lothian

Chapter 1

The historical context

Chapter 1

The historical context

What this chapter is about

This chapter presents the background context for the chapters that follow. In it, I present the historical background to attitudes to children in general, and to children in residential care in particular.

I describe the environment in which the regulatory framework (the various laws, rules and regulations) developed during the period of my review, 1950-1995. I draw attention to important influences during this period and consider themes and areas that I found relevant.

My conclusions, in the final section of this chapter, highlight areas I consider important for future consideration. I identify several issues relevant to attitudes to children, especially those in residential care:

The chapter has the following sections:

1. The lessons and limitations of history
2. How society's view of child welfare changed after 1945
3. How attitudes to children and childhood changed
4. Reform in the 1960s: Kilbrandon and the Social Work (Scotland) Act 1968
5. Major changes that followed the 1960s
6. How society's views of child abuse developed
7. How residential child care changed after 1948
8. Abuse in residential child care 1948-1990
9. My conclusions

The sources I've based this chapter on

I highlight developments – which I've found particularly relevant to my review – in social policy, in attitudes to children and in the literature of historical child abuse. I drew on two pieces of work commissioned for the review. One considers social policy trends and society's attitudes to children and young people in 1950 to 1995. It was prepared by Susan Elsley and is included in full as Appendix 1. The second is a review of the literature on historical abuse in residential child care in Scotland, which was prepared by Robin Sen, Andrew Kendrick. Ian Milligan and Moyra Hawthorn and is included in full as Appendix 2.

The review on social policy trends and society's attitudes to children drew primarily on academic literature, focusing on various texts relating to Scotland. Again, some references are to UK-wide policy and practice; this acknowledges the range of influences on child welfare in Scotland. This review is attached as Appendix 1.

The literature review on residential child care considered materials published on historical abuse in residential schools and children's homes between 1950 and 1995. It drew on sources that focused on Scotland but also, where there were gaps, on research material from the UK. The literature review is attached as Appendix 2.

Both reviews emphasise that extensive material was available, some of which could not be covered in detail for this review. There are also areas where there was little empirical research (research that draws from observation and experience) or a lack of published literature on Scotland.

I am grateful to Susan Elsley for her assistance in editing this chapter.

1. The lessons and limitations of history

- Challenges in understanding the past
- Understanding children's lives in the past

■ Scotland's experience and its impact on child welfare

Challenges in understanding the past

The review covers a lengthy period, so it's only possible in this chapter to highlight major developments and emphasise, in retrospect, significant changes in policy and attitudes that affected children and young people and residential child care.

Although my remit is to look at the period from 1950 to 1995, it's important to recognise the considerable impact of earlier decades. The influence of the Victorian Poor Law, the impact of child welfare developments from the beginning of the 20th century and during the two world wars all had a significant role in laying the foundations for what came at the start of the period of our review.

Analysing the experience of children in the past can be biased by our 21st century perspectives. What seems inappropriate and out of date now may have been seen entirely differently in a previous time. The difficulty in balancing our present-day knowledge and understanding with that of the past is another recurring and important theme in our work, to which we refer later in this chapter.

Another challenge in undertaking a historical review of this kind, is the availability of research material in some areas. Those who have explored this period and the history of children's lives have emphasised the lack of research in Scotland, as well as the scarcity of research, drawn from observation and experience, that has examined children's experiences. The lack of research material suggests that understanding children and their needs and rights was not a priority for much of the period. This is particularly relevant for us in terms of the experiences of children and young people who were looked after in residential care. This lack of direct evidence has been challenging for us.

Later chapters highlight the impact of these and other challenges on the task of examining a long period of history. A legal framework that developed over some

45 years adds significant complexity to understanding the past. The nature, extent and retention of records is another significant area: in the absence of good record keeping and records-retention, the potential value of records can be compromised significantly.

Understanding children's lives in the past

The reviews I've used as the basis of this chapter make it clear that understanding attitudes to children and childhood over time is complex. Researchers draw attention to the fact that the situation for children cannot be considered in isolation from that of adults, the state and social trends and that the influences on child welfare are diverse and extensive (Foley, 2001; Frost and Stein, 1989).

Each child's life in the past, as today, was different and it's difficult to identify one definitive understanding of childhood during this period (Hendrick, 2003). Children's experiences were also influenced by factors such as gender, class, disability and culture. In addition, society's awareness and recognition of matters affecting children vary over time. This is particularly relevant to the area of cruelty, neglect and abuse, which is highlighted in this chapter and in different contexts throughout this report.

It's clear that the position of children did change during this period, although contradictions in society's attitudes to children still existed: children were regarded as innocent and helpless, but also as threats to wider society. As Frost and Stein (1989) comment, children were the objects of society's good intentions but were also the oppressed minority who didn't have a voice and were subject to abuse.

It's difficult to define how children were regarded at any point in history as few texts examine the history of their lives. Children's perspectives were rarely recorded and not even actively sought. Research that explored experiences and ideas about children and childhood wasn't common until recently (Abrams, 1998; Hendrick, 2003). This in turn means that much of the historical knowledge of children's lives relies on adults' accounts of their own childhood and adults' interpretations of the past. Much has also been forgotten.

Scotland's experience and its impact on child welfare

What happened in Scotland in child welfare during this period was regarded as reflecting social trends, policy and professional practice in the rest of the UK. But research shows there was something about Scotland's unique urban and industrial experience that helped to make it distinct (Abrams, 1998). Murphy (1992) suggests that there were three main influences on Scottish attitudes:

- Scotland was a poor country.
- A strong, Calvinist religious tradition was dominant.
- Education was influenced by both of these.

Scotland's experience in the Second World War influenced the work of the Clyde Committee, which examined – and, in turn, had a major influence on – Scottish child welfare and education policies (Stewart and Welshman, 2006). I discuss the Committee's work in more detail later in this chapter. Although there were similarities in the philosophies between Scotland and the rest of Britain during this period, the way policy was implemented differed, and led to different outcomes (Murray and Hill, 1991).

What this tells us is that Scotland's experience was both distinctive and similar to what was happening in the rest of Britain. The process of better understanding child abuse, for example, was influenced by the same discoveries and debates.

2. How society's view of child welfare changed after 1945

- After the Second World War
- The work of the Curtis and Clyde Committees
- The Children Act (1948) in Scotland

After the Second World War

There was a strong focus on families and children following the Second World War as part of the process of rebuilding Britain (Cunningham, 2006; Heywood, 1959). The government demonstrated its commitment to investing in families through services for children in health, welfare and education (Abrams, 1998; Foley, 2001). There was a wider concept of what the government was responsible for and a move towards getting the state more involved in families.

By the end of the war Scottish children's health and well-being, which had previously been poor, was improving (Smout, 1987). Since the 1890s England and Wales had seen significant developments in education for young children. But Scotland didn't have the same commitment to child-centred education. Instead, an authoritarian attitude to children was still dominant in the period up to 1950 (Smout 1987).

People's experiences during the war and, in particular, of evacuation, had had a major impact on public opinion. At the end of the war groups such as the Scottish Women's Group on Welfare (1944), sought a more prominent role for the family in society. They asserted the importance of the child guidance movement (a service which aimed to prevent mental ill-health in children), nursery education and co-operation between home and school.

In the 1930s there had been little evidence of concern about the mistreatment of children. However, towards the end of the war the topic of child welfare and, by implication, child abuse, had become more of an issue. There was a pressing need to deal with children who had been evacuated and who couldn't return to their homes (Hendrick, 1994). This was given added weight by the campaigning work of Lady Allen, who highlighted major shortcomings in the care system in a letter to The Times in 1944. These concerns centred attention on the poor state of residential child care and the lack of co-ordination of childcare services.

The work of the Curtis and Clyde committees

In 1944, following public outcry on the situation of deprived children, the House of Commons called for an inquiry into the conditions in residential homes for children. This led to two committees being set up in 1946:

- The Care of Children Committee in England and Wales, led by Curtis.
- The Committee on Homeless Children in Scotland led by Clyde.

Their work was instrumental in leading to the 1948 Children's Act and provided an important insight into the circumstances of children living away from home. Their findings are well documented; together with tragic cases involving children in care, including the case of two brothers in Fife, they highlighted the shortcomings in child care services and the shortage of suitably qualified staff.

Both committees advocated foster care rather than residential care. In Scotland, boarding out had always been the more common. In 1945, for example, records show that 5,377 children cared for under the Poor Law in Scotland were boarded out. Only 959 children were in voluntary homes and 749 in Poor Law institutions (Clyde Report, 1946). And of 1,561 children considered in need of care and protection under the terms of the Children and Young Persons' (Scotland) Act 1937, over two-thirds (1,077) were boarded out and 484 were in children's homes. The Clyde Committee also found that a further 4,788 children were in voluntary homes, 3,476 of whom were not in the care of any type of public authority. This indicated the extent to which religious and charitable groups intervened in childcare.

Although they expressed reservations about the quality of some foster care with their report speaking of "isolated instances of cruelty",the members of the Clyde committee still preferred foster care, describing large institutions as "an outworn solution". Yet they acknowledged the need for residential homes in certain circumstances; examples included children with specific care needs,

who were part of a family unit too large to place in one foster home or what they called "specially difficult" children. The Clyde committee made recommendations for improving residential accommodation, advocating that large institutions should limit the number in a building to no more than 30 children.

Neither committee found examples of child abuse but they came across examples of extremely poor childcare practice and insensitive treatment of children. However, those who described their experiences to the Curtis committee spoke of the "danger" of "harsh and repressive tendencies or false ideas of discipline".

Later research by Magnusson (1984) and Hendrick (2003) reported that many allegations were made of abuse in residential child care during the time of the Clyde Committee. Former residents, some from Scotland, reported repeated beatings for bedwetting, being force-fed food and made to eat their own vomit (Abrams, 1998).

There were also complaints about extreme corporal punishment, which visitors had identified in one institution. This indicates that some form of monitoring existed and could be effective (quoted in Magnusson, 1984 p.109). But this has to be set against the observation (quoted in Magnusson, 1984) that life in individual units in some large homes was so self-contained that cruel mistreatment of a child could go unnoticed. This isn't to deny that children had good experiences in residential child care: there are testimonies that they did (for example, letters to Sunday Mail 1984 and interviews for this review). Some former residents who had been abused described some aspects of their care in favourable terms, highlighting the benefits provided to them. However, we don't know the extent of good experience or of abuse at that time in residential child care in Scotland. This lack of information is an ongoing theme in the review and makes it difficult for us to draw definitive conclusions.

Evidence suggests concerns about corporal punishment in the later 1940s. The Scottish Home Department questioned its use for girls (Abrams, 1998) and a local councillor requested an inquiry into a Scottish boys' residential school in 1947, noting allegations of excessive beatings (The Scotsman 15 October, 1947). A subsequent inquiry into alleged excessive punishment and beatings in the school resulted in a report that found against the allegations and included, interestingly, comments to the effect that the work of approved schools was extraordinarily difficult (The Scotsman 10 December 1947). These remarks appear to suggest that this justified such treatment.

The Children Act (1948) in Scotland

Although the 1948 Children Act is discussed in Chapter 2, I feel it's important to note some of its key aspects here.

The Act was a response to the examples of poor quality of care that the Curtis and Clyde reports revealed. It gave local authorities a duty to receive into care children who could not live with their parents. Local authorities were to place children in foster care, where possible, using residential care only if fostering was not appropriate and only as a temporary measure.

A significant aspect of the Act was its emphasis on the child's best interests, making a child's welfare central. This showed that society was placing greater importance on child care that centred on children's needs (Stewart, 2001;Ball, 1998). Children in care were to be treated as individuals rather than as a category of young people and were to have access to the same facilities as all other children (Packman, 1981). This Act was regarded as a major step forward for child welfare, paving the way for services over the next 20 years.

Most of the Act's legal provisions applied to Scotland as well as England and Wales but it didn't lead to the same level of children's service developments in Scotland in the 1950s. The approach to children's service was part-time and piecemeal. Even where children's officers were appointed, the structure was

poorly developed and affected the service adversely throughout the 1950s (Murphy, 1992). Scotland, says Murphy, didn't take the opportunity to develop a new professionalism among people working with children.

White's study (1973) highlighted how slowly some Scottish local authorities reacted. For example, Edinburgh took up to 20 years to respond to the ideas behind the Clyde report. While the Clyde report and the 1948 Act sought to tighten up the practice of boarding out, there was no attempt to look at the childcare system from the child's point of view (Abrams, 1998). Murphy's and Abrams's comments touch on two key issues identified by this review: the lack of commitment to develop a fully qualified workforce for residential child care and the need to talk to and listen to children.

3. How attitudes to children and childhood changed

- Attitudes to children and childhood
- New understandings of children
- Children's rights
- Families and parenting

Attitudes to children and childhood

Attitudes to children and childhood changed during this period. More attention was paid to children's welfare and more liberal views emerged about children's status in society. Despite this, however, childhood remained an area rife with contradictions. Commentators on childhood point out that:
- childhood has long been viewed as a time in life when children are both dependent and powerless (Stein, 1989); and
- children have continued to have low status up to the present day, being seen as a minority social group (Mayall, 2006).

In the first part of the 20th century, children were expected to be silent and didn't have a voice

(Cunningham, 2006). After the Second World War, children had greater importance to society as citizens as well as members of families but this didn't mean that they were seen as individuals (Hendrick, 1997). As the century progressed, attitudes did change due to factors such as improved standards of living, decline in strict religious views, new approaches in education and an increased respect for children's rights (Hendrick, 2003). Concern for the welfare of young people increased and led to new approaches to young offenders (Murray, 1983).

However, attitudes to children continued to differ widely. On one hand, children were regarded as special and the focus of society's attentions. On the other, children had no voice and were subject to exploitation. Power wasn't equal between adults and children; adults used their power to forward their own interests at the expense of children (Abrams, 1998).

There was also a tension between new understandings of children and the more long-standing view that linked neglect and deprivation with being depraved. Stein (2006) records that many young people in residential child care had no adults to turn to when they had been abused. The experiences of victims and survivors of abuse in residential child care reflected embedded social attitudes towards young people who were "troubled and troublesome" and were seen as a threat to society (Colton and others, 2002). Seeing children as threatening often led to the reality of their experiences as victims being disregarded by society. Contributors to our review identified this as an important issue and we return to it in later chapters.

New understandings of children

Greater understanding of the children's needs developed during this period through the work of psychologists, psychiatrists and sociologists. Work undertaken between 1920 and the late 1940s by, for example, Burt on individual differences in children, and Isaacs on child development, was developed in the 1950s and 1960s. Bowlby's work on bonding and attachment was particularly important for new

theoretical approaches to child welfare (Stevenson, 1998). These developments contributed to a greater awareness of children's well-being and mental health (Hendrick, 1997).

The new understandings of children and children's minds had an impact on child welfare in the 1950s and 1960s, influencing the professional practice of those working with children as well as public attitudes. However, there was some question about how and when these new understandings of children permeated through to professionals. Abrams (1998) suggests that it took until the 1960s before there was a major shift in child welfare services in Scotland, while Stevenson (1998) – reflecting on social work in England – states that learning from psychology didn't necessarily reach a wider group of social workers.

The Education (Mentally Handicapped Children) (Scotland) Act 1974 was an example of legislation which did reflect new understandings of children. At its heart was the basic principle that no child was "ineducable or untrainable". The Act led to teachers being appointed to work in junior occupational centres, day care centres and what were then known as "mental deficiency hospitals".

Children's rights

Children's rights did not emerge as a founding principle of children's services until towards the end of our review period. However the law began to incorporate limited elements of what we now recognise as children's rights as early as the 1908 Children Act. In 1924, the League of Nations passed the Declaration of the Rights of the Child followed by the United Nations' adoption of the Declaration of the Rights of the Child in 1959. The 1960s and 1970s brought a growing awareness of children's rights through people who spoke out for children's liberation and for more understanding of children's position in society (Archard, 1993; Franklin,1986).
The UN designated 1979 the International Year of the Child which contributed to a developing awareness of children's rights. The UN Convention on the Rights of

the Child (UNCRC) came into being in 1989 and was ratified by the UK government in 1991.

The slowly growing awareness of children's rights during the period of our review, was reflected in the introduction of the Children's Hearing system through the Social Work (Scotland) Act 1968. However that awareness didn't necessarily ensure a children's rights approach to services. Instead, the focus was still mainly on children's welfare, that is, on their needs, rather than their rights (Hill, Murray and Tisdall, 1998).This position continued until the Children (Scotland) Act in 1995, which was the first piece of legislation in Scotland to take greater account of children's rights in its principles. In the period since the UNCRC ratification in 1991 and the Children (Scotland) Act in 1995, there has been an increase in the understanding of children's rights at a professional level and, in a more moderate way, in public opinion.

The Cleveland Inquiry in England in the late 1980s highlighted that children's rights in care were poorly implemented. It indicated that professionals had not listened to children in the community (Asquith, 1983). Skinner's report 'Another Kind of Home' (1992) confirmed a clearer commitment to children's rights in care. This report emphasised that children's rights should be central to their care while they were looked after and that children should have a say.

There are examples, however, of a commitment to listening to children earlier in the review period. Our legal research has identified regulations that provided for children to be heard. Under 1930s legislation, visitors and inspectors could interview children. This was strengthened gradually but slowly over the period of our review. We return to this in chapter 4.

Families and parenting

Family practices of parenting and discipline evolved during the 1950s and 1960s, influenced by greater understanding of what children needed to help them develop. Research in the 1960s found that higher living standards had had an impact on families' well-being.

There was a move away from strict discipline of children; children were able to communicate more easily with parents (Newson and Newson, 1965). Those who didn't fit the norms of good parenting were regarded as problem families. This, in turn, had an impact on how professionals worked with disadvantaged families.

In the 1970s the government debated the notion of the cycle of deprivation which proposed that people who lived on low incomes had few opportunities to escape from poverty According to this view, the problem was families' failings, rather than a lack of resources and inequalities arising from the structure of society (Holman, 1988). Families who abused children were considered as having some underlying condition, which meant that parents passed on poor child rearing practices from one generation to another (Parton, 1985; Holman, 1988). Between the 1970s and the 1990s the impact of increased unemployment and changes in family make-up had significant implications for society (Fox Harding, 1997).

Although child care experts in the 1930s had come to the view that corporal punishment was likely to do more harm than good, it was still very common after the war with the widely held view that physical punishment was a necessary part of rearing children. Discipline in the home and school was frequently harsh and society was generally in favour of it (Murphy 1992).

Corporal punishment continued in Scottish schools until it was banned in 1986, following a ruling of the European Court. Newson and Newson's studies on discipline, which they carried out in the 1960s and again 20 years later, showed that 81% of parents in the 1980s said they hit their children, but half thought they shouldn't (Newson and Newson, 1989). Physical punishment of children by adults was therefore a continuous backdrop during this period but its use diminished over time. The law on physical punishment was amended in Scotland in the Criminal Justice (Scotland) Act 2003. This didn't outlaw adults hitting children but did put some restrictions in place.

4. Reform in the 1960s: Kilbrandon and the Social Work (Scotland) Act 1968

The 1960s saw major reform across Britain of how child welfare was administered. The Children and Young Persons Act 1963, which applied to England, Wales and Scotland, gave local authorities a duty to help families to keep children out of care (Murray and Hill, 1991). In 1950s Britain there was concern about the rising level of juvenile delinquency (Hendrick, 2003). This led to the different parts of Britain exploring how to respond to this trend.

In Scotland, the Kilbrandon Committee was established in 1961 to examine measures for dealing with young people who needed care and protection. The Kilbrandon Report (1964) was followed by the Social Work (Scotland) Act 1968. This brought together services that had previously been separate and established procedures for the children's hearings system. The new system aimed to make sure that children and young people didn't have to experience the adult criminal justice system. When children got into trouble the focus was on their needs, not their deeds. This approach was based on several principles that were linked to each other (Lockyer and Stone, 1998). These included:

- what was in children's best interests;
- the influence of home or wider environments;
- a central emphasis on family and prevention

The new children's hearings system and unified social work departments, were seen as a radical departure for Scotland's child welfare system. The child centred approach to responding to children's needs anticipated a future children's rights focus to services (Lockyer and Stone, 1998).

5. Major changes that followed the 1960s

From 1969, reforms of the social work profession proceeded rapidly. The number of field social workers who had qualifications rose from 30% in 1969 to 97% in 1989 (Murphy, 1992). Local government re-organisation in Scotland in 1975 created nine regional and 53 district councils in addition to the three unitary island authorities. Regional councils were responsible for education and social work; district councils for housing and recreation.

Inquiries and concerns about child abuse in the 1970s, 1980s and 1990s led to changes in policy and practice. The Cleveland abuse inquiry in England in the late 1980s and the Orkney inquiry in Scotland in 1991 revealed that it was difficult to protect children's rights while, at the same time, balancing parental rights and responsibilities (Asquith, 1993). The two inquiries added to more long-standing demands for changes in child care law, which reflected growing concern about poor quality care. There was a need (Asquith, 1993) to:

- improve the knowledge base of professionals in child abuse;
- explore the adequacy of training was for social workers;
- ensure parents had the right to appeal quickly against children being removed from home; and
- encourage the various agencies and organisations who were involved in providing services to work together effectively.

The Cleveland inquiry was followed by the Children Act (1989). This applied to England and Wales, although some aspects were relevant to Scotland in relation to children. To carry out a similar legal overhaul in Scotland, the Child Care Law Review Group was set up in 1988. The group recommended no substantial changes, but the Orkney 'scandal' and a child care inquiry in Fife awakened public concern. By the 1990s Scotland was following England in reforming child care laws, publishing a white paper 'Scotland's Children' in 1993. This presented the government's proposals for childcare policy and law in Scotland. It set out eight clear principles to "incorporate the philosophy of the United Nations Convention on the Rights of the Child" (Scottish Office, 1993 p6) and, in turn, led to the Children (Scotland) Act 1995.

By the 1990s, statutory bodies such as local authorities had a central role that was quite unrecognisable from the one they had at the beginning of the period of our review (Murray and Hill, 1991). Local government was re-organised in 1995 into 32 unitary authorities.

6. How society's views of child abuse developed

- Changes in understanding of child abuse
- Definitions of abuse
- Historical abuse

Changes in understanding of child abuse

People's understanding of what child abuse was changed during the period of our review. Up to the late 1940s there was little recognition of abuse in the public mind (Abrams, 1998). But this didn't mean that child abuse was a new phenomenon. Rather, people's focus in the early 20th century was on delinquency, neglect and so-called problem families, rather than on abuse (Parton, 1979).

From the 1960s to the mid 1980s, child abuse began to be more widely known, with greater understanding of emotional, physical and sexual abuse. What was then termed "battered baby syndrome" was prominent in the 1960s, but was largely a medical profession concern. Social workers continued to focus on neglect and casework with the family (Parton, 1979). In Scotland, child abuse was not well developed as a professional or public concept; indeed the first professional course in childcare only became available in 1960 (Murphy, 1992).

Child abuse was given a high profile by the inquiry into the death of seven-year-old Maria Colwell, who died after being beaten in the early 1970s (Fox Harding, 1997). The inquiry report signalled a change in child welfare and public attitudes to abuse. It also sharply highlighted society's anxieties about the family and increasing violence and permissiveness

(Stevenson, 1998; Parton,1985). There was a lot of public debate on child abuse in the 1970s and 1980s. However there was little reliable evidence that could help to identify the most effective form of intervention. Parton (1985) reports social workers feeling inadequate to the task of dealing with child abuse as there were so many contradictions in determining abuse.

The focus on child abuse in the 1980s raised questions about whether child abuse had increased during this period or if there was simply greater awareness of its existence. In the 1980s, inquiries began to focus on sexual abuse, with the Cleveland and Orkney inquiries the most prominent. By the 1990s, awareness of child abuse had moved to the experience of those who had been living in residential care (Colton and others, 2002).

Definitions of abuse

The Department of Health, summarising child protection research, comments on the many definitions of abuse and the importance of the context in which the abuse takes place. This highlights the difficulty of identifying abuse, as what people might consider normal at one time they might consider abnormal at another (Department of Health, 1995).

Defining child abuse, therefore, is complex; what the term covers has evolved over time and continues to evolve. Gil provides the following definition:

> "Any act of commission or omission by individuals, institutions or society as a whole, and any conditions resulting from such acts or inaction, which deprive children of equal rights and liberties, and/or interfere with their optimal development" (Gil, 1970, p.16)

The Scottish Office's guidance document 'Protecting Children – a Shared Responsibility' (1998) defines five categories of child abuse: physical, sexual, non-organic failure to thrive (this describes children who fail to develop normally but no physical or genetic reasons explain why), emotional and physical neglect.

The literature review at Appendix 2 states that "institutional abuse" can be defined as any kind of child abuse described in these five categories that happens in an institutional setting such as a residential school or children's home. However, there has been debate and disagreement about definitions of institutional abuse (Stanley and others, 1999). One of the most commonly used definitions is by Gil (1982) who differentiates between three forms of abuse:

■ overt or direct abuse of a child by a care worker;
■ programme abuse of children due to approaches taken in that setting; and
■ system abuse, where the childcare system has failed to meet children's needs.

In terms of the focus of this review, historical abuse refers to abuse that has taken place in the past. The Lothian and Borders Joint Police/Social Work Protocol identifies historical abuse as that which:

> "...will include all allegations of maltreatment whether of serious neglect or of a sexual or of a physical nature which took place before the victim(s) was/were 16 years (or aged 18 in some circumstances) and which are made after a significant time has elapsed" (Lothian and Borders and others, 2001, p.5)

These different definitions highlight the complexity of defining abuse. In the context of our review, it is important to identify the responsibilities of adults and institutions to protect children's welfare and rights as well as to take account of prevailing attitudes to children, child abuse and childcare. I sought to do so in this report.

Historical abuse

Is it fair to judge what happened 30 or more years ago on the basis of what is known as abuse today?

One complication is that knowledge and understanding about what actually happened to children in children's residential establishments are limited, particularly in the earlier years of the review period. There was little research and public awareness about abuse of children in institutions until the 1980s. The voices of people who lived in children's residential establishments have not had prominence within Scotland, so very little is known about the extent and type of abuse that took place years ago.

It is also evident that past abuse – whether society accepted it as normal or not – remains abuse, and that certain practices we recognise as abusive today were also regarded as unacceptable practices hundreds of years ago. For example, in 1669 a children's petition suggested that teachers who resorted to corporal punishment were "taking on them an office which they have not the ability to manage". In 1889, militant schoolboys met on London's Albert Embankment; one of their demands was "No Cane" (The Heatherbank Museum of Social Work, Factsheet 12, University of Glasgow Caledonia Archives).

To suggest that what society accepted as normal should determine practices that we consider abusive today, is to overlook that children in state care were entitled to protection by law . The Children and Young Persons (Scotland) Act 1937, for example, provided most of the fundamental regulation for the welfare and protection of children and young people during the 1950s and 1960s, making it an offence to harm children. Importantly, this Act shows what was known to be harmful to children in 1937.

The Children Act 1948 which followed imposed a general duty on local authorities to ensure that they '...exercise their powers with respect to him so as to further his best interests, and to afford him opportunity for the proper development if his character and abilities' (Section 12.1). The principle of a child's best interests is also fundamental to the Children (Scotland) 1995 Act, which currently applies, and the UNCRC.

The review found evidence of people who, in the 1950s and onwards in Scotland, showed concern about children's welfare and opposed practices such as corporal punishment. For example, the managers of a voluntary children's home in the 1950s record in their minute book that they took

"a serious view of behaviour recorded in the School Log Book on the part of Mr. X, a housemaster, in the punishment of one of his boys and having also heard from Mr G (note: a committee member) of Mr M's behaviour witnessed by him on another occasion instructed the Warden to take steps to dismiss Mr M."

Just as we don't know the extent of abuse in children's residential establishments, we don't know how many people working directly with children had concerns about their welfare. Evidence does show, however, that some adults had such concerns and recognised certain practices, or adult behaviour toward children, as inappropriate and abusive. What remains unknown – which is what I've tried to understand in this review – is why these concerns didn't prevent children from being harmed while in residential places.

7. How residential child care changed after 1948

- Attitudes to residential child care
- Residential child care and child emigration after 1945
- Attitudes to residential child care

Residential care wasn't the preferred option for children after the 1948 Children Act. The influence of the work of Bowlby (1951), who emphasised the importance of a child's attachment to its mother, reinforced a preference for foster care for children unable to live with their parents. This resulted in, for example, a large number of residential nurseries being closed in Britain, although Edinburgh still had residential nursery places in 1973 (White, 1973). The 'Edinburgh Report' for 1954 required that: "careful investigation takes place before children are separated from their parents" (quoted in White, 1973, pp.171-172). In Scotland, where fostering had long been the preferred choice with 61% of children boarded out in 1949,

the situation continued largely unchanged. In 1968, of children in care, 58% were still boarded out (White, 1973). Only 16% of those in residential care in 1968 were in local authority, rather than voluntary sector, care (White, 1973).

At the beginning of the 20th century, most children in residential child care in Scotland were orphans (Abrams, 1998; Magnusson, 1984). During the first half of the century, the proportion of children coming into care who had parents still living but who were unable or unwilling to provide appropriate care for them, grew. This number continued to grow after 1948. Illegitimacy became a significant reason for children coming into care, with the proportion of children higher in Scotland than England and Wales (White, 1973). Residential care was used where foster care wasn't appropriate, mainly for older children, those with disabilities and those with severe problems (Tresiliotis, 1988, Frost and others, 1999). After 1948, residential child care improved; homes were smaller and had better buildings and furnishings. Family group homes were developed. Progress was also made in providing children with food, clothes, activities and facilities comparable to those that other children enjoyed (Sen, Kendrick, Milligan and Hawthorn, 2007).

Research literature has little information about changes in the residential sector across Scotland during this period. However White's study (1973) shows that developments in the residential sector varied considerably by region. He notes that, in Edinburgh, the local authority took up to 20 years to respond to the ideas behind the Clyde Report and the 1948 Children Act. The size and use of homes in Edinburgh remained the same. Family group homes were developed, but only from 1962 onward.

Children's Committees in England improved practice by forbidding inhumane practices such as shutting children in dark cupboards, using excessive corporal punishment and depriving them of proper food (Packman, 1981). Evidence of comparable progress in Scotland wasn't available to us. But perhaps an indication of progress was the action of one residential home in Scotland which held its first Boys' and Girls' Council in 1967 to allow the children to have some say in the running of their home (Magnusson, 1984). Local authorities, through child care committees, were viewed as having a positive influence on children's emotional development, regulating punishment and strengthening the child-centred focus of residential child care.

The literature on residential child care between 1945 and 1970 portrays a period of optimism, reflecting confidence in the ability of public intervention to make a positive difference to children's lives (Corby and others, 2001; Hendrick, 2003; Milligan, 2005; Packman, 1981). But underneath this optimism there seems to have been some concern. In the 1960s, preventative work with families focused on keeping children with families, while there was increasing criticism of institutional settings (Goffman, 1961; Foucault, 1973). There was little research into children's experiences in residential establishments and where it existed, it wasn't always encouraging (Tresiliotis,1988). A study of 44 children's units found that "a sizeable proportion of children have a comparatively poor experience of daily care in residential life" (Berry, 1975, p.157).

In the late 1970s there were fewer residential establishments for children (Crimmins and Milligan, 2005). This reflected:
- lower government spending;
- continuing reservations about the suitability of residential child care; and
- the emphasis on keeping children with their families.

The number of children in residential child care in Scotland fell from 6,209 in 1977 to 2,364 in 1989 (from Kendrick and Fraser, 1992). The largest decrease was in the number of children under 12 years in residential establishments.

In the 1990s, the number of children in residential child care in England continued to fall, with an average length of stay decreasing from two years in 1985 to 10 months in 1995 (Berridge and Brodie, 1998). The number of residential establishments also

reduced, with homes becoming smaller and larger residential schools dividing into smaller units.

In the 21st century, most of Scotland's local authorities continue to directly manage at least one residential children's home. There is a small number of private providers. There is a large number of residential schools run mainly by the voluntary sector (Sen,Kendrick, Milligan and Hawthorn, 2007). The size, style and management of residential care facilities have changed strikingly over our 45-year review period. The research literature indicates an increasing awareness not only of the physical needs of children in care, but also of their emotional and psychological well-being and their human rights.

Residential child care and child emigration after 1945

We have also noted child emigration from residential child care – mainly to Canada, but also to Rhodesia, (now Zimbabwe), South Africa, New Zealand and Australia – which continued up to 1967. This practice, which began in 1869 in England, was taken up in Scotland by William Quarrier in 1872. There were strongly held economic, political and religious reasons for child emigration and these ensured public support for it. But concerns about the welfare of the migrant children was expressed as early as 1875 and continued, prompting the introduction of the Ontario Act 1897, which provided for greater monitoring and regulation of child emigration schemes. Around 150,000 British children were sent abroad. The exact numbers of children sent from Scottish residential institutions isn't known, however 7,000 child emigrants were sent by Quarrier's, 50 from Aberlour, 200 from Whinwell Children's Home in Stirling and an unknown number from Scottish local authority establishments (Abrams, 1998).

While the number of children sent after the war was comparatively small, some suffered severe abuse. Those sent to Australia suffered physical, emotional and sexual abuse. On top of this, the level of care that many received consistently failed to meet basic needs

(The Australian Senate Legal and Constitutional References Committee 2001; Bean and Melville, 1989; House of Commons, Health Committee, 1997-98; Humphreys, 1994; Gill,1998).

With good reason, Bean and Melville comment that the "history of child migration in Australia is in many ways a history of cruelty, lies and deceit" (1989, p.111). Children were told their parents were dead when they weren't. Family members weren't told that children were being sent abroad or were misinformed about the nature of the scheme. Family members' objections to a child being sent were overridden. Contact between the children and their family in Britain was discouraged, with letters censored and sometimes withheld. And siblings sent to Australia together were frequently separated when they arrived (Bean and Melville 1989; BBC Radio 4, 2003 a).

In the UK there were concerns about child migration schemes from just after the war. While earlier waves of child migration had been greeted with fanfare and publicity, those after the war were undertaken with as little of either as possible (Abrams, 1998). In response to the concerns the 1948 Children Act contained regulations specific to child emigration. For example, the Home Secretary had to approve the emigration of each child and be persuaded it was in their best interests. The child's parents had to be consulted and, if this wasn't possible, the child had to give clear consent.

The Lord Chancellor, Viscount Jowitt, in the Parliament's debate on the bill that led to the Children Act 1948, gave explicit assurances that the Home Office would ensure no child would be sent abroad "unless there is absolute satisfaction that proper arrangements have been made for the care and upbringing of each child." The extent to which this assurance proved hollow is striking. The conditions awaiting the child emigrants in Australia received low priority: the first formal government assessment of these conditions was only carried out in 1956. The inter-departmental committee on migration policy was highly critical of the care provided to child migrants in Australia (Bean and Melville, 1989).

In Scotland, the Scottish Office refused permission for a number of children to be sent abroad on the grounds it was it was not in their interests. It gave permission for a child to emigrate only after its parents' consent had been received (Abrams, 1998).

By 1956 it was widely accepted that young people would be better off in residential child care homes than being sent overseas, so few local authorities sent children after this time, although some voluntary organisations continued to do so. By the 1960s the prevailing public opinion was against these emigration schemes and they ceased in 1967.

The House of Commons Health Committee inquiry (1997-98) on child migration and the Australian Senate Inquiry (2001) Report into the treatment of child migrants in Australia recognised the abuse that many child migrants had suffered. Both inquiries attributed collective responsibility for the abuse to all the governments and agencies that had been involved in the child migration schemes.

8. Abuse in residential child care 1948-1990

- Awareness of child abuse in residential child care 1948-1990
- Major inquiries into abuse in residential child care after 1990
- The evidence of abuse in residential child care in the UK
- Abuse of young people by other young people
- Factors in abuse in residential child care

Awareness of child abuse in residential child care 1948-1990

Child abuse wasn't a major public concern up to the early 1960s (Hendrick, 2003). As I've highlighted, this began to change following awareness of what became known as battered baby syndrome in the 1960s. The focus on abuse across the UK in the early part of the period was on children living in their parents' care, rather than children living in residential establishments. Public recognition of child abuse in institutions began in USA in 1977 (Gil and Baxter 1979) but was slower to develop in the UK. It wasn't until 1990 that awareness of institutional abuse increased in research literature and among the public (Bibby, 1996; Corby and others, 2001; Kendrick, 1997; Stanley, 1999). Little of what was written before 1970 referred to child abuse. Between 1970s and the late 1980s there was no significant mention of institutional child abuse.

The Kilbrandon Report (1964), which established the children's hearing system, didn't refer to abuse in residential child care but did criticise approved schools because too many children were admitted. These children were sometimes too young, had what was then called a 'mental handicap' or were placed because nowhere else was more suitable. Kilbrandon noted that the public viewed approved schools as punitive although he didn't agree with this perspective.

Concern about harsh corporal punishment had been raised since the late 1940s, although it wasn't called abuse. While the Criminal Justice Act of 1948 removed courts' ability to sentence young people to be birched, corporal punishment remained legal in children's homes in Scotland until The Social Work (Residential Establishments – Child Care) (Scotland) Regulations 1987 came into effect (Black and Williams, 2002). Strathclyde Regional Council's Report 'Room to Grow' (1978/9) considered childcare and relevant social policy in the region. Although no reference is made to abuse, the report did recommend that no instrument should be used to administer corporal punishment. It was also unsure about the appropriateness of smacking children reflecting public views at the time. The majority of staff thought some smacking was necessary but they were against violence to children.

Child sexual abuse only really became a significant issue for the public in the mid 1980s. The 'Second Report from the Social Services Committee' referred to its existence, highlighting: "there is now some

professional awareness of the extent and effects of sexual abuse" (HMSO, 1984, Para 52). Government guidance for Scotland acknowledged sexual abuse only in 1986 (Directors of Social Work in Scotland, 1992). A small number of publications at the time mentioned sexual attraction in residential child care (Anthony, 1958 in Todd, 1968; Henry, 1965; Will,1971). Kahan (2000) says the response to sexually inappropriate behaviour by staff was to move the offender. Managing the incident in-house was seen as the preferred option to avoid bad publicity and minimise disruption. Holman (1996) reported that from 1948 to 1971 there were six internal investigations into alleged sexual abuse by Manchester Children's Department. While noting that these were promptly investigated, he adds: "actual or suspected abusers were swiftly pushed out but rarely prosecuted" (Holman, 1996, p.180). Davis (1980) considered what would be appropriate if a young person made an allegation of sexual misconduct against a staff member. He would prefer such incidents to be "bravely and professionally examined internally" although in some cases the staff member was dismissed and the police informed. These different examples highlight that, although sexual abuse was not a public concern at this time, it was still recognised that staff could be sexually attracted to children. There was still no dominant approach to dealing with what would now be termed sexual abuse.

To give children and young people in care a voice, the National Children's Bureau organised a conference in 1975 where young people in England and Wales could describe their experiences. As a result, the 'Who Cares? Young People's Working Group' was set up, subsequently producing a publication. Contributors referred to positive experiences as well as revealing a range of abuse, both emotional and physical, which they and others had endured in residential child care (Page and Clark, 1977). The editors commented on the young people's puzzlement that they should suffer mistreatment in places that were meant to protect them. While their accounts of humiliating punishment and physical abuse are graphic and disturbing, there was no evidence of any formal investigations or of any steps to ensure that incidents didn't happen again. However the young people commented that some staff were sacked (Page and Clark, 1977). The picture painted by Kahan (1979) of the experiences of 10 adults who had been in residential care from 1948 to 1969, is very similar to the children's descriptions of humiliating abuse and of their complaints being disregarded.

In the 1980s some attention was being paid to the rights of those living in residential care. Clough (1982) recommended a code of practice, residents' participation and a range of measures such as complaints procedures and inspection to ensure that residential establishments used good practice and were seen to be well run.

As in other cases, a scandal that was widely reported in the media highlighted abuse in residential child care. In 1981, three staff from the Kincora Boys' Hostel in Belfast were jailed for a series of sexual assaults. In 1985 the officer in charge of Leeways Children's Home in Lewisham was convicted of indecency. The inquiry into the Kincora 'scandal' uncovered a long history of offences and a failure to investigate allegations of abuse (Corby and others, 2001). The Leeways inquiry also found a long history of abuse (Corby and others, 2001).

Despite these revelations, it was still widely believed that these were one-off cases rather than indicating any wider systemic problem, "aberrations rather than the tip of the iceberg", according to Hopton and Glennister (Butler and Drakeford, 2003). An inquiry into excessive physical restraint used at Melanie Klein House for Girls in 1988 passed with little public comment.

Major inquiries into abuse in residential child care after 1990

There were 72 inquiries in the UK between 1945 and 1996 (Corby and others, 2001). However, it's worth noting that Scotland had only two major enquiries into abuse in residential child care, both after the period of my review. These were the Edinburgh Inquiry in 1999 and the Fife Inquiry in 2002. There were, however, two major reviews: 'Another Kind of Home, a review of residential child care' (Skinner, 1992); and

the 'Children's Safeguards Review' (Kent, 1997).

Abuse in residential child care had begun to gain attention at the end of the 1980s. The Children Act 1989 in England and Wales was the first law that recognised institutional child abuse in the UK. The 1991 'Working Together under the Children Act' guidance included sections on the abuse of children living away from home (Creighton 1992). The previous guidance issued in 1988 had only contained one sentence on the subject.

Public interest in abuse in residential care rose and dwindled in the 1980s until what became known as "pindown" hit the headlines in 1991. This practice involved punishing children who had absconded or who refused to attend school by confining them in a sparsely furnished room and depriving them of their possessions and all company. The practice had operated in children's homes in Staffordshire from 1983 to 1989. It had been devised and openly implemented by managers and senior management. A television programme exposing the practice led to a damning inquiry (Stanley, 1999). The Utting Report (1991) into residential care in England was a direct consequence of the Pindown Report. In considering abuse, it recognised that "children in residential care are vulnerable to exploitation by adults and to both physical and sexual abuse" and "may need protection from other children as well as from adults" (Utting 1991).

In Scotland 'Another Kind of Home' (Skinner 1992) set out to examine what residential child care was being provided and of what quality. It also considered training, control and sanctions, children's rights and inspection. While it didn't focus specifically on abuse, this topic did arise in relation to issues such as complaints procedures. In a section on complaints, Skinner recommended that there should be an independent element of any investigation into allegations of abuse by staff. Police should be informed if there was 'reasonable cause to believe that a child may have been the victim of abuse'.

A series of high-profile cases of cruelty and sexual

abuse in England and Wales occurred in the 1990s. There were inquiries into an approved school in Wales, an independent special school for boys in England and a regime put in place by an officer in charge of children's homes in England. These contributed to a government decision to commission reports into the dangers faced by children living away from home and the different forms of protection provided to them.

In Scotland, the Scottish Office commissioned the Kent Report (1997) to consider the dangers faced by children living away from home. The report would also consider evidence of different kinds of abuse against them, and what safeguards existed. Kent noted the worrying number of cases of abuse being brought to Scottish courts and warned against complacency. The Report, published in 1997, had 61 recommendations. Some twenty of these recommendations are ones that the review recognises as being of particular significance to its work. These include;

- complaints procedures;
- vetting staff;
- the responsibility and accountability of staff to report concerns about children's well-being;
- keeping staff files for not less than 20 years; and
- external monitoring.

In Wales, in 1996, a Tribunal of Inquiry into allegations of abuse in children's homes in Gwynedd and Clwyd found that there was widespread sexual abuse of young boys in several homes and physical abuse (Corby and others, 2001; Parton 2006; Waterhouse 2000). It also concluded that some men were targeting teenage boys within and outwith the homes for paedophilic activities and that many of these paedophiles were known to each other and met together.

As I've noted, the two independent inquiries into residential care in Scotland were the Edinburgh Inquiry in 1999 and the Fife Inquiry in 2002. The Edinburgh Inquiry was set up when two men were convicted of sexual abuse of children living in children's homes in Edinburgh and Lothian between 1973 and 1987. The inquiry team had to investigate

whether victims' complaints had been properly handled in the past, to investigate how adequate procedures were at the time to protect children and to determine what further safeguards were needed.

The inquiry report included recommendations to provide further safeguards which relate to matters relevant to this review. These include:

- staff recruitment;
- staff training;
- staff resignations;
- appropriate and clear record-keeping of incidents involving young people;
- prioritising whistleblowing;
- meeting young people to raise concerns about management; and
- authorised visitors.

The Fife Inquiry followed the conviction of an employee in Elie and Leven on 30 charges of sexual abuse of children from 1959 to 1989. Allegations were made against this person in the early 1970s but no steps had been taken to prosecute him, even though the police had been informed. Even though he was suspended from his first post, he was allowed to work elsewhere as a social work assistant and indeed be appointed as housefather in a residential school.

The recommendations of this inquiry also emphasised the need to:

- make staff recruitment and selection processes more rigorous;
- improve and maintain staff awareness of abuse issues and safeguarding children; and
- provide ways for children and young people to express their views about their care.

Other recommendations included better inspection and monitoring processes for care facilities.

Other allegations have been made of historic abuse in residential child care in Scotland, some leading to convictions. Many claims for compensation have been made.

The evidence of abuse in residential child care in the UK

The National Association of Young People in Care made an early attempt to highlight abuse in the care system. They found that 65% of a sample of 50 young people who had made complaints to them in a three-month period had been sexually abused while in care. Over 75% reported physical abuse while in care.

The NSPCC carried out a survey of its teams and projects in March 1992. The authors (Westcott and Clement 1992) acknowledged that the sample was unrepresentative and that the cases identified were particularly severe. They identified 84 cases of alleged abuse in residential or educational settings over the previous year. Of these, 63% were male and 88% were aged 10-17. Most had suffered sexual abuse. In 50% of the cases, the perpetrator was a peer and in 43% a member of staff. Of the staff perpetrators, 81% were male and most were aged over 40.

In 1995 an analysis of calls made to Childline in England, Wales and Scotland provided more evidence of abuse in residential establishments over the first six months of the line's operation (1992-1993). Bullying and violence from other residents were reported as was sexual abuse, perpetrated by both residents and staff.

The most comprehensive survey of institutional abuse in England and Wales was carried out by Gallagher, Hughes and Parker in 1996 in a national survey of organised sexual abuse. This defined institutional abuse as "a case in which an adult has used the institutional framework of an organisation for children to recruit children for sexual abuse." While the authors had doubts about the reliability of all their findings, they reported that, of the 211 cases submitted, there were 45 cases of institutional abuse and 16 (8%) were in residential establishments.

Other research dealing more generally with residential child care has provided some information on abuse. Grimshaw and Berridge (1994) in their study of 67

children who had been in residential special schools for at least a year, concluded that: "For a proportion of the children, admission to a residential school did not mean that they were fully protected from abusive experiences." The research found that 20% of the children were reported to have experienced some form of suspected or confirmed abuse.

A comment by Lindsay in 1997 in a Scottish context is worth repeating here: "[A]buse by staff is not a great problem in frequency of occurrence, but it is a great problem in terms of the seriousness of the offence, and of the uncertainty and anxiety the whole issue causes throughout the service as a whole."

Abuse of young people by other young people

Reported evidence tells of children bullying other children whom they described as "different". A 1992 survey of 84 children in the UK found that over 50% of the reported abusers were the victim's peers. In 1999, MacLeod estimated that over 50% of sexual assaults against children and young people in care could be committed by other children and young people. The 'Report of the Committee of Enquiry into Children and Young People who Sexually Abuse Other Children' (1992), identified that children needed to be appropriately placed to protect them from further abuse. Despite this, a 1999 survey showed that this had been done in fewer than one third of cases studied. The same survey found that, in fewer than 50% of cases, information about a young person's history of abusing or of being abused was passed on to carers at the start of a placement.

The most detailed piece of research on this form of abuse was conducted by Barter and her colleagues in 14 English children's homes (Barter, 2007; Barter and others, 2004). They interviewed 71 young people aged 8-17 and 71 residential staff members. Their research aim was to clarify the context within which particular types of violence occur, rather than to measure how frequently violent incidents happened. They identified

(Baxter, 2007, p.141) four forms of peer violence:

- direct physical assault, such as punching, grabbing hair and beatings;
- physical, non-contact attacks, which harmed young people emotionally rather than physically, for example, destruction of personal belongings;
- verbal abuse; and
- unwelcome sexual behaviour, such as flashing, inappropriate touching and rape.

Factors in abuse in residential child care

Research has identified various factors that may lead or contribute to abuse in residential child care. These factors suggest areas which need to be addressed so that children can be safeguarded in residential settings. They are grouped and summarised below.

a) Denial of abuse

- An attitude of "It can't happen here" (Bloom, 1992, p133).
- Reluctance to report incidents of abuse because of fear of damaging the institution's reputation and possible loss of credibility, referrals and licence (Durkin, 1982a; 1982b; Gil and Baxter, 1979; Harrell and Orem, 1980; Powers, Mooney and Nunno, 1990).

b) Children's isolation and vulnerability

- Social isolation can reduce the chance of identifying the abuse (Berridge and Brodie, 1996) and can lead to resistance to experiences and ideas from outside (Levy and Kahan, 1991, p.154).
- The institution can be isolated from the wider network of care (Doran and Brannan, 1996).
- Physical and geographical isolation reduces the likelihood of visits from professionals and family, so there is greater potential for the denial of abuse (Hughes, 1986; Levy and Kahan, 1991, Kirkwood, 1993; Marshall and others, 1999).
- Entering residential care reinforces children's feelings of not belonging to society, leading to feelings of displacement, loss and lack of control. (Hayden, Goddard, Gorin and Van Der Spek, 1999; Kendrick, 2005).
- Children are particularly isolated, especially

because of the power imbalance between adults and children in residential establishments, and this increases children's vulnerability (Westcott, 1991; Nunno and Motz, 1988; Stein, 2006; Wardhaugh and Wilding, 1993).

- Children's feelings of isolation inhibit them from reporting abuse (Hughes, 1986; Levy and Kahan, 1991, Kirkwood, 1993; Waterhouse, 2000).
- Children in institutions can feel insecure and be slower to develop, which can make them more reliant on adults (Siskind, 1986, p.15). Disabled children are particularly vulnerable (Doran and Brannan, 1996; Kendrick, 1997; Marshall, 1999; Stanley, 1999; Stein, 2006).
- Isolation of residential homes can mean that the public has an incomplete picture. (Colton, 2002).

c) Management and organisation

- Management failure and the absence of clear lines of accountability have been identified as factors in institutional abuse (Wardhaugh and Wardling, 1993).
- An administrative style, which discourages staff and residents from taking part in decision-making, has been identified with patterns of institutional abuse (Siskind, 1986).
- Reliance on theoretical or ideological models tends to distance and dehumanise relationships between the residents and the staff. (Siskind, 1986; Wardhaugh and Wilding, 1993).
- An oppressor mentality promotes hostility towards women, children or minorities (Siskind,1986; Wardaugh and Wilding, 1993).

(d) Training and conditions of residential staff

- In 1946 the Curtis Committee stated that staff training was highly important in improving the quality of residential child care. However, by the time of the Williams Committee census in 1963, only 15% of staff in local authority children's establishments had the appropriate childcare qualifications and 70% had no formal qualifications (Packman 1981, p.43). The Skinner and Kent Reports stressed the need for training. But major concerns continued about the rate of progress in training residential staff and ensuring they've attained the qualifications necessary for registration (Colton, 2002).

- Recent cross-national, comparative research clearly links the level of qualification of residential child care staff with the outcomes and well-being of children and young people in residential care. (Cameron and Boddy, 2007)
- Institutional work over time may bring out the worst in childcare workers (Durkin, 1982a; Baldwin, 1990, p. 150).
- Residential workers are often overworked and underpaid and have little say in decision-making (Baldwin, 1990; Gil and Baxter, 1979; Nunno and Rindfleisch, 1991; Wardhaugh and Wilding, 1993).
- Hierarchical structures in institutions make it difficult for front-line staff to register complaints (Wardhaugh and Wilding, 1993).
- Care workers suffering from burn-out may abuse children and develop increasingly negative attitudes towards them (Edwards and Miltenberger, 1991; Maslach and Jackson, 1981; Mattingly, 1981; Stein, 2006).

e) Sexuality, gender and the targetting of residential care

The lack of a focus on gender and sexuality in relation to the abuse of children and young people in residential child care has been highlighted by a number of authors (Green, 2005; O'Neill. 2007)

The anxieties of residential child care staff in dealing with sexuality have been highlighted as also have been the implications of this for practice.

- Pringle discusses the broader issues of abuse by men (Pringle, 1993, p.16) arguing: "if the male potential for abuse is so organically linked to both masculinity and entrenched patriarchal structures, as suggested in this paper, then the role of men in care services must be questioned".
- Berridge and Brodie (1996) found a macho, or masculine, culture to be a significant factor in the reports of three inquiries they examined. Wolmar (2000) argued that the increase in the number of male staff in residential homes after the 1960s was

a major factor in abuse at that time. Male staff are necessary as good role models but where they are employed, greater safeguards against abuse are needed (Wolmar, 2000 in Colton, 2002).

- Research shows that paedophiles target work settings and activities that will give them access to children whom they can abuse (Gallagher, 2000; Sullivan and Beech, 2002).

(f) Status of residential child care and children in residential child care

Much of the literature we reviewed alludes to the stigma attached to residential child care and the continuing connection in the public mind with the poorhouse and Poor Law aid. Abrams (1998) refers to the boys and girls in a children's home as "Scotland's forgotten children". The widespread assumption is that only so-called problem children are sent to a children's residential establishment. The assumption that residential child care was the option of last resort made it very difficult for the sector to function well. The high-profile scandals in some residential facilities have given rise to the notion that children are more likely to be abused in residential care than in foster care or other institutions. The available evidence, which admittedly isn't very extensive, doesn't support this view. There is evidence from research (Lambert and Millham 1968) and Childline that abuse occurs in other institutional child care settings – for example, in boarding schools – but class and socio-economic factors work against the reputation of residential care services.

9. My conclusions

This chapter's aim has been to present the historical background to attitudes to children and children based in residential care. In doing so, I've identified a number of issues:

- Looking back over a long period of time poses difficulties, such as:
  - the risk of imposing 21st century perspectives;
  - having to look at what preceded the review period; and
  - children's perspectives not having been recorded.

- There's a lack of consistent evidence:
  - there's a scarcity of research material in Scotland about children's lives, about how changes in society have impacted on them, and about children's experiences in residential care.
- Attitudes to children have changed:
  - attitudes changed gradually. The early emphasis on welfare was complemented by concerns to meet children's needs and, later, to listen to them and take account of their views. However, the full acknowledgement in law of children's rights wasn't achieved until the 1990s.
- Attitudes to punishment have been inconsistent:
  - people raised concerns about harsh punishment throughout the period of our review, yet corporal punishment was retained for most of the time.
- The understanding of what constituted abuse changed:
  - child abuse took place but wasn't always acknowledged.
  - public awareness of abuse in residential child care developed later in the review period, yet evidence indicates that abuse was known about from the beginning of the period.
- There was a lack of qualified staff and carers:
  - it was common for staff and carers to have no qualifications, little or no organised training and to work unsupervised.
- Procedures for selecting and assessing staff, and for dealing with staff who abused children, were inadequate:
  - procedures weren't rigorous enough and the ways of dealing with staff who abused children were wholly inadequate.
- Residential child care had low status:
  - the status of residential child care remained low, as did its priority in the public mind.

Chapter 2

The Regulatory Framework

Chapter 2

The Regulatory Framework

"Against the background of the abuse suffered by children up to the age of 16 in residential schools and children's homes in Scotland over the period from 1950 to 1995 the Independent Expert is instructed...to present a report...with the following objectives: (1) to identify what regulatory requirements and powers were in place from time to time over that period and which provided for the provision, regulation and inspection of such schools and homes and for the welfare and protection from abuse of children resident in them..."

Introduction

Identifying any legal framework over more than 50 years involves examining in detail a vast set of laws and constantly evolving rules and regulations.

The review focused on the legal requirements and powers in place for providing, regulating and inspecting residential schools and children's homes in Scotland between 1950 and 1995. In particular, the review considered the children's welfare and how they were protected from abuse.

I am pleased to acknowledge the work of my legal researcher, Roddy Hart, who researched and prepared this chapter. To the best of my knowledge, this is a unique piece of work which I hope many will find helpful.

This chapter describes key aspects of the law as it applied to children and their carers in various ways. It covers:

- primary legislation (Acts of Parliament);
- secondary legislation (the rules and regulations that implement Acts);
- aspects of the common law and European law, and some guidance[1].

The review also carefully considered some overlapping issues:

- child protection and welfare through social work, health, education and the criminal law; and
- discipline, punishment and record-keeping.

This chapter, therefore, seeks to map out the legal framework in the light of these sources and issues. The review tried to do this by considering two significant periods:

- 1950–1968 (that is, before the Social Work (Scotland) Act 1968); and
- 1968–1995 (from the 1968 Act up to, and including, the Children (Scotland) Act 1995).

The review also felt it was relevant and important to consider any developments that have shaped or influenced how the legal framework developed, before and after the period specified in our remit. Only by doing this can we consider fully how well the whole system worked.

This type of study is by definition historical, and must be viewed against the background of inevitable social change over the period we've examined.

---

[1] While not part of the formal regulation, reports such as that produced by the Kilbrandon Committee prove an invaluable aid in identifying any shortcomings in the law. *Report of the Committee on Children and Young Persons, Scotland* (1964) (Cmnd 2306)

The chapter comprises the following parts and sections:

Part one: 1950-1968

Section 1: How laws have sought to protect children and their welfare

Section 2: How laws provided for residential schools
- What was in place for residential (approved) schools?
- How were approved schools run?
- How were pupils treated in approved schools?
  - Education, discipline and punishment
  - Health and safety
  - Inspections and record-keeping

Section 3: How the law provided for children's homes
- Local authority homes
- Voluntary homes
- How local authority and voluntary homes were managed and administered
- How pupils were treated in local authority and voluntary homes
  - Education, discipline and punishment
  - Health and safety
  - Inspections and record-keeping

Section 4: How laws provided for other institutions
- Children and young people who were labelled "mentally defective"
- Children with disabilities
- Special schools
- Remand homes
- Other institutions

Part two: 1968-1995

Section 5: How social work principles changed from the 1960s
- The Social Work (Scotland) Act 1968

Section 6: How the law provided for residential establishments

Section 7: How residential establishments were regulated in practice
- A note on approved schools
- The Social Work (Residential Establishments – Child Care) (Scotland) Regulations 1987
- Secure accommodation
- Children and young people with mental disorders

Section 8: Further developments in the 1980s and 1990s

Section 9: The Children (Scotland) Act 1995

Part three: 1995-present day

Section 10: Developments since 1995
- Children cared for in residential establishments
- Secure accommodation
- The Regulation of Care (Scotland) Act 2001

Part one: 1950-1968

Section 1: How laws have sought to protect children and their welfare

My remit required me to consider the laws and regulations specific to residential schools and children's homes between 1950 and 1995. However, it is important to first identify the basis in law of the child protection and welfare framework, and to do this we must look beyond the period specified in the remit.

The way the legal system traditionally dealt with ill-treated children who had unsuitable parents was grounded in the Poor Law, which focused on boarding out children to people who were regarded as appropriate carers [2]. This approach changed in the 20th century as laws began to focus on child welfare. As a result, early recognition [3] that the law should prevent cruelty to children (for example, in laws such as the Children Act 1908 [4]) was continued and extended under The Children and Young Persons (Scotland) Act 1937 [5]. This Act laid the foundations for the modern law on child protection, and substantially increased the legal responsibilities of public authorities [6], such as local councils. From here on, we refer to it as "the 1937 Act".

The 1937 Act – and the amendments to it since 1937 – provided most of the fundamental rules for the protection and welfare of children and young people [7] during the 1950s and 1960s. Section 12 [8] recognised the need to make more detailed provision on child cruelty:

"**Section 12** Cruelty to persons under 16 - (1) If any person who has attained the age of sixteen years and has the custody, charge, or care of any child or young person under that age [9], wilfully assaults, ill-treats, neglects, abandons, or exposes him, or causes or procures him to be assaulted, ill-treated, neglected, abandoned or exposed, in a manner likely to cause him unnecessary suffering or injury to health (including injury to or loss of sight, or hearing, or limb, or organ of the body, and any mental derangement), that person shall be guilty of an offence...

"(2) For the purposes of this section - (a) a parent or other person legally liable to maintain a child or young person [10] shall be deemed to have neglected him in a manner likely to cause injury to his health if he has failed to provide adequate food, clothing, medical aid or lodging for him, or if, having been unable otherwise to provide such food, clothing, medical aid or lodging he has failed to take steps to procure it to be provided under the Acts relating to the relief of the poor...

"(7) Nothing in this section shall be construed as affecting the right of any parent, teacher, or other person having the lawful control or charge of a child or young person to administer punishment to him."

---

[2] For example, the Poor Law Amendment Act 1845. See also the attempts to tackle abuse and neglect, most evident in the Glasgow and Edinburgh Societies "for the Prevention of Cruelty to Children" in 1889 joining to form the Scottish Society (RSSPCC), as recognised by Alison Clelland and Elaine Sutherland in the Stair Memorial Encyclopaedia *The Laws of Scotland: Child and Family Law*.

[3] Under common law, maltreatment of infants and children was already punishable - see, for example, *McIntosh* (1881) 8 R (J) 13; 4 Coup 389

[4] c67

[5] c37

[6] . See Caroline Ball (1998) 'Regulating child care: from the Children Act 1948 to the present day' in Child and Family Social Work Vol. 3 pp 163 - 171, as referenced in Jackie McRae 'Children looked after by local authorities: the legal framework' Social Work Inspection Agency, 2006

[7] "Child" (except as provided in s37) meaning someone under 14 years, and "Young Person" meaning someone who has reached 14 years and is under 17 years. See s110(1) of the Children and Young Persons (Scotland) Act 1937

[8] later amended by the Children (Scotland) Act 1995, s105(4), Sch 4 para 7(2) and the Criminal Justice (Scotland) Act 2003, s51(5).

[9] The words from "has the custody" to "that age" substituted with "who has parental responsibilities in relation to a child or to a young person under that age or has charge or care of a child or such a young person," by the Children (Scotland) Act 1995

[10] "[O]r the legal guardian of a child or young person" inserted after "young person" by the Children (Scotland) Act 1995

This section effectively meant that anyone over 16 years could be found guilty of an offence for assaulting, ill-treating, neglecting or abandoning a child (section 12 (2) (a) defining "neglect" as failing "to provide adequate food, clothing, medical aid or lodging" for the child). Thus, the provision emphasised the duty of parents **and others caring for children** to look after their physical welfare, although notably failed to deal with psychological or emotional abuse[11]. However, it is worth noting, in relation to assault, that section 12 (7) explicitly preserved the right of parents to physically punish a child[12].

It is also important to note that the Act acknowledged the need to protect children against sexual activity: section 13 protected 16-year-old girls from being seduced, encouraged to have sexual intercourse, prostitution and indecent assault. This is in addition to the great number of sexual offences designed to protect both boys and girls, such as rape, indecent assault, lewd and libidinous practices, and shameless indecency[13].

If an offence were committed under these provisions, the Act provided for children to be removed to a "place of safety". Section 110(1) defined this as "any remand home, poor house, or police station, or any hospital, surgery, or any other suitable place, the occupier of which is willing temporarily to receive a child or young person". Section 47 stated that a justice of the peace could issue a warrant authorising a police constable to search for and remove a child, if he or she suspected that:

- a child was being assaulted, ill-treated or neglected in a manner likely to cause him or her unnecessary suffering or injury to health; or
- a so-called "Schedule 1" offence was being committed against the child. A Schedule 1 offence covered:
  - any offence under the Criminal Law Amendment Act 1885;
  - incest;
  - any offence under sections 12, 13, 14, 15, 22 and 33 of the 1937 Act; and
  - any other offence involving bodily injury to a child or young person[14].

To protect children in the long term, juvenile courts had the power to order alternative care for children who needed "care and protection", which was defined by section 65[15].

Furthermore, provision existed under The Children Act 1948[16] for those children who were orphaned or deserted, but who weren't the victims of an offence. Section 1 provided that local authorities had a duty to put a child under 17 into care in the interests of its welfare if it appeared that:

- the child had neither parent nor guardian;
- the child had been abandoned by parents or guardians; or
- the parents or guardians were unable, due to mental, physical or other incapacity, to provide for the child's proper accommodation, maintenance and upbringing.

---

[11] Indeed, it has been held that the equivalent English provision was not intended to deal with spiritual or emotional needs. See R v Sheppard [1981] AC 394 at 404, [1980] 3 All ER 899 at 902, per Lord Diplock

[12] We discuss the issue of corporal punishment later in this chapter

[13] Sexual offences were contained in various statutes and existed in the common law, and a number of them were consolidated under the terms of the Criminal Law (Consolidation) (Scotland) Act 1995 (c. 39), and latterly the Sexual Offences Act 2003, and the Protection of Children and Prevention of Sexual Offences (Scotland) Act 2005. It is worth noting, however, that Scots Law failed to recognise male rape - instead, any sexual act against a boy was, and is, tried under indecent assault, a form of aggravated assault. This position is currently under review by the Scottish Government.

[14] Schedule 1 of the 1937 Act was repealed by Schedule 10 of the Criminal Procedure (Scotland) Act 1975. Replaced by Schedule 1 of that Act

[15] Children and young people coming under the definition if they had no parent or guardian, if the parent or guardian was "unfit", if they were falling into bad associations, being exposed to moral danger or beyond control. Section 65 was repealed by Schedule 9 of the Social Work (Scotland) Act 1968 c.49

[16] c.43. later repealed by the Social Work (Scotland) Act 1968

At this general level, therefore, it seems clear there was at least some basis in law for adequately protecting children and young people. For example, section 49 of the 1937 Act further developed the principle of unsuitable carers, by stating that courts had to take account of a child or young person's welfare and, if appropriate, take steps to remove them from "undesirable surroundings". This suggests the law protected children and young people from those who had charge or control over them[17]. But it seems more likely that the law was geared towards shielding them from the dangers of their own abusive household, the implication being that, once a child or young person was removed to a "place of safety" they would be free from the risk of harm.

Section 2: How laws provided for residential schools

This section considers:

- What was in place for residential (approved) schools?
- How were approved schools run?
- How were pupils treated in approved schools?
  - Education, discipline and punishment
  - Health and safety
  - Inspections and record-keeping

What was in place for residential (approved) schools?

Firstly, it's important to establish what the term "residential school" means.

The state recognised as early as 1854 that children and young people could be sent to certain types of schools by order of a court. However, until 1933 these schools were divided into two types: reformatory and industrial. Reformatory schools dealt with delinquents while industrial schools were charged with turning destitute children into respectable and useful citizens[18]. Not until The Children and Young Persons (Scotland) Act 1932[19] (we call this the 1932 Act from here on) was this distinction abolished, and the term "approved school" given to them all[20]. Generally speaking, the function of such schools was to provide education and training on a residential basis for children and young people not aged more than 16 on committal, who had been sent to them by the courts because they had committed an offence or were in need of care or protection[21]. School managers could apply to the Scottish Education Department (SED) to approve the school to care for the children. The SED, after making such enquiries as they saw fit, could approve the school for such a purpose and issue a certificate of approval to the managers[22].

Five years later these provisions were consolidated by The Children and Young Persons (Scotland) Act 1937. Section 61[23] preserved a court's right to send to an approved school[24] any child or young person found guilty of an offence, and section 62[25] gave the Secretary of State more powers to send some juvenile offenders – for example, those detained in a Borstal institution[26] - to approved schools. Children and young people could be brought before a court by an education authority[27], constable, or authorised person[28], or even a parent orguardian[29]. And if the court felt they

---

[17] This is the definition given to the term "guardianship" in s110(1) of the 1937 Act

[18] This information is taken from the S.E.D. Memorandum "Approved Schools in Scotland: Social Work, Scotland Vote" (Class VI, 22). Circulated with agenda for 18/12/1970

[19] c.47

[20] Essentially a school approved by the Secretary of State for the purposes of the Act

[21] Memorandum "Approved Schools in Scotland: Social Work, Scotland Vote" (Class VI, 22). Circulated with agenda for 18/12/1970

[22] The Children and Young Persons (Scotland) Act 1932, Schedule 1, paragraph 1

[23] Repealed by Schedule 9 of the Social Work (Scotland) Act 1968 c.49

[24] Finding definition in s110(1) as "a school approved by the Scottish Education Department under section eighty-three of this Act"

[25] As amended by the Criminal Justice (Scotland) Act 1949, the Social Work (Scotland) Act 1968, and the Criminal Procedure (Scotland) Act 1995

[26] Meaning "an institution established under Part I of the Prevention of Crime Act 1908, c.59" - Children and Young Persons (Scotland) Act 1937, s110(1). Section 62 as amended by the Criminal Justice (Scotland) Act 1949

[27] Later "local authority" under the Children Act 1948

[28] Children and Young Persons (Scotland) Act 1937, s66 (later repealed by the Social Work (Scotland) Act 1968, Schedule 9)

[29] *ibid* s68 (later repealed by the Social Work (Scotland) Act 1968, Schedule 9)

needed "care and protection"[30] it could order them to be placed in an approved school[31].

The court or SED was responsible, where practicable, for choosing a school, depending on the child's religion. Indeed the SED could choose a school based on several factors. These included:

- the child's religion;
- what kind of education and training the school provided;
- where the school was located; and
- anything else that they thought would make sure the child was sent to a school appropriate to his or her case[32].

How were approved schools run?

As with the 1932 Act, the managers of a school intended for the residential education and training of children and young people could apply to the SED for approval under the 1937 Act. The SED would make such enquiries as they saw fit and could issue a certificate of approval to the managers[33].

The managers tended to be the education authority or joint committee representing two or more education authorities, or other "persons for the time being having the management or control" of a school[34]. However, although the education authorities did have a role to play – for example, under section 84[35] of the 1937 Act, they were responsible for providing approved schools if more accommodation

was needed – in practice, they managed a small minority of schools. The rest were administered by voluntary organisations[36].

Regardless of the type of management, the general principles of administration were similar. Schedule 2 of the 1937 Act[37] set out how the schools should be administered and how children should be treated[38]. Firstly, it gave the SED power to make additional rules for management and discipline at approved schools under paragraph 1(1), but crucially allowed schools a wide margin for manoeuvre by stating that different rules could be made "as respects different schools or classes of schools"[39].

Furthermore, the Schedule allowed school managers to make supplementary rules for managing and discipline in an approved school, but only with the SED's approval[40]. Lastly, the management was given significant responsibility over the children in the school's care by vesting in them the same legal rights and powers as a parent[41].

However, it was the supplementary rules introduced under the 1932 Act[42] that in fact provided the backbone for day-to-day regulation of approved schools in Scotland until 1961[43]. This set of regulations – the Children and Young Persons (Scotland) Care and Training Regulations 1933[44] (we call these the 1933 regulations from here on) – governed how approved schools were managed during the first 11 years of our review period.

---

[30]   *ibid* s65. See n15 above
[31]   *ibid* s66
[32]   *ibid* s85 (1). Later repealed by the Social Work (Scotland) Act 1968, Schedule 9
[33]   *ibid* s83. Later repealed by the Social Work (Scotland) Act 1968, Schedule 9
[34]   *ibid* s110(1)
[35]   Repealed by the Social Work (Scotland) Act 1968, Schedule 9
[36]   See S.E.D. Memorandum "Approved Schools in Scotland: Social Work, Scotland Vote" (Class VI, 22). Circulated with agenda for 18/12/1970. By the end of the 1960s only three from a total of 27 approved schools in Scotland were managed by an education authority (Glasgow Corporation). Although it should be noted that in both cases under s107 of the 1937 Act, sums could be paid from the exchequer on stated conditions towards the expenses of managers of an approved school
[37]   Schedule 2 later repealed by Schedule 9 of the Social Work (Scotland) Act 1968
[38]   Children and Young Persons (Scotland) Act 1937, s85. Repealed by the Social Work (Scotland) Act 1968, Schedule 9
[39]   *ibid* Schedule 2, paragraph 1(1)
[40]   *ibid* Schedule 2, paragraph 1(2)
[41]   *ibid* Schedule 2, Paragraph 12(1), which went on to say: "provided that, where a person out on licence or under supervision from an approved school is lawfully living with his parents or either of them, the said rights may be exercisable by the parents [or parent]...but it shall be the duty of any such parent so to exercise those rights and powers as to assist the managers to exercise control over him"
[42]   Made in accordance with Paragraph 8(1) of the First Schedule to the 1932 Act
[43]   It wasn't until 1961 that paragraph 1(1) of Schedule 2 and s83 of the 1937 Act were invoked to introduce the Approved Schools (Scotland) Rules 1961 (SI 1961/2243)
[44]   SI 1933/1006. Revoked by the Approved Schools (Scotland) Rules 1961 (SI 1961/2243)

Under these regulations, the SED retained some control over the management. Paragraph 1 provided that each manager's name and address had to be sent to the Department, who could appoint additional managers if they felt it necessary. The provisions also required managers – or a committee of managers – to meet as often as needed "for the efficient management of the school"[45]. Frustratingly this phrase wasn't defined, but at least shows the beginnings of a monitoring function for managers of approved schools. This was further highlighted in the requirement that managers carry out school visits from time to time[46] (although, again, the scope and purpose of this requirement wasn't fully explained). Indeed, the overall responsibility of the management was clear: although headmasters and headmistresses were responsible – admittedly, to the managers – for overall conduct and discipline in school, it was the managers who had the power to appoint and dismiss staff, subject to the SED approving qualifications[47].

It seems fair to say that the 1933 regulations, introduced at the dawn of the approved school era, did little to promote the need for school managers to fulfil a welfare-orientated role. It wasn't until the rules were revoked in 1961 that a shift took place towards regulating schools in more specific ways. The change occurred under the Approved Schools (Scotland) Rules 1961[48] (which are called the 1961 rules from here on).

The 1933 regulations had introduced the requirement for the SED to have details of each manager[49]. The 1961 rules maintained this; paragraph 2(1) set down guidelines for managers visiting schools:

"The Managers, or a Committee consisting of not less than four of them shall normally meet not less often than once a month. They shall arrange for the school to be visited by one or more of their number at least once a month, and more frequently if circumstances appear to warrant it, to ensure that the conditions of the school and the welfare, development and rehabilitation of the pupils under their care are satisfactory. The visiting Manager shall sign the log book and may enter such observations as he sees fit."

Under the 1961 rules, the management of approved schools was to be "in the interests of the welfare, development and rehabilitation of the pupils"[50].

Not only should visiting managers take the opportunity to speak to individual pupils[51], but they should also discuss with the headmaster any complaint that a pupil made[52].

Furthermore, managers of approved schools were now subject to tighter guidelines. Before, they had to make "periodic" visits; now they had to visit at least once a month to ensure the satisfactory welfare and development of the children and young people under their care. And, while managers still had the right to hire and fire staff[53], a full report on the circumstances of a dismissal had to be sent to the Secretary of State if it was because of the "character or conduct" of a member of staff[54].

However, it's worth noting that, while the 1961 rules applied to all approved schools in principle, the Secretary of State still had the right to waive any provision as he saw fit[55], effectively meaning that parts of the regulations didn't have to apply to all schools in all circumstances. This is an important power and raises more questions about what authority the Secretary of State had over how approved schools were managed.

---

[45] Children and Young Persons (Scotland) Care and Training Regulations 1933 (SI 1933/1006), paragraph 2

[46] *ibid*

[47] *ibid* paragraph 7

[48] SI 1961/2243. Brought in under the Children and Young Persons (Scotland) Act 1937, s83 and Schedule 2, paragraph 1(1). Amended by the Approved Schools (Scotland) Amendment Rules 1963 (SI 1963/1756)

[49] Approved Schools (Scotland) Rules 1961 (SI 1961/2243), paragraph 1

[50] *ibid*, paragraph 4

[51] *ibid*, paragraph 2(1)

[52] *ibid*, paragraph 2(4)

[53] *ibid*, paragraph 10(2), subject to s81 of the Education (Scotland) Act 1946

[54] *ibid*, paragraph 10(3)

[55] *ibid*, paragraph 51. Such a provision was also found in the 1933 regulations, paragraph 26

Under the 1937 Act[56], the Secretary of State could order that pupils be discharged, transferred to another school, or placed in the community on licence[57]. But if the SED was dissatisfied with the condition of an approved school or how it was being run, its only legal remedy was to withdraw the school's certificate of approval, under section 83 (2) of the 1937 Act[58]. This was the case until 1963, when the Criminal Justice (Scotland) Act 1963[59] introduced wider directions for how approved schools should be managed.

The 1963 Act retained the right to withdraw a school's certificate of approval[60] and order a pupil's release[61]. Under section 21(1) of the Act the Secretary of State could consider an approved school's:

- premises and equipment;
- number and grades of staff; and
- education, training and welfare of the children under the managers' care.

If he felt any of these weren't adequate or suitable he could give managers whatever directions he felt were needed to achieve the proper standard.

Section 22 further allowed the Secretary of State to regulate the constitution and proceedings of the school managers, and to appoint new managers. This seems a significant increase in the power available to the Secretary of State, and perhaps indicates a shift in the 1960s towards clearer regulation aimed at improving how the management of schools was monitored.

How were pupils treated in approved schools?

Education, discipline and punishment

As already noted, pupils at approved schools could be young offenders ordered there by a court[62] or transferred by the Secretary of State[63]; or people considered to be "in need of care and protection"[64].

There is no doubt that children from such different backgrounds were, in practice, placed together – and questions arise as to whether this was appropriate to their educational and welfare needs. But in terms of the legal framework it is clear that the SED had at least some responsibility to place pupils in a school suited to their needs. As mentioned earlier, not only was the religious persuasion of the child or young person relevant[65], the schools could be classified depending on the pupils' age, the location, the character of the education and training, or what was considered appropriate to individual pupils' cases. However, it should be noted that this provision was generally classified as a power available to the Department, rather than a legal duty requiring it to act[66].

Regardless of how children were placed, and who with, we clearly need to identify what framework was in place to properly treat pupils once they were in approved schools.

As noted earlier Paragraph 12 of the second Schedule to the 1937 Act gave school managers certain parental rights, and subsection (2) stated that managers were obliged to clothe, maintain and educate the children

[56] Paragraphs 6(2) and 9 of the second Schedule
[57] Essentially a form of probation
[58] Or indeed if they considered its continuance as an approved school unnecessary. Section 83 was repealed by Schedule 9 of the Social Work (Scotland) Act 1968
[59] c.39
[60] Criminal Justice (Scotland) Act 1963, s21(2) in accordance with s 83(2) of the Children and Young Persons (Scotland) Act 1937.
[61] *ibid*, s18(1)
[62] Children and Young Persons (Scotland) Act 1937, s61. Repealed by the Social Work (Scotland) Act 1968, Schedule 9
[63] *ibid* s62, as amended by the Criminal Justice (Scotland) Act 1949, the Social Work (Scotland) Act 1968, and the Criminal Procedure (Scotland) Act 1995
[64] *ibid* s65. See n15 above
[65] *ibid*, s72(2). Repealed by the Social Work (Scotland) Act 1968, Schedule 9
[66] This was similar to the argument put forward by counsel for the Lord Advocate (as modern representative for the SED) in *M v Hendron* 2005 SLT 1122

under their care. This educational right was a crucial component of the overall function of approved schools. (It also sat alongside the various regulations set out by the Education (Scotland) Acts[67].) Yet the 1933 regulations put little emphasis on it.

Paragraph 8 of the 1933 regulations (headed "education, training, etc") stated that details of the education, training, food and timetables of school routine had to be sent to the SED for approval **"as required"**.

This remained the case until the 1961 rules took effect. These stated that inspectors had to approve:

- the school's daily routine (for example, getting-up time, schoolroom instruction and practical training) "from time to time"[68]; and
- the timetable and syllabus.[69]

The rules also stated that the school should provide:

- full-time education appropriate to the age, ability and aptitude of school-age pupils; and
- further education as long as children remained in the school"[70].

However, both the 1933 regulations and 1961 rules provided extensively for disciplining and punishing pupils in approved schools.

Under the 1933 regulations, the discipline of the school was to be maintained by the personal influence of the headmaster or headmistress, and of the staff. They had to keep all forms of punishment to a minimum[71]. Punishment would reflect both the seriousness of the offence and the offender's temperament and physical condition[72]. Offenders would lose:

- privileges or rewards;
- conduct marks, recreation or freedom; or
- loss of rank[73].

The 1933 regulations stated that any pupil being punished should be deprived of recreation for no more than one day at a time[74]. If isolation was considered the best method of what was termed "correction and reform", this should be:

- for no longer than six hours;
- in a room that the regulations stated should be "safe for the purpose"; and
- with regular visits and means of communication with staff[75].

Managers could authorise the principal teacher and assistant teacher to administer minor punishment[76] for offences committed during an ordinary school-room lesson. But they weren't to inflict the same punishment more than once for the same offence[77].

The 1961 rules were almost identical, but included the extra punishment of not allowing home leave for pupils who committed a serious offence[78]. Furthermore, they added an important condition by stating that the Secretary of State's permission was needed[79] for any other forms of punishment, including corporal punishment (which we discuss later).

---

[67] For example: Although "approved schools" were not within the definition of "school" for the purposes of the Education (Scotland) Acts, the Acts generally provided that "it shall be the duty of every education authority to secure that there is made for their area adequate and efficient provision of school education and further education": see the Education (Scotland) Acts 1946 and 1962, s1 (as amended)

[68] Although "time to time" is given no definition, Approved Schools (Scotland) Rules 1961 (SI 1961/2243), paragraph 20

[69] *ibid* paragraph 21(2)

[70] *ibid* paragraph 21 (1)

[71] Children and Young Persons (Scotland) Care and Training Regulations 1933 (SI 1933/1006), paragraph 11

[72] *ibid* paragraph 12

[73] *ibid* paragraph 11

[74] *ibid*

[75] *ibid* paragraph 13

[76] All other punishment to be administered by the headmaster or headmistress. *Ibid* paragraph 16

[77] *ibid* paragraph 17

[78] Approved Schools (Scotland) Rules 1961 (SI 1961/2243) paragraphs 28 - 30

[79] *ibid* paragraph 29

They also expanded, in a separate paragraph, the detail necessary for using segregation as punishment. Segregating a pupil for more than 24 hours, or more than two nights in a row, required written permission by one of the managers and a report to the SED[80]. Further requiring the Secretary of State's approval, which marked an increased role, was the obligation to obtain permission to use part of a school as a special section for abnormally unruly pupils.

This meant that:
- no pupil could be transferred to such a section without the Secretary of State's authority; and
- the rules on managing and running an approved school were to be applied, unless otherwise stated, to the special sections[81].

It should be noted that although the review is to consider what may have allowed children and young people to suffer abuse in a specific[82] period, it has to be seen within the culture of what was regarded at the time as acceptable punishment.

So, while the 1937 Act made it an offence for any child or young person to suffer an assault at the hands of a parent or carer,[83] it also gave parents the right to chastise[84]. This right passed on to school managers when they assumed parental rights under the Second Schedule to the Act[85]. At this time, people accepted corporal punishment as fundamentally important in maintaining discipline to educate youngsters properly. The right of schoolteachers to physically chastise children was normally viewed as independent of the parents' right[86]: "reasonable chastisement"[87] of a child by a teacher was not considered an actionable assault unless the punishment was excessive or involved an improper instrument[88].

As a result, the 1933 regulations and 1961 rules both allowed corporal punishment in approved schools. The 1933 regulations stated that only a "light tawse" (a leather strap) could be used for corporal punishment. Paragraph 14 stated that:
- a cane or any form of cuffing or striking was forbidden;
- corporal punishment should rarely be imposed on girls; and
- the medical officer's consent was needed before punishment was inflicted on a boy or girl who showed any sign of physical or mental weakness[89].

---

[80] *ibid* paragraph 33

[81] *ibid* paragraph 34

[82] The law still avoids any specific definition of child "abuse" or neglect, other than the partial definition of child cruelty that appears in the Children and Young Persons (Scotland) Act 1937, and which is primarily concerned with physical injury. The extent to which modern child protection law has developed its understanding of child cruelty can be seen in the guidelines that are available to agencies working with children throughout Scotland. See Alison Clelland and Elaine Sutherland in the Stair Memorial Encyclopaedia The Laws of Scotland: Child and Family Law, para 275 onwards

[83] Children and Young Persons (Scotland) Act 1937, s12 (1)

[84] *ibid* (section 12 (7)).

[85] "[A]ll rights and powers exercisable by law by a parent shall as respects any person under the care of the managers of an approved school be vested in them" - CYP(S)A 1937, Schedule 2, paragraph 12 (1)

[86] Although an analogous right - see *McShane v Paton* 1922 JC 26

[87] What amounts to "reasonable" has long been debated by the courts. See, e.g. *Cowie v Tudhope* 1987 GWD 12-395; *B v Harris* 1990 SLT 208; *Peebles v MacPhail* 1990 SLT 245. The European Court of Human Rights saw a potential link between the right to physically chastise a child and what constituted abuse, and found the law lacking in this area: *A v UK* 1998 Fam LR 118, [1998] EHRLR 82; 1998-VI; 27 EHRR 611. The Scottish Parliament introduced legislation that has limited the parental right of chastisement, while not abolishing it - Criminal Justice (Scotland) Act 2003 (asp 7), s 51(1)

[88] This was the case right up until, and including, the Education (Scotland) Act 1980. As a result of the decision in *Campbell v Cosans* (1982) 4 EHRR 293, subsequent amendments to the Act (see s40A) provided that the former right of teachers to administer corporal punishment was no longer justified, although it was specifically stated not to be an offence if in pursuance of a right exercisable by a member of staff by virtue of his position as such; if the punishment given were held to be excessive or improper, then an offence would still be committed. Not until the Standards in Scotland's Schools etc Act 2000, s16 was the right to administer corporal punishment deemed unjustifiable in any circumstances. See The Stair Memorial Encyclopaedia, Vol. 8: Education

[89] Children and Young Persons (Scotland) Care and Training Regulations 1933 (SI 1933/1006), paragraph 11. The role of the medical officer was, it is suggested, a crucial one and will be considered in the section on "Health and Safety"

Paragraph 15 detailed the punishments:

"In girls' schools corporal punishment may be inflicted only on the hands and the number of strokes shall not exceed three in all on any one occasion. In boys' schools corporal punishment may be inflicted only on the hands or on the posterior over ordinary cloth trousers, and the number of strokes shall not exceed on any one occasion:
(a) **for boys under 14 years of age:** two strokes on each hand, or four strokes on the posterior over ordinary cloth trousers;
(b) **for boys who have attained the age of 14 years:** three strokes on each hand, or six strokes on the posterior over ordinary cloth trousers."

The principal teacher could punish only boys, not exceeding three strokes on the hands for an offence committed during an ordinary lesson. Otherwise the headmaster or headmistress should administer all punishment[90]. Again, no punishment could be inflicted more than once for the same offence[91].

The guidance on this area of discipline for the first 11 years of our review period was, therefore, quite specific and detailed. It continued almost identically under the 1961 rules.

Curiously, however, paragraph 17 of the 1933 regulations stated that no child should receive corporal punishment in the presence of other children – but didn't stipulate who else should be present. This seems a clear gap in the efficient regulation of approved schools at the time – and was picked up by the 1961 rules. Paragraph 31 of these rules stated that an **adult witness must be present** if the punishment

wasn't carried out in the presence of a class in a schoolroom.[92] The 1961 rules also stated clearly that anyone who broke the rules in this area could be dismissed or subject to other disciplinary action[93] – something the 1933 regulations didn't contain.

The 1961 rules therefore recognised an apparent need to monitor more efficiently the way in which corporal punishment was administered in approved schools. They did this by incorporating the basic rules from the 1933 regulations, but more clearly, with more certainty and clarity – and, we suggest, with some important additions.

So, except for a few crucial items that we've outlined, the 1933 regulations and 1961 rules both laid down an almost identical framework as guidance on corporal punishment. Both also recognised it was vital to keep a punishment book as a monitoring device. The 1933 regulations require the headmaster or headmistress to detail, in the punishment book, all punishments, including those given in the schoolroom. The details had to include the:

- date of punishment;
- offender's name and age;
- nature of the offence;
- name of the officer who administered the punishment;
- nature of the punishment (and in the case of corporal punishment, its exact amount); and
- medical officer's observations, if any.[94]

The 1961 rules replicated these, but added that any witness to corporal punishment should also be noted down.[95]

---

[90] *ibid* paragraph 16.
[91] *ibid* paragraph 17
[92] Approved Schools (Scotland) Rules 1961 (SI 1961/2243) paragraph 31
[93] *ibid*
[94] Children and Young Persons (Scotland) Care and Training Regulations 1933 (SI 1933/1006), paragraph 18
[95] Approved Schools (Scotland) Rules 1961 (SI 1961/2243) paragraph 32 (2)

It's notable that the 1933 regulations' requirement to enter all punishments into the book was replaced in the 1961 rules. These stated that it was necessary to enter only "particulars of each occasion on which home leave is stopped or corporal punishment inflicted". They also stipulated that any teacher who inflicted corporal punishment, under the conditions that were allowed, should report the punishment to the headmaster to be entered in the punishment book.[96]

Health and safety

The laws on maintaining health and safety of pupils in approved schools changed little between 1950 and 1968. Under the 1937 Act (paragraph 12 (2) of the Second Schedule), school managers had to provide for the clothing and maintenance of pupils in their care. Paragraph 4 allowed pupils who needed medical attention to be sent to and kept in a hospital, home or other institution where they could receive the necessary attention[97].

The 1933 regulations (paragraphs 6-9) and 1961 rules (paragraphs 3-6) both placed strict requirements on those responsible for ensuring that schools were properly managed. They laid down the following:

- School buildings had to be maintained in a satisfactory condition, which covered lighting, heating, ventilation, cleanliness, sanitary arrangements and fire-safety[98].
- School buildings had to provide adequate accommodation both for residential and teaching needs[99].
- Managers were responsible for consulting the local fire authority about "suitable and necessary" fire precautions[100].

- The Secretary of State had to approve the instructions to be followed if a fire broke out and "frequent/regular" fire drills had to take place[101].
- The number of pupils in a school was not to exceed the number specified by the Secretary of State or SED. (The 1933 regulations stated "save in exceptional circumstances"; this was removed by the 1961 rules[102].)

The 1961 rules provided more thoroughly for pupils' welfare. Under the heading "Care of Pupils", they stated that schools should provide each pupil with:
- a separate bed in a room with sufficient ventilation;
- suitable clothing; and
- a diet of "sufficient, varied, wholesome and appetising food…adequate for the maintenance of health".

Managers were to draw up the diets after consulting the headmaster and the medical officer and they had to be approved by an inspector[103]. Schools could not withhold a meal from a pupil as a form of punishment[104]. The 1933 regulations contained nothing like this.

The rules and regulations also covered pupils' dental hygiene. Under the 1933 regulations, schools had to arrange for a dentist to examine each pupil when they were admitted, and at least once a year after that[105]. The 1961 rules tightened this to examinations at least every six months, using the School Health Service or the general dental service provided under the National Health Service (Scotland) Act 1947.[106] Both sets of regulations required schools to keep a record of inspection and treatment.

---

[96] *ibid* paragraph 32 (1)
[97] And that person, while so detained, was for the purposes of the Act deemed to be under the care of the managers of the school, and for the purposes of s10 of the Mental Deficiency and Lunacy (Scotland) Act 1913 - later s71 of the Mental Health (Scotland) Act 1960" as inserted by Schedule 4 of the Mental Health (Scotland) Act 1960 - deemed to be detained in the school: Children and Young Persons (Scotland) Act 1937, c.37, Schedule 2 paragraph 4
[98] SI 1933/1006 paragraph 6 (1), and SI 1961/2243 paragraph 3
[99] *ibid*
[100] SI 1933/1006 paragraph 7, and SI 1961/2243 paragraph 4
[101] *ibid*
[102] SI 1933/1006 paragraph 8, and SI 1961/2243 paragraph 5
[103] SI 1961/2243 paragraphs 18 and 19
[104] *ibid* paragraph 19 (1)
[105] SI 1933/1006 paragraph 21
[106] SI 1961/2243 paragraph 42

Arguably, however, it was the medical officer's role[107] that provided the most significant monitoring function affecting pupils' health and safety at approved schools during this period. These officers were required under the 1933 regulations (paragraph 20), which said their duties should include:

■ a thorough medical examination of every pupil when admitted to and shortly before leaving school;

■ a quarterly routine inspection of every pupil;

■ treating the pupils as required; and

■ giving advice on dietary and general hygiene.

The 1961 rules repeated these, but added a further crucial requirement that – as well as inspecting each pupil every quarter – the officer should visit the school at least once each week[108].

Both the 1933 regulations and the 1961 rules required the medical officer to keep whatever records were needed and inform the managers about the school's health.[109] The 1961 rules stated that the medical officers should also provide whatever reports and certificates "as the Managers may require".[110]

However, perhaps most significant was the requirement under the two sets of rules and regulations that the medical officer should examine the punishment book at each visit and draw the managers' attention to any apparent case of excessive punishment.[111] This highlights an interesting and important supervisory responsibility that medical officers were given – and one that required a joint effort with managers to uphold pupils' welfare. Whether, of course, the practice met the principle is something we discuss elsewhere in the report.

Inspections and record-keeping

In considering what other inspection procedures approved schools were subject to, it is necessary to examine parts of the 1937 Act.

In general, section 106 provided for the powers of the Secretary of State and the SED to appoint inspectors:

"(1) The Secretary of State and the Scottish Education Department may, for the purposes of their respective powers and duties under the enactments relating to children and young persons, appoint such number of inspectors as the Treasury may approve and may pay to the persons respectively appointed by them such remuneration and allowances…and the Department may authorise or require any of His Majesty's Inspectors of Schools to exercise any power or perform any duty which might be exercised or performed by an inspector appointed in pursuance of this section."[112]

The SED, through their inspectors, had a specific duty[113] to review the progress of pupils detained in approved schools, with a view to ensuring that they were placed out on licence as soon as they were fit to be[114]. The 1933 regulations and 1961 rules expanded these inspection powers.

---

[107] Given no definition under the 1933 regulations, but defined in the 1961 rules as "the medical practitioner appointed under Rule 40" - SI 1961/2243 paragraph 53 (1)

[108] *ibid* paragraph 40 (d)

[109] SI 1933/1006 paragraph 20; SI 1961/2243 paragraph 40

[110] SI 1961/2243 paragraph 40 (g)

[111] SI 1933/1006 paragraph 20; SI 1961/2243 paragraph 40

[112] c.37, s106(1). In general, the Education (Scotland) Acts provided for inspection procedures as well. Although approved schools were not within the definition of "school" for the purposes of the Acts, "educational establishments" (including residential institutions conducted under endowment schemes) were within its remit and schools providing boarding for children were also covered. Thus, for example, the Education (Scotland) Act 1962, s67 (restating the same principle contained in the Education (Scotland) Act 1946 as amended) determined that it was "the duty of the Secretary of State to cause inspection to be made of any educational establishment". This duty of inspection was replaced with a discretionary power under amendments made by s11 of the Education (Scotland) Act 1969. This remains the position to the present day, for example recognised in s66(1) of the Education (Scotland) Act 1980

[113] As recognised by counsel for the Lord Advocate (as modern representative for the SED) in *M v Hendron* 2005 SLT 1122

[114] Children and Young Persons (Scotland) Act 1937, c.37, Schedule 2 paragraph 6 (2)

Under the 1933 regulations[115], approved schools had to be open at all times to inspection by His Majesty's Inspector of Schools or by any officer that the SED appointed to carry out an inspection. School records had to be available for examination, and inspectors could note in the log book any visit paid to the school and any details that needed attention".[116]

The 1961 rules continued these general powers of inspection, but with an important addition: managers had to have arrangements available for inspectors to interview staff and pupils.[117]

This was a relatively minor but still significant increase in authority. Furthermore, the managers themselves were placed under a duty to visit the school at least once a month (as opposed to merely "periodically" under the 1933 regulations[118]). They had to make sure that school conditions and the pupils' welfare, development and rehabilitation were satisfactory[119]. This shift towards a more welfare-oriented system of regulating schools was also evident in a requirement that inspection visits had to be signed in the log book and any remarks noted[120].

In addition to the various monitoring duties given to inspectors and managers, the rules and regulations also recognised the need to allow forms of communication with parents and guardians.

The 1933 regulations stated that pupils were allowed letters and visits from parents or guardians at "reasonable intervals" that managers could decide. These "privileges" could be suspended if they interfered with school discipline, although any suspension had to be noted in the log book[121].

The 1961 rules echoed these provisions[122], but they attached more importance to letters as means of communication. They stated that pupils could receive letters, but added that pupils should be actively encouraged to write to their parents at least once a week[123]. Every letter to or from a pupil could be read by a member of staff delegated by the headmaster, and withheld if appropriate (although the facts and circumstances of any letter withheld had to be noted in the log book, and the letter kept for at least a year).[124] Importantly however, schools could not withhold a letter to a school manager, the Secretary of State or any of his officers or departments.[125]

It can therefore be argued that writing letters and receiving visits played a small but important part in allowing people other than inspectors or managers to monitor pupils in approved schools.

The 1933 regulations and 1961 rules included additional requirements on schools to keep records. Under the 1933 regulations, headmasters and headmistresses had to keep whatever records as may be required. These included (under paragraph 23):

- a general record of all pupils admitted, licensed and discharged;
- individual records of pupils under the care of the managers;
- a log book, recording:
  - any written report on the school communicated to the managers;
  - visits of any managers; and
  - all events connected with the school that "deserve to be recorded";
- a punishment book[126]; and
- a separate register of pupils attending the school to be taught.

---

[115] Introduced under the Children and Young Persons (Scotland) Act 1932, c.47

[116] SI 1933/1006 paragraph 24

[117] SI 1961/2243 paragraph 48

[118] SI 1933/1006 paragraph 2

[119] SI 1961/2243 paragraph 2 (1)

[120] *ibid*

[121] SI 1933/1006 paragraph 19.

[122] SI 1961/2243 paragraph 36

[123] *ibid* paragraph 35. For this purpose postage stamps were to be provided free, once a week, by the managers

[124] *ibid*

[125] *ibid*

[126] See also SI 1933/1006 paragraph 18

The 1961 rules incorporated these requirements but, notably, also required schools to keep "an adequate record" of each pupil's progress, and a record of every time a pupil absconded from the school[127]. In addition:

- the records had to be available to managers at all times;
- the log book had to be presented at every management meeting; and
- the chairman had to certify that he had read items recorded since the last meeting[128].

This increase in responsibility under the 1961 rules shows more recognition of the importance of record keeping and its role in monitoring. Indeed, all returns called for by the Secretary of State were to be duly made and managers had to arrange to keep all necessary records[129].

Section 3: How the law provided for children's homes

This section of the report considers:

- Local authority homes
- Voluntary homes
- How local authority and voluntary homes were managed and administered
- How pupils were treated in local authority and voluntary homes
  - Education, discipline and punishment
  - Health and safety
  - Inspections and record-keeping

As seen earlier, the legislation provided an obvious definition for "residential schools" – namely approved schools – but it's less clear what the term "children's homes" meant. For the purposes of this review, the term will be seen to cover both homes provided by local authorities for children in their care, and homes helped by voluntary contributions.

However, other institutions existed to care for children with mental defects or physical disabilities, and the question also arises as to how "remand homes" were regulated (that is, institutions created to provide accommodation and care specifically for juvenile delinquents).

The review's approach has therefore been, firstly, to examine local authority and voluntary homes – how they were provided, maintained and regulated – and then to consider other types of institution providing residential care for children during this period.

Local authority homes

The 1937 Act played a part in properly regulating children's homes between 1950 and 1968, but it was the Children Act 1948[130] (which we call the 1948 Act from here on) which proved most crucial in laying the framework for guidance in this area.

The 1948 Act amended parts of the 1937 Act, but its most significant role was in formalising child services and for the first time creating specific duties owed to children[131]. As we have seen, local authorities had a duty to take orphaned or deserted children in their area into care[132], and could assume significant parental rights for children in their care[133]. The Act ensured there was no overlap with any similar rights that those in charge of approved schools might assume. Therefore if any child under the care of a local authority became the subject of an approved school order, the parental rights that the local authority had would cease and would be transferred to the body in charge of the approved school[134]. The 1948 Act also provided that any children out on licence or in local authority care with the consent of the managers of an approved school would still be considered under the managers' care[135].

---

[127] SI 1961/2243 paragraph 11(1)(b) and (f). The details to be shown in the punishment book were outlined under paragraph 32

[128] *ibid* paragraph 11(3)

[129] *ibid* paragraph 49

[130] c.43. Later repealed by the Social Work (Scotland) Act 1968

[131] "child" being generally defined under the Act as a person under the age of eighteen: the Children Act 1948, c.43, s59

[132] This chiefly applied to children under the age of seventeen: the Children Act 1948, c.43, s1

[133] *Ibid* s2

[134] *ibid* s6(3)(a)

[135] And therefore still within the terms of the 1937 Act. *Ibid* s6(4)

Part II of the 1948 Act covered:

■ local authorities' powers over and duties towards children they took into care under section 1 of the Act; and

■ children placed in their care by order of court under the 1937 Act.

It placed a general duty on local authorities to use their powers in a way that furthered the children's best interests, and to give them the opportunity to develop their character and abilities.[136]

In addition to these welfare principles, section 15 of the 1948 Act made it a duty for local authorities to provide homes to accommodate children in their care. This included separate accommodation, for temporarily receiving children, with facilities necessary for "observation of their physical and mental condition"[137]. However, if a local authority was unable to provide this accommodation itself, it could discharge its obligation under the 1948 Act in a number of ways. It could:

■ arrange with another local authority to provide homes[138];

■ board the child out[139]; or

■ place the child in a voluntary home where managers were willing to receive the child[140].

This was still an important responsibility, introduced under the 1948 Act, and was bolstered by the power given to the Secretary of State to make regulations about how local authorities should carry out their functions and run the homes, and for securing the welfare of the children in the homes[141]. In particular, these regulations could impose requirements covering accommodation, health, facilities that catered for children's religion, and the appointment of staff[142].

The Secretary of State also had the power to serve a notice on the local authority not to use a property as a home if he considered that the property was unsuitable or not being run in line with the regulations made by him[143].

It's worth noting that local authorities' powers to promote children's welfare were confined to caring for:

■ the children they received into care under the 1948 Act; and

■ children committed to their care by a court order under the 1937 Act.

This remained the position until the Children and Young Persons Act 1963[144], which extended local authorities' powers. Section 1 stated that every local authority had a duty to make available any advice, guidance and help needed to promote children's welfare. This was aimed at diminishing the need to put children into care under the 1937 or 1948 Acts, or bringing them before a juvenile court, by placing the local authority under a duty to take action while a child was still in its own home. This duty was the responsibility of local authorities' children's committees; but in practice it was carried out by voluntary groups such as the Family Service Units, Save the Children Fund, Family Welfare Association and the Women's Voluntary Service.

---

[136] *ibid* s12(1)

[137] *ibid* s15(1), (2)

[138] *ibid* s15(3)

[139] *ibid* s13(1)(a)

[140] *ibid* s13(1)(b). Amendments under Schedule 8 of the Social Work (Scotland) Act 1968 provided: '...at the end of section 13(1) there shall be inserted the words "and arrangements may be made under this subsection for boarding out a child in Scotland, or for maintaining him in a residential establishment provided, or the provision of which is secured, or which is registered, under Part IV of the Social Work (Scotland) Act 1968"'.

[141] *ibid* s15(4)

[142] *ibid* s15(4)(a) - (d)

[143] *ibid* s15(5)

[144] c. 37

Voluntary homes

Local authorities had clear duties to provide suitable accommodation for children who were in their care for whatever reason[145]. As mentioned, one way of doing this was to put the child in a voluntary home[146]. For the period of the review, the 1937 Act began to provide for these. It defined voluntary homes as:

"any home or other institution for the boarding, care, and maintenance of poor children or young persons, being a home or other institution supported wholly or partly by voluntary contributions"[147].

However, this term didn't include any institution or house that the General Board of Control for Scotland certified under the Mental Deficiency and Lunacy (Scotland) Act 1913 – unless children were taken into these but weren't what this Act termed "mental defectives"[148].

The 1937 Act provided for voluntary homes to be inspected[149] (which we'll discuss later), and gave the Secretary of State an important monitoring function. He could give any instructions to managers to ensure children's welfare if he felt that the management, accommodation or treatment of children posed a danger to their welfare[150].

The terms of the 1937 Act largely stayed in force between 1950 and 1968, although the monitoring function described was an exception. Section 29(9) of the 1948 Act replaced it with more extensive powers. Regulations could now extend to:

- the accommodation and equipment that voluntary homes provided;
- medical arrangements for protecting children's health; and
- consultation with the Secretary of State on people applying to take charge of a home[151] (although it's worth noting that this consultation wasn't always required under the regulations).

The Act stated that a child in local authority care shouldn't be placed in a voluntary home if it couldn't provide facilities for the child to receive a religious upbringing in keeping with his or her religion[152]. Perhaps most importantly, however, the 1948 Act required that voluntary homes had to be registered with the Secretary of State[153]. If a home wasn't registered – or if a home was to be removed from the register – the child had to go into the local authority's care.[154] This requirement went hand in hand with section 16 of the 1948 Act, which gave the local authority the right (and indeed duty if required by the Secretary of State or the managers of the home) to remove children from a voluntary home.

How local authority and voluntary homes were managed and administered

The 1948 Act allowed for regulations to be made that covered areas such as how local authority and voluntary homes were run and maintained, and yet the first set of regulations to be introduced under this power didn't occur until 1959. So the question arises as to what rules governed the day-to-day operation of such homes before this.

[145] i.e. whether those children were orphans, deserted, or placed by order of court

[146] The Children Act 1948, c.43, s13(1)(b)

[147] The Children and Young Persons (Scotland) Act 1937, s96 (later repealed by the Social Work (Scotland) Act 1968, Sch 9). This reference was taken to include a reference to a home or other institution supported wholly or partly by endowments, not being a school within the meaning of the Education (Scotland) Act 1946 - as added by the Children Act 1948, s27

[148] ibid. From the words "any institution" to the end of the section was later substituted by the words "any private hospital or residential home for persons suffering from mental disorder within the meaning of Part III of the Mental Health (Scotland) Act 1960" by Schedule 4 of the Mental Health (Scotland) Act 1960

[149] The Children and Young Persons (Scotland) Act 1937, s98 (later repealed by the Social Work (Scotland) Act 1968, Sch 9)

[150] ibid s99. Repealed by s29(9) of the Children Act 1948

[151] The Children Act 1948, s31(1). The Secretary of State was also empowered to prohibit the appointment of any particular applicant unless the regulations dispensed with such consultation

[152] ibid s16(2). This provision applied to voluntary homes and local authority homes equally, and was carried through to The Administration of Children's Homes (Scotland) Regulations 1959 SI 1959/834, paragraph 5

[153] ibid s29(1)

[154] ibid s29(6)

The Children (Boarding-Out Etc.) (Scotland) Rules and Regulations 1947[155], covered institutions not classed as poor houses, remand homes or approved schools[156]. So it would have been relied on in relation to the operation of local authority and voluntary homes.

If a local authority was responsible for a child and chose not to place it with a foster parent, the rules generally recognised that the local authority could place the child in:

- an institution subject to being inspected by the Secretary of State under the Children and Young Persons (Scotland) Act 1937 or the Education (Scotland) Acts; or
- an institution that the Secretary of State had specially approved in line with these rules and regulations[157].

Before placing a child, therefore, local authorities had fairly wide powers to make sure that the institution they chose suited the child's needs best[158]. Their powers also meant that that they would be provided with reasonable facilities for visiting the institution and satisfying themselves about arrangements for the child's welfare[159].

Local authority officers had to visit – or arrange a visit by someone with the right qualifications – every child within a month of the local authority placing the child in an institution. Subsequent visits were required at least once every six months[160]. This was reinforced by what we could argue was the most crucial duty placed on the local authority: to arrange visits to these children by members of the authority at least once a year, with the visiting officer reporting to the local authority on:

- the child's health, well-being and behaviour;
- the progress of the child's education; and
- any other matters about the child's welfare that they felt they should report[161].

If a local authority took action on one of these reports, they were required to send a copy of the report and a note of the action taken to the Secretary of State. This highlights an important relationship between the local authority and the Secretary of State, as a result of which:

- no child could be placed in an institution without giving consent[162];
- any person could be visited at any time by any person acting on their behalf[163]; and
- a local authority – if the Secretary of State asked – could be required to remove a child from the care of any institution it was placed in[164].

A final requirement ensured that local authorities should, if asked to do so, send the parents of a child placed in an institution reports from time to time about the child's welfare and progress. And parents were to be allowed to communicate with the child – unless the local authority felt this would be against the child's best interests[165].

---

[155] SI 2146/1947. Made under section 10 of the Poor Law (Scotland) Act 1934, and section 88 (2) of the Children and Young Persons (Scotland) Act 1937

[156] SI 2146/1947, paragraph 2(1)

[157] *ibid* paragraph 23

[158] *ibid* paragraph 24

[159] *ibid* paragraph 26

[160] *ibid* paragraph 27

[161] *ibid*

[162] *ibid* paragraph 29

[163] *ibid* paragraph 30

[164] *ibid* paragraph 31

[165] *ibid* paragraph 33

These 1947 regulations were an important step in providing for homes, but offered very little detail on homes' day-to-day operation. In 1959, however, a new set of regulations was introduced under the 1948 Act[166], known as The Administration of Children's Homes (Scotland) Regulations 1959[167] (we've called them the 1959 regulations from here on). Effectively replacing the terms of the 1947 regulations in this specific area, they sought to deal with the conduct of:

■ children's homes provided by a local authority, and
■ voluntary homes.

However, they didn't cover:

■ remand homes; or
■ voluntary homes that could be inspected by a government department not covered by the provisions of the 1937 Act[168] or used solely for providing holidays of less than one month.

The 1959 regulations – like those introduced for approved schools – covered areas such as children's medical and dental care, standards of sleeping accommodation, fire precautions, discipline, records, and information provided to the Secretary of State. The general standards imposed required the "administering authority" (defined by the regulations as the local authority or people carrying on a home[169]) to make sure the home was run in ways that secured the well-being of the children in its care[170]. This involved two important monitoring functions:

■ The home had to be visited at least once every month by what the regulations described as an "authorised visitor". This person had to satisfy themselves that that the home was being run in line with the regulations and had to enter their details in the home's log book[171].

■ The Secretary of State was to be given any information he required about the home's accommodation and staffing arrangements .

Although the administering authority had the power to appoint someone to be in charge of the home[173], having to consult with the Secretary of State was in line with the procedures laid down in the 1948 Act[174]. In voluntary homes, the person in charge was to be responsible to the administering authority for the home's conduct, and the authority had to notify the Secretary of State if the person in charge changed[175].

How pupils were treated in local authority and voluntary homes

Education, discipline and punishment
Before examining the rules and regulations governing discipline and punishment in children's homes, it's worth noting that some homes had an additional educational function.

This applied to homes that included a school which was a public school, a grant-aided school or an independent school as defined in the Education (Scotland) Acts 1939 to 1956[176], and later 1962. For these, the 1959 regulations provided that most of the rules (including those covering visits, supervision by the medical officer, discipline, punishment and record keeping[177]) "[should] not apply to the part of the home used as a school"[178].

---

[166] The Children Act 1948, s15(4) and s31
[167] SI 1959/834. Revoked by the Social Work (Residential Establishments-Child Care) (Scotland) Regulations 1987
[168] That is, Part VI dealing with homes supported by voluntary contributions
[169] SI 1959/834 paragraph 21(1)
[170] *ibid* paragraph 1
[171] *ibid* paragraph 2
[172] *ibid* paragraph 3
[173] *ibid* paragraph 4
[174] The Children Act 1948, s15(4)(d) and s31(1)
[175] SI 1959/834 paragraph 16
[176] See 9 & 10 Geo. 6, c.72, s143, and 4 & 5 Eliz. 2. C. 75, s13(1), sch 1
[177] But more specifically: Regulations 2, 6(2), 7, 10, 11, and 13-15
[178] SI 1959/834 paragraph 20

The various Education (Scotland) Acts regulated these schools and procedures such as inspections and record keeping[179]. There was, therefore, clearly a distinction between regulating homes in their overall capacity of caring for children on a residential basis (covered by the 1959 regulations), and regulating schools within the home (covered by the various Education (Scotland) Acts and their corresponding rules and regulations). Any school that the Education Acts didn't cover could still, however, seemingly be regulated by the 1959 regulations.

The 1959 regulations covered discipline in homes outside of any school setting. They stated that the general discipline of the children was to be maintained "by the personal influence of the person in charge of the home"[180]. Although rather undefined, this responsibility was still significant. It required the person in charge to report any case of a child being punished with abnormal frequency to the administering authority (the local authority or whoever ran the home), who then had to arrange an investigation of the child's mentality[181].

Any punishment administered to a child had to be recorded in the log book.[182] In general, any punishment for misconduct could only take the form of a temporary loss of recreation or privileges[183] - with one exception, corporal punishment. This had a prominent role in disciplining children in residential care, and the regulations took account of it. Therefore:

■ administering corporal punishment was permitted only in "exceptional" circumstances;

■ it had to be administered by someone who'd been given the power to do so by the home's administering authority; and

■ it had to be in line with whatever rules the administering authority had laid down for the form the punishment would take, and any limits to the punishment[184].

One final condition covered any child known to have any physical or mental disability. In such a case the home's medical officer had to agree before corporal punishment could be administered[185].

Health and safety

As noted that the Children Act 1948 (sections 15(4) and 31(1)) provided for regulations that covered accommodation, equipment and medical arrangements in local authority and voluntary homes.

The 1959 regulations provided for basic sleeping arrangements: each child should have a separate bed in a room with enough ventilation and lighting, and easy access to suitable and sufficient toilets and washing facilities[186]. The home's administering authority had a duty to consult the local fire authority about fire precautions for the home. Regular fire drills and practices were required to ensure staff and children were well versed in the proper evacuation procedure[187]. The administering authority also had to notify the Secretary of State of any outbreak of fire that had required children being removed from the home or from a part of it affected by fire[188].

---

[179] For example, The Education (Scotland) Act 1946, s61, and later The Education (Scotland) Act 1962 s67. "School" was defined as "an institution providing primary or secondary education or both" but did not include an approved school within the meaning of the Children and Young Persons (Scotland) Act 1937: see s143 and s94 respectively. However, although approved schools were not within the definition of "school" for the purposes of the Acts, "educational establishments" (including residential institutions conducted under endowment schemes) were within its remit and schools providing boarding for children were also covered. Thus, for example, the Education (Scotland) Act 1962, s58 and s67 (restating the same principles contained in the Education (Scotland) Act 1946 as amended) determined that it was the duty of the education authority to provide for medical inspection at appropriate intervals of all pupils in educational establishments, and "the duty of the Secretary of State to cause inspection to be made of any educational establishment". This latter wide duty of inspection was replaced with a discretionary power under amendments made by s11 of the Education (Scotland) Act 1969. This remains the position to the present day, for example recognised in s66(1) of the Education (Scotland) Act 1980

[180] SI 1959/834 paragraph 10(1)

[181] *ibid* paragraph 10(4)

[182] *ibid* paragraph 10(3)

[183] *ibid* paragraph 10(2)

[184] *ibid* paragraph 11

[185] *ibid* paragraph 11(b): the sanction could be given in relation to that child either generally or in respect of a particular occasion

[186] *ibid* paragraph 8

[187] *ibid* paragraph 9(1) and (2)

[188] *ibid* paragraph 9(3)

On the subject of maintaining children's health, the 1959 regulations required the home's administering authority to arrange for children's dental care. They could use the school health service, the general dental service provided under the National Health Service (Scotland) Act 1947 or the special arrangements that local authorities made through their maternity and child welfare services for children of pre-school age[189].

Perhaps of greatest significance, however, was the requirement to appoint a medical officer for the home, under paragraph 6 of the regulations. Medical officers had a general supervisory role to ensure the health of the children and staff, and hygiene in a home. They also had to supervise the compilation of a medical record for each child. These detailed the child's:

- medical history before being admitted to the home;
- physical and mental condition when admitted to the home;
- medical history in the home; and
- condition before leaving the home[190].

The medical officer was also responsible for giving advice to the person in charge of the home on anything that affected the health of the children or staff, or hygiene in the home, and had to provide any medical attention that children needed[191].

It's possible to argue that the most important duty of the medical officer was to attend the home at regular intervals, and "with sufficient frequency" to ensure that he was "closely acquainted with the health of the children"[192]. Although the regulations didn't define "regular intervals", the importance of this duty was strengthened by a requirement that each child had to be examined when admitted

to the home, and, after that, at intervals of no less than 12 months[193]. Furthermore, a home's administering authority could appoint more than one medical officer – and even divide the various duties among them[194].

It seems clear that medical officers' duties therefore played a prominent and crucial role in monitoring not only the health but – by implication – the safety of children in local authority and voluntary homes.

Inspections and record-keeping

As noted, medical officers had a clear role in monitoring the welfare of children in local authority and voluntary homes. In addition, a home's administering authority had to arrange monthly visits by what the regulations termed an "authorised visitor"[195] to ensure homes were being run in a way that ensured the children's welfare. Parents and guardians could also visit, and the 1959 regulations stated that the Secretary of State had to be given any information he required about facilities for parents and guardians to visit and communicate with children accommodated in voluntary homes[196].

Overall powers of inspection were, however, granted by The Children Act 1948, working closely with the general terms of the Children and Young Persons (Scotland) Act 1937. Section 54 of the 1948 Act provided that the general provisions on the appointment and duties of inspectors contained in s106 of the 1937 Act would apply[197]. This meant that any inspector appointed under section 106 could go into any local authority home under Part II of the 1948 Act[198], or any place where a child was being boarded by a local authority or a voluntary organisation, and inspect the home and the children[199].

---

[189] *ibid* paragraph 7

[190] *ibid* paragraph 6(2)(a), (b), (g)

[191] *ibid* paragraph 6(2)(c), (f)

[192] *ibid* paragraph 6(2)(d)

[193] And immediately before discharge: ibid paragraph 6(2)(e)

[194] *ibid* paragraph 6(3). In particular, the administering authority could arrange for a medical officer/practitioner to provide children with medical services under Part IV of the National Health Service (Scotland) Act 1947

[195] *ibid* paragraph 2

[196] *ibid* paragraph 17. The Secretary of State could also give directions as to the provision of such facilities

[197] That is, any references to the enactments relating to children and young persons were to include references to the 1948 Act, and later Part I of the Children Act 1958 as added by the Children Act 1958, Schedule 2. The terms of s106 of the 1937 Act are discussed in the "inspection procedures and record keeping" section on approved schools, above

[198] Or any premises under s13(2) or (3): The Children Act 1948, s54(2)(b)

[199] *ibid* s54(2)

Under the 1948 Act, local authorities had a duty to ensure children in voluntary homes received visits. Anyone authorised by a local authority could go into any voluntary home to check on the children's well-being[200]. This was to go hand in hand with the 1937 Act's more detailed procedures for inspecting voluntary homes, which gave the Secretary of State the power to inspect any voluntary home unless it was the subject of inspection by – or by authority of – a government department.[201] Anyone appointed by the Secretary of State had the power to go into a home and examine how it was being managed and the condition and treatment of the children[202].

This was further reinforced by a clear and telling clause that if a home refused to let an inspector in, this would be regarded as a reasonable ground for suspecting that a child was being neglected and his or her health suffering as a result[203].

It's worth noting that, while the inspection procedure for local authority-run homes was no doubt similar, it wasn't expressed quite as extensively in either the 1937 or 1948 Acts or the 1959 regulations.

The 1959 regulations did, however, cover record-keeping in both local authority and voluntary homes[204]. Schedule 2 stated that the following records should be kept:
- A register with the date when every child was admitted to, and discharged from, the home.
- A log book recording every important event at the home, including:
  - visits and inspections;
  - punishments administered to each child;
  - every fire drill or practice;
  - the fire precautions recommended to the administering authority; and
  - how these recommendations had been implemented.

- Enough detail about food provided for children for anybody inspecting the records to judge whether the diet was satisfactory.
- A personal history of each child in the home, including:
  - medical history;
  - the circumstances in which the child was admitted to the home (in the case of a child in the care of a local authority, why it was impracticable or undesirable to board the child);
  - details of the child's progress in the home, including visits by parents, relatives or friends and any emotional or other difficulties experienced by the child); and
  - the child's destination when discharged from the home.

The person in charge of the home was responsible for compiling the records. These were to be open to inspection by anyone visiting the home under powers granted to the Secretary of State or by legal requirements that the home's administering authority had to meet[205]. Similarly, the person in charge of the home was responsible for the medical record of every child in the home. They had to make the records available at all times to the medical officer and to anyone authorised by the Secretary of State or the home's administering authority to inspect them .

The Voluntary Homes (Return of Particulars) (Scotland) Regulations 1952[207] also stipulated that certain details of voluntary homes had to be sent to the Secretary of State. These included:
- the home's name and address;
- the name of the person in charge;
- the number of children in the home according to age;
- the number of children receiving education, training or employment in the home and outside the home;

---

[200] *ibid* s54(3)
[201] The Children and Young Persons (Scotland) Act 1937, s 98(1). Repealed by Schedule 9 of the Social Work (Scotland) Act 1968
[202] *ibid* s98(3)
[203] *ibid*. Indeed, any obstruction to the execution of those duties of inspection could result in a fine.
[204] SI 1959/834 paragraph 14
[205] *ibid*
[206] *ibid* paragraph 15
[207] (SI 1952/1836). Exercised under section 97 of the Children and Young Persons (Scotland) Act 1937, revoking the Children and Young Persons (Voluntary Homes) Regulations (Scotland) 1933 (SI 1933/923)

- the name of any government department or departments – other than the Scottish Home Department – inspecting the home; and
- the date of the last inspection by each such government department[208].

Overall, the evidence shows that legal procedures at least existed to ensure that events were properly recorded in both local authority and voluntary homes. It also suggests that these went some way towards making these homes more accountable: homes had to keep records and make them open to inspection at any time.

Section 4: How laws provided for other institutions

As already mentioned, institutions other than local authority or voluntary children's homes existed to care for children and young people throughout our review period. So it's important to determine how they were regulated by law during this time.

In this section of the report the following areas are considered:

- Children and young people who were labelled "mentally defective"
- So-called "mentally defective" children and young people
- Children with disabilities
- Special schools
- Remand homes
- Other institutions

Children and young people labelled "mentally defective"

The Mental Deficiency and Lunacy (Scotland) Act 1913 (called the 1913 Act from here on) – with some minor amendments made by the Mental Deficiency (Scotland) Act 1940 – governed the treatment of "mental defectives"[209] until repealed by the Mental Health (Scotland) Act 1960.

Section 4 of the 1913 Act allowed so-called "defectives" under 16 years to be put into an institution for defectives or under guardianship. To achieve this, written consent was needed from two qualified medical practitioners, and from the parent or guardian, or school board or parish council – also with the parent or guardian's consent[210]. Once children were placed in care, responsibility for overseeing how they were supervised, protected and controlled[211] fell to the General Board of Control. The Board's duties included co-ordinating and supervising how school boards, parish councils and district boards administered their powers and duties under the Act.

The Board also had to certify, approve, supervise and inspect:

- institutions and houses for "defectives"; and
- all the arrangements that these institutions and houses made to care for and control the people in them[212].

This monitoring role was strengthened by a requirement on inspectors and commissioners to visit and inspect people in these institutions and houses at least twice a year[213]. They had to report at least every year, but the Secretary of State could also ask for special reports[214]. The Board could also grant a certificate to managers of these institutions to receive children – provided they were satisfied that the premises and the people who maintained them were suitable[215].

---

[208] *ibid* Schedule 1 and paragraph 11
[209] Defined fully in s1 of the Act
[210] The Mental Deficiency and Lunacy (Scotland) Act 1913, s 4(1)(a)-(c)
[211] *ibid*, s24
[212] *ibid* s24(1)(b) and (c)
[213] *ibid* s24(1)(d) and (2). This was without prejudice to their powers and duties under any regulations which the Secretary for Scotland may make for further or more frequent inspection and visitation
[214] *ibid* s24(1)(g)
[215] *ibid* s29(1) - a "certified institution"

Finally, the 1913 Act required children in these institutions to be treated properly. It did this by making it an offence for any member of staff to:

- ill-treat or neglect a child in their care; or
- commit an act of sexual immorality[216].

Members of staff included superintendents, officers, nurses, attendants, servants, anyone else employed in the institution or anybody in charge of a child.

The Mental Health (Scotland) Act 1960 (called the 1960 Act from here on)[217] repealed the 1913 Act, and provided fresh guidance for dealing with, caring for and treating people suffering – or appearing to be suffering – from "mental disorder", the term that replaced "defective". The Act stated that local authority services should provide, equip and maintain residential accommodation for people suffering from mental disorder, and care for residents"[218]. (This requirement covered local health authority arrangements under section 27(1) of the National Health Service (Scotland) Act.)

Furthermore, a local authority under the terms of the Children Act 1948 (a "children authority"), could accommodate children that were being provided with care or after-care by that or any other local health authority for persons suffering from mental disorder[219], as provided for by the Children Act 1948 and section 27 of the National Health Service (Scotland) Act 1947. Local authorities could also assume parents' rights under section 79 of the 1937 Act or section 3 of the 1948 Act, and if they did so, they had to:

- arrange for visits to be made by them to any child admitted to a hospital or nursing home for any treatment; and
- take whatever other steps "would be expected of a parent"[220].

The 1960 Act's general provisions also stated that local authorities had to provide, or arrange for "suitable training and occupation" for under 16s who had been reported to the education authority as not being suitable for education or training in a special school[221]. (However, this duty didn't affect how section 1 of the Education (Scotland) Act 1946[222] should operate.)

The 1960 Act laid down more specific rules for private hospitals and residential homes caring for anybody suffering from mental disorder. It stated that every private hospital[223] had to be registered[224], and importantly required the people responsible for running them to open the hospital to inspection at all "reasonable times", and keep any registers and records that the Secretary of State may stipulate[225]. Any failure to carry out these requirements was an offence under the Act. Additional duties were placed on the Secretary of State, to make sure – through regular inspection – that private hospitals were being run properly[226]. Furthermore, anyone authorised by

---

[216] *ibid* s45 and s46 respectively

[217] Amended principally by the Mental Health (Amendment) (Scotland) Act 1983, and repealed by the Mental Health (Scotland) Act 1984

[218] The Mental Health (Scotland) Act 1960, s7(1)(a)

[219] *ibid*, s9(1). Repealed by the Social Work (Scotland) Act 1968, Schedule 9. It should be noted that a line could be drawn between care by a local authority and by a mental health body: s8 of the Children Act 1948 stated "If a child who is in the care of a local authority under section one of this Act comes under the control of any person or authority under the provisions of [in Scotland]...the Mental Deficiency (Scotland) Acts, 1913 to 1938, or the Lunacy (Scotland) Acts, 1857 to 1919, he shall thereupon cease to be in the care of the local authority under this Act..."

[220] *ibid* s10(1) and (2)

[221] And those persons over the age of 16 suffering from a mental deficiency. The Mental Health (Scotland) Act 1960, s12(1)

[222] Which, among other things, imposed a duty on educational authorities to provide educational facilities for pupils who suffered from disability of mind

[223] defined as "any premises used or intended to be used for the reception of, and the provision of medical treatment for, one or more patients subject to detention under this Act...not being (a) a hospital provided under Part II of the National Health Service (Scotland) Act 1947; (b) a State hospital; or (c) any other premises managed by a Government department or provided by a local authority": The Mental Health (Scotland) Act 1960, s15(3)

[224] ibid s15(1). Indeed, the Secretary of State could, at any time, cancel a registration of a private hospital on any ground on which he might have refused an application for such a registration of that hospital, or on the ground that the person carrying on the hospital had been convicted of an offence against the Act: see s18(1)

[225] ibid s17(1) - such registers and records being open to inspection at any time

[226] ibid s17(2)

him could – by producing documents showing his or her authorisation – inspect a private hospital under the Act[227] and interview any patient in private[228].

The 1960 Act also covered residential homes for people suffering from mental disorder[229]. Generally, sections 37-40 of the National Assistance Act 1948 were to go hand in hand with the provisions on residential homes for people suffering from mental disorder, and apply as if they were intended for such a home[230]. The National Assistance Act related to the registration, inspection and conduct of homes for disabled people and elderly people. This meant that the Secretary of State had the power (under section 40 of the National Assistance Act 1948) to make regulations about the records kept, and reports to be given, by residential homes about the people they took into care[231]. Furthermore, section 39 of the National Assistance Act 1948 included the power to inspect any records and interview any of the home's residents in private[232].

Finally, the 1960 Act extended to placing children from approved schools into the guardianship of a local health authority or someone directed by the Secretary of State[233]. This would occur in circumstances where the Secretary of State was satisfied that the child was suffering from a mental disorder to the extent that he or she needed to be placed in the care of such a guardian.

Children with disabilities

Homes that provided residential care for disabled children not covered by the 1937 Act were chiefly regulated by the National Assistance Act 1948. Generally, the local authority had to provide residential accommodation for anyone who needed care and attention because of age, ill health or any other circumstances[234]. Importantly, they had take into account the welfare of everyone they provided accommodation for[235]. Section 29 of the Act laid down welfare arrangements for what it termed "blind, deaf, dumb and crippled persons", and the local authority had the power to make rules about how the premises it managed were be run[236].

There was also a strict requirement for anyone running a home for disabled people to register the home[237]: any failure to do so could result in a fine, prison or both[238]. They also had to keep the registers available for inspection at all times[239]. Section 39(1) of the Act reinforced these powers of inspection, stating that anybody authorised by the Secretary of State could "at all reasonable times" inspect any premises used as a home for disabled people.

---

[227] ibid

[228] ibid s17(3)

[229] defined as "an establishment the sole or main objective of which is, or is held out to be, the provision of residential accommodation, whether for reward or not, for persons suffering from mental disorder, not being - (a) a nursing home within the meaning of the Nursing Homes Registration (Scotland) Act 1938;(b) a hospital as defined by this Act; or (c) any other premises managed by a Government department or by a local authority..." and "deemed not to be a voluntary home within the meaning of Part VI of the Children and Young Persons (Scotland) Act 1937, or Part IV of the Children Act 1948": The Mental Health (Scotland) Act 1960, s19(2) and (3)

[230] *ibid* s19(1) (repealed by the Social Work (Scotland) Act 1968, Sch 9)

[231] *ibid* s21(1) (repealed by the Social Work (Scotland) Act 1968, Sch 9)

[232] *ibid* s21(2) (repealed by the Social Work (Scotland) Act 1968, Sch 9)

[233] *ibid* s71(1) (repealed by the Social Work (Scotland) Act 1968, Sch 9)

[234] And such accommodation was not otherwise available to them: The National Assistance Act 1948, s21(1)(a)

[235] *ibid* s21(2)

[236] *ibid* s23(1)

[237] Defined as "any establishment the sole or main objective of which is, or is held out to be, the provision of accommodation, whether for reward or not, for persons to whom section twenty-nine of this Act applies (not being persons to whom that section applies by virtue of the amendment thereto made by the Mental Health Act 1959 or by the Mental Health (Scotland) Act 1960 [added by Schedule 4 of the Mental health (Scotland) Act 1960])... or for the aged or for both" but not including: any hospital maintained in pursuance of an Act of Parliament; any institution for persons of unsound mind within the meaning of the Lunacy and Mental Treatment Acts 1890 to 1930 or hospital within the meaning of the Lunacy (Scotland) Acts 1857 to 1913; any institution, house or home certified or approved under the Mental Deficiency (Scotland) Acts 1913 to 1940; and any voluntary home as defined in...Part VI of the Children and Young Persons (Scotland) Act 1937. See The National Assistance Act 1948, s37(9)

[238] The National Assistance Act 1948, s37(1)

[239] *ibid* s37(8)

Special schools

It's worth noting that the various Education (Scotland) Acts provided for institutions caring for what the legislation termed "mental defectives", and also special schools.

The Education (Scotland) Act 1946 generally stated that – with approval from the Secretary of State and the General Board of Control for Scotland – councils could provide and maintain institutions and schools under the Mental Deficiency Acts and Education (Scotland) Acts[240]. It was accepted that the Secretary of State had the power to make regulations that defined:

- the categories of pupils who needed "special educational treatment"[241]; and
- what special educational arrangements were appropriate for pupils in each category[242].

Generally, education authorities had to find out which children in their area needed special educational treatment[243], and had to issue a report to the local health authority if they thought any child wasn't suitable for a special school because they had a mental disability[244]. Such special schools were also subject to the general powers of inspection established under the Acts[245]. Their position has changed little over the years[246], and the principles were contained in the Education (Scotland) Act 1980[247].

Remand homes

The arrangements for regulating remand homes – as for approved homes – originated in the Children and Young Persons (Scotland) Act 1937. Under the 1937 Act local authorities had to provide remand homes for their area[248]. Any authority, or anyone responsible for managing an institution other than a prison, could arrange to use the institution – or part of it – as a remand home[249]. Generally, the Act provided that if a child could be remanded into custody it could be remanded to any remand home in the area[250].

Crucially, the Criminal Justice (Scotland) Act 1949 imposed tighter rules, most importantly stipulating that no premises could be used as a remand home unless a certificate of approval had been issued by the Secretary of State"[251]. This permitted the Secretary of State to apply to remand homes – with any modifications he felt appropriate – sections 83 and 109(3) of the 1937 Act, which laid down rules for the approval of schools[252]. Further to this, no individual could take charge of a remand home unless the Secretary of State had approved the appointment[253].

Section 82(3) of the 1937 Act[254], which the Criminal Justice (Scotland) Act 1949 amended, also provided for:

- inspecting, regulating and managing remand homes;
- classifying, treating, employing, disciplining and controlling residents; and
- visits to residents by people appointed "in accordance with the rules"[255].

---

[240] The Education (Scotland) Act 1946, s19, as amended by the Education (Scotland) Act 1949 and 1956

[241] Defined, for example, in the 1962 Act as "education by special methods appropriate to the special requirements of pupils who suffer from disability of mind or body and shall be given in special schools approved by the Secretary of State": The Education (Scotland) Act 1962, s5 (later amended by Sch 2 of the Education (Scotland) Act 1969)

[242] *ibid* s62, replacing s53 of the Education (Scotland) Act 1946

[243] The Education (Scotland) Act 1962, s63(1)

[244] *ibid* s65(1)

[245] For example, the Education (Scotland) Act 1962, s67

[246] Although the definition of "special schools" contained in the 1962 Act was amended to by the Education (Scotland) Act 1969, Sch 2 to mean "education appropriate to the requirements of pupils whose physical, intellectual, emotional or social development cannot...be adequately promoted by ordinary methods of education, and shall be given in special schools"

[247] For example section 5

[248] The Children and Young Persons (Scotland) Act 1937, s81(1). Repealed by the Social Work (Scotland) Act 1968, Sch 9

[249] *ibid* s81(2). Repealed by the Social Work (Scotland) Act 1968, Sch 9

[250] *ibid* s81(3). Repealed by the Social Work (Scotland) Act 1968, Sch 9

[251] The Criminal Justice (Scotland) Act 1949, s51(1)

[252] *ibid* s51(2)

[253] *ibid* s51(3)

[254] Eventually repealed by the Social Work (Scotland) Act 1968, Sch 9

[255] The Criminal Justice (Scotland) Act 1949, amendment to s82(3) of the Children and Young Persons (Scotland) Act 1937

Rules on the day-to-day operation of remand homes were already in force under the Remand Home (Scotland) Rules 1946[256] (called the 1946 Rules from here on). These came into force on 1 July 1946 and replaced the Remand Home (Scotland) Rules of 1933.

In terms of welfare, the rules generally said that each "inmate" – to use their terminology – should be thoroughly washed and examined by a doctor within 24-48 hours after being admitted[257]. They also required that a doctor be appointed at each remand home to act as medical officer and administer any necessary medical treatment to inmates[258]. Reflecting the importance of this role, the medical officer had to regularly visit the remand home and generally ensure the premises were hygienic, supervise the inmates' health and provide any medical attention that was needed[259].

The superintendent (that is, the person in charge of the home[260]) also had responsibilities under the 1946 Rules. First, he or she was required to inform the clerk of court, council and the inmate's parents if an inmate had to be taken to hospital, clinic or other safe place to be medically treated or examined, or if the medical officer felt the inmate shouldn't be detained in the remand home on medical grounds. If the inmate had been committed to the home under section 58 of the 1937 Act, the superintendent also had to inform the Secretary of State[261]. Finally, the superintendent had to report any death, serious illness, infectious disease or accident to the inmate's parent or guardian, the council and the Secretary of State[262].

Homes had, as far as possible, to arrange for schoolroom instruction – on or off the premises – for inmates of school age[263], and in general the discipline of the remand home was to be maintained by "the personal influence" of the superintendent[264]. When punishment was necessary to uphold discipline, the rules stipulated it should take the form of:

■ temporary loss of recreation or privileges;
■ reduction in food; or
■ separation from other inmates (but only for those aged over 12, and provided they had some way of communicating with a member of staff).[265]

Corporal punishment was allowed if these punishments proved ineffective, but could only be administered to boys[266] and under the following conditions:

■ It should be administered by the superintendent or, if the superintendent wasn't available, by whoever was left in charge.
■ Only punishments described by the rules were allowed: striking, cuffing or any shaking were forbidden.
■ Only a strap approved by the council could be used:
  - for no more than three strokes on each hand; or
  - for no more than six strokes on the bottom, over trousers[267].

---

[256] SI 1946/693
[257] The Remand Home (Scotland) Rules 1946 SI 1946/693, paragraph 8. Furthermore, in the case of an inmate known to be awaiting removal to an approved school, a medical examination was to take place within 48 hours before such removal
[258] The Remand Home (Scotland) Rules 1946 SI 1946/693, paragraph 9
[259] *ibid*
[260] *ibid* paragraph 23(1)
[261] The Remand Home (Scotland) Rules 1946 SI 1946/693, paragraph 9
[262] And any sudden or violent death was to be reported immediately by the council to the Procurator Fiscal: The Remand Home (Scotland) Rules 1946 SI 1946/693, paragraph 11
[263] *ibid*, paragraph 12
[264] *ibid*, paragraph 16
[265] *ibid*, paragraph 17(a)
[266] *ibid*
[267] *ibid* paragraph 18

In terms of monitoring arrangements, the 1946 rules provided that homes had to be open for inspection by an inspector at all times.[268] This was in addition to the general powers of inspection in the Children and Young Persons (Scotland) Act 1937[269]. Homes also had to have arrangements in place for regular visits by council-appointed visitors, which were to take place at intervals of no more than three months, with at least two visits a year unannounced[270]. It is significant that these visitors were to include women, and that a further channel of inspection was now available: the home should be open "at all reasonable hours" to visits by justices and magistrates of the juvenile courts that sent children to the home[271]. In addition, reasonable facilities were to be given for inmates to receive visits from their relatives or guardians and friends, and to send or receive letters[272].

The rules also covered record-keeping. The superintendent was required to keep a register of inmates admitted to and discharged from homes, and had to keep log books, which had to detail "every event of importance" connected with the home[273]. These included details of all visits and dates of inspection, and all punishments. The latter was reinforced by a requirement on owners to record punishments immediately and to inform the Secretary of State every quarter of corporal punishments[274]. Registers and log books had to be open to inspection by the council, on the council's behalf or by an inspector. They also had to be inspected regularly at intervals of no more than three months[275].

It may be relevant to note that some children were under probation orders – that is, they were subject to an extra method of monitoring through a probation officer.

It is not necessary to examine the rules in detail. But, for example, under the Probation (Scotland) Rules 1951[276] a probation officer would have to make sure there were proper records for everyone he or she supervised[277]. That officer would, subject to the terms of the probation or supervision order, have to keep in close touch with the person under his supervision and meet him or her frequently[278]. These requirements applied both to children in school (the probation officer would be required to make enquiries of the head teacher from time to time about the child's attendance and progress, but the child was not to be visited on the school premises[279]) and those residing in institutions (whether or not an approved probation hostel or home)[280].

Other institutions

Finally, it's worth noting that there were other establishments whose role was to deal on a daily basis with the maintenance and welfare of children and young people. Many institutions were dealt with under the provisions of the Children (Boarding-Out Etc.) (Scotland) Rules and Regulations 1947[281], which have been outlined in the section on children's homes above. But other regulations existed to govern other types of institutions.

---

[268] *ibid* paragraph 2

[269] I.e. s82(3) as amended by the Criminal Justice (Scotland) Act 1949. Later repealed by the Social Work (Scotland) Act 1968

[270] The Remand Home (Scotland) Rules 1946 SI 1946/693, paragraph 19

[271] *ibid*

[272] *ibid*, paragraph 14

[273] *ibid* paragraph 20

[274] *ibid* paragraph 17(b)

[275] *ibid* paragraph 20

[276] Introduced under the Criminal Justice (Scotland) Act 1949, revoking probation rules of 1931, 1932, 1937, 1945, 1946 and 1949

[277] The Probation (Scotland) Rules 1951, s35(1)

[278] *ibid* s38(1)

[279] *ibid* s39

[280] *ibid* s54(1)

[281] SI 2146/1947. Made under section 10 of the Poor Law (Scotland) Act 1934, and section 88 (2) of the Children and Young Persons (Scotland) Act 1937

For example, the Criminal Justice (Scotland) Act 1949 covered institutions that weren't approved probation hostels or approved probation homes. People were sent to these homes by probation orders or supervision orders and the institutions could be inspected if the Secretary of State requested[282]. Anyone appointed to inspect these institutions could investigate, in any way they felt was appropriate, how residents were being treated. Obstructing an inspector was deemed to be an offence[283].

The nursery school system also shows how young children were cared for, and was initially regulated under the Nurseries and Child-Minders Regulations Act 1948[284].

Generally, local health authorities had to keep a register of premises in their area where children were looked after during the day, for most of the day or for longer periods of not more than six days[285]. The register also had to include people who were paid to look after children under five in their home[286], on the same basis as above. The local authority could refuse to register a property if they felt anyone employed (or proposed to be employed) to look after a child wasn't fit to do so. They could also refuse if they felt the property was unsuitable[287].

The local health authority could also impose conditions to ensure that:

- feeding arrangements and diet were adequate;
- children were under medical supervision; and
- records were kept for any children – and containing any details – that the authority could specify[288].

To ensure the children's conditions were monitored, the Act provided that a register had to be open to inspection "at all reasonable times[289]". And anyone authorised by the authority could – also at all reasonable times – inspect the property, the children, the arrangements for their welfare and any records kept under the terms of the Act[290]. This isn't fully within the terms of our review, but is still an interesting point of reference. The requirements for registering and inspecting nurseries can be viewed alongside those for regulating children's homes during this period of the review.

Part Two: 1968-1995

Section 5: How social work principles changed from the 1960s

As part one of this report shows, the framework of laws, rules and regulations that regulated how children should be cared for in residential institutions between 1950 and 1968 was extremely complex.

Arguably, competing definitions in various laws and uncertainty about the scope and extent of the framework inevitably led to confusion in the system. So by the 1960s, it was widely agreed that the social work principles should be modified. Three significant reports during the 1960s recognised this need to change:

- The McBoyle Committee presented its report Prevention of Neglect of Children in January 1963[291].
- The Kilbrandon Committee produced a report making recommendations that included setting up children's panels in each education authority for juvenile offenders and young people in need of care or protection[292].

---

[282] Unless it was, as a whole, subject to inspection by a government department: The Criminal Justice (Scotland) Act 1949, s13(1)

[283] *ibid* s13(2)

[284] c.53

[285] The Nurseries and Child-Minders Regulations Act 1948, s1(1)(a)

[286] *ibid* s1(1)(b)

[287] *ibid* s1(3)

[288] *ibid* s2(4)

[289] *ibid* s1(1)

[290] *ibid* s7

[291] *Report of the Committee of the Scottish Advisory Council on Child Care* (1963) (Cmnd 1966).
   Although it concerned mainly recommendations for dealing with the neglect of children in their own homes

[292] *Report of the Committee on Children and Young Persons, Scotland* (1964) (Cmnd 2306)

■ The government, under the Secretary of State for Scotland's guidance, made proposals for change in *Social Work and the Community*[293], suggesting social work departments with wide responsibilities.

Together, these proposals led to the Social Work (Scotland) Act 1968[294] being introduced (we call this the 1968 Act from here on). The Act retained some of the requirements of the previous laws on child protection, whereby the measures put in place by The Children and Young Persons (Scotland) Act 1937 and subsequent amendments to protect children, stayed the same. This meant that children would still be provided with substitute care only when parents could not provide an adequate standard of care.

However, the Act also introduced several new important features. The Children Act 1948, as it applied to Scotland, was repealed by the 1968 Act., which meant that local authorities' duties to children were restated in the new Act. This effectively changed the way decisions about children who needed protection were made. Under the new Act, local authorities were no longer able to authorise children to be removed to substitute care. This was now the remit of the new children's hearings, as set up by Part III of the 1968 Act.[295]

The Act aimed to:
■ put further measures in place to promote social welfare in Scotland;
■ bring together existing laws on the care and protection of children; and
■ set up children's panels to deal with children who needed compulsory measures of care[296].

Parts I and II of the Act therefore sought to bring together the existing legislation covering services for child care, welfare, social support for people who were ill, and supervising offenders. It created local authority social work departments covering these areas. It also imposed a duty on those subject to the Act to promote social welfare and give advice and help to people who need it.

Part III of the Act set up a system of children's panels to deal with children who committed offences, or who for other reasons needed compulsory measures of care and protection. Juvenile courts were abolished, although all decisions of the children's panels could be appealed in court. Local authorities were required to promote social welfare by making advice, guidance and assistance available and by providing facilities including residential and other establishments.

Finally, Part IV of the Act dealt with residential and other establishments. This part of the Act is examined in greater detail below. But it is this move to bring together services dealing with the welfare and care of children in residential institutions that proves most significant in our understanding of how the legal framework developed.

The Social Work (Scotland) Act 1968

Before examining how the 1968 Act changed the way residential establishments were run, it is important to consider the Act's general impact on the establishment of crucial social work services.

Part I of the 1968 Act[297] placed a duty on local authorities to "enforce and execute" the Act in their areas[298]. To do this, each local authority had to set up a Social Work Committee[299]. These committees were responsible for local childcare and child welfare services, together with the duties that probation committees had previously carried out[300]. Generally,

---

[293] (1966) (Cmnd 3065)

[294] c.49. The Act received royal assent on 26 July 1968, and much of it came into force on 17 November 1969

[295] A. Clelland and E.E. Sutherland, Stair Memorial Encyclopaedia The Laws of Scotland: Child and Family Law, para 287

[296] Preamble to the Act: The Social Work (Scotland) Act 1968, c.49

[297] Section 1. Amended by the Local Government (Scotland) Act 1973 (c 65), ss 161, 214(2), Sch 20, Sch 27, Pt II, para 183). For the regional and islands councils, see SW(S)A 1968, Sch 1, Pt I. Also amended by the Children Act 1989 (c 41), s 108(7), Sch 15, the Local Government etc (Scotland) Act 1994 (c 39), s 180(1), Sch 13, para 76(2); the Children (Scotland) Act 1995 (c 36), s 105(4), Sch 4, para 15(2)

[298] "[O]r Part II of the Children (Scotland) Act 1995" later inserted by Schedule 4 of the Children (Scotland) Act 1995

[299] The Social Work (Scotland) Act 1968, s2(1). Later repealed by Local Government (Scotland) Act 1994, Sch 14

[300] That is, services to the courts and the supervision of persons who are subject to statutory after-care and parole. Probation and children's committees were thus abolished

therefore, the performance of each of the local authority's functions under the various Acts would now be referred to the Social Work Committee[301]. This was reinforced by a requirement on local authorities to appoint a director of social work[302] (later changed to a requirement to appoint a "Chief Social Work Officer"[303]), with a duty placed on the Secretary of State to set down what qualifications these officers should have.[304]

The Secretary of State, therefore, had an important role. Local authorities had to perform their functions under the 1968 Act[305] under his general guidance[306]. He had the power to make regulations covering how local authorities performed their functions under the Act, and this could cover any activities by voluntary organisations that came under the Act[307]. The Secretary of State also had the authority to appoint an advisory Council on Social Work, to advise him on anything to do with how he performed his functions in relation to social welfare, how local authorities performed theirs, and any activities of voluntary organisations linked to those functions[308].

In terms of consolidating the relevant provisions for caring for and protecting children in need, the 1968 Act re-established a number of the principles introduced in the Children Act 1948. Thus, in repealing the 1948 Act, the 1968 Act was able to re-assert the framework with amendments in a clearer format. Indeed, the requirements placed on local authorities in relation to issues such as their assumption of parental rights, and duty to provide for and assert the best interests of the child, remained until repealed by the Children (Scotland) Act 1995[309].

So, under the 1968 Act, a local authority was required (so long as doing so was in the interests of the child's welfare) to take into care a child under 17 years old:

■ who had no parent or guardian;

■ who was lost or abandoned; or

■ whose parent or guardian was unable to provide for the child's accommodation, maintenance and upbringing[310].

This duty would remain as long as necessary for the child's welfare, or until the child reached 18 years[311]. However, if the child's welfare was best served by placing them in the care of their parent or guardian (or a relative or friend), the local authority was required to so place them[312].

The 1968 Act also restated the principles that the 1948 Act recognised governing how local authorities should assume parental rights. They would assume these rights if:

■ the child's parents were dead;

■ the child had no guardian; or

■ the parent and guardian couldn't care for the child for reasons that the law explained[313].

---

[301] The Social Work (Scotland) Act 1968, s2(2). The Acts referred to include Part IV of the Children and Young Persons (Scotland) Act 1937, the Nurseries and Child-Minders Regulation Act 1948, and latterly the Children Act 1975 (amendment made under Schedule 3 of the Children Act 1975)

[302] The Social Work (Scotland) Act 1968, s3(1)

[303] SW(S)A 1968, s 3 substituted by Local Government (Scotland) Act 1994, s 45

[304] The Social Work (Scotland) Act 1968, s3(2); Qualifications of Directors of Social Work (Scotland) Regulations 1978, SI 1978/1284. See now the Qualifications of Chief Social Work Officers (Scotland) Regulations 1996, SI 1996/515

[305] "[A]nd Part II of the Children (Scotland) Act 1995" inserted by Schedule 4 of the Children (Scotland) Act 1995

[306] The Social Work (Scotland) Act 1968, s5(1)

[307] *ibid*, s5(2). Amended by Schedule 3 of the Children Act 1975: "For section 5(2) there is substituted - (2) The Secretary of State may make regulations in relation to - (a) the performance of the functions assigned to local authorities by this Act; (b) the activities of voluntary organisations in so far as those activities are concerned with the like purposes; (c) the performance of the functions referred to social work committees under section 2(2)(b) to (e) of this Act; (d) the performance of the functions transferred to local authorities by section 1(4)(a) of this Act". Such regulations could, as stated in s5(3) of the 1968 Act (later amended by Schedule 4 of the Children (Scotland) Act 1995), make provision for the boarding out of persons by local authorities and voluntary organisations

[308] The Social Work (Scotland) Act 1968, s7(1)

[309] The Children (Scotland) Act 1995, Schedule 5

[310] The Social Work (Scotland) Act 1968, s15(1). Repealed by the Children (Scotland) Act 1995, Schedule 5

[311] *ibid* s15(2). Repealed by the Children (Scotland) Act 1995, Schedule 5

[312] *ibid* s15(3). Amendments made by the Children Act 1975, s73. Repealed by the Children (Scotland) Act 1995, Schedule 5

[313] *ibid* s16(1). Repealed by the Children (Scotland) Act 1995, Schedule 5

This remained the case until the Children Act 1975 amended and extended the rules: under the 1975 Act, a local authority could assume parental rights itself. It could also permit voluntary organisations that were incorporated bodies or trusts to assume these rights, in some circumstances[314]. However, it could only do this if it seemed in the child's best interests[315]; the local authority retained the power to re-assume parental rights if not exercised suitably by the voluntary organisation[316].

Undoubtedly, welfare-orientated principles were at the centre of the 1968 Act, reflected in how local authorities were now required to look after children in their care. So, any local authority looking after a child was now explicitly required to "exercise their powers with respect to him so as to further his best interests, and to afford him opportunity for the proper development of his character and abilities".[317]

It's worth noting that the Children Act 1975 extended this: any decision by a local authority about a child in its care had to take account of the need to safeguard and promote the child's welfare throughout its childhood. Local authorities had, as far as possible, to consult the child's wishes and feelings and take these into account, given the child's age and understanding.[318]

The 1968 Act also introduced a requirement on local authorities to review the case of any child in their care no less than six months after the child came into care or after a previous review[319]. In addition to this, the Act gave the Secretary of State the power to make regulations about how cases should be reviewed and to vary the minimum interval for reviews, bringing Scots law into line with the English position (namely section 27 of the Children and Young Persons Act 1969).

It's also worth noting that, in line with these principles, local authorities had a duty to advise, guide or assist children over school age (but not yet 18), so long as doing this was in the child's welfare. This applied to children who were no longer in the care of the local authority or a voluntary organisation[320].

As already noted that the 1968 Act (Part III)[321] abolished juvenile courts in favour of children's hearings by members of a children's panel[322]. The rules that governed these hearings replaced and changed the requirements that had been made under the Children and Young Persons (Scotland) Act 1937[323]. Hearings could decide (similar to juvenile courts) if children brought before them needed what the Act called "compulsory measures of care"[324]. The 1968 Act again made sure that a police constable, or

---

[314] Namely that the parents of the child are dead, he has no guardian, or that the parent or guardian: (a) has abandoned the child; or (b) suffers from some permanent disability rendering him incapable of caring for the child; or (c)...suffers from a mental disorder...which renders him unfit to have the care of the child; or (d) is of such habits or mode of life as to be unfit to have the care of the child; or (e) has so persistently failed without reasonable cause to discharge the obligations of a parent or guardian as to be unfit to have the care of the child: see The Social Work (Scotland) Act 1968, s16(1) and (2) (inserted by The Children Act 1975, s74). Repealed by Schedule 5 of the Children (Scotland) Act 1995

[315] The Social Work (Scotland) Act 1968, s16 (4) (inserted by the Children Act 1975, s74). Repealed by Schedule 5 of the Children (Scotland) Act 1995

[316] The Social Work (Scotland) Act 1968, s16A (1) (inserted by the Children Act 1975, s75). Repealed by Schedule 5 of the Children (Scotland) Act 1995

[317] The Social Work (Scotland) Act 1968, s20 (1) (later amended by s79 and 80 of The Children Act 1975; and The Health and Social Services and Social Security Adjudications Act 1983, Schedule 2, paragraph 5; Repealed by Schedule 5 of the Children (Scotland) Act 1995)

[318] The Social Work (Scotland) Act 1968, s20 (1) (inserted by s79 of The Children Act 1975). Repealed by Schedule 5 of the Children (Scotland) Act 1995

[319] The Social Work (Scotland) Act 1968, s20A (1) (inserted by The Children Act 1975). Repealed by Schedule 5 of the Children (Scotland) Act 1995

[320] The Social Work (Scotland) Act 1968, s26 (1)

[321] Part III ceased to have effect under Schedule 4 of the Children (Scotland) Act 1995, with the exception of subsections (1) and (3) of section 31 and the amendments provided for by the said subsection (3) and contained in Schedule 2 to that Act

[322] The Social Work (Scotland) Act 1968, ss33 and 34. Schedule 3 to the 1968 Act gives details of the appointment, recruitment and training of panel members

[323] So, for example, with the ending of juvenile courts as provided for by the 1968 Act a number of changes were required in Part IV of the 1937 Act. These changes are set out in Schedules 2, 8 and 9 to the Act of 1968. The revised provisions of the 1937 Act continued to apply to the few children who are brought before the courts.

[324] Defined in s32 of the 1968 Act, as amended by Schedule 3 to the Children Act 1975. Examples include: the child is falling into bad associations or is exposed to moral danger, the lack of care is likely to cause him unnecessary suffering, or any Schedule 1 offences contained in the 1937 Act (and latterly the Criminal Procedure Act 1975) have been committed against the child.

someone authorised by a court or Justice of the Peace, could take a child to a "place of safety"[325] if:

- the child was being ill-treated to the extent that this was causing unnecessary suffering or injury to health; or
- a so-called "Schedule 1 offence"[326] (such as general criminal sexual offences, incest, or bodily injury) had been committed against a child.

Once again, the Children Act 1975 expanded this. Amendments in the Act placed an important duty on local authorities to "cause enquiries to be made" if they received information suggesting that a child may need to be taken into care[327]. This was a significant development. As stated by the general notes to the Act, it stressed the central role of local authority social service departments in matters of child abuse[328].

Section 6: How the law provided for residential establishments

As has now been seen, under Part III of the 1968 Act, juvenile courts were replaced by a system of children's hearings able to decide on the measures appropriate to deal with children brought before them in need of compulsory measures of care. In cases where the hearings decided that a child must be removed from home, they could now call upon any one of the range of establishments for children, including local authority and voluntary homes. Part IV of the 1968 Act governed such establishments, and was most significant in effectively consolidating the rules and regulations covering various residential institutions for children and young people.

So, gone were the various definitions and requirements established under a mass of legislation, replaced instead by a more streamlined framework intended to regulate what were now called "residential establishments". The 1968 Act defined these as "an establishment managed by a local authority, voluntary organisation or any other person, which provides residential accommodation for the purposes of this Act"[329]. Local authorities had to provide and maintain these residential (and other[330]) establishments or arrange for them to be provided[331]. They could do this by providing establishments themselves or jointly with another local authority. Or they could arrange for voluntary organisations or other local authorities to provide them[332].

Regardless of any agreements made about placing a child in a residential establishment, the local authority could remove the child at any time, and indeed would have to if required by the Secretary of State or the person responsible for the establishment[333].

Section 59 ensured that the residential establishments that social work authorities had to provide for now included:

- children's homes (local authority and voluntary-run, previously provided under the Children Act 1948);
- homes for disabled people (previously provided under the National Assistance Act 1948);
- accommodation for the mentally disordered (previously provided under section 7 of the Mental Health (Scotland) Act 1960); and
- temporary accommodation for the homeless (previously provided under Part III of the National Assistance Act 1948).

[325] The Social Work (Scotland) Act 1968, s37. Amended by The Children Act 1975, s83. Such a place was defined in the Act "as any residential or other establishment provided by a local authority, a police station, or any hospital, surgery or other suitable place": s94 (1). This definition ceased to have effect under Schedule 4 of the Children (Scotland) Act 1994

[326] Or any offence under s21(1) of the 1937 Act. Schedule 1 of the 1937 Act was later replaced by Schedule 9 of the Criminal Procedure (Scotland) Act 1975

[327] The Social Work (Scotland) Act 1968, s37 (1A) (as inserted by The Children Act 1975, s83)

[328] General note to section 83 of The Children Act 1975, relating to the newly inserted s37 (1A) of the Social Work (Scotland) Act 1968

[329] The Social Work (Scotland) Act 1968, s94(1). Amended by The Children (Scotland) Act 1995, Sch 4

[330] Defined as "an establishment managed by a local authority, voluntary organisation or any other person, which provides non-residential accommodation for the purposes of this Act, whether for reward or not": The Social Work (Scotland) Act 1968, s94(1)

[331] The Social Work (Scotland) Act 1968, s59(1). Later amended by the Regulation of Care (Scotland) Act 2001, s72

[332] *ibid*, s59(2)

[333] *ibid*, s22

The 1968 Act widened local authority duties to providing not just residential establishments but also other establishments such as day centres. This allowed them to provide residential and day accommodation in one establishment and to provide facilities in a single building for more than one type of person requiring assistance[334].

Section 59 was, therefore, very important and was subsequently amended in various ways over the years[335] , perhaps most significantly by the Health and Social Services and Social Security Adjudications Act 1983[336]. This required section 59 to be read with a newly inserted section (58A) ensuring that local authorities had to provide for young people who needed secure accommodation[337].

In terms of monitoring residential establishments, the 1968 Act enabled the Secretary of State to make regulations that covered how they were run and the welfare of the people resident and accommodated in them[338]. This was similar to arrangements established under the Children and Young Persons (Scotland) Act 1937 and the Children Act 1948. Furthermore, anybody who contravened or failed to comply with a regulation or any requirement or direction that it made, faced a fine[339]. We examine regulations made under the authority of the 1968 Act later in this chapter.

Under the 1968 Act, establishments not run by a local authority had to apply to the local authority to be registered before they could admit residents[340]. The local authority had to visit these establishments and, before deciding whether to register them, had to be satisfied that:

■ the applicant was fit to manage the establishment;
■ there were enough staff to run it;
■ the premises were suitable for its purpose; and
■ the establishment was being properly run[341].

The local authority could refuse to register the establishment if:

■ the applicant wasn't fit because of age or character;
■ the property wasn't suitable; or
■ proposed staffing levels weren't sufficient.

The Act also allowed for existing establishments to be registered, and provided for important transitional arrangements for these establishments in the run-up to the Act taking effect[342].

Having to register was therefore clearly very important, and the 1968 Act's requirements remained more or less unchanged until amendments made by the Registered Establishments (Scotland) Act 1987 and the Children (Scotland) Act 1995. One effect of the 1987 Act was to refine the definition of "establishment"[343]. But perhaps most importantly, it

---

[334] See the general note to s59 of the Social Work (Scotland) Act 1968

[335] Amended by the National Health Service and Community Care Act 1990, s66(1), Sch 9, para 10(7); the Children (Scotland) Act 1995, s105(4), Sch 4, para 15(15);the Regulation of Care (Scotland) Act 2001, s72; and the Mental Health (Care and Treatment) (Scotland) Act 2003, ss25(4), 331(1), Sch 4, para 6

[336] Section 8(4)

[337] These secure units were required for young people where physical and structural controls were necessary to prevent further deterioration of the young person's behaviour. Specific powers were given to the Secretary of State to make grants to local authorities to ensure that this kind of accommodation was available: s59A of the Social Work (Scotland) Act 1968, added by the Children Act 1975, s72

[338] The Social Work (Scotland) Act 1968, s60 (1). Section 60 was amended by the National Health Service (Scotland) Act 1978, s109, Sch 16, para 29, and the Health and Social Services and Social Security Adjudications Act 1983, s8(3). Repealed by the Regulation of Care (Scotland) Act 2001, s80(1), Sch4

[339] *ibid* s60(3)

[340] *ibid* s61. Amended by section 1 of the Registered Establishments (Scotland) Act 1987, and by section 34 of the Children (Scotland) Act 1995. Repealed by the Regulation of Care (Scotland) Act 2001, s80(1), Sch4

[341] *ibid* s62(3). Repealed by the Regulation of Care (Scotland) Act 2001, s80(1), Sch4

[342] The Social Work (Scotland) Act 1968, Schedule 7, paragraph 1

[343] Namely that it "does not include any establishment controlled or managed by a Government department or by a local authority or, subject to sections 61A and 63B below, require to be registered, or in respect of which a person is required to be registered, with a Government department or a local authority under any other enactment": The Social Work (Scotland) Act 1968, s61(1) and (1A) as inserted by The Registered Establishments (Scotland) Act 1987, s1. Repealed by the Regulation of Care (Scotland) Act 2001, s80(1), Sch4

added the possibility that grant-aided and independent schools could – but weren't required to – apply to be registered[344]. (This referred to schools within the meaning of the Education (Scotland) Act 1980, which provided personal care or support, whether or not "combined with board, and whether for reward or not"[345]). The 1995 Act further refined the definition of "establishment"[346], and redefined requirements for voluntary registration[347].

The 1968 Act also consolidated the procedures for inspecting residential establishments. Under the Act, local authority officers with the authority to do so could go to any establishment that was registered under the Act. They could examine any aspect of its condition, how it was being run and the condition and treatment of residents. The officers could inspect any records or registers that had to be kept in line with the Act[348].

The Children (Scotland) Act 1995 developed this idea in amendments made to the 1968 Act. Officers would now also be able to inspect premises that they had reasonable cause to believe were being used as a residential establishment[349], and were given wider powers to examine records and registers. They could now examine those that related to the premises, or to any individual who was – or had been – receiving services under the 1968 Act, parts of the Mental Health (Scotland) Act 1984 or the Children (Scotland) Act 1995[350].

Finally, it's worth noting that the 1968 Act placed an important duty on local authorities to arrange that residents in establishments in their areas should, from time to time, be visited in the interest of their general well being[351].

Section 7: How residential establishments were regulated in practice

This section considers:

- A note on approved schools
- The Social Work (Residential Establishments – Child Care) (Scotland) Regulations 1987
- Secure accommodation
- Children and young people with mental disorders

A note on approved schools

The Social Work (Scotland) Act 1968 was undoubtedly effective in bringing together a mass of legislation regulating various institutions providing residential care for children and young people. Our research shows that one of the Act's main strengths was to uniformly provide for residential establishments against the background of a newly formed social work framework. This meant, for example, that institutions such as children's homes and those caring for the disabled or mentally ill – whether run by local authorities or voluntary organisations – were now governed by one Act.

---

[344] The Social Work (Scotland) Act 1968, s61A(1) as inserted by The Registered Establishments (Scotland) Act 1987, s2(1). Repealed by the Regulation of Care (Scotland) Act 2001, s80(1), Sch4. Further, in the definition of "school" contained in s135 (1) of the Education (Scotland) Act, the words "not includ[ing] an establishment or residential establishment within the meaning of the Social Work (Scotland) Act 1968" were omitted: s2(2)

[345] ibid, s61(1) as amended by the Registered Establishments (Scotland) Act 1987, s1.
Repealed by the Regulation of Care (Scotland) Act 2001, s80(1), Sch4

[346] Adding to the definition contained in footnote 327 above, "but an establishment is not excluded for those purposes by paragraph (a) above by reason only of its being registrable by the Registrar of Independent Schools in Scotland;": The Social Work (Scotland) Act 1968, s61(1A), as amended by The Children (Scotland) Act 1995, s34(2)(b). Repealed by the Regulation of Care (Scotland) Act 2001, s80(1), Sch4

[347] The Social Work (Scotland) Act 1968, s61A, as inserted by The Children (Scotland) Act 1995, s34(3). See also s62A, as inserted by s34(4) of the 1995 Act. Repealed by the Regulation of Care (Scotland) Act 2001, s80(1), Sch4

[348] The Social Work (Scotland) Act 1968, s67

[349] The Social Work (Scotland) Act 1968, s67(1), as substituted by the Children (Scotland) Act 1995, s34(6).
Repealed by the Regulation of Care (Scotland) Act 2001, s80(1), Sch4

[350] The Social Work (Scotland) Act 1968, s67(2), as substituted by the Children (Scotland) Act 1995, s34(6).
Repealed by the Regulation of Care (Scotland) Act 2001, s80(1), Sch4. The relevant provisions as mentioned above are ss7 and 8 of the Mental Health (Scotland) Act 1984 and Part II of the Children (Scotland) Act 1995.

[351] The Social Work (Scotland) Act 1968, s68(1). Repealed by the Regulation of Care (Scotland) Act 2001, s80(1), Sch 4

The question arises, however, as to the status of approved schools – later referred to as "List D" schools – after the introduction of the Act. Generally, when Part III of the Act became law, social work departments took over and managed approved schools that were provided by education authorities[352], and from the same date managers of voluntary schools had to be registered under Part IV of the Act. Under transitional arrangements in Schedule 7 to the Act, the Secretary of State retained his powers to:

- withdraw approval for a school;
- change the classification of a school;
- give directions about the conduct of a school; and
- in the case of voluntary schools, appoint managers and alter the constitution of the managing body.

The schools continued to be subject to the Approved Schools (Scotland) Rules 1961[353]. They were also bound by the more general regulations on conduct and administration that applied to all local authority and voluntary establishments that came under the 1968 Act.

But these rules and regulations applied only to the approved schools existing immediately before Part III of the Act took effect. No new approved schools could be set up after this and any new residential establishments that local authorities or voluntary bodies set up that were similar to approved schools, were to be subject only to the 1968 Act[354]. And as a step towards implementing the new law, school aftercare officers transferred to the employment of the local authority social work departments from 17 November 1969, when these departments came into

being. Local authorities, on behalf of school managers, now undertook aftercare and liaison with the families of pupils in the schools[355].

The Social Work (Residential Establishments – Child Care) (Scotland) Regulations 1987

As noted above, the day-to-day regulation of existing approved schools continued under the 1961 rules. Similarly, children's homes remained governed by the Administration of Children's Homes (Scotland) Regulations 1959[356]. These arrangements stayed in force until 1987, when the Secretary of State exercised his power under the 1968 Act to make regulations relating to the conduct of residential establishments, and for securing the welfare of their residents[357].

The Social Work (Residential Establishments – Child Care) (Scotland) Regulations 1987[358] (we've called them the 1987 Regulations from here on) replaced the 1959 Regulations and 1961 Rules. They concerned the general residential care of children that local authorities and voluntary organisations were responsible for under the Social Work (Scotland) Act 1968. Therefore, the 1987 Regulations applied[359] to any residential establishment providing accommodation for children that:

- was controlled or managed by a local authority;
- had to be registered under section 61 of the 1968 Act[360]; or
- was a school voluntarily registered in line with section 61A of the 1968 Act[361].

---

[352] The Social Work (Scotland) Act 1968, s1(5). Section 1 amended by the Local Government (Scotland) Act 1973 (c 65), ss 161, 214(2), Sch 20, Sch 27, Pt II, para 183). For the regional and islands councils, see SW(S)A 1968, Sch 1, Pt I. Also amended by the Children Act 1989 (c 41), s108(7), Sch 15, the Local Government etc (Scotland) Act 1994 (c 39), s 180(1), Sch 13, para 76(2); the Children (Scotland) Act 1995 (c 36), s 105(4), Sch 4, para 15(2)

[353] SI 1961/2243

[354] Information taken from "Approved Schools in Scotland: Social Work, Scotland Vote", Memorandum by the Scottish Education Department (Circulated with Agenda for 18/12/70). The Social Work (Scotland) Act 1968, Sch 7, paragraphs 1-4 deal with the transitional provisions for approved schools

[355] *ibid*

[356] SI 1959/834. Revoked by the Social Work (Residential Establishments-Child Care) (Scotland) Regulations 1987

[357] Under s5(2) and 60(1) of the Social Work (Scotland) Act 1968, as amended by the National Health Service (Scotland) Act 1978, s109, Sch 16, para 29, and the Health and Social Services and Social Security Adjudications Act 1983, s8(3). Eventually repealed by the Regulation of Care (Scotland) Act 2001, s80(1), Sch4

[358] 1987/2233. In force from the 1st June 1988. Superseded by the Residential Establishments - Child Care (Scotland) Regulations 1996 (SI 1996/3256) and the Arrangements to Look After Children (Scotland) Regulations 1996 (SI 1996/3262)

[359] As determined by paragraph 3 of the Regulations (1987/2233)

[360] As amended by section 1 of the Registered Establishments (Scotland) Act 1987

[361] Inserted by section 2 of the Registered Establishments (Scotland) Act 1987

The managers[362] of such an establishment were considered to have a duty to provide for the care, development and control of each child resident there in such as way as would be in the child's best interests[363]. If a local authority provided a residential establishment the person in charge would be an officer appointed by the local authority. If the establishment wasn't provided by the authority, its managers had a duty to appoint a person to be in charge. They could, in writing, delegate any duties under the 1987 Regulations as they saw fit[364].

However, perhaps the most significant difference from the 1959 Regulations and 1961 Rules was the requirement placed on managers (of a local authority establishment or the person in charge of a non-local authority establishment[365]) to prepare a "statement of functions and objectives"[366]. This was to include details specified in schedule 1. These covered:

■ arrangements for meeting the needs and development potential of children resident in the establishment, including their emotional, spiritual, intellectual and physical needs;

■ arrangements for educating the children;

■ measures to be taken to safeguard the physical care of the children;

■ disciplinary and other arrangements for caring for and controlling children;

■ arrangements for the residential establishment to:
  - work with care authorities to help children develop their potential while in care and after leaving care;
  - take into account the needs and wishes of children and their parents; and
  - formulate procedures, in co-operation with care authorities, to deal with complaints by children, their parents or other relatives;

■ arrangements for keeping records, including:
  - procedures for selecting children to be admitted to the establishment;
  - details of children admitted to, and discharged from, the establishment;
  - procedures for access to records for staff, children and parents; and
  - records about how children and parents were involved in decisions taken about the welfare of children while residents of the establishment;

■ arrangements for visits by children's relatives and friends;

■ the establishment's policy on involving children and parents in decisions about the child's future while in residential care;

■ policies and practice for recruiting and training qualified staff to ensure the establishment's objectives are achieved – and taking into account services such as social work, health and education;

■ healthcare arrangements; and

■ details of all fire practices and fire alarm tests carried out in the establishment.[367]

These statements were, therefore, now recognised as a crucial component in regulating residential establishments efficiently. Managers had a duty to keep the preparation and implementation of the statement under review[368]. They also had to make sure the person in charge of the establishment reported in writing to them, at intervals of not more than six months, on how the statement was being implemented[369].

Managers also had to make sure that visits took place at least twice a year on their behalf at every residential establishment they provided to report on how the statement was being implemented[370].

---

[362] Meaning "(a) in the case of a voluntary organisation, the management committee to whom powers are delegated within the organisation for management of the residential establishment; (b) in the case of a local authority, those officers having delegated powers under section 2 of the Act, as read with section 56 of the Local Government (Scotland) Act 1973, for the management of the residential establishment: The Social Work (Residential Establishments - Child Care) (Scotland) Regulations 1987 (1987/2233), paragraph 2(1)

[363] *ibid* paragraph 4

[364] *ibid* paragraph 7. Indeed, the managers could also specify the persons to have charge of the establishment in the absence of the person in charge

[365] Meaning "the person in charge of a residential establishment who is responsible to the managers of the residential establishment": *ibid* paragraph 2(1)

[366] *ibid* paragraph 5

[367] *ibid* Schedule 2

[368] *ibid* paragraph 5(2)

[369] *ibid* paragraph 5(2)(a)

[370] *ibid* paragraph 5(2)(b)

Visits could take place at any other times considered necessary[371]. Managers kept the power to amend the statement, and could arrange for it to be made available to any care authority or children's hearing considering placing a child in a residential establishment[372].

As well as making these statements of functions and objectives necessary, the 1987 Regulations laid out minimum requirements for notifying incidents, fire precautions, discipline, records, education and healthcare[373].

It's worth noting how they provided for discipline. Under regulation 5(1) managers had the power to make arrangements relevant to caring for and controlling children, in line with the statement of functions and objectives[374]. But, perhaps most significantly, these arrangements could not authorise corporal punishment[375]. Managers of each establishment also had to make sure (in consultation with the education authority) that each child of school age in the establishment who wasn't getting a school education outwith the establishment, should receive "adequate and effective education"[376]. This was in addition to the requirement that every child should be able to attend religious services and receive religious instruction as appropriate to the child's religion[377].

Furthermore, managers had a duty to make sure that the establishment had arrangements in place to maintain conditions "conducive to the good health" of the children. They also had to, in consultation with

the care authorities responsible for the child's welfare, make sure each child could get medical and dental treatment[378].

In terms of monitoring children in such establishments, the 1987 Regulations added to the requirements of the statement of functions and objectives, and to the procedures required for inspections by the 1968 Act[379]. The Regulations required that if a registering authority issued a certificate of authority under the 1968 Act[380] it had to visit yearly and be satisfied that the establishment was still being run in line with the standards it had to meet when it was registered.[381] The authority also had to make sure that the children's safety and welfare were being maintained.

On the subject of record-keeping, the basic requirements of the 1987 Regulations were that managers (in consultation with the person in charge) had to make sure all necessary records – including health details – were properly maintained for every child resident in the establishment[382]. Managers (again in consultation with the relevant person in charge) also had a duty to ensure that a log book was kept, and maintained. Its contents included day-to-day "events of importance or an official nature" and details of disciplinary measures imposed[383].

The 1987 Regulations not only placed requirements on managers and people in charge of establishments, but also gave guidance about what arrangements a care authority had to make to put a child in residential care[384]. If a care authority was responsible

---

[371] *ibid* paragraph 5(3)

[372] *ibid* paragraph 5(4) and (5)

[373] *ibid* paragraphs 8-15

[374] *ibid* paragraph 10(1)

[375] *ibid* paragraph 10(2). Corporal punishment was for this purpose to have the same meaning as in section 48A of the Education (Scotland) Act 1980 (as inserted by the Education (No.2) Act 1986, section 48)

[376] The Social Work (Residential Establishments - Child Care) (Scotland) Regulations 1987 (1987/2233), paragraph 11(1)

[377] *ibid* paragraph 12

[378] *ibid* paragraph 13 and 30

[379] The Social Work (Scotland) Act 1968, s67. See above

[380] *ibid* s62(3)

[381] And in doing so shall have regard to the statement of functions and objectives: The Social Work (Residential Establishments - Child Care) (Scotland) Regulations 1987 (1987/2233), paragraph 16(a)

[382] *ibid* paragraph 14

[383] *ibid* paragraph 15

[384] *ibid* Part III

for a child under the regulations[385] for six weeks or more immediately before the placement, it could place the child in:

- a residential establishment;
- a school within the meaning of the Education (Scotland) Act 1980 (where the child would normally reside for the duration of the placement); or
- a hospital, convalescent home, private nursing home or other establishment within the meaning of the National Health Service (Scotland) Act 1978[386].

A placement could proceed so long as the care authority was satisfied that it was appropriate to the child's needs. This meant taking into account the information required by the regulations themselves[387] and the authority's duty under section 20 of the 1968 Act, namely to further the best interests of a child in their care and to give the child the opportunity to properly develop[388].

The care authority also had to be satisfied that the residential placement proposed for the child was appropriate to the child's needs as set out by the statement of functions and objectives required by the regulations[389]. Similar requirements applied to care authorities that had not been responsible for a child for more than six weeks before placement. Again, there was great weight on the need for the placement to correspond with the child's welfare and best interests[390].

When a care authority did place a child, the 1987 Regulations imposed a duty to give written notice and details of the placement to the local authority in the area the placement took place (if this differed to the care authority's area)[391]. The care authority also had to notify the area's education and health authorities,[392] although this wasn't needed if the care authority didn't intend the placement to last more than 28 days[393]. However such a notification was needed if the placement did last for more than 28 days[394], or if the authority learned that the child:

- had significant medical or educational needs[395];
- had a medical problem important to its future care[396]; or
- was below compulsory school age[397].

The child's parents or guardians also had a right to be notified of the placement, unless the care authority considered this wasn't in the child's interests[398].

The care authority's responsibility for providing information extended to having to give written details to the person in charge of the establishment about the child's background, health, and mental and emotional development. The details also had to include any other information considered relevant, including information about the child's wishes and feelings about the placement itself[399]. Both the care authority and the person in charge were to agree about the care the establishment would provide, including the arrangements for contact between a child and its family[400]. They also had to make sure that

---

[385] *ibid.* See paragraph 17(3) for the relevant application

[386] Again where the child would normally reside there for the duration of the placement.
Ibid paragraph 17(1) and 18

[387] Especially the particulars set out in Schedule 1

[388] The Social Work (Residential Establishments - Child Care) (Scotland) Regulations 1987 (1987/2233), paragraph 18

[389] *ibid*

[390] *ibid* paragraph 19(1)

[391] *ibid* paragraph 22(1)(a)

[392] *ibid* paragraph 22(1)(b) and (c)

[393] *ibid* paragraph 22(2) and (3)

[394] *ibid* paragraph 22(2)(b) and (3)(c)

[395] *ibid* paragraph 22(2)(a)

[396] *ibid* paragraph 22(3)(a)

[397] Within the meaning of section 31 of the Education (Scotland) Act 1980: ibid paragraph 22(3)(b)

[398] *ibid* paragraph 22(1)(d): this was decided with regard to section 20 of the 1968 Act and the code of practice issued by the Secretary of State under section 17E of the 1968 Act (as inserted by the Health and Social Services and Social Security Adjudications Act 1983, section 7(2))

[399] *ibid* paragraph 29(a)

[400] In accordance with the code of practice issued by the Secretary of State under section 17E of the 1968 Act (as inserted by the Health and Social Services and Social Security Adjudications Act 1983, section 7(2))

the child received adequate and efficient education (in line with the regulations) and proper medical and dental treatment[401].

Further monitoring arrangements under the Regulations included a duty on the care authority to take whatever steps it felt were needed to be certain that any placement made under the Regulations continued to be in the child's interests[402]. This required visiting the child within one week of the placement and, after this, at intervals of no more than three months from the last visit. However the authority could visit as often as it considered necessary, to supervise the child's welfare[403]. Such visits carried out in line with the Regulations had to be followed up by written reports, for the care authority to consider[404]. If a care authority felt it was no longer in the child's best interests to remain in a residential establishment, it could end the placement as soon as practicable, giving written notice[405].

Secure accommodation

As seen earlier, the 1968 Act successfully consolidated several principles concerned with regulating various types of residential establishment. However it seems that, in practice, some of these establishments remained governed by legislation introduced before the 1968 Act[406]. The 1987 Regulations effectively pulled together the laws relating to how a number of individual residential establishments operated, placing them under the one roof. But other regulations still existed to govern institutions not ostensibly covered by them.

Perhaps the most notable of the legal provisions not already mentioned are those relating to secure accommodation – that is, accommodation in residential establishments that restricted children's liberty[407]. Previously, legal provisions were within the context of the regulations governing individual establishments. For example, the Approved School (Scotland) Rules 1961 contained requirements on sectioning unruly pupils (for example, placing them in solitary confinement)[408].

Specific regulations relating to the provision and use of secure accommodation were made after the Health and Social Services and Social Security Adjudications Act 1983[409] amended the Social Work (Scotland) Act 1968. The Secure Accommodation (Scotland) Regulations 1983[410] (we've called these the 1983 Regulations from here on) stated that children could only be accommodated in residential establishments[411] providing secure accommodation approved by the Secretary of State[412]. The person in charge also had to make sure that a child placed and kept in such accommodation received care appropriate to its needs[413]. The regulations also covered:

- detaining children for no longer than seven days without the authority of a children's hearing or sheriff;
- the standards to be applied before a child subject to a supervision requirement could be placed;
- arrangements for an interim placement in secure accommodation of children in care under Part II of the 1968 Act;
- reviewing the conditions of the secure accommodation; and
- requirements for children being cared for by local

---

[401] The Social Work (Residential Establishments - Child Care) (Scotland) Regulations 1987 (1987/2233), paragraph 29(b) and (c)

[402] *ibid* paragraph 23

[403] *ibid* paragraph 23(a)

[404] *ibid* paragraph 23(b)

[405] *ibid* paragraph 24

[406] For example, children's homes and approved schools (still in operation) were subject to the 1959 Regulations and 1961 Rules respectively until revoked by The Social Work (Residential Establishments - Child Care) (Scotland) Regulations 1987 (1987/2233)

[407] The Secure Accommodation (Scotland) Regulations 1983 (SI 1983/1912) paragraph 2(1)

[408] 2243/1961 paragraphs 33 and 34

[409] Section 8 inserted the new sections 58A to 58G into the 1968 Act

[410] SI 1983/1912. Paragraph 19 revoked rules 33 and 34 of the Approved Schools (Scotland) Rules 1961

[411] Having the same meaning applied to it as s94(1) of the 1968 Act: SI 1983/1912 paragraph 2(1)

[412] *ibid* paragraph 3

[413] *ibid* paragraph 4

authorities in secure accommodation:
- because a court sent them under the Criminal Procedure (Scotland) Act 1975; or
- under place of safety warrants under the Social Work (Scotland) Act 1968)[414].

But perhaps most notable in terms of monitoring children was the duty placed on the person in charge to keep a record of the child's placement. This had to include details about the supervision requirement and any reviews of the placement required by the 1968 Act[415]. These records had to be open at all times for inspection by the Secretary of State, who could ask for copies to be sent to him[416].

The Secure Accommodation (Scotland) Amendment Regulations 1988[417] (we've called these the 1988 Amendment Regulations from here on) significantly amended the elements of the 1983 Regulations that applied to secure accommodation. (The 1988 Amendment Regulations followed the introduction of the Social Work (Residential Establishments-Child Care) (Scotland) Regulations 1987.) The amendments placed managers[418] of a residential establishment that provided secure accommodation under a new duty to make sure, in consultation with the person in charge[419], that the establishment provided appropriate standards of care for children, taking account of Part II of the 1987 Regulations[420].

In line with this best-interests principle, the regulations extended the general duties of

directors of social work under the 1983 Regulations, when deciding about placing a child in secure accommodation subject to a supervision requirement[421]. What's more, a child could now only be placed if the director of social work and the person in charge of the residential establishment were satisfied the child's needs were being met in line with the requirements of the newly amended 1983 Regulations[422]. These requirements were that the placement was considered appropriate to the child's needs, taking account of any relevant information and the statement of functions and objectives[423].

Changes to the 1983 Regulations included the following new elements:
- If a children's hearing was considering whether a condition should apply to a supervision requirement allowing a child to be detained in secure accommodation, a local authority could recommend such a condition only if it was satisfied that the placement was in the child's best interests, in line with the procedures set out in 1987 Regulations[424].
- A condition permitting a child to be put into secure accommodation as part of a supervision requirement made by a children's hearing under section 58C of the 1968 Act[425] had to be reviewed every three months. This required that in calculating the prescribed interval of three months, account should be taken of any review for other purposes under the 1968 Act that also reviewed such a condition.

[414] *ibid* paragraphs 5-15

[415] *ibid* paragraph 16(1)

[416] *ibid* paragraph 16(2)

[417] SI 1988/841

[418] The definition of which was added to the 1983 Regulations by the 1987 Amendment Regulations, meaning: "(a) in the case of a voluntary organisation, the management committee to whom powers are delegated within the organisation for management of the residential establishment providing secure accommodation; (b) in the case of a local authority, those officers exercising powers standing referred to the Social Work Committee under section 2(2) of the 1968 Act or subject to an arrangement under section 161(3) of, and Schedule 20 to, the Local Government (Scotland) Act 1973 for the management of the residential establishment providing secure accommodation": SI 1988/841, paragraph 3

[419] Now defined as "the person in charge of a residential establishment providing secure accommodation who is responsible to the managers of that establishment": *ibid*

[420] *ibid*, paragraph 4

[421] *ibid* paragraph 5. The director of social work, in following the prescribed procedures, now being required to satisfy himself as to the matters set out at regulation 18(b) and (c) of the 1987 Regulations

[422] *ibid* paragraph 6. That is, in accordance with the matters set out at regulation 18(b) and (c) of the 1987 Regulations

[423] A similar requirement was added by the amendment made to paragraph 15 of the 1983 Regulations dealing with a number of situations where a child was detained in a place of safety under a warrant issued by a hearing or a sheriff not authorising the use of secure accommodation under section 58E of the 1968 Act: SI 1988/841, paragraph 10

[424] *ibid* paragraph 7 (inserting a new paragraph 9A into the 1983 Regulations)

[425] *ibid* paragraph 8 (inserting a new paragraph 12 into the 1983 Regulations)

A further change gave a child or its parents the right to a review by a children's hearing within 21 days of asking for one in writing. This applied if a condition imposed by the hearing had not taken effect for six continuous weeks[426]. Finally, apart from various transitional provisions governing the implementation of changes effected by the new regulations[427], the 1988 Amendment Regulations required that the managers of such establishments consult with the person in charge about the need to keep records[428].

These changes to the 1983 Regulations represented a general tightening of the legal framework governing secure accommodation, and arguably put more stress on welfare. They also highlighted the important role that Social Work (Residential Establishments – Child Care) (Scotland) Regulations 1987 had in altering how residential establishments were run and regulated.

However, additional legal measures were needed to govern how secure accommodation was used in Scotland for children who were ordered by a court to be detained in residential care under section 413 of the Criminal Procedure (Scotland) Act 1975[429]. As a result, the Residential Care Order (Secure Accommodation) (Scotland) Regulations 1988[430] were introduced. Generally, these stated that a child could only be detained in secure accommodation[431] under section 413 if the relevant local authority's director of social work and the person in charge of the establishment were both satisfied it was in the child's best interests. They had to take account of certain circumstances that the Regulations[432] set out and they had to agree how long detention was necessary[433].

The Regulations also allowed for reviews. The director of social work and the person in charge of the establishment had to review cases when they felt it was necessary and appropriate in light of the child's progress[434] – but at intervals of no more than three months[435]. Furthermore, the Regulations significantly stated that the child's best interests were paramount[436] in any decisions about whether the child should remain liable to be detained. Decisions had to take account of what the Regulations described as "all relevant circumstances". These had, if possible, to include the child's opinion and that of its parents[437].

Managers[438] also had a duty to maintain children's welfare by ensuring that children placed and kept in secure accommodation received care appropriate to their needs[439]. And, just as previous legislation had, the Regulations laid down important rules for keeping records. The person in charge had to maintain a record of the child's placement and this had to include:

■ details of any reviews carried out under the Regulations;
■ the date and time of the child's placement, release, or both; and

---

[426] *ibid* (inserting a new paragraph 12A into the 1983 Regulations)

[427] *ibid* paragraph 12

[428] *ibid* paragraph 11 (amending paragraph 16 of the 1983 Regulations)

[429] Section 413(1), as substituted by section 59(1) of the Criminal Justice (Scotland) Act 1987

[430] SI 1988/294

[431] Defined as "accommodation provided in a residential establishment for the purpose of restricting the liberty of children": SI 1988/294, paragraph 2(1)

[432] Namely "(a) he has a history of absconding, and-(i) is likely to abscond unless he is kept in secure accommodation; and (ii) if he absconds, it is likely that his physical, mental or moral welfare will be at risk; or (b) he is likely to injure himself or other persons unless he is kept in secure accommodation; and in either case it is in the child's best interests that he be kept in secure accommodation": *ibid* paragraph 4(1)

[433] *ibid* paragraph 4(2)

[434] *ibid* paragraph 5(1)(a)

[435] *ibid* paragraph 5(1)(b)

[436] *ibid*

[437] *ibid* paragraph 5(2)

[438] Defined under paragraph 2 of these Regulations, but soon amended by The Residential Care Order (Secure Accommodation) (Scotland) Amendment Regulations 1988 (S.I. 1988/1092) paragraph 3, to mean "(a) in the case of a voluntary organisation, the management committee to whom powers are delegated within the organisation for management of the residential establishment providing secure accommodation; (b) in the case of a local authority, those officers exercising powers standing referred to the Social Work Committee under section 2(2) of the Social Work (Scotland) Act 1968, or subject to an arrangement under section 161(3) of, and Schedule 20 to, the Local Government (Scotland) Act 1973, for the management of the residential establishment providing secure accommodation;"

[439] SI 1988/294, paragraph 6

■ the child's full name, sex and date of birth[440].
These records had to be available for inspection by
the Secretary of State, who could ask for copies to be
sent to him[441].

Children and young people with mental disorders

The modern regulation of residential care for children
with a mental disorder has its basis in the Mental
Health (Scotland) Act 1984[442]. This consolidated the
Mental Health (Scotland) Act 1960, which was
amended principally by the Mental Health
(Amendment) (Scotland) Act 1983.

The 1984 Act was intended to regulate how people
suffering – or appearing to suffer – from mental
disorder[443] were taken into care, cared for and
treated, and continued the important monitoring
function of the Mental Welfare Commission
established under the previous legislation. Its duty
was to inquire about cases of ill-treatment, poor
standards of care and treatment, or cases where
mentally disordered people had been wrongly
detained. The Commission also had to regularly visit
patients detained in hospitals or under a guardian,
and all these duties continued under the 1984 Act[444].

The Commission's role in protecting patients was
deeply rooted in the new law. It had the power to
interview any patient in private and inspect any
patient's medical records[445], and continued to have a
duty to inform hospitals and local authorities about
any case that was relevant to:
■ secure a patient's welfare;
■ prevent a patient being badly treated; or
■ deal with any shortcomings in how a patient was
cared for or treated.[446]

Furthermore, the Commission could notify the
Secretary of State and any other relevant body about
any concerns it had[447].

In terms of local authority services, powers under the
1984 Act extended to:
■ providing residential accommodation for people
suffering from mental disorder;
■ local authorities' functions as guardians; and
■ the supervision of people suffering from mental
handicap but not who weren't detained or placed
in a guardian's care[448].

Local authorities – as with previous laws – had a duty
to provide after-care services and training facilities[449].
If they had parental rights over a child, they had to
visit the child and take what the Act described as
"such other steps" while the child was in a hospital or
nursing home that would be expected of a parent[450].

---

[440] *ibid* paragraph 7(1)
[441] *ibid* paragraph 7(2)
[442] c. 36
[443] The Mental Health (Scotland) Act 1984, c. 36, s 1(1). "Mental disorder" was defined in s1(2) as "mental illness or mental handicap however caused or manifested"
[444] *ibid* s3
[445] *ibid* s3(2)(b), (5) and (6)
[446] *ibid* s3(2)(d)
[447] *ibid* s3(2)(e) and (f)
[448] *ibid* s7, derived from ss7 - 12 of the Mental Health (Scotland) Act 1960 and ss6, 7(1) of the Mental Health (Amendment) (Scotland) Act 1983
[449] The Mental Health (Scotland) Act 1984, s8
[450] *ibid* s10 - parental rights vesting in a local authority as defined by that section

The 1984 Act imposed a duty on local authorities to provide or arrange for suitable training and occupation for people suffering from mental handicap who were over school age[451]. (This didn't affect how the Education (Scotland) Act 1980 operated, which placed a duty on education authorities to provide educational facilities for pupils suffering from mental disability.) The Act also carried on the requirement, established by the 1960 Act, that all private hospitals had to be registered and open to inspection at all times[452]. (Part IV of the Social Work (Scotland) Act 1968 replaced the 1960 Act's requirements for residential homes.)

The 1984 Act also largely retained the 1960 Act's legal provisions on caring for and treating patients. For example, it was an offence under the 1984 Act for anyone –including an officer, employee or manager – to ill-treat or deliberately neglect a patient being treated for mental disorder as an in-patient or out-patient[453]. Furthermore, women received more protection; it was an offence for a man to have, procure or encourage unlawful sexual intercourse with a woman or girl protected under the Act[454].

Inspections were also of great importance. Section 109 (1) of the Act made it an offence for anyone to refuse to allow premises to be inspected, obstruct a visit to, interview with or examination of a patient, or fail to produce records. Indeed, mental health officers and medical commissioners could demand, at all reasonable times, to enter and inspect a premises and remove a patient if they believed the patient was being ill-treated or neglected[455].

Overall, therefore, the 1984 Act clearly continued the effective measures put in place by the 1960 Act and 1983 amendment Act, attempting to ensure that children with mental disorders were properly protected.

Section 8: Further developments in the 1980s and 1990s[456]

The latter half of the review period shows that there had been significant advances in efficiently regulating how children and young people were cared for and treated in residential establishments. The way the various laws, rules and regulations were applied made the legal framework clearer and more transparent. It brought together a vast number of requirements and began to place child welfare at the centre of a system of regulation that was increasingly streamlined.

But one can criticise the fact that, after the Social Work (Scotland) Act 1968 was introduced, the power to make regulations for such establishments was largely unused until the 1980s. This effectively meant that many of the older and potentially outmoded legal provisions – such as the 1959 Regulations and the 1961 Rules – remained in force and at the core of how establishments were regulated. In other words, what seemed on the surface to be an extensive overhaul and consolidation of the main principles may have had little effect on how these establishments were run in practice.

What is apparent, however, is that the legal developments mirrored closely an increasing awareness in England and Scotland that vulnerable children might be exposed to risks in the very places where they should be safe[457]: residential establishments.

In England, concerns about the quality of care in such establishments led to 'The Report of the Committee Inquiry into Children's Homes and Hostels' in 1985, which uncovered systematic sexual abuse of children in residential care[458]. Another significant inquiry – the 'Pindown Report'[459] – was published in the early 1990s, and revealed methods of restraining children that were unsuitable and not appropriate to a caring environment. These reports led to new procedures in

---

[451] Within the meaning of the Education (Scotland) Act 1980. The Mental Health (Scotland) Act 1984, s11(1)

[452] *ibid* ss12, 14

[453] *ibid* s105(1)

[454] That is, a woman or girl "suffering from a state of arrested or incomplete development of mind, which includes significant impairment of intelligence and social functioning". The Mental Health (Scotland) Act 1984, ss106, 107

[455] *ibid* s117

[456] Taken primarily from the Stair Memorial Encyclopaedia *The Laws of Scotland: Child and Family Law*, para 292 onwards

[457] *ibid* para 292

[458] *ibid*. The phrase "systems abuse" has been coined to describe the abuse or neglect that children suffer at the hands of organisations dealing with their education and care. See J Cashmore 'Systems Abuse' in M John *A Charge Against Society: The Child's Right to Protection* (1997)

[459] *The Pindown Experience and the Protection of Children: the Report of the Staffordshire Child Care Inquiry* (1991)

England for recruiting and training staff in residential homes. They also influenced policy and practice north of the border.

Taking account of developments in England, the Secretary of State commissioned a review of residential childcare in Scotland, known commonly as 'The Skinner Report'[460]. This was charged with outlining changes in how residential childcare had been provided during the 1970s and 1980s, and stated the eight fundamental principles necessary for effective residential care (including individuality and development, good basic care and a feeling of safety). The report made 66 recommendations[461]. Also important during this period were the findings of the 'Fife Inquiry'[462], and hearings into several complex child protection cases in Scotland[463]. These led to further inquiries[464] into how the 1968 Act operated.

As various commentators have recognised[465], the effect of all the conclusions and recommendations of these inquiries – and growing awareness of the significance of children's and parents' rights in child protection[466] – led to substantial reforms under the Children (Scotland) Act 1995[467].

Section 9: The Children (Scotland) Act 1995

The Children (Scotland) Act 1995 radically overhauled Scottish law relating to children. (We've called it the 1995 Act from here on.)

The 1995 Act provided for adoption of children and young people who had been looked after as children by local authorities. It covered how residential establishments should be regulated, and introduced new regulations covering the relationship between parents and children, and between guardians and children. It continued an existing emphasis on finding care for children whose parents couldn't adequately care for them[468], and also continued to recognise the importance of protecting children. Children could therefore be referred to children's hearings if they were the victim of a "Schedule 1 offence", meaning Schedule 1 to the Criminal Procedure (Scotland) Act 1975[469].

Schedule 1 of the Criminal Law (Consolidation) (Scotland) Act 1995 listed a range of sexual offences against children, for example, incest[470] and intercourse between someone in a position of trust and a child under 16[471]. This was designed to reinforce the protective measures that the 1995 Act laid down. At a general level, the 1995 Act also responded to the many inquiries into child cruelty and child protection policies by putting more emphasis on

[460] Another Kind of Home: A Review of Residential Child Care (1992) (the Skinner Report)

[461] Mostly concerning local authorities' policies and procedures: Stair Memorial Encyclopaedia *The Laws of Scotland: Child and Family Law*, para 292 onwards

[462] *Report of the Inquiry into Child Care Policies in Fife* (the Kearney Report) (HC Papers (1992-93) no.191) dealing with Fife Regional Council's policy to place children, where possible, on home supervision, seemingly at the expense of denying residential placements to those children who might benefit from them, and therefore undermining the authority of the children's hearing system. The Inquiry concluded that the implementation of the region's policy was characterised by over-simplification of issues affecting children and their families and that 'this approach was dangerous and inimical to good social work practice'

[463] *Sloan v B* 1991 SLT 530; *L, Petrs* 1993 SCLR 693, 1993 SLT 1310 and 1342

[464] *Report of the Inquiry into the Removal of Children from Orkney in February 1991* (The Clyde Report) (HC Papers 1992-93) no.195) which concentrated on the legal provisions for emergency protection of children and the decision-making processes of the various agencies (specific to the case) involved in child protection.

[465] Stair Memorial Encyclopaedia *The Laws of Scotland: Child and Family Law*, para 293

[466] The United Kingdom had ratified the United Nations Convention on the Rights of the Child on 16 December 1991 and a challenge to the children's hearing system had been made under the European Convention on Human Rights in *McMichael v United Kingdom* (1995) A 307; 20 EHRR 205: *ibid*

[467] See E Kay M Tisdall *The Children (Scotland) Act 1995: Developing Policy and Law for Scotland's Children* (1997)

[468] For example, local authorities were placed under a duty to promote the upbringing of children by their families, and involve parents in decision-making etc: The Children (Scotland) Act 1995, s22(1)(b) and s17(4)

[469] 'Any offence involving the use of lewd, indecent or libidinous practice or behaviour towards a child under the age of 17': See the Children (Scotland) Act 1995, s52(2)(d). See also the Criminal Law (Consolidation) (Scotland) Act 1995, Sch 1

[470] Criminal Law (Consolidation) (Scotland) Act 1995, s1.

[471] Ibid, *ibid* s3: although this was geared towards individuals living at home with children, see below for residential home provisions

listening to children's views and treating them with respect. This meant that courts, children's hearings and local authorities had a duty to take account of these views.[472]

Part I of the 1995 Act gave parents a range of duties towards a child[473]. This included being responsible for:

■ safeguarding the child's health;

■ the child's development and welfare[474];

■ providing direction and guidance to the child[475]; and

■ if the child didn't live with them, keeping in regular, personal touch with the child[476].

Fulfilling their responsibilities under the Act meant that parents generally had the right to:

■ have the child living with them – or to make other arrangements for where the child could live[477]; and

■ control, direct or guide the child's upbringing in ways appropriate to the child's stage of development[478].

And if the child wasn't living with the parent, he or she had the right to maintain personal relations and direct contact with the child regularly[479].

Parents' rights and responsibilities under the 1995 Act replaced any similar rights and responsibilities they may have had under common law[480]. Anyone deemed to have parental responsibilities or rights under the 1995 Act could not renounce those responsibilities or rights, but could arrange for some or all of them to be exercised on his or her behalf. Even young people who didn't have any parental rights or responsibilities, but who had reached 16 years and had care or control over a child under 16 had a duty, namely to do what was reasonable in the circumstances to safeguard the child's health and welfare[481].

Perhaps the greatest change that Part I of the 1995 Act made in this area was to the need to take a child's views into consideration. This was the case for anybody who made any major decision about taking responsibility for a child as a parent, or about caring for a child. In doing so, they had to allow for the child's age and maturity; a child aged 12 or over was considered old and mature enough to form a view[482]. This shows a definite shift towards a more child-centered legal framework than before: further evidenced by the fact that a court could only grant an application for guardianship if it felt that doing this was in the child's best interests[483].

Indeed this principle underpins the 1995 Act. Part II dealt with how local authorities and children's hearing should promote children's welfare, and stated that if a children's hearing or court decided any matter with respect to a child, the child's welfare throughout their childhood had to be their paramount consideration[484].

The language was therefore very clear about how the law should be applied. The duties of local authorities looking after children[485] (in any way that the Secretary of State allowed) were also clear: they had to safeguard and promote the child's welfare, which also had to be their paramount consideration. Local authorities were therefore required to do whatever was necessary, practical and appropriate to promote regular, direct contact and personal relations between

---

[472] The Children (Scotland) Act 1995, ss16-17

[473] Defined as a person under the age of 16 or 18 depending on the relevant provisions relied on: see The Children (Scotland) Act 1995, s1(2)

[474] *ibid* s1(a)

[475] *ibid* s1(b)

[476] *ibid* s1(c)

[477] *ibid* s2(1)(a)

[478] *ibid* s2(1)(b)

[479] *ibid* s2(1)(c)

[480] *ibid* s1(4) and 2(5)

[481] *ibid* s5(1), but "nothing in this section shall apply to a person in so far as he has care or control of a child in a school ("school" having the meaning given by section 135(1) of the [1980 c. 44.] Education (Scotland) Act 1980)": *ibid* s5(2)

[482] *ibid* s6

[483] *ibid* s11(7)(a)

[484] *ibid* s16(1)

[485] "Look[ing] after" referring to a child for whom a local authority are providing accommodation for under s25 of the Act, who is subject to a supervision requirement, or who is subject to a warrant or order under the Act: The Children (Scotland) Act 1995, s17(6)

a child and anybody with parental responsibilities for the child[486]. Their duties could include giving advice and help to prepare the child for when it was no longer looked after by the local authority[487].

Decisions about any child whom the authority was looking after[488] had to take account of the views of the child, its parents, anybody with parental rights and anyone else the authority considered relevant. The decision could also have to take account of the child's age, maturity, religion, race and cultural and linguistic background[489]. This promotion of welfare would extend not only to children in local authorities' care, but also to children in their area who were in need[490].

Local authorities' duties under the 1995 Act included having to prepare and publish plans[491], the contents of which could be directed by the Secretary of State. The authority was required to review these plans regularly[492] and in consultation with their local health boards, NHS trusts and any other organisations considered appropriate under the Act. Furthermore, they had to make more information publicly available. This included what services they provided to children in their area and, if appropriate, services that voluntary organisations[493] provided for them[494].

Under the 1995 Act, local authorities had to provide accommodation in line with the obligations laid down in the 1968 Act. Therefore, authorities were required to provide for children who lived in or were found in their area and who apparently needed accommodation because:

■ nobody had parental responsibility for them;
■ they were lost or abandoned; or
■ whoever was caring for them couldn't provide suitable accommodation and care[495].

Again this was underpinned by the general principle that a local authority could provide accommodation simply if they considered it would safeguard or promote a child's welfare[496]. As before, they had to take account of the child's views as far as practicable[497].

This duty to provide accommodation was not to apply under these general provisions if anyone with parental responsibilities for, or rights over, the child could:

■ care for the child; and
■ was willing to either provide, or arrange to have provided, accommodation for the child[498].

Therefore, anyone in this position could at any time remove the child from accommodation provided by the local authority under these provisions[499].

In terms of the manner of accommodation to be provided, the 1995 Act stated that a local authority

---

[486] *ibid* s17(1)(c)

[487] *ibid* s17(2)

[488] *ibid* s17(3)

[489] *ibid* s17(4)

[490] *ibid* s22(1). Being "in need" defined as being in need of care and attention because "he [the child] is unlikely to maintain, or to have the opportunity of achieving or maintaining, a reasonable standard of health or development unless they are provided for him...his health or development is likely significantly to be impaired, or further impaired, unless such services are so provided...he is disabled; or...he is affected adversely by the disability of any other person in his family...": The Children (Scotland) Act 1995, s93(4)

[491] *ibid* s19(1)

[492] *ibid* s19(3)

[493] Defined as "a body (other than a public or local authority) whose activities are not carried on for profit" - the Children (Scotland) Act 1995, s93 (1)

[494] *ibid* s20

[495] *ibid* s25(1)

[496] *ibid* s25(2). Furthermore a local authority could provide accommodation for any person within their area between the ages of 18 and 21, if they considered it necessary to promote their welfare: The Children (Scotland) Act 1995, s25(3)

[497] *ibid* s25(5)

[498] *ibid* s25(6)(a), but not applying if any child over 16 agreed to be provided with such accommodation or where a residence order had been made but it was agreed that the child should be looked after in accommodation provided by the local authority: The Children (Scotland) Act 1995, s25(7)

[499] *ibid*, s25(6)(b), although not applying where accommodation has been provided for a continuous period of at least six months unless the person removing the child had given the local authority for the time being making such provision at least fourteen days' notice in writing of his intention to remove the child: The Children (Scotland) Act 1995, s25(7)

could provide accommodation for a child looked after them by:

- boarding them out (that is, placing them with an individual or family who would have responsibility for the child)[500];
- maintaining the child in a residential establishment[501]; or
- making any other arrangements that the local authority considered appropriate[502].

Furthermore, local authorities also had a duty to review the case of any child in their care at certain intervals and in ways laid down by the Secretary of State[503]. They retained the right to remove any child placed in residential establishments at any time – and had to if asked by the person responsible for the establishment[504].

Local authorities could insist that a child had to go into care under the 1995 Act if it appeared, for example, that the child:

- was beyond the control of what the Act described as a relevant person[505];
- was falling into bad company or exposed to moral danger;
- was likely to suffer unnecessarily or suffer serious health or development problems because of a lack of parental care; or
- had been the victim of a so-called Schedule 1 offence[506], which covered offences such as indecent behaviour.

If a local authority received information suggesting that a child would have to be placed in care, it could make whatever inquiries were needed and inform the Principal Reporter[507]. These investigations also allowed a sheriff to grant a child assessment order: this meant an assessment could be made of the state of the child's health or development, or how the child had been treated[508].

Children could be given emergency protection under child protection orders. These allowed a sheriff to remove a child to a place of safety[509] if, for example, there were reasonable grounds to suspect that a child was being ill treated, neglected or suffering significant harm. A child protection order was also possible if enquiries were under way to allow a local authority to decide whether they should take any action to safeguard a child's welfare[510]. The 1995 Act also ensured that children at risk of harm could be given short-term refuge if a child asked for it[511]. The child could be placed in residential establishments both controlled or managed by a local authority, or one registered under the 1968 Act and approved by the local authority.

It's clear, therefore, that the welfare of children was more obviously at the heart of the legal framework under the 1995 Act. However, the Act was significant not just for introducing legal measures to properly govern standards of alternative care, but also in its relationship to what was already in force under existing laws. Worth noting in particular is the vast number of ways it amended the Social Work (Scotland) Act 1968. These amendments updated the 1968 Act's requirements and tightened up

---

[500] *ibid* s26(1)(a)

[501] *ibid* s26(1)(b). Defined in s93(1) as an establishment (whether managed by a local authority, by a voluntary organisation or by any other person) which provides residential accommodation for children for the purposes of the Children (Scotland) Act 1995 or the Social Work (Scotland) Act 1968

[502] *ibid* s26(1)(c)

[503] *ibid* s31(1)

[504] *ibid* s32

[505] "relevant person" in relation to a child meaning - (a) any parent enjoying parental responsibilities or parental rights under Part I of the 1995 Act; (b) any person in whom parental responsibilities or rights were vested by, under or by virtue of the 1995 Act; and (c) any person appearing to be a person who ordinarily (and other than by reason only of his employment) had charge of, or control over, the child

[506] *ibid* s52. "Schedule 1" to the [1975 c. 21.] Criminal Procedure (Scotland) Act 1975 (offences against children to which special provisions apply)

[507] *ibid* s53. "The Principal Reporter" means the Principal Reporter appointed under section 127 of the Act of 1994 or any officer of the Scottish Children's Reporter Administration to whom there is delegated, under section 131(1) of that Act, any function of the Principal Reporter under the 1995 Act: The Children (Scotland) Act, s93(1)

[508] *ibid* s55

[509] Meaning a residential or other establishment provided by a local authority, a community home within the meaning of s53 of the Children Act 1989, a police station, or a hospital surgery or other suitable place, the occupier of which is willing temporarily to receive the child: The Children (Scotland) Act 1995, s93(1)

[510] *ibid* s57

[511] The Children (Scotland) Act 1995, s38 (1)

the framework of laws, rules and regulations that regulated services for children. So, for example, section 34 of the 1995 Act amended how residential establishments should be registered. It refined the scope of what had been possible under the 1968 Act[512] and required new details about the process of voluntary registration[513].

The 1995 Act also tightened the law on inspecting establishments (amending section 67 of the 1968 Act), allowing someone who'd been authorised by a local authority to go into a registered establishment – or premises suspected of being used as one – at all reasonable times[514]. In line with 1968 Act's wording, an inspection could be made under the 1995 Act to examine "the state and management of the establishment or place, and the condition and treatment of the persons in it, as the person so authorised thinks necessary"[515].

More significantly, however, is how the 1995 Act changed access to records. Under the 1968 Act, inspectors could examine "any records or registers required to be kept". Now they could inspect any records or registers in whatever form they were held relating the place or to anyone in the establishment receiving services under the 1968 Act, the Mental Health (Scotland) Act 1984, or the 1995 Act[516].

A final significant amendment ensured that the actions of local authorities could be properly scrutinised. The change meant that an inquiry could be called into the local authority's functions, under the 1968 Act, which related to children. Although it was the local authority that would be required to carry out the inquiry[517], it was an important revision of the law, and complemented the Secretary of State's power to order an inquiry into:

- the functions of a local authority or voluntary organisation under the 1968 Act;
- the detention of a child under the Children and Young Persons (Scotland) Act 1937 or the Criminal Procedure (Scotland) Act 1975; or
- the functions of the Principal Reporter under the Local Government (Scotland) Act 1994 or the Children (Scotland) Act 1995[518].

The 1995 Act also made an important contribution to how the various education Acts introduced in Scotland operated over the years. From 1946[519] until 1995[520] no mention was made specifically of schools providing residential accommodation[521], and the 1995 Act inserted a new legal provision into the Education (Scotland) Act 1980. It affected whoever was responsible for a school providing residential accommodation: for the first time, they were under a duty to safeguard and promote the welfare of children in their accommodation. They also had, under the Act, to comply with the amended rules on inspections[522]. Again, this emphasis on the child's welfare is important. It could also be seen in a requirement that affected children accommodated in establishments such as hospitals and nursing homes.

---

[512] Applying more extensively now "(a) to any residential or other establishment the whole or a substantial part of whose functions is to provide persons with such personal care or support, whether or not combined with board and whether for reward or not, as may be required for the purposes of this Act [that is, the 1968 Act] or of the Children (Scotland) Act 1995; (b) in the case of a residential establishment which is a grant-aided or independent school (as respectively defined in section 135(1) of the [1980 c. 44.] Education (Scotland) Act 1980), to that establishment if any part of its functions are as described in paragraph (a) above" The Children (Scotland) Act 1995, s34 (amending s61 of the 1968 Act). Repealed by the Regulation of Care (Scotland) Act 2001, s80(1), Sch4

[513] Inserting a new s61A into the Social Work (Scotland) Act 1968. Certificates of registration as regards grant-aided or independent schools were dealt with in the newly inserted s62A. Both were repealed by the Regulation of Care (Scotland) Act 2001, s80(1), Sch4

[514] The Social Work (Scotland) Act s67(1), as inserted by the Children (Scotland) Act 1995, s34

[515] *ibid* s67(2)(a) as inserted by the Children (Scotland) Act 1995, s34

[516] *ibid* s67(2)(b)

[517] The Social Work (Scotland) Act 1968, s6B as inserted by the Children (Scotland) Act 1995 s100

[518] The Social Work (Scotland) Act 1968 s6A, as amended by the Children (Scotland) Act 1995, Sch 4, s15

[519] That is, The Education (Scotland) Act 1946

[520] Chiefly governed by the Education (Scotland) Act 1980

[521] "School" was defined consistently as excluding approved schools and latterly establishments or residential establishments within the meaning of the Social Work (Scotland) Act 1968. "Educational Establishments" could include residential institutions conducted under an endowment scheme. See, for example, the Education (Scotland) Act 1946 s143(1), and the Education (Scotland) Act 1980 s135(1)

[522] The Education (Scotland) Act 1980, s125A, as inserted by the Children (Scotland) Act 1995, s35

Here, too, steps had to be taken to make sure the child's welfare was being safeguarded and promoted[523].

Overall, therefore, the 1995 Act undoubtedly placed children at the core of its legal provisions, making some vital changes to the existing framework of laws, rules and regulations. It also, arguably, sharply refocused the objectives of the system, and made sure the new provisions worked effectively alongside the important provisions still in force under the Social Work (Scotland) Act 1968. However, although the changes made by the 1995 Act were seen as a welcome and important development, they weren't absolute. As we'll see, further refinements were needed.

For example, the Regulation of Care (Scotland) Act 2001 brought further measures relating to the standards of residential care for children; it required that all care home services had to be registered with the Commission for the Regulation of Care[524]. (Care home services provide accommodation and nursing care or some form of personal support to people who are vulnerable or in need[525]. The term includes residential care homes for children.) And, although the 1995 Act amended the 1968 Act in the areas of registration and inspection procedures, the 2001 Act tightened the regulations. Residential homes had to be registered and inspected to ensure adequate standards of care, with a requirement for twice-yearly inspections[526].

Furthermore, under the 2001 Act, a new Care Commission was required to take national standards into account when deciding whether standards of care were "adequate".[527]

Part three: 1995 – present day

Section 10: Developments since 1995

This period isn't in my remit and therefore it's not necessary to analyse it extensively. However, it is relevant to examine some developments since the changes introduced by the 1995 Act, as it offers a valuable insight into how the legal framework has progressed. This section considers the following:

■ Children cared for in residential establishments
■ Secure accommodation
■ The Regulation of Care (Scotland) Act 2001

Children cared for in residential establishments

The Residential Establishments - Child Care (Scotland) Regulations 1996[528] covered residential establishments into which local authorities could place children they looked after[529]. The regulations replaced the Social Work (Residential Establishments - Child Care) (Scotland) Regulations 1987.

At their heart was a requirement that managers of these establishments had a duty to make sure that a child's welfare was safeguarded and promoted in accordance with the child's best interests[530]. Managers

---

[523] The Children (Scotland) Act 1995, s36
[524] The Regulation of Care (Scotland) Act 2001, s7(1)
[525] *ibid* s2(3)
[526] *ibid* s25(3)
[527] *National Care Standards for Care Homes for Children and Young People* (Scottish Executive, 2002), available via www.scotland.gov.uk
[528] S.I. 1996/3256. Superseded themselves by the Regulation of Care (Requirements as to Care Services) (Scotland) Regulations 2002 No 114
[529] Applying to any residential establishment controlled or managed by a local authority, one which required registration under s61 of the 1968 Act, or a school voluntarily registered in accordance with s61A of the 1968 Act: S.I. 1996/3256, paragraph 3
[530] *ibid*, paragraph 4

had, as before, to prepare a statement of functions and objectives, setting out their responsibilities[531] and reviewing them to make sure their obligations were being implemented[532]. Minimum requirements – again almost identical to those of 1987 Regulations – covered fire precautions[533], sanctions[534], education[535], the need to keep log books and personal records[536], religious instruction[537] and health and medical care[538].

Arrangements for monitoring registered establishments were reinforced, requiring the authority to visit at least once a year and make sure that the establishment was:

- complying with the statement of functions and objectives; and
- maintaining residents' safety and welfare[539].

The similarities with the 1987 Regulations had two notable exceptions.

Firstly, a new requirement meant managers had to have in place procedures for appointing and vetting staff[540]. This was significant in recognising the need to tighten provisions governing monitoring in this area. Secondly, some of the measures in the 1987 Regulations were moved to the Arrangements to Look After Children (Scotland) Regulations 1996[541], which dealt with the nature of child placements and how these were reviewed and ended. This ensured that the Residential Establishments - Child Care (Scotland) Regulations 1996 offered a streamlined and more focused set of rules to govern the practicalities of running residential establishments.

The Arrangements to Look After Children (Scotland) Regulations 1996 are also significant, in that they required local authorities to make a care plan before taking a child into care. Obviously an important development, these plans had to cover the child's immediate and longer-term needs and had to aim to safeguard and promote the child's welfare[542]. Among other things[543], the care plan had to include:

- the local authority's immediate and longer term plans for the child;
- details of any services to be provided to meet the child's care, education and health needs;
- the responsibilities of the local authority, the child, anyone with parental responsibility, or another relevant person[544];
- the type of accommodation (for example, residential establishment, foster home);
- the address;
- the name of whoever was responsible for the child at the establishment on the local authority's behalf:
- how the child's parents were contributing to the child's day-to-day care;
- contact arrangements; and
- how long care was expected to last[545].

The plan had to be in writing and the local authority had to agree it with a parent or whoever was in charge of the child[546].

---

[531] *ibid* paragraph 5(1) and the Schedule to the Regulations
[532] *ibid* paragraph 5(2) and (3)
[533] *ibid* paragraph 9
[534] *ibid* paragraph 10. Generally, to be determined by the managers in accordance with their statement of functions and objectives, specifically excluding corporal punishment having the same meaning as in s48A of the Education (Scotland) Act 1980
[535] S.I. 1996/3256, paragraph 11
[536] *ibid* paragraphs 12 and 13
[537] *ibid* paragraph 14
[538] *ibid* paragraph 15
[539] *ibid* paragraph 16
[540] *ibid* paragraph 8
[541] S.I. 1996/3262
[542] S.I. 1996/3262 paragraph 3
[543] *ibid* paragraph 4 and 5
[544] *ibid* paragraph 6(1) and Schedule 2 Part I
[545] *ibid* paragraph 6(2) and Schedule 2 Part II
[546] *ibid* paragraph 6(4) and (5)

The regulations also introduced other safeguards. Local authorities had to give written notice of any placement[547] - and information about the placement – to:

- the education authority responsible for the area the child would live[548] in;
- the local health board[549];
- (in some circumstances) the parent or person in charge of the child[550]; and
- any other local authority if different from the placing authority (this was usually an authority in a different area)[551].

Stringent reviews of the placement and the care plan were required, and local authorities had to do these frequently[552] and record their findings[553].

The emphasis on having to keep records was stressed by requiring local authorities to keep a written case record for each child it looked after by. This had to include:

- a copy of the care plan;
- a copy of any report they had that concerned the child's welfare;
- review documents; and
- details of any arrangements for anyone to act behalf of the local authority that placed the child[554].

A case record had to be kept until the 75th birthday of the person it related to. If a child died before reaching 18, the record had to be kept for 25 years from the date of death[555]. Local authorities were responsible for keeping case records safely and confidential, although confidentiality could be lifted under legal provisions or if a court ordered it[556]. These obligations undoubtedly strengthened record-keeping for children in local authority care.

The regulations also strengthened arrangements for monitoring children in care. Local authorities had to make sure that a registered medical practitioner (such as a doctor) examined children before they were placed. They also had to provide children with health care during the placement[557]. Furthermore, they had to make sure that the child was visited within a week of being placed. After this, visits had to take place at least every three months, or whenever local authorities felt it was necessary to safeguard or promote the child's welfare. Local authorities had to keep written reports on visits[558].

A local authority could, by giving written notice, end a placement if it felt it was no longer in the child's best interests[559].

---

[547] Not required if the placement was only intended to last not more than 28 days, unless the child had significant medical or educational needs or the placement did in fact last for more than 28 days: S.I. 1996/3262 paragraph 7(2)

[548] *ibid* paragraph 7(1)(b) if the child was of compulsory school age within the meaning of section 31 of the Education (Scotland) Act 1980

[549] *ibid* paragraph 7(1)(c)

[550] *ibid* paragraph 7(1)(d) except where they have already received a written copy of the care plan, or where the local authority consider it against the interests of the child, or where a supervision requirement, order or warrant prevents disclosure

[551] S.I. 1996/3262 paragraph 7(1)(a)

[552] *ibid* paragraphs 8 and 9, namely six weeks within the date of first placement, three months within the date of the first review and thereafter periods of six months within the date of the previous review

[553] S.I. 1996/3262 paragraph 10

[554] *ibid* paragraph 11

[555] *ibid* paragraph 12(1), the requirements being met by either retaining the original written record or a copy of it, or in some other accessible form (such as a computer record): S.I. 1996/3262 paragraph 12(2)

[556] *ibid* paragraph 12(3)

[557] *ibid* paragraph 13(1) and (2)

[558] *ibid* paragraph 18

[559] *ibid* paragraph 19. The regulations also made provision for a looked after child to be cared for by his own parents in certain circumstances, and set out minimum requirements for planned short term placements: S.I. 1996/3262 paragraphs 16 and 17

Secure accommodation

New regulations were also introduced to govern how secure accommodation should be provided in residential establishments, designed to work alongside the Residential Establishments-Child Care (Scotland) Regulations 1996 and replaced the previous sets of secure accommodation regulations[560].

The new regulations (the Secure Accommodation (Scotland) Regulations 1996[561]) covered any child looked after by a local authority or for whom the local authority was responsible under criminal procedure laws. Consolidating the previous legislation in this area, they again required the Secretary of State to approve any arrangements to use part of a residential establishment as secure accommodation[562]. And, as before, managers and owners had to make sure to safeguard and promote the welfare of a child placed in secure accommodation[563]. A record of the child's placement also had to be kept, including details of the child and any reviews of the child's placement under section 73 of the 1995 Act[564].

The most notable change that the regulations introduced was to reduce the maximum period that a child could be kept in secure accommodation without the authority of a children's hearing or a sheriff. This was cut from seven days to 72 hours. The period for calling a children's hearing to consider a child's case was also shortened[565]. Finally, local authorities could now set up secure placement review panels. These could review the case of any child detained by a local authority in secure accommodation under the Criminal Procedure (Scotland) Act 1995[566].

The Regulation of Care (Scotland) Act 2001

Perhaps the most significant recent development in the care provided for children and young people has been the Regulation of Care (Scotland) Act 2001 (we've called this the 2001 Act from here on).

Various consultation papers were published before the Act took effect, making detailed proposals for new arrangements to regulate care services and the social services workforce. These papers considered:

- how to modernise social work services in Scotland;
- the first and second sections of draft national care standards covering, amongst other things, older people, people with mental health problems, and children and young people; and
- the future of care homes under the new legislation[567].

As a result, the 2001 Act established a new independent body to regulate care services in Scotland, known as the Scottish Commission for the Regulation of Care (also known as the Care Commission)[568]. This created a system under which care services were to be registered and inspected against a set of national care standards, and subject to enforcement action. Furthermore, the Act established another independent body, the Scottish Social Services Council, to regulate social service workers and promote and regulate their education and training.

---

[560] Chiefly, The Secure Accommodation (Scotland) Regulations 1983 (SI 1983/1912); The Secure Accommodation (Scotland) Amendment Regulations 1988 (SI 1988/841); The Residential Care Order (Secure Accommodation) (Scotland) Amendment Regulations 1988 (S.I. 1988/1092)

[561] S.I. 1996/3255

[562] *ibid* paragraph 3

[563] *ibid* paragraph 4

[564] *ibid* paragraph 16

[565] *ibid* paragraphs 5, 8 and 9

[566] *ibid* paragraphs 13-15

[567] See: *Modernising Social Work Services: A Consultation Paper on Workforce Regulation and Education*, published in November 1998; *Aiming for Excellence: Modernising Social Work Services in Scotland* (Cm 4288), published in March 1999; *Regulating Care and the Social Services Workforce: A Consultation Paper*, published in December 1999; *Draft National Care Standards: First Tranche*, published in June 2000; *The Way Forward For Care: a policy position paper*, published in July 2000; *Draft National Care Standards: Second Tranche*, published in April 2001; *The Future for Care Homes in Scotland: A Consultation Paper*, published in April 2001

[568] www.carecommission.com

It's interesting and significant that the explanatory notes to the 2001 Act[569] described the way that care services were regulated before 2001 as "patchy", and considered that many of the services were regulated under laws, rules and regulations that seemed to be outdated. The need for change highlighted in the Act recognised that not all care services had to be registered or inspected: those that were, were regulated and inspected by different bodies. We've seen, for example, that private and voluntary sector residential care homes were regulated by local authorities; private nursing homes by health boards; and secure accommodation for children by the Social Work Inspectorate. Some services, such as residential care homes run by local authorities and support services for people at home weren't subject to registration at all.

It was also widely recognised that the various standards weren't being consistently applied, and that there was a lack of efficient integration between different services being provided by the same establishment. The 2001 Act, therefore, aimed to "modernise and standardise" how care services were regulated, to ensure people's trust and confidence in the effectiveness of the system. These care services included:

- residential care for children;
- children's early education, day care and child-minding;
- adoption and fostering services; and
- care and welfare in boarding schools, school hostels and in accommodation for offenders.

For the first time, all local authority care services had to register and meet the same standards as the independent sector provided.

The Act therefore set out to plug gaps in the framework for regulating care services. In doing this, it changed existing legislation in various ways. Most notably for our purposes, this included replacing sections 60-68 of the Social Work (Scotland) Act 1968; schedule 9 of the Children Act 1989 (as it applied to Scotland); and some other minor changes and repeals.

Notable features of the 2001 Act

The 2001 Act provides us with the most modern, significant piece of legislation for regulating care services for children and young people. Alongside the 1968 Act and 1995 Act, it forms a crucial part of the modern legal framework. So it's important to examine some of its provisions more carefully to help us understand the current position.

The Act is divided into seven parts, and Part One is perhaps most noteworthy for creating the Scottish Commission for the Regulation of Care[570], an independent, non-departmental public body accountable to Scottish Ministers. The Commission's job includes promoting improvements in care services in Scotland[571], and acting in line with instructions given to it by, and under the general guidance of, Scottish Ministers[572]. It therefore has a crucial role to play in how care services are regulated today. Indeed its aim was to replace a fragmented and inconsistent system of regulating services with a comprehensive system of registration and enforcement in line with published standards[573].

---

[569] Asp 8

[570] The Regulation of Care (Scotland) Act 2001, s1(1)

[571] *ibid* s1(1)(b)

[572] *ibid* s1(2). Subsection (3) gives effect to Schedule 1 which sets out the constitutional arrangements and general provisions for the establishment and operation of the Commission

[573] General Note to s1 of the Regulation of Care (Scotland) Act 2001, asp 8

The Commission took over the tasks of registration, inspection and enforcement previously undertaken mainly by local authorities and health boards. However, it has no role in overseeing or supervising how to decide what services are needed or provided. This remains a legal duty for local authorities under the Social Work (Scotland) Act 1968.

The 2001 Act also deals with the range of care services that have to be registered with the Commission[574]. Section 2(3) defines a "care home service" as one which provides accommodation – along with personal care, personal support or nursing – for anyone, including children, because of their vulnerability or need. Local authority care homes have to be registered, and nurses can be employed to provide nursing care[575]. The care and accommodation must be inextricably linked[576] for a care service to be considered a care home. If this isn't the case, the Commission registers and inspects the care being delivered as a support service under section 2(2). The importance of such a section on care home services is that it brings together the previously separate definitions of residential care homes and nursing homes under the single definition of a care home.

The Act then goes on to deal with other possible types of care service, perhaps most importantly defining "school care accommodation" and "secure accommodation for children". School care accommodation is classified as residential accommodation provided for school pupils by a local authority or by an independent or grant-aided school, and covers services to children boarding at an independent school, school hostels provided by local authorities and special schools[577].

Secure accommodation for children is recognised as residential accommodation approved by Scottish Ministers in line with regulations under section 29(9)(a) of the Act[578], catering for some of the most vulnerable children and young people in Scotland. The Commission now regulates these services, but Scottish Ministers remain responsible for approving secure accommodation under section 29(9).

The Commission's chief priority is obviously to enforce the regulations that apply to these services overall. Section 4 of the 2001 Act provides greater accountability by requiring the Commission to publish information about the availability and quality of care services. This can include details of what types of services are available as well as the results of the Commission's inspections of care services[579]. The Act also requires procedures to be put in place to deal with complaints by the people who use care services regulated by the Commission, their relatives, advocates or staff[580].

However, perhaps the Commission's greatest obligation under the Act is that of enforcing the registration and inspection procedures. Generally, the Commission has to take national care standards[581] – focusing on the needs of people who use care services – into account when making any decisions about registering, inspecting and enforcing care services. This is the case whether the services are registered under Part 1 or Part 2 of the Act[582]. Under section 7, anyone seeking to provide a care service must apply to the Commission to register the service[583], giving whatever information the Commission asks for and identifying who will manage the service[584]. If someone provides more than one care service they

---

[574] The Regulation of Care (Scotland) Act 2001, s2
[575] *ibid* s72
[576] To be determined by the Commission, with guidance from Scottish Ministers
[577] The Regulation of Care (Scotland) Act 2001, s2(4)
[578] *ibid* s2(9)
[579] *ibid* s4(1) and (2)
[580] *ibid* s6(1)
[581] http://www.scotland.gov.uk/Topics/Health/care/17652/9328
[582] The Regulation of Care (Scotland) Act 2001 s5
[583] *ibid* s7(1)
[584] *ibid* s7(2)

must apply to register all services[585]. This is also the case for anyone providing a care service from two or more settings: they have to register each setting as a separate service[586].

These stringent requirements ultimately tighten the regulation of these care services. The Commission can serve an improvement notice on any care service that doesn't meet the standards imposed[587], and any service that fails to comply with an improvement notice can have its registration cancelled[588]. The Commission can also cancel or deny registration if someone commits an offence under the Act, such as:

- describing a service as a care service but without being registered[589];
- failing to display a certificate of registration[590]; or
- failing to comply with any of the regulations introduced under section 29 of the 2001 Act[591].

It's also an offence to intentionally obstruct an inspection[592] – and inspections are thoroughly dealt with under the 2001 Act. It allows inspectors authorised by the Commission to inspect at any time any premises used or believed to be used in connection with a care service[593]. Crucially, the Act states that all care services offering 24-hour care away from home should have at least two inspections a year, with one or both being unannounced[594]. Unannounced inspections are, therefore, an important

part of the current system of regulation. Those services subject to two inspections a year under the Act are care homes, school care accommodation, secure accommodation and independent health care services that offer 24-hour care[595]. The Commission must ensure that all other care services are inspected at least once every 12 months[596].

Inspectors' duties underline the importance placed on inspections. They can ask to see records or other documents, wherever these are kept, and can ask whatever questions they feel are appropriate about how the service is run or how residents are treated[597]. They also have an extremely important power to interview, in private, the manager, employees, or any resident who agrees to be interviewed[598]. Inspectors who are medical practitioners or registered nurses can also examine a resident, or their medical records, if there's any concern – or if they believe – that the resident may not be getting proper care[599]. The examination is in private, and inspectors need the resident's agreement. Inspectors may also remove any material that could be used as evidence that a care service may not be meeting its requirements[600]. And any inspection under the Act requires the Commission to prepare a report to be sent to the registered person and made available to the public[601].

---

[585] *ibid* s7(3). This would mean, for example, that someone who provides a care home and a separate home care service would have to make a separate application for each. But someone who provides a care home which includes some day care provision might only need to apply once

[586] The Regulation of Care (Scotland) Act 2001 s7(4) and (5). This is to cover situations whereby an organisation or business operates a number of care services but effectively manages them each individually on a day to day basis

[587] The Regulation of Care (Scotland) Act 2001 *ibid* s10

[588] *ibid* s12

[589] *ibid* s21(1)

[590] *ibid* s21(2)

[591] *ibid* s12

[592] *ibid* s25(13)

[593] *ibid* s25(2). However, inspectors are not authorised to enter the home of a person receiving a support service in their own home

[594] *ibid* s25(3)

[595] *ibid* s25(4)

[596] *ibid* s25(5)

[597] *ibid* s25(6), (7) and (8)

[598] *ibid*

[599] *ibid* s25(9). Subsection (10) makes the same provision in respect of dentists. Subsection (11) defines an appropriate examination and consent for the purposes of these sections

[600] *ibid* s27(1)

[601] *ibid* s27(5) and (7)

The Act also introduces an interesting new measure to inspections. It requires the Commission's inspectors to collaborate with inspectors of schools where services have both care and educational components[602], such as school care accommodation, secure accommodation and day care of children[603]. The 2001 Act, therefore, is clearly much more detailed and thorough in what it requires of inspections, and gives inspectors wide and varied powers.

However, one fundamental difficulty for the Act is the difficulty it has in striking the right balance between effective powers to investigate – to enable it to regulate services in a meaningful way – and respect for the rights to privacy and property of the people who provide care services[604]. The Commission is a public authority under the terms of the Human Rights Act 1998[605]. So it must act in line with the rights that people who provide care services have under the European Convention of Human Rights[606]. The 2001 Act makes it possible to interfere with these rights. As a matter of principle, it is possible to justify this as necessary to protect the rights of the people who receive care services, but in practice many difficult and sensitive decisions have to be made[607].

Nonetheless, the Act goes as far as providing extensive powers to make regulations that cover care service premises and how the services are managed, staffed and run. And it does so in far more detail than previous laws. The Act gives a general power to make regulations to impose any requirements that Scottish Ministers request[608]. Regulations may, for example:

■ make sure that care services are suitably managed, staffed and equipped and that premises are fit for their purpose[609];

■ safeguard the welfare of people who receive care services (indeed they may specifically promote and protect residents' health and regulate how services control and restrain residents)[610]; and

■ prohibit someone from being appointed to manage or work in a care service if they're not on a register of social care workers maintained by the Scottish Social Services Council[611].

Scottish Ministers can also dictate, through regulations, how care services should be provided. This covers areas such as facilities and services, record-keeping, notifying significant events and how to deal with complaints[612]. The Act, therefore, gives much wider scope to regulating care through both primary legislation (Acts of Parliament) and secondary legislation (how Acts are implemented).

However, one issue has yet to be addressed relating to recent regulations introduced under such powers. The Regulation of Care (Requirements as to Care Services) Scotland Regulations 2002[613] set out the requirements that providers of care services must now comply with under the 2001 Act. The regulations specify, amongst other matters, people who are not fit to provide, manage or be employed in care services. They also extend to residents' welfare, the fitness of premises and the need to keep records[614]. However, they also state that a care service must comply with certain general principles and require the provider of the service to prepare a written statement of the "aims and objectives" of the care service[615]. It is here that potential confusion may arise in its relationship with the Residential Establishments – Child Care (Scotland) Regulations 1996, discussed above.

---

[602] *ibid* s26(1)
[603] *ibid* s26(2)
[604] General note to s25 of the Regulation of Care (Scotland) Act 2001
[605] c.42 s6
[606] Particularly Art 8 and Protocol 1, Article 1
[607] General note to s25 of the Regulation of Care (Scotland) Act 2001
[608] *ibid* s29(1)
[609] *ibid* s29(2)
[610] *ibid* s29(6)
[611] *ibid* s29(4) and (5)
[612] *ibid* s29(7)
[613] SI 2002/114
[614] *ibid* paragraphs 4 - 10, and 19
[615] *ibid* paragraphs 2 - 5

The implication seems to be that, with the introduction of the 2001 Act, there's uncertainty about whether the 1996 regulations still apply. The understanding in practice may be that the 1996 regulations only apply to homes directly run by local authorities, and that the 2002 regulations supersede the inspection procedures in all other areas. In other words, one is governed by the terms of the Social Work (Scotland) Act 1968, and the other by the terms of the 2001 Act. If this is the case, however, then inspectors can only enforce the need to provide a written statement of aims and objectives required under the 2002 regulations: there's no such requirement that all residential care services provide a statement of functions and objectives to be reviewed annually, as in the 1996 regulations. This could potentially lead to questions over whether an inspector from the Care Commission can rightfully inspect a home's statement and check that it's been reviewed, and, crucially, that it's operational. Such a gap, we suggest, could hinder the provision of quality care[616].

Overall, however, it's apparent that the 2001 Act marks important advances in regulating care services for children and young people, both in detail and efficiency. Operating alongside the main legal provisions of the Social Work (Scotland) Act 1968 and the Children (Scotland) Act 1995 that are still in force[617], there is no doubt that the 2001 Act implements some crucial changes, and establishes itself as one of the core components in the legal framework for regulating care services.

[616] See the work of Jackie McCrae, Children looked after by local authorities: the legal framework, published by SWIA (September 2006)
[617] Indeed, the 2001 Act makes some minor amendments and repeals to both Acts outlined in their respective sections above

Chapter 3

The regulatory framework: Observations, conclusions and recommendations

Chapter 3

The regulatory framework: Observations, conclusions and recommendations

These observations are based on my consideration of the findings of the review's research into the legislation. They also take into account:

- the literature reviews that I commissioned and the records research undertaken by my researcher;
- information given to me by people my researcher and I interviewed during the review; and
- information found in files in the National Archives of Scotland (NAS) and other archives.

They are my personal responses to what I have learned about the regulatory framework from 1950 to 1995.

This chapter has the following sections:

1. Understanding and implementing the legislation. The challenge
2. Observations on the Regulatory Framework
3. Conclusions

1. Understanding and implementing the legislation: The challenge

A vast number of legal requirements and powers governed how children's residential establishments were provided, regulated and inspected in Scotland from 1950 to 1995. They were complex and, in some cases, vague. The many regulations and rules had their origins in different government policies and were amended and repealed. As a result, it is very difficult to identify precisely what was current at any given point in time, a challenge which those delivering children's residential services must have faced and which may well have given rise to confusion and misunderstanding.

Some of the people we interviewed had professional experience in social work, education and health and had worked in the residential child care sector during the review period. They said that managers and staff in children's residential establishments were often unsure about, if not unfamiliar with, the relevant regulations and rules. Detailed guidance from government departments was said to compound uncertainty, particularly in the first half of the review period, when opportunities to brief and train managers and staff were very limited.

The Social Work (Scotland) Act 1968 recognised the need to consolidate and streamline legal provisions. Yet – as was also the case with the Children Act 1948 – the powers to modernise regulations for residential schools and children's homes weren't taken up for many years after the enactment of the primary legislation. This added to the potential for confusion among managers and staff and cannot have been in the best interests of the welfare and safety of the children in residential establishments.

A significant feature of the lengthy period that the review spanned was upheaval in the 1970s. This resulted from:

- major structural changes in social work services in Scotland introduced by the Social Work (Scotland) Act 1968;
- the re-organisation of local government in the mid 1970s; and
- the impact of problems in employment and the economy on services.

Such extensive and intensive change, which affected other public services such as health at that time, may well have drawn attention away from the needs of residential child care. It may have left those in the sector relatively unsupported as they sought to respond to new legislation; certainly that view was expressed by a number of those whom I interviewed during the review.

In considering the legislation I couldn't avoid asking these questions:

- What consideration was given by those introducing changes to the law, to the challenges that implementing the laws posed for the staff, managers and the authorities that provided residential schools and children's homes?
- When guidance was being written, was the lack of qualifications and training throughout the residential child care taken into account?

A number of the people we interviewed said that often legal requirements were misunderstood, there were ill-considered responses to changes in the law and, in some instances, the legislative requirements were ignored.

2. Observations on the Regulatory Framework

I identified several themes that helped me to formulate my observations on the legislative requirements and powers. I chose these because of their particular relevance to the welfare and safety of children in residential schools and children's homes. The themes are:

(i) Talking and listening to children.
(ii) Meeting children's needs.
(iii) Protecting children in residential establishments from abuse.
(iv) Ensuring accountability for children's welfare and safety.
(v) Monitoring and inspecting children's welfare and safety.

I recognise that the legislation of some 50 years ago was drawn up when society's attitudes and expectations were very different from those of today. Perceptions of these themes will have changed over time. And yet the themes seem to me to be relevant to children in residential schools and children's homes throughout the review period.

(i) Talking and listening to children

The laws that governed children's residential establishments during the review period only slowly developed to ensure that children in residential schools and children's homes were:

- treated with dignity;
- listened to; and
- had their views taken seriously.

Awareness and discussion of children's rights weren't evident in the 1950s and 1960s. The 1961 Approved Schools rules provided for children to be interviewed by inspectors, but there was no indication of the purpose of such interviews. The 1961 rules also required representatives of the managers to visit a school at least monthly and to speak to individual pupils. It's interesting to note that there is an associated reference to discussing with the headmaster any complaint made by a pupil. Beyond that, no detail is given.

The 1937 Act doesn't specifically require children to be interviewed or spoken to by authorised visitors or inspectors. However, presumably those who were involved in monitoring the welfare of the children placed in those homes by local authorities had opportunity to talk to the children. As we've seen in chapter 2, the terms of these rules and regulations remained unchanged through to 1987.

In interviews with retired government inspectors and from information in files held in the NAS, I learned that children were interviewed as part of the government inspection process throughout the review period. An NAS file dating from the 1960s has a prolonged exchange of minutes and correspondence between the then Secretary of State and the chairman of the managers of an approved school about the action of a government inspector in talking to children in the school without the presence of a teacher. The correspondence concludes with the Secretary of State affirming the appropriateness of the inspector's action, which, it's worth noting, resulted in an inappropriate punishment regime being discontinued.

The next development that strengthened the rather vague legal provisions for listening to children came in the Social Work (Scotland) Act 1968. This was in the context of introducing children's hearings. These, as we've already noted in this report, were a significant advance in the government's commitment to meet children's needs. They offered the prospect of placements that centred on children as opposed to being simply focused on children. The Children Act 1975 and the Social Work (Residential Establishments – Child Care) (Scotland) 1987 regulations further strengthened the legal provisions for listening to children. However, it wasn't until the Children (Scotland) Act 1995 was introduced that children's rights were embraced by the legislation including legislation governing residential schools and children's homes. The 1995 Act ensured that children's views should not only be sought and listened to, but should also be given credence and treated as an important consideration in ensuring their welfare and safety.

(ii) Meeting children's needs

The regulatory framework didn't ensure that children's residential care services responded sufficiently to the needs and entitlements of children requiring these services in the period from 1950 to 1968. It allowed children to be placed in residential establishments that were inappropriate to their needs.

The Social Work (Scotland) Act 1968 and the Education (Mentally Handicapped Children) (Scotland) Act 1974 indicated the developing commitment by the government to improving residential child care and tackling inadequacies in meeting children's needs. The 1974 Act acknowledged that "no child is ineducable or untrainable" and resulted in significant developments in residential special education. And yet I've learned that the interaction of established factors for determining children's placements – for example religious persuasion, age, gender and the availability of potentially suitable establishments in the child's family locality – continued to result in children being placed where their needs were not best met.

As I've noted earlier, the Social Work (Residential Establishments - Child Care) (Scotland) Regulations 1987 represented a significant step forward in addressing weaknesses in regulation. Children's placements improved as a result. But the fundamental developments in legislation – which were needed to ensure that the needs of children and young people being placed in residential establishments were met appropriately – only occurred at the end of the period under review, beginning with the Children (Scotland) Act 1995.

(iii) Protecting children in residential establishments from abuse

The regulatory framework, throughout the period of my review, reflected concern for the welfare and safety of children in children's residential establishments, and contained many provisions to that effect. Section 12 of The Children's and Young Persons Act (1937), for example, set out clearly a wide range of actions and neglect that were regarded as harmful to children and were against the law. The list, understandably, is set in language of its time but includes most of the forms of unacceptable treatment of children that we'd now include in a definition of abuse. It's reasonable to conclude that, had these provisions been observed as intended, the amount of abuse that has occurred in residential schools and children's homes across the review period would have been reduced.

The regulatory framework's schedule of what constituted abuse didn't alter over most of the review period. Legal provisions relating to sexual misconduct with boys were contained in legislation outwith that for residential childcare. Like the legal provisions for mistreatment, cruelty and neglect, they were originally framed with reference to abuse in the community. So although the law catered for protecting boys from sexual abuse, I believe it was unhelpful that there was no unified specification of abuse to inform managers and staff of residential schools and children's homes – as well as parents, guardians and children – throughout the review period. Those legislating were slow to take account of what was being learned about abuse in general.

Throughout most of the review period the legislation permitted corporal punishment in residential schools and children's homes; it wasn't until 1986 that this was prohibited in Scotland. Before then the legislation set limits on the amount of corporal punishment that could be administered. The tightening of these limits, particularly in the Approved School rules in 1961, suggests a concern and reflects a determination to moderate and contain this form of punishment. Corporal punishment was disapproved of by many of those who worked with children from before the beginning of the review period. There's also evidence that officers in the SED discouraged its use in the 1960s. An SED file dated 4 October 1968 includes minutes of a meeting about punishment in children's homes. An officer stated that corporal punishment should be abolished in children's homes: "to permit corporal punishment in children's homes only within a framework of rules is to deny that it really is a home". In another file containing the minutes of a meeting with representatives of the association of Approved School Headmasters Scotland, civil servants proposed that corporal punishment should not be used in approved schools. The minutes record the vigorous resistance from the heads of approved schools to this proposal. They viewed corporal punishment as a necessary part of disciplining and controlling children, a view which – it's important to note – was shared throughout schools, particularly secondary schools, at that time.

That corporal punishment continued to be permitted cannot have been conducive to protecting children in residential establishments from physical abuse. Some of those who contributed to our review, both professionals and former residents, spoke of the harsh regimes in some residential schools and children's homes, where corporal punishment was practised and used to excess. Their view was that in some residential schools and children's homes the permitted limits were ignored. In files in NAS, I found evidence of inspectors drawing attention to weaknesses in recording information about punishments in log

books. For example, in files relating to a children's home in the 1960s, I found comments by an inspector who noted that no punishments were recorded in the log book. In another file, also from the 1960s, an inspector refers to telling the house father that he should keep records of punishments and fire practices. Monitoring corporal punishment depended on accurate and efficient record-keeping. Punishments, including corporal punishments, were to be recorded in the log book, which was to be examined by the medical officer, the managers and inspectors. In situations where record keeping was inefficient, those monitoring the entries would have been unable to make adequate assessments of the nature, frequency and type of punishments being given. It is also conceivable that some of the reported poor record-keeping about corporal punishment could have been because it was not seen to be wrong, or because the intention was to conceal what took place.

Legal provisions for responding to concerns about possible abuse were inadequate. The regulations did not require sufficiently specific and robust approaches to developing policies and arrangements for protecting children in children's residential establishments from abuse until late in the 1980s. Furthermore the regulatory framework did not promote collective and collaborative action for protecting children in residential establishments amongst the people who provided and monitored services to children until after 1995. This was despite calls for such action from the 1980s. The possibility of such action was illustrated by the inspections of secure accommodation undertaken by government inspectors from social work and education backgrounds.

(iv) Ensuring accountability for children's welfare and safety

The staff in children's residential establishments, the managers, the authorities who administered the establishments and the government were all accountable for children's welfare and safety. The administering authorities were directly responsible, as they assumed parental rights. Given that responsibility, it is interesting to note the prominence and detail of legal provisions relating to punishing and controlling children. Although these were extremely important, they contrast with references to ensuring children's welfare and safety, which, for the most part, are broad and undefined.

The regulatory framework from 1950 to 1987 is limited, vague or silent about three key areas of accountability for children's welfare and safety:

- the qualifications of those delivering the care services;
- the suitability of staff for work with children in both care and education; and
- national standards of care.

Qualifications of staff

Clyde (1946), in highlighting the shortcomings in child care services, comments on the shortage of suitably qualified staff. However, the regulatory framework makes no reference to the need for staff in residential child care to have qualifications. The Children Act (1948) refers to the Secretary of State having powers to make regulations that he could be consulted about "the applicants for appointment to the charge of a home". No mention is made of qualifications. Evidently the criteria for appointing staff were left to the discretion of the administering authorities and to managers.

The absence of a requirement for all care staff to have recognised qualifications and appropriate continuing professional development, allowed unqualified care staff to be employed in residential schools and children's homes throughout the review period. In contrast, the 1933 rules governing Approved Schools specified that the qualifications of education staff were subject to approval by SED. The 1961 rules included a requirement that the managers, in consultation with the headmaster, should decide staff qualifications, subject to the Secretary of State's approval.

Changes in legislation for education, introduced in the 1960s, required that anyone employed as a teacher in a permanent post in any grant-aided school had to have recognised qualifications. The contrast between requirements for care and education is stark. It reflects

the attitudes and values of the day and yet significantly illustrates the low status accorded to residential child care.

Some of the retired professionals who contributed to the review were of the opinion that, particularly in the first part of the review period, there was no expectation that people working in residential childcare needed qualifications. The reality was that for all of the period under review, the proportion of unqualified care staff in residential establishments remained high. This posed challenges in ensuring the quality and effectiveness of delivering services to children. In this regard the legislation did not ensure provision which was in the interests of either the staff or the children in residential establishments. As our literature reviews have shown, concern about this has been raised in reports of other reviews and inquiries into residential child care before, during and since the period spanned by this review. It is inexcusable that so little was done in response to these concerns and associated recommendations during the period spanned by the review. The lack of regulation to ensure that children were cared for by appropriately qualified staff was a weakness for which the government was accountable. To say that this judgement amounts to applying today's standards to yesterday's services is to deny the insights and the recommendations of many others in the past.

Suitability of staff

The regulatory framework was, at best, vague on the need to select staff suitable for working with children in residential establishments in terms of both character and temperament. Problems could and did result for children in residential establishments from adults appointed to positions of trust and authority who couldn't cope with the challenges of meeting the needs of children and managing their behaviour. A number of contributors to our review commented on problems of this kind. I have also read inspection reports, for example, that highlighted weaknesses in the leadership of residential schools. Recent research has shown the link between staff selection and effectiveness of services (Cameron and Boddy, 2007). The legislation gave no lead to recruiting, selecting and supervising staff. This didn't reflect an adequate response to ensuring the welfare and safety of the children and young people in residential establishments.

The risk of predatory paedophiles infiltrating the residential childcare sector was being recognised more openly during the last 15 years of the review period. But, as indicated in the literature review, there is evidence from reviews and inquiries, research, and other sources such as the press, of the sexual abuse of children in residential establishments in Scotland in earlier decades of the review period. Examples are The Edinburgh Inquiry into Abuse and Protection of Children in Care (1999), and research such as that undertaken by Kahan (2000). These have shown that individual abusers were known about and dealt with quietly or not at all. Despite this, and although detailed guidance on vetting applicants for employment in the sector was issued by the SWSG, for example in 1992, it wasn't until 2002 – some seven years after the review period – that legislation was introduced to establish a national vetting system. This was an unacceptably slow response to a major threat to children's safety. Accountability for failure to act appropriately in recruiting, selecting and reviewing staff rested with boards of managers, administering authorities and government. Improvements in recruitment, vetting and supervision procedures were developing in the latter years of the review period and have been introduced since 1995. These point to the importance of effective management in this critical element of protecting children in residential establishments. Sadly that lesson was learned at the expense of the children in the care of the state.

National standards of care

The lack of national care standards weakened accountability at the level of boards of managers, administering authorities and monitoring and inspection. Without these standards, it would have been particularly difficult to ensure consistency in assessing care. In these circumstances, standards of service could differ from institution to institution and from authority to authority, denying children and young people comparable levels of welfare and safety

across Scotland. I've been told in interviews with senior professionals who worked in the residential child care sector during the period from 1970 to 1995, that the need for shared standards had been recognised by professionals and policy makers. A paper presented to the North East Branch of the British Association of Social Workers in November 2001 referred to development work on standards. This had gone on since the 1980s amongst professional staff in both the regional and voluntary authorities, with support from national bodies and associations (Hartnoll, 2001). It is to the credit of those who undertook this work that such good foundations for national standards had been laid. But the legislation to introduce national care standards wasn't introduced until 2002, seven years after the review period and some 10 years after the publication of *Another Kind of Home* (Skinner, 1992), the report that set out key principles for care services.

(v) Monitoring and inspecting children's welfare and safety

Throughout most of the period spanned by the review, there were specific if relatively narrow requirements in the regulatory framework to guide the focus of monitoring and inspecting children's residential establishments. Much was left to be determined at government department, administering authority or manager level.

A wide range of people monitored and inspected establishments. They included members of boards of managers, authorised visitors, medical officers, local authority children's officers, advisors and inspectors and government inspectors. Each observed and commented on particular aspects of services but, as noted in the preceding section, there were no prescribed standards of care to inform their evaluations, so they had to determine their own benchmarks or indicators. The legislation appears to reflect an assumption that these people would:

- know what to look at when they reviewed how establishments provided for children's welfare and safety;
- know how to assess what they saw; and

- be able to reach reliable conclusions.

That approach, although perhaps reflecting attitudes and expectations of the time in the period from 1950 to 1980, did not promote consistency in standards of care and weakened the accountability of monitoring and inspection. The regulatory framework did not foster a strategic approach to monitoring and inspection, including record-keeping, in children's residential establishments and among management authorities, until the final years of the review period.

This isn't to deny that individuals and certain organisations fulfilled a worthwhile role in evaluating and advising on quality and standards. Several of those who provided us with information mentioned and emphasised the work of children's officers and government inspectors. Their work, they told us, helped to identify weaknesses and promoted improvement. But, generally, the rigour, consistency and accountability of monitoring and inspection approaches for the care services were weakened by the lack of national standards or indicators of quality.

Developments in the last 15 years of the review period, prompted in part by other government policy initiatives to improve public services, led to substantial changes in monitoring and inspection approaches. They made inspections more transparent and more accountable to the people who used the services, more focused on outcomes and more independent. The establishment of arms-length inspection units was one example of the changes. The developments in general encouraged new ways of evaluating effectiveness and promoting improvement.

As noted earlier, the regulatory framework did not require levels of collaboration and co-operation between the various monitoring and inspection approaches and agencies which, in my judgement, were necessary in the interests of the welfare and safety of the children in residential child care. There continued to be concern that inspection was too closely linked to the providers' interests at both government and local authority levels. The legislation to introduce changes and establish independent inspection services was introduced 7-10

years after the review period and resulted in the establishment of the Care Commission, Social Work Inspection Agency (SWIA) and Her Majesty's Inspectorate of Education (HMIe).

3. Conclusions

- The regulatory framework was extensive, in many respects impressive, and of its time. It developed in response to changing understanding of the needs and entitlements of children. Over the review period it moved from a child focused to a child centred philosophy, from an approach to residential child care based on welfare to one based on rights, needs and welfare.

- It's all too easy to apply today's standards, understanding and expectations to the services provided yesterday, and it's important to avoid that risk. However, across the review period, the legislation largely made it clear what the required responses were from the people who provided residential child care, to ensure the welfare and safety of the children in their care. It also specified the limits of punishment. If the legislation been honoured in spirit and letter when it was being implemented, if the work of residential schools and children's homes had been supervised and managed as expected, then it's reasonable to conclude that the incidence of abuse would have been lower and the experiences and outcomes for many would have been better.

- The shortcomings that this review identifies in the legislation support the case made to me by most of those I interviewed that government didn't give residential child care sufficiently high status or priority. Intentions were sound, but implementation didn't always match the vision and possibilities. Chapter 6 provides information about survivors' experiences which further endorse this case.

- Most of the gaps and inadequacies in the legislation for providing, regulating and inspecting residential schools and children's homes identified by this review from 1950-1995 were addressed by or after the Children Act 1995. The extent of additional regulation since then indicates the determination of government to refine the legislation and respond to changing circumstances in the best interests of the children in the care of the state.

4. Recommendations

Some 12 years after the review period the regulatory landscape has changed dramatically. Now legal provisions are founded on children's rights and are designed to ensure that their needs are met and their welfare is assured. It wasn't part of my remit to comment on the adequacy of the legislation from 1995 onwards or its outcomes. However, at this stage an audit would be timely, to consider the effectiveness of:

- the new legislation; and
- arrangements for monitoring and inspecting children's residential establishments.

The audit would ascertain the extent to which what has happened (the outcomes) match the intentions. And it would gauge the extent to which children in residential establishments are safer. I recommend that a National Task Group be established to undertake such an audit. It would be part of the role of such a group to:

i.   audit annually the outcomes (those agreed through the Government's Vision for Children and Young People) for looked-after and accommodated children and report on the findings;

ii. audit the recommendations of previous reviews and inquiries to determine what action is outstanding and why;

iii. review the adequacy and effectiveness of the arrangements, including advocacy support, in place for children who wish to complain about the services they receive;

iv. monitor the progress in meeting the target of a fully qualified complement of staff in residential child care services, including the identification of barriers to reaching this target, and ways of overcoming them;

v.   audit the quality and appropriateness of training and development for those employed in residential childcare;

vi. identify ways of making employment in residential child care a desirable career option;

vii. identify and disseminate best practice in recruitment and selection of staff in residential child care;

viii. ensure that monitoring and inspection focus on those aspects of provision and practice that will help to keep children safe and enable them to achieve their potential;

ix. monitor the extent to which self-evaluation is becoming established practice in residential schools and children's homes;

x.   identify the most effective ways, through research and inspection findings and drawing on Scottish and international experience, of ensuring children's welfare and safety in residential establishments;

xi. review the quality and standards of accommodation for residential establishments and recommend improvements as necessary; and

xii. make recommendations for research and development.

Chapter 4

Compliance, monitoring and inspection

Chapter 4

Compliance, Monitoring and Inspection

"Against the background of the abuse suffered by children up the age of 16 in residential schools and children's homes in Scotland over the period from 1950 to 1995 the Independent Expert is instructed ... to present a report ... with the following objectives:

(2) to identify, and review the adequacy of any systems, whether at national, local or organisational level , intended to ensure compliance with those requirements and with any proscribed procedures and standards from time to time including systems of monitoring and inspection;

(3) to review the practical operation and effectiveness of such systems."

Introduction

Chapter 2, which sets out the regulatory framework for the review period, contains the details of the law's requirements for monitoring and inspection in residential schools and children's homes across the review period. In this chapter I include:

- an overview of monitoring and inspection
- my observations on the legal requirements for monitoring and inspection
- the challenges which the review faced in identifying the practice of monitoring and inspection and assessing its effectiveness
- my conclusions and recommendations.

This chapter has the following sections:

1. What do compliance, monitoring and inspection mean?
2. What was to be monitored and inspected?
3. What forms of monitoring and inspection were required?
4. With what frequency were monitoring and inspection to take place?
5. What other opportunities were there for monitoring the welfare and safety of children in residential schools and children's homes?
6. How adequate were the legal provisions?
7. How were monitoring and inspection done in practice? The challenges of finding evidence.
8. How effective were monitoring and inspection? The challenges of determining effectiveness.
9. Conclusions and recommendations.

1.What do compliance, monitoring and inspection mean?

These terms aren't defined in the legislation. However, throughout the legislation are legal provisions that assign responsibility for actions that fall within the ambit of what I understand to be monitoring and inspection. These include requirements for visiting, recording information about and inspecting residential schools and children's homes.

The legislation specifies, in varying degrees of detail, what monitoring and inspection should focus on. This indicates the government's concern with, and approach to, making sure that schools and homes complied with the law.

For the purposes of this review, I've defined compliance, monitoring and inspection as follows:

Compliance is the act of adhering, and demonstrating adherence, to laws. Monitoring and inspection are the means by which compliance is observed, assessed and reported on.

Monitoring is any means specified within the legislation by which information is gathered to confirm that residential schools and children's homes are complying with regulations and standards, however defined. The information gathered would include details about the children, staffing and premises in individual schools and homes, and how these are organised and managed. Monitoring should focus on – the child, the residential establishment, the administering authority, the government department, and ultimately, should help to secure the welfare, needs and rights of the child.

Inspection is the formal process of:
- seeing whether the needs of children are being met;
- examining residential schools and children's homes to find out how they comply with regulations;
- assessing standards; and
- evaluating the quality and appropriateness of outcomes – that is, what happens to children during and as a result of their stay there – to promote improvement in the children's welfare, safety and educational attainment

Monitoring and inspection are inter-related. In one view, inspection is one of a range of monitoring activities, part of a continuum of monitoring; in another, in my experience, it can often be viewed by those whose establishment is being inspected as a separate form of external evaluation rather than a periodic part of the monitoring process.

2. What was to be monitored and inspected?

In children's homes, the health, wellbeing, behaviour and the progress of the children in their education were to be monitored and inspected (1947 Act, 1959 Regulations). These were central to monitoring in children's homes throughout the review period to 1987. The welfare, development and rehabilitation of the children were at the heart of monitoring and

inspection in approved schools (1937 Act). Broadly similar requirements continued throughout much of the review period for approved, later List D schools.

In addition, and, presumably, as an indication of what the government saw as contributing to the children's welfare and safety, other aspects of schools and children's homes were to be monitored including:

In an approved school:
- the provision of clothes and maintenance of the children (1937 Act)
- the maintenance of the premises (1933 Regulations)
- the provision of separate bedrooms (1961 Rules)
- diet (1961 Rules)
- fire precautions (1933 Regulations)
- the daily routine and suitability of the education provided (1933 Regulations; 1961 Rules)
- health, including dental health (1933 Regulations)
- punishment and discipline, including corporal punishment (1933 Regulations; 1961 Rules)

In a children's home:
- the provision of separate bedrooms (1959 regulations)
- fire precautions (1959 Regulations)
- diet (1959 Regulations)
- health, including dental health (1959 Regulations)
- punishment and discipline, including corporal punishment (1959 Regulations)
- where provided on site, education provided (1959 Regulations)
- health and safety (1987 Regulations)

For a remand home or other types of residential school, similar aspects of provision were identified for monitoring.

In addition to these providing a focus for monitoring and inspection, the Secretary of State had powers and duties which, in exercising them, would have required monitoring and inspection activities to enable him to make decisions. For example, the Secretary of State could serve notice on a local authority not to use a home for the placement of children if the property was unsuitable. He could also give instructions to the managers if the management posed a danger to the children placed there. Such decisions would have had to be based on information he received from monitoring and inspection.

3.What forms of monitoring and inspection were required

Monitoring and inspection activities provided for by the law included the following:

In a children's home:

(a) Visits

- visits by inspectors approved of by SED(1948 Act);
- visits by medical officers (1959 Regulations);
- visits by children's officers of the local authority and local authority members (1947 Rules)
- visits from 1959 by an 'authorised visitor' from the administering authority – local or voluntary and
- visits from parents and guardians (1959 Regulations)

(b) Records

- a log book had to be kept in which visits, punishments and other information had to be recorded (1959 Regulations)
- other records relating to individual children, staff and accommodation had to be maintained and information sent to the administering authority and as required, to SED or the Secretary of State. (1959 Regulations)

In an approved school:

(a) Visits

- visits by an SED inspector or any appointed officer (1937 Act);
- visits by managers, the medical officer, a dentist (1933 Regulations);
- interviews with an inspector (1961 Rules);
- visits by parents, guardians, relatives or friends (1937 Act)

(b) Records

- a log book had to be kept (1933 Regulations);
- other records relating to individual children had to be maintained and information made available for

inspection and, as required, forwarded to the SED or Secretary of State (1933 Regulations).

4. With what frequency were monitoring and inspection to take place?

Detailed information about the frequency of monitoring and inspection is contained in Chapter 2. Here are some examples.

MEMBERS FOR CHURCH OT SCOTLAN

In children's homes:

- a local authority officer was to visit at least once every six months (1947 Rules);
- members of the authority were to visit at least once a year (1947 Rules);
- an authorised visitor was to visit monthly (1959 Regulations);
- the medical officer was to examine every child yearly and visit the institution regularly (1959 Regulations); and
- an officer of the care authority was to visit every three months (1987 Regulations).

Establishments had to be open to inspection at all times (1948 Act) but no reference is made in the legislation to the frequency of inspectors' visits.

Visits by parents and guardians were also allowed for (1959 Regulations) but, again, no reference is made to the frequency of the visits.

In approved schools:

- a manager was to visit periodically (1933 Regulations)
- a manager was to visit every month (1961 Rules)
- the medical officer was to examine each child every three months and visit the school weekly (1961 Rules)
- the dentist was to examine each child yearly (1933 Regulations) and the every six months (1961 Rules)

The school had to be open at all times for inspection by His majesty's Inspectors of Schools (1937) but no reference is made to the frequency of these visits.

Visits by parents, relatives, guardians and friends were permitted but no reference is made in the legislation to the frequency of these visits.

5. What other opportunities were there for monitoring the welfare and safety of children in residential schools and children's homes?

In addition to contact with visitors, administering authority officers, medical officers and government inspectors, children in residential establishments may have needed the services of others from time to time – educational psychologists, psychiatrists, GPs, social workers, nurses, police officers, clergy.

When this was the case, these professionals should have been in a position to observe and, as necessary, raise concerns about certain individual children or their circumstances with the Headmaster, Headmistress or person in charge of the institution, and with managers and external management authorities.

6. How adequate were the legal provisions?

As indicated in Chapters 2 and 3, the law provided for a range of monitoring and inspection in residential schools and children's homes throughout the review period. Some had clear focus and purpose, others were undefined. They had potential to ensure the children's welfare and safety. How adequate they were depended on;

- their scope – what they required to be monitored and inspected;
- how they were implemented;
- the management of monitoring and inspection; and
- how the information they provided was used.

The legislation relating to monitoring and inspection was strengthened across the review period. But as

noted in the previous chapter, it did **not** provide for –

Agreed national standards for care: This meant that the focus of what those involved in monitoring and inspection observed and the consistency of the assessments they made were subject to variation. And this weakened the value of their findings.

A statement of purpose or a specification for visits by managers and authorised visitors: Too much was left to the interpretation of those carrying out the monitoring and inspection practice. The lack of definition of the purpose of visits may have failed to emphasise the value and importance they had in monitoring and inspecting the children's welfare and safety.

Local authority residential establishments to be registered before 1987: This was a significant gap in ensuring comparable standards of service across all residential establishments. It lessened the obligation on these institutions to be subject to regular monitoring and inspection visits and may have left them less closely supervised, thereby increasing the risk that abuse could go undetected.

Public accountability: Inspection at government level wasn't accountable to parents and the wider public until the 1980s when reports had to be published. Publication was intended to enable parents and guardians to challenge the quality and standards of residential schools.

Independent monitoring and inspection: The law's requirements for monitoring and inspection involved staff who were appointed by the administering authorities or by government departments. This meant there was the risk of lack of objectivity and less scrupulous monitoring and inspection.

Listening to children: For the first part of the period of the review, there was no specific requirement to talk and listen to children during monitoring and inspection – although the provision for inspectors to "inspect the place and the children therein" (The Children Act 1948) suggests that they were expected to do so. The 1961 Rules required the managers to give inspectors facilities for interviewing staff and pupils and children's hearings were introduced following the 1968 Act. But requirements to take account of children's views were not in place until the 1987 Regulations and it wasn't until the 1995 Act that children's views were sought, given credence and treated as an important consideration in ensuring their welfare and safety.

It is significant that the Skinner Report (1992), the Kent Report (1996), the Edinburgh Inquiry (1999) and the Fife Independent Inquiry (2002) all refer to the lack of attention paid to listening to children and taking them seriously.

Co-operation: There was no specific requirement for those involved in monitoring and inspection to co-operate, for example, in sharing expertise and information in the interests of ensuring the welfare and protection of children. The need for this multi – disciplinary working was recognized in the 1980s and advocated in the Skinner Report in 1992. But there were no legislative changes to require such working in the interests of the protection of children in residential establishments until the end of the review period.

7. How were monitoring and inspection done in practice? The challenges of finding evidence

My remit required me to review the practical operation and effectiveness of systems that were meant to make sure residential schools and children's homes complied with laws, rules, regulations, procedures and standards. It covered systems at national level and in local organisations. And it included systems of monitoring and inspection.

In approaching this my researcher and I sought information from:
- local and voluntary authorities' records;
- government records, including those relating to residential schools and children's homes, HMI,

SWSG, and SWSI and including circulars and reports of inspections;
- interviews with retired administrative and professional staff from local and voluntary authorities, government departments and agencies;
- interviews with former residents and staff of residential schools and children's homes;
- reports of public inquiries and reviews focused on residential childcare in Scotland;
- the literature reviews commissioned for this review; and

As the literature reviews indicate, there is a lack of research into residential child care in Scotland that might shed light on practice on monitoring and inspection in the review period.

Chapter 5 and Appendix 3 of this report give information about the questionnaire sent by the review to all local authorities and to selected voluntary and religious organisations. For the period 1950 – 1969 all the local authorities who responded said they had no inspection records and many didn't know if they had specific policy and practice guidelines. For the period 1970 – 1985 they all said they had no inspection reports and none knew if they had specific policy or practice guidelines, for example for whistleblowing and inspection. For the period 1986 – 95 most said they had records, including inspection records and some said they had specific policy and practice guidelines. Similar responses were received from voluntary and religious organisations.

The difficulties the review faced in getting information from local and voluntary authority records and the large volume of potentially relevant records meant that it wasn't possible to investigate those sources to inform the review about practice in monitoring and inspection. That remains work to be done.

Government records for residential schools and children's homes contain minutes and some reports of inspectors' visits and inspections and it's possible to get from these an indication of the focus and structure of monitoring and inspection activities in the 1950s and 1960s. But the volume of these records, and the form of cataloguing used, meant that it was extremely difficult and time-consuming to identify which files would be most useful to the review.

Much more work would be required to establish comprehensively the focus and form of monitoring and inspection undertaken by government inspectors at that time. A detailed account of the challenges faced by the review in searching for information is given in Appendix 3.

In other government files, for example those relating to HMI and SWSG, the review was unable to find papers giving details of frameworks, standards or indicators relating to monitoring and inspection as a whole or in relation to residential schools and children's homes. In interviews with retired inspectors we learned that there was no policy to retain papers about such matters. As changes in practice in monitoring and inspection were introduced, they said, the out-dated papers were destroyed.

Some of the files examined by the review contain papers relating to policy, for example, on the use of corporal punishment in residential schools in the 1960s, and on the number of HMI and strategy for inspection of schools (of all kinds) in the 1970s. These are of value in shedding light on the kinds of factors which would have been influencing practice in monitoring and inspection during the review period, but the amount of work involved in searching through such files – and in the many others held in NAS – was not feasible within the resources and time span of the review.

We also found that there is no central collection of inspection reports for any of the government inspectorates that spans the period of the review. Current national inspection agencies such as SWIA and HMIe don't hold extensive records of the bodies that preceded them. And, while they were extremely helpful in suggesting possible sources of information and providing information where they could, they weren't in a position to provide comprehensive information about monitoring and inspection practice before they were set up and across the review period.

Retired government inspectors, whom we interviewed, said that when new inspectors were appointed – at least from the 1970s onwards – they received guidance materials on carrying out inspections including checklists of what to cover. These materials, they said, were up-dated regularly throughout the 1980s and 1990s, becoming ever more sophisticated and prescriptive. They also said that talking to children and young people was central to inspections of residential schools and children's homes across the review period and in the 1970s a practice known as day-profiling was used in inspection of schools generally. This involved following a child for a day during an inspection to observe what he or she experienced. In the 1980s child protection featured in inspections for the first time, and inspectors received guidance on what action to take if any issues were suspected. Following the Cleveland inquiry in 1987 and the Orkney inquiry, child protection became a central issue for inspectors and all received intensive training on the subject.

My conclusion is that there's a need for further research to find out more fully the nature, range and basis of monitoring and inspection in the past. That task would depend on action being taken to gather records, catalogue them and make them accessible for further research – which is one of this chapter's recommendations.

8. How effective were monitoring and inspection? The challenges of determining effectiveness

Assessing monitoring and inspection practice depends on the quality and quantity of information available or which can be collected about these. It's complex and difficult even when done in ideal circumstances, namely where:

■ the monitoring or inspection took place relatively recently and access to all kinds of related information is possible;

■ an agreed framework and process are in place for the monitoring or inspection activity to be assessed;

■ the process followed by visitors, officers or inspectors is informed by an agreed set of standards or indicators of performance, quality and ethos;

■ those undertaking the work are appropriately trained and experienced

■ there is an agreed form of recording information and evaluations and, in the case of inspectors, an agreed format for reporting to the stakeholders in the institution being inspected;

■ a record is made of any actions taken in response to the findings of monitoring and inspection and of any follow-up activity.

As noted earlier, there are no national standards or indicators of performance for residential child care across the review period. And there appears to be no specific information recorded about monitoring and inspection frameworks or the approaches adopted by visitors, officers from administering authorities and inspectors, both local authority and national.

Some may argue that detecting abuse is a valid indicator of effectiveness. But there is no way of knowing what abuse was prevented by monitoring and inspection or indeed of knowing what abuse may yet be disclosed. So assessing effectiveness based on detecting abuse is problematic.

The research undertaken by the review into records and through interviews indicates that with further work it would be possible to learn more about practice in monitoring and inspection in the past. For example, it would be possible to examine minutes of children's committees or social work committee meetings to see what, if anything, is recorded about reports of abusive practice or concerns about staff, and to identify the action taken in response.

Similarly, further work would allow information to be gathered about the focus of inspection reports, the extent to which they addressed the welfare and safety

of the children and the results of any action taken in response to the inspection findings.

I believe that research in a selected sample of locations would provide valuable insights into practice in monitoring and inspection and the effectiveness of the methods used. For example, even with the limited research into government records that the review was able to undertake, a number of records were found which indicate that monitoring and inspection detected excessive punishment. There are papers dated 1967 which refer to two HMI looking for signs of irregular or excessive punishment. They detected failings in a few approved schools which led to the removal of one headmaster and the issue of a severe warning to another. The review also found a report of a survey of punishment in children's homes undertaken by the Child Care inspectorate in 1968. The survey was undertaken as part of a SED review of Discipline Punishment Policy and indicates the SED's use of such monitoring to inform policy.

But a challenge to be faced in any such work is the unknown, namely the extent to which all that was monitored and inspected was recorded and the extent to which the recorded information was accurate.

Positive results of monitoring and inspection in terms of children's protection from abuse must be set against instances where abuse took place and wasn't detected. The implication is that it requires more research to find out why monitoring and inspection were effective in detecting abuse in some places but not in others. And it has to be kept in mind that monitoring and inspection were expected to contribute to raising standards of care, education and health, as well as assessing the welfare and safety in residential schools and children's homes. They were about preventing rather than detecting abuse, which wasn't acknowledged until late in the review period as a serious problem that could be found in residential child care.

9. Conclusions and recommendations

I have learned through the work of the review that, despite the fact that many records are missing, a very large number of valuable records exist in a wide range of locations, and in varying states of organisation. These records could add to our understanding of practice in monitoring and inspection in residential childcare in the past and may well give insight into effectiveness. The records need to be assembled and catalogued and made available for research and investigation. As that process proceeds it would be possible to glean evidence of practice.

As indicated earlier, I have also learned that considerable numbers of people who lived and worked in children's residential services across the review period could and would be willing to talk about their experience and the practice of monitoring and inspection and other aspects of the organisation and management of residential child care as they knew it.

I recommend that:
- all local authorities and voluntary organisations ensure that their records are identified, catalogued and stored properly; and
- research is commissioned to gather information from people who lived and worked in children's residential services across the review period, as a contribution to our knowledge of practice in the past.

These recommendations are incorporated into the overall recommendations in Chapter 7.

Chapter 5

Records of residential schools and children's homes in Scotland

Chapter 5

Records of residential schools and children's homes in Scotland

The review depended on the availability of records to fulfil the remit. In practice, however, many aspects of records – from their accessibility to their very existence – proved extremely challenging.

The remit itself yielded unexpected problems. Former residents told the review of the frustrations, surprises, shocks and disappointments involved in their search for records. The review's research showed that many laws were in force to govern records, but revealed that the practice of generating and keeping records was a different matter entirely. The review also found that record-keeping and the availability of records across all organisations and across Scotland has, and remains, very patchy indeed.

This chapter sets out:

1 Why records are important
2 The challenges the review faced in fulfilling the remit
3 Former residents' experiences of accessing records
4 The legal background to records
5 The review's search for information and what was found

Focusing on these main topics, I asked my researcher to undertake a study of records with the objective of contributing to a better understanding of the importance of children's residential establishment records and the need to ensure these are preserved and made accessible. Her report is included in full in appendix 3, which I consider a valuable contribution to the work of the review. This chapter draws on that report.

Many people made invaluable contributions to the review's search for records. Others shared highly personal experiences with us. My researcher and I are deeply grateful to all of them.

1. Why records are important

Learning from the past

The review's work, like that of any inquiry into the past, can't proceed without the existence of properly preserved records. Records are essential for society to gain an insight into, and learn from, people's experiences.

Records of children's residential services are an essential part of ensuring children's safety and well-being. They're also significant to people who lived in children's residential establishments – they're essential to their sense of identity.

Keeping children safe in residential care involves:
- preventing problems from occurring;
- monitoring how children are cared for and their well-being; and
- responding to any issues and problems that may arise.

Current and past records are vital to all of these actions.

Preventative and monitoring approaches rely on suitably generated records, such as those created through assessments, reviews, incidents, complaints and inspection reports. Reactive approaches – often taking the form of investigations and inquiries – also rely on properly maintained records, past and present, to review current and past practices that may have been harmful to children.

Analysing the information held in records, inspections and inquiries can reveal what happened and what can be improved upon to ensure that people's experiences, and the lessons to be learned from these, aren't lost. In other words, records are extremely important for contributing to informed decision-making about keeping children safe and responding to claims of abuse.

They are essential, along with research, statistics and inspection, to the evaluation and development of policy and practice in children's residential services.

Records are crucially important to former residents

Former residents who inquire about their past are also responding to a basic human need to search for family and to better understand what happened during their childhood. They live in a society of people who grew up in family homes, knowing their siblings, parents and extended family. Their lack of such knowledge can make them feel isolated, so records can help them trace their own family connections and develop a common sense of belonging to a family.

The review found that records are important to former residents for reasons that are not always revealed or fully understood and acknowledged by people who work in organisations, local authorities and central government departments that hold records.

Former residents told the review that records about their lives and children's residential establishments have enormous significance to them for many reasons, including the following:

- They valued not just information from their own records, but also general information about the places they lived in, the people involved in children's residential services and the social and historical context that establishments operated in.
- For the many former residents unable to find their own records, general historical records may contain the only information that verifies their childhood experiences in a children's residential establishment.
- Survivors of child institutional abuse, in particular, want to know how abuse was allowed to happen and depend on records to provide them with information about the circumstances surrounding their abuse.
- Some former residents want their family members and descendants have access to records.
- There is evidence to suggest that people involved in running residential establishments put little value on giving information to children, who were often silent and too afraid to ask about matters important to them or to express their concerns.
- Former residents have huge gaps in what they know about their families. Many children were isolated from or had little contact with siblings, families and friends. There is also evidence to suggest that authorities placed restrictions on family members who tried to access children and that children weren't told about their family members' inquiries about them.
- People who lack basic information about their lives can face difficulties in areas that others take for granted: getting passports, birth certificates and medical records; knowing their mother's maiden name.
- Many of the former residents who contributed to the review reported that they had, and continue to have, no understanding about why they were placed in children's residential establishments away from their family. Some want to trace other family members, as they were often separated from siblings and parents at a young age and had no contact with family members while living away from their family home. Some said they'd never received information about their families while residing in children's residential establishments or the information was wrong.
- Survivors of institutional child abuse place huge importance upon records for insights into their circumstances, for information to help with any legal proceedings they are involved in and for helping them to heal from the long-lasting effects of child abuse.
- Records also ensure that former residents can realise their rights, specifically those under human rights, freedom of information and data protection laws.

Records are important to organisations

Maintaining accessible records is in the interest of all the organisations involved in providing, monitoring and regulating residential establishments. It enables them to maintain a corporate memory: when individuals with important knowledge and experience leave, that knowledge and experience doesn't leave with them.

Records are vital for public accountability. They make possible contemporary and historical analyses, investigations, monitoring and audits – internal and external. All of these hold organisations, local authorities and central government accountable for the quality of their services.

Records are important to social history

Records of children's residential services contribute to a better understanding of Scotland's social history; for example, the wider contribution to society made by people who lived in children's residential establishments.

However there is a lack of research about abuse in children's residential establishments. Records can help fill the research gap and add to a body of historical knowledge about childhood experiences. Social research can improve our understanding about what happened in children's residential establishments and give us information about what needs to change to improve the lives of children in residential care today.

2. The challenges faced in fulfilling the remit

The review's remit

Point four of the remit states that, in addition to the information that is publicly available, the independent expert would:

"(1) have access to all documentary records of the former Scottish Office in so far as in the possession of Scottish Ministers from the period under consideration and in so far as relating to residential schools and children's homes which will be subject to redaction[1] to ensure that no individual can be identified;

"(2) be expected to seek the co-operation of local authorities and other organisations with responsibility for the management and administration of residential schools and children's homes in making available to

him such documentary records and explanation of such records as he considers to be necessary for his purposes."

The remit appears to presume that all relevant information would be found in the former Scottish Office records as well as information that's publicly available. It anticipates that local authorities, voluntary and religious organisations would hold information potentially useful to the review, and implies that this information is not publicly available.

There was no legal requirement for local authorities and organisations to help the review by granting access to information. However in the Scottish Parliament debate, held on 1 December 2004 on institutional child abuse, the Minister for Education and Young People, Peter Peacock, had encouraged organisations to open their files and it was within this spirit that many local authorities and organisations helped us.

It's worth highlighting that, during the debate, the Minister announced that the Scottish Executive Education Department was "working to open all files that are relevant". The difficulty of defining what was relevant became an important theme in the review's efforts to locate and gain access to records.

The challenges faced

The review sought to identify and locate records that were relevant to fulfilling my remit. In practice, this process was fraught with challenges:

■ **How to find fundamental information?**
No information existed describing what regulatory framework was in existence between 1950 and 1995, which made the search for related policy, guidance and standards difficult. No central government database records the names of children's residential establishments, their location, dates of operation, their purpose or their management structures. No central database identifies what records are associated with children's residential services and where they are located.

---

[1] Redaction means editing out information, such as people's names.

- **How to define "residential school" and "children's home"?** Many formal and informal terms were used to describe residential establishments where children lived without parental care, making it challenging to define these terms. The imprecise definitions, which altered in meaning throughout the review period, also affected the search for records.

- **A complex picture of services:** The review's research found that residential services provided to children between 1950 and 1995 were extensive and extremely complex. Hundreds of children's residential establishments existed, with many places changing function, location and management at various times or closing down. Policies and guidance were extensive, complicated, changing and from many sources: central government, local government, voluntary and religious organisations. Other services were involved, for example. in areas such as health, psychology, the courts, churches and education. So it was impossible to identify all records that might have existed and related to children's residential services throughout the review period and with the resources available.

- **Which records should exist – and which do exist?** No schedules exist of which records have been kept or disposed of. No laws required these types of schedules to be kept. Poor records management practices mean that records are missing, have been destroyed or weren't generated in the first place. We had to find out what records people thought existed in various locations, and distinguish these from records that actually did exist. Many records relating to one topic could have been made in different locations, such as a children's residential establishment and a social work department. Record-keeping varied immensely from establishment to establishment, within organisations and local authorities and at central government level. In the earlier years, in particular, the records that were made weren't always managed properly and archived.

- **What is a public record?** The term "public record" has particular meaning under the Public (Scotland) Records 1937 Act. Disclosing records in public is also subject to the terms of the Freedom of Information (Scotland) Act 2002 and the Data Protection Act 1998. These legal issues made it difficult for organisations and governments to comply with the proposed spirit of opening up their files and to grant the review unfettered access to all records relating to children's residential services.

- **Records aren't always open:** Some potentially significant records in archives were closed. Voluntary, private and religious organisations had no legal obligation to give us access. There were also geographical problems: records are stored in various locations throughout Scotland and England. There were no clear, standardised access policies in all the locations where records were held. So the review had to learn about a multitude of access requirements in a multitude of locations.

- **What is "relevant"?** The review had to identify records held by local authorities, organisations and central government and where they might be located, which was very time-consuming. But it was impossible to determine what was "relevant" without examining the records – an enormous task for the review, organisations and local authorities working with limited time, staff and funding. When the review asked for information, local authorities, organisations and central government needed to make their own individual and varying interpretations about what might be "relevant". And the issues of what and who decided what was relevant in the past have had major implications for what records have been kept.

- **Where are records kept?** Records are kept in a vast number of locations throughout Scotland and England. Records relating to one establishment might be in several locations: central offices; local authority departments; regional, local, national or university archives; private storage facilities; museums and libraries. They've often been moved, for example when services close, or move, or management changes and for lack of storage space. When this happened the transfer wasn't tracked, making it difficult, if not impossible, to know where records were sent.

- **How many records are there?** There are massive volumes of records about children's residential services due to the number of services and the years involved. Not all have been identified, located or archived. Some are at varying stages of discovery. Some were found in boxes in basements or other unidentified locations. It is apparent, however, that far more records exist than is currently known as many records have not been properly identified and put into records management systems for transfer to archives.

- **What type of records should be held?** It was extremely difficult, if not impossible, for various organisations and local and central government to locate, identify and make accessible records specific to children's residential services without guiding criteria, such as a records retention schedule. (This is a system that makes clear what records must be retained and preserved.)

- **Attitudes to records varied:** The review found that many people recognised the importance of records relating to children's residential services. However they were often constrained in their attempts to locate and preserve records due to lack of staff and funding, lack of value placed on such records, and legal concerns. The review also found negative attitudes and misunderstandings about the significance of records. Some people in key positions, such as senior managers, seemed to lack understanding about the significance of records, what records existed and where. Some senior people in local authorities, voluntary and religious organisations were guarded and even unwilling to help. The review also learned that senior people had ordered records to be destroyed.

3. Former residents' experiences

Former residents have rights associated with records. These include the legal entitlement to view records relating to their childhood experiences in residential placements. Poor records management in the past has meant that some former residents are unable to realise their legal entitlements to access records.

The review found that former residents had, and continued to have, difficulty in identifying, locating and accessing records. For example:

- There is no central location in Scotland where people can ask for information and guidance about records – about their experiences, their family history and about children's residential establishments in general – and how to search for records.
- Information may be held in several locations and in many types of records. Some records are unidentified; others are unknown.
- Former residents may be prevented from getting access to records without agreeing to support services such as counselling from organisations and local authorities concerned about the possible effects that reading file contents may have on them.
- Some former residents can't afford to travel to the locations where records are kept; others don't have access to computers or the computer literacy skills needed to find information online.
- Some former residents found it hard to read photocopied records and incomplete information, where pages were missing or information blocked from view.

Once they gain access to their records, however, they are often disappointed or distressed by what they learn for the first time in their lives. Records often don't contain the information that former residents expect, or hope, to see.

The challenges faced by former residents contacting our review were consistent with those highlighted in other inquiries, such as those into child migration and institutional child abuse.

What records show in general

The information in records show how isolated some children became after they were placed in residential establishments. Many records reveal a dearth of information about family contact and relationships with outside professionals.

Many children died while living in children's residential establishments. Some organisations have identified the children in graveyards. But in other cases searches have yielded few records identifying children or information about why they died. The lack of information suggests that little importance was placed on the children's identity and their value to their extended families.

The review learned that individual records offer substantial insights into approaches to keeping children safe in residential placements and, in particular, monitoring practices relating to individual children. The review also identified that organisations, local authorities and central government need to understand how the legacy of poor practices in the past is reflected in the records of former residents.

What individuals' experiences revealed

Scant and incomplete information: A former resident of a children's home for 18 years was surprised by how little information his record showed. He had spent time in hospital and been medically examined, but his file contained no medical information. He felt the record had been doctored and did not reflect a complete picture of his stay at the home. He had been abused sexually and physically and felt that criminal acts had been covered up.

No family information: A former resident of a large children's home for 16 years only learned from reading her files many years later that she had a twin brother and three cousins, all of whom had stayed at the same home. She is haunted by the screams of a girl who was beaten, and whom she only learned

years later had been her cousin. She was not told that her father was contributing weekly to her upkeep and only found out years later that her mother was still alive and had an extended family.

Inability to find information: A man who had been placed in an approved school has spent almost five years trying to find records to tell him why he had to spend three years at the school. He feels the social work department, school, religious organisation and educational authorities all should have records. Despite writing several letters he has not located any records that verify he was at the approved school, or any information about that part of his childhood. Another former resident of a children's home has spent almost a decade writing to and telephoning local authorities, social work departments and a religious organisation and has found no record about him and no information about his childhood experiences in the home.

Conflicting information: A woman who had lived as a young child with her brother and sister in a children's home was told her records had been lost in a fire. But her brother received records from the organisations responsible for the home. His records included personal information about her. She later visited the organisation – with her sister, who also sought information – and learned that records did indeed exist about her. But information she expected to find was wrong or absent. Information in the records for her, her sister and brother conflicted.

Suspicion: Some former residents found it difficult to return to the organisation responsible for running the establishment they had lived in. Some felt that organisations and local authorities treated information about them as belonging to the institution. Others felt that local authorities put up barriers, such as insisting that social workers should see their records first and sit with them while they reviewed the records. Others suspected that organisations would remove information from records that might damage the organisation.

Disappointment: Some former residents were disappointed at the poor quality of record-keeping, inaccuracy and missing pages. Some found their names had been changed, their family names were spelled incorrectly and dates of birth were altered.

Improvements that former residents feel should be made

The following are steps that former residents feel would benefit people trying to find and access records. It was compiled by an organisation that represents former residents of children's establishments.

- Information should be provided within 40 days, in line with the Data Protection Act 1998. All care institutions and organisations should comply with the law.
- The entire process, including any costs, should be fully explained in writing when someone first makes contact with the former care home, organisation or local authority.
- Finding information about yourself for the first time in your life can be traumatic. So former residents should be offered independent help, such as counselling.

4. The legal background

Records associated with children's residential services allow insights into how these services were provided and, more specifically, how abuse was allowed to happen. The review's search for records included finding out what the law said about generating and maintaining records since 1950. The answers suggest that important legal issues are associated with records – issues that must be addressed to ensure that records for children's residential services are preserved and made accessible in the future.

The regulatory framework for children's residential services shows how children's residential **establishments** needed to generate more records in later years. At the same time, this regulatory framework doesn't take account of all the records generated in association with children's residential **services**. From 1950 to 1995, the law specified what records needed to be generated within approved schools, children's homes, residential placements for children with what at the time was called "mental disorders" and remand homes, for example. The law outlined managers' and the Secretary of State's duties and powers relating to records. It imposed a responsibility for overseeing – through records – the welfare of individual children and children's residential establishments.

Regulating records for children's residential services was, and remains, an extremely complex undertaking. Many organisations have generated, and continue to generate, records. They include: individual children's residential establishments, local authorities, voluntary organisations, religious organisations, professional bodies, the children's hearing system, justice, education and health care systems, inspection agencies and central government.

The review has identified comprehensive sets of laws, rules and regulations covering the generation of records for children's residential establishments. Local authorities, voluntary organisations, religious organisations, central government and those who provided services were responsible for complying with the legislation. Later in this chapter their response to the law is considered.

Laws on generating records 1950-68:

A series of laws stipulated what records had to be generated by:
- approved schools;
- children's homes;
- voluntary homes;
- homes for children with mental disabilities; and
- remand homes.

Each law had specific requirements but in general they required information such as:
- records of all children admitted and discharged;
- individual records of children;

- log books containing details such as visits, inspections, punishments and any other events that the law said "deserve to be recorded" or were considered important;
- a register of children attending schools;
- personal histories with details such as medical histories, why the child was admitted to a home, visits by parents, relatives and friends;
- letters from parents and guardians to be placed in individual files;
- records of food – with enough detail to judge whether the diet was satisfactory
- a note of every time a pupil absconds.

The laws were as follows:
- The Children and Young Persons (Scotland) Care and Training Regulations 1933.
- The Approved Schools (Scotland) Rules 1961.
- The Administration of Children's Homes (Scotland) Regulations 1959.
- The Voluntary Homes (Return of Particulars) (Scotland) Regulations 1952.
- The National Assistance Act 1948
- The Remand Home (Scotland) Rules 1946

Laws on generating records 1969-95:

Further laws were introduced in this period, applying to residential establishments and secure accommodation. Again, each had specific requirements but in general covered details such as:
- procedures used to select children to be admitted;
- details of children admitted to and leaving an establishment;
- procedures for access to records for staff, children and parents;
- records on any involvement of children and parents in decisions about a child's welfare while living in the establishment;
- records, including health details, for every child resident; and
- a log book detailing important and official events and other details including disciplinary measures.

The laws were:
- The Social Work (Residential Establishments – Child Care) (Scotland) Regulations 1987
- The Secure Accommodation (Scotland) Regulations 1983
- The Secure Accommodation (Scotland) Amendment Regulations 1988
- The Residential Care Order (Secure Accommodation) (Scotland) Regulations 1988

Laws on generating records after 1995:

The Children's (Scotland) Act 1995 Regulations and Guidance contains specific and very detailed requirements for the information that children's residential establishments, including secure accommodation, must record. The legal provisions they contain cover aspects of life within establishments, personal records and requirements specific to records in secure accommodation. The provisions were, therefore, more expansive, suggesting a growing reliance on records as a method for monitoring and improving services to children.

Other laws introduced in this period include the Arrangements to Look After Children (Scotland) Regulations 1996, the Secure Accommodation (Scotland) Regulations 1996 and the Residential Establishments – Child Care (Scotland) Regulations 1996. These also provided for detailed requirements on record-keeping, and the latter emphasised the need for local authorities to establish written case records for children in their care. These records must be kept until the 75th birthday of the person it relates to or, if a child dies before reaching the age of 18, for 25 years from the date of death.

How were records kept and how accessible are they?
Although thousands of records about children's residential services were generated between 1950 and 1995, the law has not been as effective in ensuring these were kept and made accessible. It has been extremely difficult for former residents, others – and for the review – to identify and locate significant historical records.

Overview of the laws in place

The Public Records (Scotland) Act 1937 is the main law in place during the period of our review for ensuring preservation of, and access to, public records. It still applies, in amended form. It was introduced to make "better provision for the preservation, care and custody of the Public Records of Scotland". However it was mainly concerned with providing for the transfer of court records to the Keeper of the Records of Scotland, who heads the National Archives of Scotland. It's worth noting that the Act allows for local authorities and other bodies to transfer their records to the Keeper but does not require them to do so.

Several other laws have a bearing on public records. These include:

- The Disposal or Records (Scotland) Regulations 1992 (and an amendment of these in 2003)
- The Freedom of Information (Scotland) Act 2002
- The Data Protection Act 1998
- The Human Rights Act 1998

In addition, the Local Government (Scotland) Act 1973 included requirements that affected records. One section governed the transfer of records from the local authorities that were replaced by Scotland's nine regional councils in 1973. It stated that the new regional councils had to make "proper arrangements" for their records. This was repealed by the Environment Act 1995.

When local authorities were reorganised in the mid 1990s, the Local Government etc (Scotland) Act 1994 provided for the transfer of records from the old to the new councils. It said councils "should" make "proper arrangements" to preserve and manage any records transferred to them under the Act, but didn't require them to do so. It also allowed local authorities to dispose of any records they did not consider "worthy of preservation".

How effective are these laws?

Scotland's laws on records don't do enough to ensure that records relating to children's residential services are preserved and that people have access to them.

The Public Records Act 1937 is very limited in its scope and outdated. Despite its name, it doesn't define "public records", so it can be difficult to understand the distinction between public and private records. This has serious implications for people responsible for preserving records and for people who entitled to have access to records.

Finding out who owns records can be challenging, especially where private organisations were contracted to provide public services.

The 1937 Act applies to courts, government departments and agencies and the NHS. But it doesn't apply to other public bodies – such as local authorities, NHS trusts and universities – or to voluntary and religious organisations. Nor does it specify how records generated by private bodies receiving public funding must be preserved and made accessible.

There is a clear need to reform the Public Records Act 1937 in Scotland.

The review has noted that local authorities must make "proper arrangements" for preserving and managing records. But this requirement is not defined and there are no sanctions to enforce it. In practice, local authorities have handed records over to the Keeper of the Records of Scotland voluntarily and by custom.

The absence of adequate public records legislation means that local authorities aren't consistent in how they deal with archives or manage records. Many have archives, but archivists complain of lack of funding and of little value being placed on their work. There is no guidance on how to identify and keep records and when it's acceptable to destroy records.

There have been significant attempts within the past decade to improve the weaknesses in laws relating to archives and archiving. These include:

The Archival Mapping Project (1999): This built a national picture of the state of archives in Scotland in both public and private organisations and concluded there was a need for significant improvements in areas that included funding, staffing and purpose-built buildings to house archives in Scotland's major cities.

The Public Records Strategy (2003-04): This was a review, by the former Scottish Executive, of laws, guidance, standards and practices relating to Scottish public records and archives. It followed the introduction of freedom of information and data protection laws.

The Code of Practice on Records Management (2003): Legislation has been drafted, but has yet to be introduced to the Scottish Parliament's legislative agenda.

Many barriers still exist that prevent people getting access to records they're legally entitled to view. The review noted many of these barriers earlier in this chapter. During the review's investigation it was learned that access policies vary hugely. Some local authorities and organisations have no access policy in place. Other organisations have individual policies in place. Former residents told the review they found these inconsistencies confusing.

The review found evidence of records that exist, but aren't accessible because they're not being managed properly or haven't been archived. Local authorities, in particular, have records in a myriad of locations and many records that haven't been archived. Some use private storage companies to store records. They don't always know what records are being stored, making these records inaccessible.

Former residents feel that the state and other organisations responsible for children's residential establishments have a duty to care to them as adults, particularly adults who were abused as children in a children's residential establishment. They feel this duty includes making it possible to establish historical accounts and learn about what happened in children's residential establishments.

5. The review's search for information

The challenges faced in searching for records

Major local government reorganisations and changes to children's services legislation in 1968 occurred during the period 1950 to 1995. These would have had an impact on the generation and preservation of records associated, directly or indirectly, with central government as well as local authorities and organisations. The reporting and policy relationship between organisations and central government would have changed throughout the years, with significant implications for records. The absence of appropriate records legislation would also have affected how records were preserved.

The review's search for information was affected by people's knowledge of what records existed. In some cases individuals knew what records were held, where they were and what they contained. But in others, individuals who knew this information had retired or were dead. In the time available to the review, it was extremely challenging for the review team– and the many people who helped – to locate records.

Adding to the difficulty was the assumption contained in the remit that:
- all the organisations the review sought records from had located and identified "relevant" records;
- these records were immediately accessible; and
- the review could review them thoroughly.

The reality was that records containing information about children's residential services are in multiple locations and in massive volume throughout Scotland and England. No central database identifies where these records are, which made it extremely difficult for the review, local authorities and organisations to identify what records existed and where they were.

Voluntary organisations, religious organisations and local authorities found it difficult, and at times impossible, to respond to our queries about past management policies and practices, including policies that relate to monitoring children's well-being and keeping children safe.

Obtaining relevant information was a major undertaking for local authorities and organisations, requiring expense and staff. Deciding what information was "relevant" to the review was difficult, if not impossible, for organisations and local authorities without viewing all the records available.

The poor overall state of records raises important issues about how voluntary organisations, religious organisations and local authorities that provided children's residential services are held accountable to children, former residents and others, for the services they provided.

The search for government records

The review began the search by identifying the most obvious places, such as the Scottish Executive Education Department, National Archives of Scotland, voluntary organisations, religious organisations and local authorities. The education department had begun searching for records on residential schools and children's homes before the review began its work, and had drawn up a list of records. The review later found that many other records relevant to its work were not on this list, which made the work more complex than anticipated. Some records also had to be reviewed by education department officials before they could be given to the review, which also made the research more time-consuming.

Other challenges included the quality of records. Government records tended to be about policies and inspections, not about individuals. The title of records could give little indication of the information they contained. Records reflected what might have appeared important when they were written, but rarely contained information that people seek now. However in many of the records we reviewed we found information relevant to our understanding of children's residential services.

Overall, the review found that the education department and National Archives of Scotland records contain considerable information that is potentially relevant to its work. But lack of time and available resources made it impossible to examine those records thoroughly. The content of the report of the review is limited by these factors.

Before the education department's records became available to us, the Scottish Information Commissioner had examined the department's process of gathering records relating to historical abuse in residential schools and children's homes. The Commissioner's report identified many issues that arose for this review.

The search for local authority, voluntary and religious organisation records

The review's information-gathering process shows how difficult, if not impossible, it is without records to gain insights into how systems contributed to children's abuse in residential establishments. In general, our search for information revealed that local authorities, voluntary organisations and religious organisations all faced similar challenges when trying to locate records, making it difficult to gain access to records.

We learned, for example, that **management records** relating to the same topic may be in many locations. Records might be absent in one location. But this didn't mean that they, or records relating to the same topic, didn't exist.

When children left residential placements, various unregulated approaches guided what happened to children's records.

Complicating this, there might be several children's records for one child, depending on what services were involved. Any or all of the following could have held **children's records**: residential establishments; local authority social work or children's departments; education authorities; health boards and voluntary or religious organisations. Records relating to children placed outwith their own local authorities could have been returned to the child's originating authority and dispersed to central offices. It's not clear what happened to the records of Scottish children placed in children's residential establishments in England.

What we did

The review circulated a questionnaire to 32 local authorities and 11 voluntary and religious organisations. Letters were written and interviews carried out. A survey was also sent to all local authority archivists to find out what records they held about children's residential services.

The questionnaire sought details such as what kind of services were provided, how they were monitored and inspected, what records, policies and guidelines were held and what these covered. The questionnaire also asked for basic details such as when residential establishments opened, where they were, how many children attended, the current status or when they closed.

What was found: voluntary organisations

The review had little information about what voluntary organisations provided residential services to children between 1950 and 1995. Six organisations were contacted, but the review may not have identified all voluntary organisations responsible for children's residential establishments during the period of the review.

Most of those contacted found it difficult to locate significant information about the establishments. Many have undergone changes – for example reorganisation or relocation – that affected their record-keeping practices. Records are in locations across Scotland and England. Some are more advanced than others in managing their records and archives; some employed archivists and others didn't. Other challenges included:
- lack of staff and time;
- inability to search documents by type;
- difficulty in deciding what was "relevant" information;
- poor filing;
- log books of limited value because their content was uninformative;
- no system for recording complaints, so none was recorded; and
- records held in multiple locations.

All voluntary organisations found it challenging to find out what management policies and practices might have existed for their children's residential services between 1950 and 1995. In general, records specific to children's residential services were difficult to locate, or didn't exist.

What was found: religious organisations

The review began with little information about the religious organisations that provided children's residential services between 1950 and 1995. It was also extremely difficult to identify which organisations had been responsible for children's establishments and should, therefore, have records.

The review contacted 16 organisations. Some said they had provided children's residential services and others said they hadn't. The extent to which they were involved in children's residential services varied, which made it difficult to identify, locate and access records specific to children's residential establishments.

Some organisations had specific, detailed information about what services they had managed but others had little or no information. Many didn't know where information might be located, or what information might exist. Many have large numbers of records throughout the UK that deal with services to children and adults.

Staff had moved on, offices had changed down the years, so it was often unclear what had happened to records. When some schools closed there was no policy on what to do with records, which then went missing. One organisation had a policy of destroying records after seven years. Labelling was inconsistent and some records were in boxes, on shelves and unsorted. Other challenges included:
- records held in several locations;
- records specific to Scotland integrated with records for projects in England;

- haphazard historic record-keeping; and
- the effect of fires and floods.

In one case the review's requests for information were dealt with solicitors, who said their client was under no obligation to give any access to archives.

The contents of records that organisations said they held varied widely. Some said they held general management records, files, registers and log books, but no policy and practice guidelines. Others said that formal processes existed in areas such as inspections, management reports and complaints, but were unable to find out if there were policies in areas such as recruitment and training, child protection, whistleblowing, formal complaints, bullying, grievances, incident reports, advocacy support records and information management and inspections.

Different information was held for different time periods, even more recent times. For example, one organisation said it had records for 1970-1985, but that these were no longer accessible. Another didn't know if it had specific policy and practice guidelines for the period 1986-1995.

What was found: local authorities

Of the 32 questionnaires the review sent to local authorities 15 were returned. Eleven other authorities replied, four didn't respond and two others had provided no children's residential establishments. Some contacted the review to discuss how to approach the task given the difficulties they faced. Others adopted an approach that best suited their circumstances.

During the time of the review local government had experienced two major reorganisations. The impact can be seen in one current local authority. Between 1975-96 it had existed entirely within the boundary of a larger regional authority. Before 1975 the area it covers today was covered by three county councils. But only part of the old county councils' areas are within the current council's boundaries.

In their responses, some local authorities speculated

that they had few records available. Other representatives made considerable efforts to find records. One individual went as far as contacting retired colleagues and went to homes for older people to find out if anyone could recall children's homes in the area. Two local authorities employed retired social workers to report on children's residential establishments run by former corporations and regional councils. One researcher found valuable information about monitoring practices by carefully scrutinising council minutes.

The review found that the relationship between local authority departments and archives was uneven. Some employees within departments worked closely with their local authority archivists. Others either didn't contact their archivist to assist with locating records or actively resisted getting the archivist involved.

As noted earlier, there is no central government database of children's residential establishments in Scotland between 1950 and 1995. Children's establishments changed function, management and even location. Many local authorities didn't know what had happened to management records and children's files when children's residential establishments closed, so it was difficult for them to identify what places had existed.

Like voluntary and religious organisations, the local authorities faced enormous challenges in their attempts to locate records that might be relevant to the review. These included:
- large volumes of records located in many locations;
- confusion about where records were sent during local government reorganisations and what records exist;
- records buried among other records because there was – and is – no system for cataloguing records; and
- no consistent processes for managing records among local authorities.

Early in the review's information-gathering work, a professional association questioned the review's remit and process of gathering information. This led to misinformation circulating about the review. As a result, some local authorities that had been willing to help decided not to continue with their search for information. It is difficult to know how much this episode affected the local authorities' co-operation in working with the review.

Most local authorities said they didn't know if they had records for the period 1950-1969. No local authority had inspection reports for children's residential services or their own departments for this period. Some had records for the period 1970-85. Again, none had inspection reports for children's residential services or their own departments for this period.

For the most recent period, 1986-1995, most local authorities said they had records for children's residential services, although a few said they had no records or didn't know if they had records. Some had records that were no longer accessible.

The review's survey of archivists revealed a mixed picture of problems and gaps that affect the availability and quality of records available now and in the future. Their responses included the following:

- One archive holds no records specific to children's residential establishments and attempts to find the information from council departments failed.
- An archivist was instructed to destroy all senior management team records in 2004.
- All records after 1996 are on recycled paper, which is unlikely to survive in the long term.
- One council appointed its first professional archivist in 1986.
- Archives are only partially listed and it's not possible to identify archives that relate to children's residential establishments.
- Not all local authorities have records managers or record management systems. In some, individual departments manage and store their own records. In others more than one system is in place.

Recommendations

The lessons of this review point to an urgent need to take action to preserve historical records, ensure that residents can get access to records and information about their location.

1. The government should commission a review of public records legislation which should lead to new legislation being drafted to meet records and information needs in Scotland. This should also make certain that no legislation impedes people's lawful access to records. This review's objectives should address the need for permanent preservation of significant records held by private, non-statutory agencies that provide publicly funded services to children.

2. All local authorities and publicly funded organisations with responsibility for past and present children's services should undertake to use the Section 61 Code of Practice on Records Management issued on behalf of Scottish Ministers and in consultation with the Scottish Information Commissioner and the Keeper of the Records of Scotland under the terms of the Freedom of Information Scotland Act 2002[2].

3. Training in professional records management practice and procedures should be available to all organisations and local authorities providing children's services. This might be provided by NAS or the Scottish Information Commissioner.

4. The government should invite NAS to establish a national records working group to address issues specific to children's historical residential services records. Appendix 4 of the report contains suggested representation and terms of reference.

5. Voluntary organisations, religious organisations and local authorities, working in partnership, should commission guidance to ensure that their children's residential services records are adequately catalogued to make records readily accessible.

6. Record management practices should be evaluated regularly where records associated with children's residential establishments are held, particularly records associated with monitoring children's welfare and safety. It is recommended that the Care Commission should consider taking responsibility for this.

---

[2] see http://www.scotland.gov.uk/Resource/Doc/1066/0003775.pdf

Chapter 6

Former residents' experiences

Chapter 6

Former residents' experiences

The purpose of this chapter is to show how the law worked in the experiences of some former residents of residential schools and children's homes. The information is drawn from written responses which a number of former residents made in answer to questions posed by the review and has been compiled by my researchers.

These responses, while clearly not a representative sample of all former residents' experiences, give insight into life in some residential schools and children's homes in the first part of the review period.

This chapter is in four parts:
- Part 1 considers abuse in a human rights and international context.
- Part 2 is a collection of extracts from people's childhood memories as told to the review. The extracts have been chosen because they relate to how the law worked in the experience of these former residents. A note of the developments which former residents would like to see is also included. The opinions expressed are those of the people who responded to the review and not necessarily those of the review itself. While Part 2 may not be strictly within the remit of the review, I believe it is helpful to our understanding of how the law was implemented in some places in the early years of the review period. It also prompted the preparation of Part 3 of this chapter.
- Part 3 presents – from a former resident's perspective – what rights he or she should have expected to receive under the various laws, rules and regulations that governed residential schools and children's homes.
- Part 4 is the review's conclusions.

"I felt like a non-person. I lived in a crazy world."

These words belong to an individual who lived for 16 years in a children's home in Scotland after she was placed there as a small child. Thousands of children lived in children's residential establishments throughout Scotland from 1950 to 1995. Today, they describe their experiences as ranging from the very good to the horrific. There is little written information, however, about children's experiences in children's residential establishments from the perspective of the children who lived through those experiences years ago.

The review acknowledges, in this report, that some former residents of children's residential establishments recall positive experiences and others had mixed experiences or painful memories that have remained throughout their lives.

Part 1. Abuse in a human rights and international context

> "All human beings are born free and equal in dignity and rights. They are endowed with reason and conscience and should act towards one another in the spirit of brotherhood." (Universal Declaration of Human Rights, 1948)

In the mid 20th century, the Universal Declaration of Human Rights (1948) emerged as the pre-eminent international human rights instrument. It was supported by such treaties as the European Convention on Human Rights and Fundamental Freedoms signed in 1950 by the European Council, which had convened in 1948 following the Second World War. Both of these instruments developed in response to the horrific experiences of individuals placed in institutions, for example, during the Second World War. "Human rights" are defined as those rights marked by certain characteristics: they can't be waived or denied, they impose obligations, they are universal and they "focus on the inherent dignity and equal worth of all human beings" (Office of the UN High Commission on Human Rights, 2006: 8).

> "Human rights are universal legal guarantees protecting individuals and groups against actions

and omissions that interfere with fundamental freedoms, entitlements and human dignity." (Office of the UN High Commission on Human Rights, 2006: 8)

Ignatieff (2000:2) suggests that, by working "their way deep inside our psyches", human rights go beyond legal instruments to situate themselves as "...expressions of our moral identity as a people." When former residents lived in children's residential establishments they had human rights entitlements, along with legal entitlements, to be protected from harm and to be treated with dignity.

People throughout the world have been disclosing incidents of abuse they experienced as children while living in residential institutions[1]. The continued abuse of children worldwide, in all circumstances, is the focus of The United Nations World Report on Violence against Children[2], presented in October 2007. This referred in particular to children in institutions providing care and associated with justice:

"Although these institutions are established to provide care, guidance, support and protection to children, the boys and girls who live in them may be at heightened risk of violence compared to children whose care and protection is governed by parents and teachers, at home and at school"[3].

The definition of violence in the report is from Article 19 in the UN Convention on the Rights of the Child, prohibiting "...all forms of physical or mental violence, injury and abuse, neglect or negligent treatment, maltreatment or exploitation, including sexual abuse"[4]. The definition is also informed by the World Report on Violence and Health (2002) as:

"...the intentional use of physical force or power, threatened or actual, against a child, by an individual or a group, that either results in or has a high likelihood of resulting in actual or potential harm to the child's health, survival, development or dignity"[5].

Survivors of institutional child abuse claim that what happened to them meets the UN definition of violence against children, constituting a violation of their human rights as children. Many survivors also say that as children they often didn't speak about their abuse or, if they did, they weren't believed and were punished. Survivors also have reported that they weren't able to talk about their abuse until they were older adults. In today's world, it's not uncommon for children to remain silent about the abuse they are suffering. In referring to the stigmatisation, the isolation and the de-socialisation that occurs when children reside in institutions, the UN report suggests that these factors make children more vulnerable to further violence and sometimes perpetrators as well[6].

All countries investigating child abuse within institutions begin from a place where the extent of child abuse is unknown. In recognition, various countries have put in place processes that make it possible to hear directly from people about their experiences as children abused within state-supported residential establishments. In Ireland, for example, the government passed legislation[7] that launched a commission of inquiry into child abuse in institutions. This process includes hearing directly from people who lived as children in state-funded institutions. Since 1999 several inquiries into institutional child abuse in Australia[8] have also heard evidence from people who experienced abuse as children living in institutions.

---

[1] See **** (references)
[2] See World Report on Violence Against Children (2007)
     http://www.violencestudy.org/IMG/pdf/I._World_Report_on_Violence_against_Children.pdf
[3] Ibid
[4] Ibid
[5] Ibid
[6] Ibid
[7] See The Commission to Inquire into Child Abuse Act 2000
[8] See references as per records special report

In Canada, a national Law Commission conducted extensive research into government responses to allegations of child abuse within institutions[9], consulting with survivors of childhood abuse about their needs and advising governments on how best to address those needs.

Most recently, the Canadian federal government announced a residential school settlement arising from claims of child abuse within residential schools where aboriginal people were placed[10]. Linked to this, the government is establishing a Truth and Reconciliation Commission[11] whose primary purpose is "…to contribute to truth, healing and reconciliation"[12] of aboriginal people abused as children in residential placements. It is intended to "…provide a holistic, culturally appropriate and safe setting…" for people who lived in residential schools to talk about their experiences.

Children were sent to live in many kinds of institutions in Scotland throughout the period under review. By listening to their experiences, much can be learned about what happened to children living in those institutions. In speaking for themselves, former residents also speak for those many children, now adults, who can't speak for themselves. Children with disabilities, for example, were sometimes placed in adult institutions such as mental health institutions and hospitals, and their voices may be among the most silent. As it is often said that societies are measured on the basis of how they treat their most vulnerable, we have a responsibility to seek ways to ensure all voices are heard, including those children who lack the skills so necessary to claiming their entitlements.

Former residents contributed to the review in various ways, through interviews, meetings, site visits, telephone conversations, letters and emails. The adults who contacted the review lived in children's residential establishments between the 1940s and the 1970s; no-one contacted the review who had lived in children's residential establishments during the 1980s or 1990s. Today, the people who provided information to the review live in Scotland and throughout the world, in places as far apart as England, Canada, the USA and Hong Kong.

The review would like to express its gratitude and appreciation to those many individuals who shared their experiences as it was extremely painful for all to recount what happened to them as children. Many people, however, said their reason for speaking was to contribute to an accurate historical account of what happened, to seek apologies for what happened and to make certain that children who live in state care today are safe and cared for.

Part 2. What children remember about life in residential establishments: 1950-1995

The following information represents written responses received from former residents to a series of questions posed by the review. The information doesn't represent all information received by the review. This chapter highlights, therefore, some of the experiences described by former residents. It sheds light on the necessity for implementation to match legislation in spirit and letter.

Did you know the reason for your placement in a residential home while you lived there?

No, I did not know.
Former resident, children's home, 1944-1960

No, and I still don't know.
Former resident, approved school, 1955-1957

Yes, mother had tuberculosis and died. My father had disappeared.
Former resident, two children's homes, 1954-1960

---

[9] Hall, M (2002). Law Commission of Canada, Restoring Dignity: Responding to Child Abuse in Canadian Institutions in The International Journal of Children's Rights, Vol 10:3, pp 295-302

[10] See Indian Residential Schools Settlement, http://www.residentialschoolsettlement.ca/English.html

[11] See Mandate for Truth and Reconciliation Commission, http://www.residentialschoolsettlement.ca/SCHEDULE_N.pdf

[12] Ibid

Yes, my father was killed in WWII and my mother had tuberculosis so she was hospitalised for one year.
Former resident, children's home, 1954-55

The only thing I was told was that I was unwanted, unloved and a child from the gutter... I later found out (as an adult) that there were indications in records available that my father was contributing to my keep and I was 12 before I found out that I had a brother (my twin).
Former resident, children's home, 1938-1956

In my 15.5 years at the [children's home] I was told matter-of-factly that I was a bastard and that I should be more than grateful for what I had and that was the sole purpose of my being there. Never, at any time did anyone explain to me how or why I was brought to the [children's home].
Former resident, children's home, 1944-1959

Did you have any family contact or contact with outside friends while you lived at the residential home?

No, I did not know of any family or even where I was born.
Former resident, children's home, 1944-1960

No, I did not see anyone.
Former resident, children's home, 1957-58 and 1963-64

None at all.
Former resident, children's home, 1938-1956

No contact was ever made between myself or immediate family. Later on, when I was about six or seven years old an elderly lady... would visit me once a month... On one of these occasions I had apparently misbehaved and was sent to bed for the day. When she arrived she was told that I was too ill to see anyone that day and she returned back to [her home]. Some after she became too frail and unable to come visit. She was then replaced with another 'Auntie' from a church group... who visited faithfully with her son and daughter till I was discharged in 1959.
Former resident, children's home, 1944-1959

Did you know who was responsible for your care?

No, I did not know who was responsible for my care.
Former resident, children's home, 1944-1960

No. I never received a visit from a social worker.
Former resident, two children's homes, 1954-1960

Before she was hospitalised with tuberculosis, my mother spoke to a social worker. I was placed in an orphanage where my mother thought I would receive good care from the nuns. I knew who was 'in charge' of the orphanage – Sister X. For this sister to get any kind of attention all she had to do was hold up her first finger and everyone just froze where you stood, if you moved an inch you where severely beaten with a long wooden stick approximately 3 ft long. This was used with brute force sometimes the stick would break and had to be replaced.'
Former resident, children's home, 1954-55

I didn't know as I was led to believe that I was an orphan by the house mother. I was never told my birthdate, nor the year I was born until I left [the children's home] and got my birth certificate.
I found out then that I had a father and mother...
I didn't know who was responsible for my care in [the children's home]. I felt like a non-person..
Former resident, children's home, 1938-1956

I had no idea of anyone other than [the children's home] being responsible for my care. I assumed that [the children's home] was responsible and that they, through faith, love and charity, would feed and clothe me until discharged. After discharge at 15 I should get myself a job and then would be responsible for taking care of myself. No-one at the [children's home] explained to us how to do anything anywhere outside of the main gates.
Former resident, children's home, 1944-1959

Were you able to talk to that person, or persons, about what made you unhappy?
If not, why not?
If so, what type of response did you get?

I didn't talk to anybody – never.
Former resident, children's home, 1942-1954

We were caned if we didn't drink our sour milk and if we didn't eat our meal it was left and added to the next meal. I was treated differently in the children's home where I was out in the parks playing. When I tried to talk about abuse, I was not believed and told "nuns don't act like that".
Former resident, two children's homes, 1954-1960

If someone done something wrong (trivial) then all the boys were punished, by being lined-up in the main drill hall. The punishment consisted of (Sister X) would have an item in her hand that she would squeeze, this would make a click sound. When you heard this click sound we would point our arms upwards towards the roof and when the click sound was heard again then we would bring our arm back down and try to line our fingers level with our shoulders. If [Sister X] saw that your fingers were not level with your shoulder, she would carry a long wooden round stick. This was used to hit us across the fingers with brute force. Sometimes this stick would break because of the pressure she used.

Some of the boys had broken and badly bruised fingers but I cannot remember any of the boys getting any medical treatment after the punishment drills.

I was sent to the kitchen to work with [Sister Y] and life became a lot better with her. She would talk to me and show respect. She was responsible for all the meals.
Former resident, children's home, 1954-55

There was no-one to talk to... other than the other boys. We never dared associate with the girls. Venturing through the girls side... was shunned. We would be asked for what purpose was the visit then we'd be strapped with the leather belt for doing so. We were never encouraged by anyone in the [children's home] to sit and talk about conditions that existed... We would never disclose our feelings fears

or problems to anyone. We were controlled by fear and intimidation. Fear to tell of the brutality on an almost daily basis, and fear for the repercussions that would follow if we did. Conversation with [our house parents] would almost always be in a question or an answer format. We would answer yes or not to them as mummy or daddy till about 12 years old then it became yes or no [Mr and Mrs] till we were discharged. I sat many times since leaving... to try and recall conversations with either one of them... They just do not exist.
Former resident, children's home, 1944-1959

Were there any adults at the residential home where you lived whom you could talk to about your concerns?
If not, why not?
If so, what was their job?
If so, what type of response did you get?

We had no-one with whom we could talk about why we were unhappy. Most of the time we lived in total fear. We had no freedom there was complete control of our every move. Absolute regimentalism was expected. When we rose and ate and when it was bed time... 6 o'clock. I was 12 years old when I had to spend an entire week in bed during the summer for talking. I felt Alone! Lost! Afraid! And Helpless! Once I was severely punished and went to see [Mr S] at his office. He did respond to my complaint. I told an older girl about and she told the house parent and I was made to spend several days in my bed. I did not know if [Mr S] did anything about the incident. We had nothing in the little lockers beside our beds.
Former resident, children's home, 1944-1960

No...same as [previous question]. I couldn't/didn't talk to anybody. This was because we were prisoners of fear and scared of being reported. We were paralysed. The level of fear of the house mother was unbelievable. She would have a strap in her hand and with that, or her bare hands, would hit you in passing. If you cowered when passing her, as we often did, she would say, "I won't disappoint you girl" and hit you. There was nobody to tell and we were too scared anyway. I never reported any of this and I feel guilty sometimes for others that I couldn't. There was no way out (we were even schooled there too) life was so

narrow with nobody to turn to. I used to lie in bed, as others did, crying for someone to love me or take me away from there.
Former resident, children's home, 1938-1956

The nuns, who were responsible for my care and my brother's care, beat my 5-year-old brother so severely that he couldn't go to school for a fortnight. I told the police and my grandfather about it. I was told "I deserved a smack every now and again" and that the "nuns were good women".

I showed my hands where I had received the strap to my teacher, who told the headmistress. The headmistress said "these girls have to be kept under control".

I told a priest about abuse and he said "God bless you my child".
Former resident, two children's homes, 1954-1960

I could not think of anyone that I could relate any problems to other than the [house parents] or to the...superintendent. In any case, either of them were to be avoided at all costs in our estimation. There was no independent agency to talk to. If my former peers were to be asked I am positive they would agree. We lived in an atmosphere that as bastards and misfits we were in a different league with [house parents] and the [children's home] management. We felt somehow subservient and huddled together and of course we were always too timid to approach anyone else about our concerns. We were never encouraged to talk about our feelings, or about ambitions or what we would like to do after our departure. That we supposed, was all part of growing up and we would have to deal with it in our own miraculous ways when we were edged into the mainstream of society upon discharge.
Former resident, children's home, 1944-1959

Were you aware of adults visiting from outside

the residential home where you lived?
If so, did you know who they were?
Were you able to talk to them?
If so, were you able to talk to them in private?
If you spoke to them about your concerns, what response did you get?

I would watch children on the first Saturday of the month have a visit from family members. The phone would ring telling which child was to go to the central hall for a visit.
Former resident, children's home, 1944-1960

I don't remember seeing a doctor – maybe once. We got a dose of Epsom salts no matter what. A dentist pulled my teeth. I was sent to the sick bay with the flu. The nun in charge told me to get up and I fainted. I was sent to school but sent home again by the teacher. I was isolated in the sick bay and had no personal contact.
Former resident, two children's homes, 1954-1960

Nobody came to visit in 16 years apart from one incident I mentioned above with the house auntie who left and I wasn't one of the ones spoken to by the two men who came to [the children's home].
Former resident, children's home, 1938-1956

The only adults that I recall who visited me were the two [aunties that is, children's home visitors]. I entered the children's home when I was three months old. I had no idea who brought me to the [children's home] until I received a letter in 1972, thirteen years after discharge[13].
Former resident, children's home, 1944-1959

Did you have contact with adults when you spent

---

[13] This former resident learned that he was born to his mother during the war when her husband was away. When her husband returned, this former resident was placed in the children's home. Originally the former resident was given a modified birth certificate and then, in 1972, he was sent his original birth certificate. This doesn't show his correct father's name, but the name of his mother's husband. This former resident was told in 1972 that there was no information about whether his parents were alive, or not, or whether he had any relatives.

time away from the residential home?
If so, who did you have contact with?
Were you able to talk to them?
If so, were you able to talk to them in private?
If you spoke to them about your concerns, what
response did you get?

I was 10 years old when I saw my first visitor (my heart
jumped!). I was introduced to a [Mrs. q] (possibly from
a church group) who lived at [x]. Sometimes she was
unable to come but always sent people to visit me on
the first of the month. There was a young boy named
[c]... who was also picked. Poor [c] one day he was not
allowed to go out because his house parent decided
to punish him. I never did find out why? I kept asking
my visitor but I only received silence. I do remember
that day and spending the visit sitting ... for hours not
moving an inch. I do remember looking back and
guessing that Mrs. [q] could not change their minds.
[c] was never chosen for a visit again.

I did tell [Mrs. q] how unhappy I was but she never
made any comments. I am certain this also distressed
her, however I felt that I was never heard. I still got a
visit and was on rare occasions allowed out on a visit
to Glasgow. However she seemed very distant. [Mrs. q]
did give me some sweets and presents at Christmas.
However, I was forced to hand them to the house
parent. Sometimes I never saw them again.
Unfortunately I did not keep in touch with [Mrs. q]
when I left the Homes.
Former resident, children's home, 1944-1960

I never saw or was taken to see any person from the
local authority.
Former resident, two children's homes, 1954-1960

The only time away I had was one year we went to
[town] for a holiday to a ...home, but we were kept
apart from other folk there. One of other house
mothers took us. If we were 'good' we got up to [city]
once a month when we were a bit older. I 'rebelled' a
bit at 15 so didn't get out much. In all the years I was
there (1938-1956) I got out once a month when over
16, up to [city] 1pm to 9pm. 9/10 I never got out.
During all of the years there would be visiting for
others once a month. The 'phone would go, names

would be shouted to go and meet visitors but it never
happened for me. The children's home provided no
comfort at these times. As children and young people
we were loyal to each other. We were made to feel
by some of the adults that it was a crime that we had
been born...
Former resident, children's home, 1938-1956

I was about twelve years old when [a children's home
visitor] invited [another boy] and myself to spend a few
days with her at her home... We were never asked by
[her] or her family about our time at the [children's home]
and we never spoke to them about things that happened
at the [children's home]. We were simply overjoyed to
be away yet unfortunately, still too meek and ashamed
to tell what was happening to us... In retrospect I
think [the children's home visitor] just wanted us to
have a nice time while we looked at what was in store
for us a world far away from the [children's home].
Former resident, children's home, 1944-1959

Did 'inspectors' or other adults from outside with
management responsibilities visit the residential
home where you lived?
If so, were you able to talk to them?
If so, were you able to talk to them in private?
If you spoke to them about your concerns, what
response did you get?

Yes we had inspections. Once we had a [special]
inspection. First [the visitors] listened to an account
of how the money was spent on the upkeep of the
home. Descriptions of the allocations for the buildings
food etc.... We were all expected to sit and listen to
this for hours not moving an inch.... The children had
to make an extra effort to make sure the home was
spotless for the visit. This was not a pleasant way to
spend our time. The visit was approximately 2 hours
with people coming and going while we kept in the
background.

Once I remember a visit of an inspector at school.
We were told to turn our pages to our best math
work. He walked around the class said nothing just
looking at our jotters.
Former resident, children's home, 1944-1960

Once, when two inspectors came to visit.
Former resident, children's home, 1938-1956

I think there were inspections, maybe yearly. The place was cleaned up, washed down including the walls and ceilings before the inspector arrived. **Former resident, two children's homes, 1954-1960**

There was no evidence of anything of this kind [inspection and monitoring system], no visits to the [children's home] by independent external agencies, nor interviews with the children.
Former resident, children's home, 1960s.

There was never any need for inspectors as all the [buildings] were scrubbed and polished clean from top to bottom 365 days a year in my time. 1944-1959. If we were to have inspectors visit us, no doubt we would be sitting with our arms folded in silence for the duration.
Former resident, children's home, 1944-1959

Did you know what 'quality of care' you could expect to receive when you lived in your residential home?
If so, how did you know?
As a child, what did you expect from those persons responsible for your care?

No, but I knew that I was not valued.
Former resident, children's home, 1944-1960

Nothing. When I lived in [the children's home] I was never allowed to be ill. If I was ill and unable to work I was told I was 'sciving' and made to feel like a criminal. We were treated like animals... we got no respect. For example, at puberty I had to knock on the door and declare to the house mother if I had my period and children who wet the bed had to do the same thing. Sometimes teachers would be told that we were in bed ill when in fact we were scrubbing floors and unable to attend school in case the teachers saw the result of the physical punishment meted out by the house mother e.g. black eyes and/or

that you were emotionally upset by it.

The carers in [the children's home] lived in relative luxury e.g. eating poultry and eggs, whilst in all the years I was there I never tasted chicken and the children had to make do mostly with powered eggs.

You couldn't sit down and talk, confide 1 to 1 with any staff member as that would have been seen as condemnation of [the founder] and that could never happen. I feel that the name of [the home] definitely came before the welfare of the children. As a child I felt like a commodity. It was all about money with religion being rammed down your throat from 4 years old. The only time talking was permitted was if it was about religion in some way e.g. chanting bits of the bible. We had no choice, we were just put there. We had no existence, no quality of life. There was no love and compassion.

What did I expect? I had nothing to compare it with so I had no expectation except that I wished that someone would take me away from it. I had wanted to be a nurse but I never got that chance. When I left [the children's home] I was 'put out to a family' to do their housework. It was an awful experience.
Former resident, children's home, 1938-1956

If you had concerns as a child living in a residential home, what options did you think you had if you wanted an adult to help you?

I had No Options! We knew no adults who we could trust or who would help us. We were taught to pray and that didn't work. I often thought of running away. Maybe I could knock on a strangers door. Surely they would feed me and give me a bed.
I knew deep down that this was impossible because children who ran away were brought back and beaten by...
Former resident, children's home, 1944-1960

It was hard to seek help even from the few outsiders you did come into contact with e.g. doctor. You just didn't trust anybody. The doctor came once a year and sometimes there would be marks on you from punishment which he must have seen – but he said and did nothing about them. People from the outside made assumptions about why you were upset e.g. 'maybe you just didn't like your job' as in my case at one point, instead of trying to find out what was really troubling me.
Former resident, children's home, 1938-1956

The lines of reporting and communication appeared to deliberately obscure and threats of severe punishment were used by some carers to deter children from making complaints… There was no evidence that management, abusers and the system were accountable to anyone. They were skilful in concealing or suppressing incidents of malpractice, complaints of cruelty and reports of abuse.
Former resident, children's home, 1960s.

By being silent it was our life-blood, our way of grasping anything just to be able to live. Saying anything to anyone of the cruelty's that happened on a daily basis might jeopardise the only home that we ever had. To speak of abuse or beatings to anyone would be the betrayal of a false loyalty we had to the [house parents] and the [children's home] that we inherently just had to accept. The consequences included beatings and/or threats of eviction from the [children's home] to Borstal. This was a choice that would be offered constantly to remind us just how grateful we should be to be part of the [children's home] under the administration of the [house parents]…
Former resident, children's home, 1944-1959

What would you recommend for children living in residential homes who want to express their unhappiness about something important to them?

This is a very difficult question. If the child has no one to turn to. The system has failed the child.
Former resident, children's home, 1944-1960

They must have contact with the outside world as we didn't and look what happened. There must be someone to build a trusting relationship with who isn't part of the place they live. Children must have this opportunity. Children need to feel confident and not fear that they can tell someone who will help them if things aren't right for them or they aren't being cared for properly. To hold back fear is a terrible thing – allowing the person doing wrong to get away with it, and having to watch them.

To protect children we need to somehow look at the inside of people, not the outside, not allow them to build up falseness unchallenged.

Got to look deeper – it can be hard for a child but if he/she builds up trust with an adult and that can be maintained this builds confidence. This shouldn't be broken as then the child can go into a corner again, as trust is taken away from him/her.

Never tell a child nobody wants them and/or deny them information about their family. Children need love and compassion not the dreaded emptiness that I have experienced.
Former resident, children's home, 1938-1956

One older former resident contacting the review summarised his response in a paragraph. He stated that his '…generation was brought up using entirely different methods than the generations of the sixties and seventies. We did not have at our disposal any social agencies to help us. We had not such thing as public services such as a police station to go to if needed. [The children's home] has it's own internal security called the strap. No other agencies were visible at any time in my fifteen years at [the children's home]. No one ever came to interview me or to ask if I needed any help'.

How childhood experiences have affected former residents' lives

Former residents described their poor sense of identity and feelings of not belonging, which they attribute to their experiences in children's residential establishments[14]. They expressed feelings of isolation, guilt, shame, despair, lack of trust and stigmatisation. They reported dysfunctional inter-personal and family relationships, suicide attempts, high death rates, and alcohol and drug abuse. According to former residents they experience feelings of betrayal, resistance to and non-acceptance of authority.

Many residents talked about the poor education they received and its life-long impact. Several managed to further their education in later years, with some winning national awards for their work and gaining employment as university professors. Others say they managed to raise healthy children, build strong, loving family relationships and to lead a productive, satisfying life despite their unhappy childhood experiences.

Many former residents, despite many unhappy childhood experiences, can also remember times in their earlier lives when they had happy or joyful moments. Former residents spoke about individuals who were kind to them, about special excursions they said were fun and about times playing with other children that made their lives manageable. Some recall brutal experiences in one children's home and caring experiences in another.

What former residents want

Former residents indicated that they have different and varying needs although there are some common elements to all. Some or all former residents indicated they would like:

- A survivors' conference to discuss funding distribution for support services
- Direct apologies from the organisations or local authorities with responsibility for them as children

- The establishment of a historical account
- Support and advocacy services for survivors of childhood abuse
- Support and advocacy services, including educational and training opportunities, for all former residents who may require such services
- Right of access to records
- Accountability by those responsible for the residential establishments where they resided
- Proper vetting, listing and reporting procedures for employees
- Effective training, monitoring and investigation procedures for employees
- An independent complaints reporting system for children
- A judicial inquiry
- The removal of the time-bar established by the 1964 law on limitation
- Making certain that the law is applied to ensure due legal process
- Legal amendments to eliminate the possibility of reductions in sentences due to technical loopholes

One individual who lived in a children's residential establishment in the 1970s, for example, told the review that she requires counselling services arising from abuse she experienced in a children's home. This person stated that her experiences as a witness at a criminal trial, resulting in the criminal convictions of adults who abused children in children's homes, had also contributed to her additional support needs.

Part 3. Former residents: key legal themes 1950-1995

This section summarises the main legal provisions affecting former residents living in children's residential establishments. Arising from questions former residents asked during their contact with the review, it is written from the perspective of former residents and intended as an aid to understanding the legal framework[15].

---

[14] This is based on information from survivors who spoke to the review and by a submission made by a former resident.

[15] See regulatory framework in Chapter 2

Why and where were we placed in children's residential establishments?

The law shows you may have been placed for various reasons. For long-term care, juvenile courts and, after 1968 the children's hearing system, had the power to order alternative care for you if you were seen as being in need of "care and protection"[16].

In the early years, if you had an offence committed against you under the Children and Young Persons (Scotland) Act 1937, namely assault, ill treatment, neglect or abandonment, then the 1937 Act could provide for your removal to a "place of safety" – which could include a remand home, poor house, police station, and hospital.

You may have been placed in a **children's home**. Whether an offence was committed against you or not, the Children Act 1948 (then later in the Social Work (Scotland) Act 1968 and Children (Scotland) Act 1995) provided that if you were orphaned or deserted, or your parents or guardian couldn't provide you with proper accommodation or care for you adequately, then the local authority had a duty to receive you into care in the interests of your welfare[17]. The authority could either provide accommodation itself, or make arrangements to board you out, place you in another local authority home, or in a voluntary home[18].

Before 1968, you may been placed in an **approved school**, intended to provide residential education and training for children and young people aged 16 years and under. You might have been an offender, ordered there by a court[19] or transferred by the Secretary of State[20]. Or, the authorities may have considered you "in need of care and protection"[21]. After 1968, approved schools became known as "List D schools" and were phased out over a period of time under the terms of the Social Work (Scotland) Act 1968.

Before 1968, if you had mental health problems, then your parent or guardian, and the school board or parish council – with the consent of your parent or guardian – could arrange for you to be transferred to a relevant institution under the legislation[22]. These placements might have included **mental health institutions, special schools** and **homes for children with disabilities**. The local education authority had to decide whether you were in need of "special educational treatment", and, if so, could provide for that education in a special school. If you suffered from a disability and needed care and attention, the local authority could place you in residential accommodation under either the 1937 Act or the National Assistance Act 1948, later dealt with under the Social Work (Scotland) Act 1968.

You may have been placed in a remand home under the 1937 Act[23]. As a juvenile offender, you may have been placed in what you knew as a Borstal institution in the years before 1968.

---

[16] Children and young people came under this definition if they had no parent or guardian, if the parent or guardian was "unfit", if they were falling into bad associations, being exposed to moral danger or beyond control: Section 65 of the Children and Young Persons (Scotland) Act 1937, repealed by Schedule 9 of the Social Work (Scotland) Act 1968 c.49

[17] The Children Act 1948, s1. Later repealed by the Social Work (Scotland) Act 1968, and replaced by s15(1), in turn later repealed by Sch 5 of the Children (Scotland) Act 1995

[18] The Children Act 1948, ss13 and 15, as amended by the Social Work (Scotland) Act 1968

[19] The Children and Young Persons (Scotland) Act 1937, s61. Repealed by the Social Work (Scotland) Act 1968, Schedule 9

[20] ibid s62, as amended by the Criminal Justice (Scotland) Act 1949, the Social Work (Scotland) Act 1968, and the Criminal Procedure (Scotland) Act 1995

[21] ibid s65.

[22] For example, various provisions contained in The Mental Deficiency and Lunacy (Scotland) Act 1913, the Mental Deficiency (Scotland) Act 1940, and the Mental Health (Scotland) Act 1960. For later provisions see The Mental Health (Scotland) Act 1984

[23] The Children and Young Persons (Scotland) Act 1937, s81(3). Replaced and repealed by the Social Work (Scotland) Act 1968, Sch 9

Who had guardianship responsibilities for us?

In the early years, your parents or family members may have placed you in a children's residential establishment. Beginning with the 1937 Act, however, the local authority could assume guardianship responsibilities for you under the legislation[24], depending upon the circumstances and what was considered to be your best interests. This usually happened if you had no living parent or guardian, or where your parent or guardian couldn't adequately care for you. The local authorities had to take steps in your care "as would be required of a parent"[25].

But if you were placed in an approved school or residential establishment not managed by a local authority, the legislation stated that the managers could assume all rights and powers that normally belonged to parents by law[26].

Were we allowed contact with family and friends?

If you were placed in an **approved school**, under the 1937 Act you were entitled to receive letters and visits from your parents, relatives, guardians or friends (although such a "privilege" could be suspended as a form of discipline)[27]. This entitlement in later law required you to be actively encouraged to write to your parents at least once a week[28]. Every letter to or from you could be read by staff under the Headmaster's authority. Those letters could be withheld (although the facts and circumstances of letters withheld had to be noted in the log book, and the letter kept for at least a year)[29]. However, any letter to a manager, or to the Secretary of State or any of his officers or departments, could not be withheld[30].

If you were placed in a **children's home** run by a local authority, the law also entitled you to parental and guardian visits[31]. If a voluntary organisation managed your children's home, you could still receive visits. The law required managers to give the Secretary of State information about the facilities provided for parents and guardians to visit and communicate with children[32].

If you were placed in a **remand home**, the law stated that "reasonable facilities" should be given for you to receive visits from your relatives or guardians and friends, and to send or receive letters[33].

Apart from family and friends, what independent visits should I have had?

Inspectors:

If you were in an **approved school**, the Scottish Education Department was responsible for reviewing your progress through an inspector[34]. Under the 1937 Act, your approved school had to be open at all times for inspection by His Majesty's Inspector of Schools or of any appointed officer. Inspectors could examine your school records and record any observations in the log book[35]. Later, in 1961 law, inspectors had the power to interview you, as well as the staff at your approved school if they wished[36].

---

[24] Initially The Children and Young Person (Scotland) 1937, s79, and The Children Act 1948, s3; and later the Social Work (Scotland) Act 1968, the Children Act 1975, and the Children (Scotland) 1995

[25] The Mental Health (Scotland) Act 1960, s10

[26] For approved schools specifically see The Children and Young Persons (Scotland) Act 1937, Sch 2 paragraph 12(1). This extended to being under a duty to provide for your clothing, maintenance and education while in care: paragraph 12(2)

[27] SI 1933/1006 paragraph 19

[28] SI 1961/2243 paragraph 35. Postage stamps were to be provided free for this, once a week, by the managers. See later SI 1987/2233

[29] ibid

[30] ibid

[31] The Administration of Children's Homes (Scotland) Regulations 1959 SI 1959/834

[32] SI 1959/834 paragraph 17. The Secretary of State could also give directions as to the provision of such facilities

[33] The Remand Home (Scotland) Rules 1946 SI 1946/693, paragraph 14

[34] The Children and Young Persons (Scotland) Act 1937, s106, and Sch 2 para 6(2); see later the Social Work (Scotland) Act 1968

[35] SI 1933/1006 paragraph 24

[36] SI 1961/2243 paragraph 48

If you were in a **children's home** the Scottish Education Department could inspect that home as the law provided[37].

If you were placed in a **mental health institution**, the law generally required that inspectors or commissioners visit you at least twice every year, and inspect your welfare and the what arrangements were in place to care for you and control you[38]. These inspection requirements were replaced by new provisions in 1960 allowing for the institution, whether a private hospital or residential home, to be inspected at "all reasonable times"[39]. The inspectors were allowed to interview you in private if they wished[40]. These provisions continued under new mental health legislation introduced in 1984[41].

If you were placed in a **home for the disabled**, the law stated that any person authorised by the Secretary of State could enter the home and inspect it at any time[42]. If you were placed in a **remand home** then the home was subject to inspection at all times by an inspector[43].

Care authorities and managers:

The managers of an **approved school** were required to visit the school to ensure that your "welfare, development and rehabilitation" was satisfactory. Initially, these visits could be periodic, but after 1961 had to be made every month[44].

If you lived in a **children's home**, the 1947 law required a children's officer to visit you within one month of your placement in the establishment and at least once every six months[45]. The local authority was also required to arrange for you to be visited by an authority member at least once a year, and for a report to be produced assessing your health, well-being and behaviour, the progress of your education, and any other matters relating to your welfare if considered necessary[46]. These requirements continued under new legal provisions introduced in 1959 (and remaining until 1987). These placed a duty on the authority that administered the home – for example a local authority or voluntary organisation – to arrange for the home to be visited every month by an "authorised visitor" (usually a children's officer) who was to be satisfied that the home was being conducted properly in securing your welfare.[47] Finally, under new legislative provisions introduced in 1987, the local authority had a duty to ensure that your placement continued to be in your "best interests". The law required the local authority to visit within one week of your placement, and at least every three months after that[48].

If you lived in a **mental health institution** and the local authority had parental rights, someone from the authority had to visit you[49] under provisions introduced in 1960 and extending to 1984.

If you lived in a **remand home**, the law provided that a local authority member should visit the home at least every three months, with at least two visits a year made without notice[50]. You were also entitled to visits from justices and magistrates of juvenile courts from which cases were received by the remand home[51].

---

[37] See The Children Act 1948, s54, and The Children and Young Persons (Scotland) Act 1937, s106

[38] The Mental Deficiency and Lunacy (Scotland) Act 1913 s24

[39] The Mental Health (Scotland) Act 1960, s17

[40] *ibid* s17(3)

[41] The Mental Health (Scotland) Act 1984

[42] The National Assistance Act 1948, s39(1)

[43] The Children and Young Persons (Scotland) Act 1937 s82(3), as amended by the Criminal Justice (Scotland) Act 1949, and later incorporated into the Social Work (Scotland) Act 1968

[44] SI 1933/1006 paragraph 2; SI 1961/2243 paragraph 2(1)

[45] SI 2146/1947 paragraph 27

[46] *ibid*. Indeed, where a local authority took action on such a report, they were required to send a copy of the report to the Secretary of State together with a note of such action

[47] SI 1959/834 paragraph 2

[48] SI 1987/2233 paragraph 23(a)

[49] See the Mental Health (Scotland) Act 1960 and 1984

[50] The Remand Home (Scotland) Rules 1946 SI 1946/693, paragraph 19

[51] *ibid*

Medical officers:

If you lived in an **approved school**, the law required a medical officer to give you a thorough medical examination when you were admitted to the school and shortly before leaving it. While you were at the approved school, the medical officer should have examined you every three months and, under rules introduced in 1961, he should also have visited the school every week[52]. You were also entitled to be seen by a dentist initially once every year, increased to once every six months after 1961[53].

If you lived in a **children's home** the law said you had to get a proper medical examination when you arrived at and left the home. The medical officer was required to visit the home regularly, and to examine children at least once a year[54]. Again, you were also entitled to dental treatment[55].

If you were resident in a **remand home**, the rules generally provided for a medical examination when you arrived at and left the home. A doctor should have been appointed to act as medical officer and administer any necessary medical treatment. This medical officer was to make regular visits to the home and generally supervise your health[56].

What was to be done to ensure my welfare, education, health and safety?

If you were placed in an **approved school**, managers had a duty to provide for your clothing and maintenance. The school premises need to be properly maintained; this covered lighting, heating, ventilation, cleanliness, sanitary arrangements and safety against fire. After 1961 the law stated that you should have a separate bed in a room with sufficient ventilation and be given suitable clothing. You also had to be supplied with a diet of "sufficient, varied, wholesome and appetising food...adequate for the maintenance of health"; the diet was to be decided by managers after consulting with the headmaster and the medical officer and approved by an inspector[57]. A meal couldn't be withheld from you as a form of punishment[58]. The relevant fire precautions also had to be taken. Furthermore, the daily routine of the school education was to be approved by the SED[59], and the education itself was to be suitable in terms of your age and aptitude[60].

If you were in a **children's home**, the law also provided that you had to be provided with a separate bed in a room with enough ventilation and lighting, and easy access to suitable toilets and washing facilities[61]. Again, the relevant fire precautions were to be taken. New rules in 1987 applied the legal provisions on health and safety to all residential establishments[62]. Some children's homes may have also had an additional educational function. If so, the school was to be run in line with the rules in the various Education (Scotland) acts, providing for your proper education.

If you were in a **remand home**, and of school age, then arrangements were to be made for suitable schoolroom instruction either on or off the premises[63]. If you were in a mental health institution or disabled home then rules applied to provide you with education in a special school. If you were unsuitable for training or education in this kind of school, then the local authority had to provide or find suitable education for you[64].

---

[52] SI 1933/1006; SI 1961/2243; and later The Social Work (Residential Establishments - Child Care) (Scotland) Regulations 1987 (1987/2233)
[53] *ibid*
[54] SI 1959/834 paragraph 6, and later SI 1987/2233
[55] *ibid* paragraph 7
[56] The Remand Home (Scotland) Rules 1946 SI 1946/693, paragraph 9
[57] SI 1961/2243 paragraphs 18 and 19
[58] *ibid* paragraph 19 (1)
[59] SI 1933/1006; SI 1961/2243; and later 1987/2233
[60] SI 1961/2243
[61] SI 1959/834 paragraph 8
[62] The Social Work (Residential Establishments - Child Care) (Scotland) Regulations 1987 (1987/2233)
[63] SI 1946/693
[64] See, for example, the Mental Health (Scotland) Act 1960, The National Assistance Act 1948 and the various Education (Scotland) acts

The law made certain types of acts criminal in all the establishments described above. This was to protect you against mistreatment, abuse, and child cruelty. For example, anyone over the age of 16 could be found guilty of an offence if he or she assaulted, ill-treated, neglected or abandoned a child[65]. "Neglect" was defined as "[failing] to provide adequate food, clothing, medical aid or lodging". Various sexual crimes applied throughout the years of the review. These included homosexual acts, indecent assault, shameless indecency, and lewd and libidinous conduct[66].

What discipline and punishment was allowable?

If you lived in an approved school, then the headmaster, headmistress or staff could punish you in certain ways according to the seriousness of your behaviour. To maintain discipline, you could be deprived of "privileges or rewards", "conduct marks, recreation or freedom", or "loss of rank", for example[67]. You shouldn't have been deprived of recreation for more than one day at a time, and if isolation was part of your punishment it was to be for no longer than six hours in a suitable room with regular visits from staff[68]. After 1961, you could be denied home leave if you committed a serious offence[69]. However, any segregation for more than 24 hours, or more than two nights in a row, now required written permission by one of the managers and a report to the SED[70].

Corporal punishment was permitted, although from 1933 only a leather strap could be used: the rules stated that a cane or any form of cuffing or striking was forbidden[71]. The punishment was also very specific. For boys under 14, only two strokes on each hand, or four strokes on the backside over trousers, was permitted[72]. Boys over 14 could be punished with three strokes on each hand or six strokes on the backside over trousers. For girls, only three strokes on the hands were allowed on any one occasion[73]. And if you showed any signs of physical or mental weakness, the medical officer's consent was required before corporal punishment was inflicted[74]. After 1961 an adult witness was also required to be present if the punishment wasn't carried out in front of a class in a schoolroom[75], and the Secretary of State's permission was required for some forms of punishment, including corporal punishment[76].

If you were resident in a **children's home**, similar rules to approved schools applied. Any punishment administered to you had to be recorded in a log book, and, in general, any punishment for misconduct could only take the form of a temporary loss of recreation or privileges[77]. Corporal punishment was allowed, but only in "exceptional circumstances" and in line with whatever rules the authority that administered the home laid down about what type of punishment and any limits to punishment[78]. Again the medical officer had to agree to any punishment of any child known to have any physical or mental disability . In general, corporal punishment was permitted until changes in law under the Education (Scotland) Act 1980[80]. New rules introduced in 1987 gave managers the power to make arrangements for your discipline and control in line with a statement of functions and objectives – that set out how the home was run – but

---

[65] The Children and Young Persons (Scotland) Act s12, later amended
[66] Contained in the various statutes on sexual offences, and to some degree in the Children and Young Persons (Scotland) Act 1937
[67] SI 1933/1006; SI 1961/2243
[68] SI 1933/1006 paragraph 13
[69] SI 1961/2243 paragraphs 28-30
[70] SI 1961/2243 paragraph 33
[71] SI 1933/1006 paragraph 11
[72] *ibid* paragraph 15
[73] *ibid*
[74] *ibid* paragraph 11
[75] SI 1961/2243 paragraph 31
[76] *ibid* paragraph 29
[77] SI 1959/834 paragraph 10(2) and (3)
[78] *ibid* paragraph 11
[79] *ibid* paragraph 11(b)
[80] As a result of the decision in *Campbell v Cosans* (1982) 4 EHRR 293, subsequent amendments to the Act (see s40A) provided that the former right of teachers to administer corporal punishment was no longer justified.

this couldn't include authorising corporal punishment[81].

If you were resident in a **remand home**, rules for discipline were similar. When punishment was necessary, it had to take the form of a temporary loss of recreation or privileges, reduction in food, or separation from other inmates (but only if you were over 12 and had a way of communicating with a member of staff)[82]. Corporal punishment was allowed if the previous punishments were ineffective, but could only be administered to boys. Striking, cuffing and shaking were forbidden, and only a strap could be used and only then for no more than three strokes on each hand or for no more than six strokes on the bottom, over trousers[83].

What powers and duties did the Secretary of State have?

If you were resident in an **approved school**, the Secretary of State had various powers and duties. He or she could:

- withdraw your school's certificate of approval, if dissatisfied with the school's condition or how it was being run[84];
- order you to be discharged, transferred to another school, or placed in the community on licence[85];
- send you to an approved school if you were a juvenile offender (for example detained in a Borstal institution)[86];
- waive any provisions contained in the rules and regulations as he saw fit[87];

- consider the school's premises and equipment, number and grades of staff, and your education, training and welfare; if he or she felt any of these weren't good enough, managers could be given directions to achieve the proper standard[88];
- regulate how your school was managed and appoint new managers[89];
- specify the number of pupils allowed in your school[90];
- appoint inspectors to inspect your school[91]; and
- call for the return of any records considered necessary[92].

The Secretary of State had to:
- review your progress in school[93];
- authorise, after 1961, any punishment other than a minor punishment; this meant that authorisation was needed if you were to receive corporal punishment[94];
- approve any part of your school that was to be used as a special section for abnormal and unruly pupils; any pupil that was to be transferred there now had to have the Secretary of State's permission[95]; and
- approve the instructions to be followed if a fire broke out[96].

If you were resident in a **children's home**, the Secretary of State could:
- make regulations about how local authorities should carry out their functions and run the home, and for securing your welfare in the home[97];

---

81   1987/2233 paragraphs 5 and 10
82   The Remand Home (Scotland) Rules 1946 SI 1946/693, paragraph 17
83   *ibid* paragraph 18
84   *ibid* s83(2)
85   The Children and Young Persons (Scotland) Act 1937, Schedule 2 paragraph 6(2) and 9
86   The Children and Young Persons (Scotland) Act 1937, s62, as amended by the Criminal Justice (Scotland) Act 1949, the Social Work (Scotland) Act 1968, and the Criminal Procedure (Scotland) Act 1995
87   SI 1933/1006 paragraph 51; SI 1961/2243 paragraph 26
88   The Criminal Justice (Scotland) Act 1963, s2(1)
89   *ibid* s22
90   SI 1933/1006 paragraph 8, and SI 1961/2243 paragraph 5
91   The Children and Young Persons (Scotland) Act 1937, s106
92   SI 1961/2243 paragraph 49
93   *ibid* Schedule 2, paragraph 6. This was recognised as being a duty by counsel for the Lord Advocate (as modern representative for the SED) in *M v Hendron* 2005 SLT 1122
94   SI 1961/2243 paragraph 29
95   *ibid* paragraph 34
96   SI 1933/1006 paragraph 7, and SI 1961/2243 paragraph 4
97   The Children Act 1948, s15(4)

- serve a notice on the local authority not to use a property as a home if the property was unsuitable or wasn't being run in line with the regulations[98];
- give any instructions to managers if the management, accommodation or your treatment posed a danger to your welfare[99];
- consult on the people applying to take charge of the home[100];
- require the local authority to order you to be removed from the home if necessary[101]; and
- appoint inspectors to inspect the home[102].

The Secretary of State had to:

- require voluntary homes to be registered[103];
- receive notification of any action taken by a local authority on a report by a visiting officer about your health, well-being and behaviour, the progress of your education, or any other matter concerning your welfare[104];
- receive any information he or she required about your home's accommodation and staffing arrangements[105];
- be told if the person in charge of your home changed[106];
- be told about any outbreak of fire in your home that meant you had to be removed from the home or the part of it affected by the fire[107];
- receive any information he or she required about facilities for your parents and guardians to visit and communicate with you[108]; and
- receive details of your home, including (if it was a voluntary home) its name and address, the

name of the person in charge, and the name of any other government departments inspecting the home[109].

If you were resident in a **mental health institution**, the Secretary of State could:

- ask for special reports on inspections[110];
- after 1960, stipulate what registers and records should be kept[111];
- make regulations about the records kept, and reports to be given, by residential homes about who they took into care[112]; and
- after 1984, be told about any concerns the Care Authority had about your care or treatment[113].

The Secretary of State had to make sure (after 1960), through regular inspections, that **private hospitals** were being run properly[114].

If you were resident in a **home for disabled children**, the Secretary of State could appoint inspectors to inspect the home[115].

If you were resident in a **remand home**, the Secretary of State could appoint inspectors to inspect the home[116]. The Secretary of State also had to:

- approve the home for the relevant purpose[117];
- approve the appointment of the person taking charge of the home[118];
- be told of your committal under the 1937 Act, and of any death, serious illness, infectious disease or accident that occurred in the home[119]; and

---

[98] *ibid* s15(5)

[99] The Children and Young Persons (Scotland) Act 1937, s99. Repealed by s29(9) of the Children Act 1948

[100] The Children Act 1948, s29(9)

[101] *ibid* s16

[102] The Children and Young Persons (Scotland) Act 1937, s98 and s106

[103] The Children Act 1948 s29(1)

[104] SI 2146/1947

[105] SI 1959/834 paragraph 3

[106] *ibid* paragraph 16

[107] *ibid* paragraph 9(3)

[108] *ibid* paragraph 17. The Secretary of State could also give directions as to the provision of such facilities

[109] SI 1952/1836

[110] The Mental Deficiency and Lunacy (Scotland) Act 1913, s24

[111] The Mental Health (Scotland) Act 1960 s17

[112] The National Assistance Act 1948, s40

[113] The Mental Health (Scotland) Act 1984, s3

[114] The National Assistance Act 1948, s40

[115] *ibid* s39

[116] The Children and Young Persons (Scotland) Act 1937, s82(3), as amended by the Criminal Justice (Scotland) Act 1949. Later repealed by the Social Work (Scotland) Act 1968

[117] The Criminal Justice (Scotland) Act 1949, s51(1), applying s83 and s109 of the Children and Young Persons (Scotland) Act 1937

[118] The Criminal Justice (Scotland) Act 1949, s51(3)

[119] SI 1946/693 paragraph 9 and 11

- be told every three months of corporal punishments[120].

Also, **after 1968**, if you were resident in **any residential establishment** within the terms of the Social Work (Scotland) Act 1968 or the Children (Scotland) Act 1995, the Secretary of State could:

- remove you from any establishment[121];
- make regulations covering your welfare and how the establishment should be run[122];
- appoint inspectors to inspect the establishment[123];
- require local authorities to review your case at certain intervals and in certain ways[124]; and
- order an inquiry into, for example, the functions of a local authority or voluntary organisation under the 1968 Act, or the detention of a child under the 1937 Act[125].

Other powers extended to approved, or List D, schools. The Secretary of State could:

- withdraw approval for the school;
- change its classification;
- direct how managers should run the school; and (for voluntary schools)
- appoint managers and change the constitution of the managing body[126].

If you were placed in **secure accommodation** in a residential establishment, the Secretary of State had to:

- approve the establishment that provided secure accommodation[127]; and
- have access to records about your placement so these could be inspected[128].

Part 4. Conclusion

"By being silent it was our life-blood, our way of grasping anything just to be able to live."
(Former resident, children's home, 1944-1959)

A major theme among former residents' experiences, as told to the review, is that they didn't talk about their abuse as children or, if they did, they weren't believed or they were punished. As children, they learned to be silent about what they experienced as grave injustices. Former residents say they often expressed their unhappiness and fear through their behaviours: by absconding, becoming ill, acting out, crying, hiding and remaining silent.

According to Pinheiro, the history of violence against children is a history of silence[129]. The UN Study on Violence against Children[130], which combined human rights, public health and child protection perspectives, included the views of children directly consulted throughout the study. The study concluded that there is a lack of knowledge and understanding about violence against children. It urged member states to fulfil their human rights obligations to protect children from violence, which the study claimed required a multi-faceted preventative approach.

It is apparent that hearing the experiences of survivors of abuse can contribute to our understanding and our knowledge about violence towards children, particularly children who are among the most vulnerable – children in state care. If there is one overriding message from all that former residents have said, it is that people who listen to, respect and treat children with dignity make the positive difference in children's lives – not laws alone.

[120] *ibid* paragraph 17(b)
[121] The Social Work (Scotland) Act 1968 s22
[122] The Social Work (Scotland) Act 1968, s60 (1). Section 60 was amended by the National Health Service (Scotland) Act 1978, s109, Sch 16, para 29, and the Health and Social Services and Social Security Adjudications Act 1983, s8(3). Repealed by the Regulation of Care (Scotland) Act 2001, s80(1), Sch4
[123] The Social Work (Scotland) Act 1968, s67
[124] The Children (Scotland) Act 1995
[125] The Social Work (Scotland) Act 1968, s6A, as amended by the Children (Scotland) Act 1995, Sch 4, s15
[126] *ibid* Schedule 7
[127] SI 1983/1912 paragraph 3
[128] *ibid* paragraph 16(2)
[129] Paulo Sergio Pinheiro, Independent Expert for the United Nations Secretary General's Study on Violence against Children, see http://www.violencestudy.org/r25
[130] See http://www.violencestudy.org/IMG/pdf/English-2-2.pdf

Chapter 7

What more can be done? Conclusions and recommendations

Chapter 7

What more can be done? Conclusions and recommendations

This chapter is structured as follows:

- My conclusions
- A strategy for achieving progress for looked after and accommodated children and for former residents
- My recommendations:
  - For establishing a National Task Group for looked after and accommodated children
  - For meeting needs of former residents
  - For records

My conclusions

The Regulatory Framework

Looking back over a long period of time poses difficulties, not least the risk of imposing 21st century perspectives on action in the past. There's a scarcity of research material about children's lives in Scotland and about their experiences in residential child care. Attitudes to children have changed gradually but only in the last 10 years or so in Scotland has there been full acknowledgement in law of children's rights.

Attitudes to punishment have been inconsistent. Although evidence indicates that abuse of children was known about throughout the review period, public awareness didn't develop until the 1980s.

Throughout the period there was a lack of qualified care staff, perhaps a symptom of the low status given to residential child care.

The review has identified the laws that were in place from 1950 to 1995 to ensure that residential schools and children's homes in Scotland were provided, monitored and inspected. During that period, the context in which residential child care services were delivered changed constantly.

The regulatory framework didn't provide adequately for talking and listening to children and taking their views into account until the end of the review period. Before that, the laws governing residential schools and children's homes developed only slowly in acknowledging children's rights.

The laws in place during the first half of the review period didn't ensure that children's residential care services responded sufficiently to the needs of the children requiring the services. It allowed some children to be placed in residential establishments inappropriate to their needs. Despite changes to the law in the late 1960s and 1970s which led to improvements, especially in providing for children with special educational needs, it was the end of the review period before the needs of children being placed in residential establishments were met appropriately.

The law responded slowly to growing awareness of the abuse of children across the review period and to strengthening the protection of children in residential establishments and children's homes. Corporal punishment was permitted in residential establishments into the 1980s despite concerns expressed for example in SED meetings recorded in papers on file in NAS which date from the 1960s. And the law did not require inter-agency working to share information as an aid to protecting children until after the review period.

Accountability for children's welfare and safety were weakened by the law's lack of insistence that children's residential care staff should be suitably qualified, by the lack of a national vetting system for residential care staff and by the lack of national care standards.

Monitoring and inspection requirements were subject to a considerable degree of interpretation across much of the review period. In the absence of national standards of care, consistency in the expectations and assessment of quality and standards in residential schools and children's homes could not be assured.

Compliance, monitoring and inspection

The law specified in varying degrees of detail what should be monitored and inspected in residential schools and children's homes to ensure the children's welfare and safety. Visits by various people, professional and lay, and records were the main approaches for monitoring and inspection mentioned in the legislation and some visits were to take place at specified intervals. However, the law did not provide for independence in monitoring and inspection, nor did it require public accountability for inspection until late in the1980s. As there were no national standards for care, assessments of the welfare and safety of the children by visitors and inspectors could be inconsistent. And the vagueness of requirements for children to have the opportunity to talk to visitors could have limited the possibility of children expressing concerns about their safety. Although there is evidence in files in NAS of government inspectors talking to children during their visits, the action taken was at the inspectors' initiative and may not have been seen by the children as an opportunity for them to speak about any concerns. The lack of requirement for co-operation and sharing of information amongst professionals, may have inhibited valuable exchanges and limited the potential of the information for protecting children.

Identifying practice in monitoring and inspection has proved very difficult. The search for information was affected by people's knowledge of what records existed, where they were located and what they contained. Furthermore the former inspectors I interviewed told me that there was no policy to retain information about practice in inspection because, as practice changed, previous guidance papers were destroyed. Nor is there a central archive of government inspection reports for the period of the review.

Former residents have a key role in contributing to our understanding of past residential child care. The experiences of those I met reinforced my understanding of the importance of listening to, respecting and treating children with dignity. This I recognise as being fundamentally important to all children and all the more so to some of the most vulnerable children in our society.

A strategy for achieving progress

The lessons learned from this review are focused on two distinct but inter-related groups in Scotland:
■ children who are looked-after and accommodated in residential establishments; and
■ former residents.

Both groups have rights and needs and we must strive to do what is best for them in 2007.

Looked-after and accommodated children

The prime objective of the former residents who contributed to the review is to do all they can to ensure that children in residential establishments in 2007 don't experience the kind of abuse which they endured and have survived. It is for those reasons that an outcome of the review should focus on looked-after and accommodated children in 2007.

Having investigated the regulatory provisions for residential schools and children's homes in the past, it's clear to me that, despite extensive and complex regulation, the requirements weren't wholly effective in ensuring children's welfare and safety.

Twelve years on from 1995 new legislation and new approaches to safeguarding children in residential establishments are in place. Monitoring and inspection have been developed to give greater attention to child welfare and safety and the inspection processes have been developed to allow input by people from many professions. In some respects you could say that everything that was identified as needing to be done in 1995 is now in place. And yet, are the same problems are occurring? Do the same needs exist and are the concerns that motivated government to legislate in 1995 still evident? And what of the arrangements for children who are being looked after in other settings; is their welfare and safety good enough?

Former residents

I'm acutely aware that former residents have a range of needs resulting from their experience in residential child care:

- Some need support services, including counselling.
- Many would like to have their experiences as a child in a residential establishment heard and recorded – a means of acknowledging and believing what they need to tell.
- Almost all the former residents who contributed to the review require easy access to records that may contain information about their childhood.
- Above all, they want to be involved in discussions and decisions about the services provided to meet their needs, including their emotional needs.

The process of relating to and responding to former residents needs to be respectful, empathetic and constructive; for some, the experience to date has been dismissive and abusive. Listening to them and believing them is essential – after all that's what so many of them were denied as children in residential child care.

There is extensive experience in other countries of responding to and meeting the needs of those who have been abused when in children's residential establishments. There is much to learn from that experience in planning the way forward in Scotland, not least in finding ways of accommodating and meeting needs that aren't adversarial or disrespectful.

My recommendations

The lessons of this review point to the need for a new drive to:

- strengthen the arrangements for the welfare and safety of children in the care of the state
- meet identified needs of former residents for a range of support services, including access to records; and
- improve provision and practice for children's residential services records

I've grouped my recommendations into three areas:

a) Current provision to ensure the welfare and safety of looked-after and accommodated children
b) Former residents' needs
c) Records

a) Current provision to ensure the welfare and safety of looked-after and accommodated children

I have learned from a wide range of sources that the needs identified in 1995 still exist.

I believe there is a need to:

- develop a culture in residential child care founded on children's rights;
- raise respect for children in the care of the state;
- raise the status of residential childcare;
- raise the status of those working in residential childcare;
- evaluate the fitness for purpose of new policy, new legislation, new structures, new ways of working and new ways of monitoring and inspecting the services provided for children in residential care of all kinds; and
- keep the services provided to children, and practice in these services, under continuous review.

1. I therefore recommend that a National Task Group should be established with oversight of services provided for looked-after and accommodated

children. The Task Group should report to the Education, Lifelong Learning and Culture Committee of the Scottish Parliament.

The Task Group should be asked to:

i. audit annually the outcomes (those agreed through the Government's Vision for Children and Young People) for looked-after and accommodated children and report on the findings;

ii. audit the recommendations of previous reviews and inquiries to determine what action is outstanding and why;

iii. review the adequacy and effectiveness of the arrangements, including advocacy support, in place for children who wish to complain about the services they receive;

iv. monitor the progress in meeting the target of a fully qualified complement of staff in residential child care services, including the identification of barriers to reaching this target, and ways of overcoming them;

v. audit the quality and appropriateness of training and development for those employed in residential childcare;

vi. identify ways of making employment in residential child care a desirable career option;

vii. identify and disseminate best practice in recruitment and selection of staff in residential child care;

viii. ensure that monitoring and inspection focus on those aspects of provision and practice that will help to keep children safe and enable them to achieve their potential;

ix. monitor the extent to which self-evaluation is becoming established practice in residential schools and children's homes;

x. identify the most effective ways, through research and inspection findings and drawing on Scottish and international experience, of ensuring children's welfare and safety in residential establishments;

xi. review the quality and standards of accommodation for residential establishments and recommend improvements as necessary;

and

xii. make recommendations for research and development.

b) Former residents' needs

2. The government in partnership with local and voluntary authorities should establish a centre, based on an existing agency if appropriate, with a role that might include:

   ■ supporting former residents in accessing advocacy, mediation and counselling services.

   ■ conducting research into children's residential services, including oral histories;

   ■ maintaining a resource centre with information about historical children's residential services in general;

   ■ maintaining a database of all past and present children's residential establishments in Scotland

   ■ developing and maintaining an index for locations where children's residential services records are held

c) Records

The lessons of this review point to an urgent need to take action to preserve historical records to ensure that residents can get access to records and information about their location.

3. The government should commission a review of public records legislation which should lead to new legislation being drafted to meet records and information needs in Scotland. This should also make certain that no legislation impedes people's lawful access to records. This review's objectives should address the need for permanent preservation of significant records held by private, non-statutory agencies that provide publicly funded services to children.

4. All local authorities and publicly funded organisations with responsibility for past and

present children's services should undertake to
use the Section 61 Code of Practice on Records
Management issued on behalf of Scottish Ministers
and in consultation with the Scottish Information
Commissioner and the Keeper of the Records of
Scotland under the terms of the Freedom of
Information Scotland Act 2002[1].

5. Training in professional records management
   practice and procedures should be available to
   all organisations and local authorities providing
   children's services. This might be provided by NAS
   or the Scottish Information Commissioner.

6. The government should invite NAS to establish a
   national records working group to address issues
   specific to children's historical
   residential services records.

   Appendix 4 of my report contains suggested
   representation and terms of reference.

7. Voluntary organisations, religious organisations
   and local authorities, working in partnership,
   should commission guidance to ensure that
   their children's residential services records
   are adequately catalogued to make records
   readily accessible.

8. Record management practices should be evaluated
   regularly where records associated with children's
   residential establishments are held, particularly
   records associated with monitoring children's
   welfare and safety. I recommend that the Care
   Commission should consider taking responsibility
   for this.

---

[1] See http://www.scotland.gov.uk/Resource/Doc/1066/0003775.pdf

A Final Observation

A Final Observation

Having conducted this review, I have come closer to understanding why abuse was 'allowed to happen'.

I am convinced that monitoring and inspection are essential components in the framework of support and assurance for the welfare and protection of children in residential establishments. They can provide invaluable insights into the effectiveness of provision and the areas needing improvement, including the children's protection and sense of safety and they may contribute to the identification of abuse and abusers.

Although more work is needed to research the past and investigate practice, I believe that: the best protection for children in residential establishments comes from within:

- within the child – through the development of self-respect and confidence and from support through advocacy

- within the staff – through on-going development of their professional knowledge, understanding and skills and their sense of being valued as members of a team

- within the establishment – through the development of a culture based on the rights, needs and welfare of the children, which promotes open and constructive questioning of practice and relationships and objective appraisal, reflective practice and self – evaluation

- within the management – through support and training in good governance; through promoting and supporting self- evaluation and through constructive responses to the findings of internal and external evaluations including inspection

- within the external providing authority – through informed supervision and monitoring; through support for the establishment informed by objective needs analysis; through well focused and managed record keeping and through engagement with the institution in responding to evaluation from whatever source

- within the government – through good legislation, good communication, clear guidance, resources for training and development and effective monitoring of outcomes – and, above all, through support in raising the status of residential child care in society.

Appendices

Appendices 1 and 2 were commissioned to provide the context for and inform the work of the review. The contents of these appendices do not form part of the findings of the review and any opinions expressed are those of the authors and not the review itself.

Appendix 1

Societal Attitudes to Children and Social Policy Changes 1950 to 1995

Susan Elsley October 2007

Appendix 1

Societal Attitudes to Children and Social Policy Changes 1950 to 1995

Susan Elsley – October 2007

1. Challenges in undertaking a review

There are major challenges in undertaking a review of social policy trends and societal attitudes to children and young people between 1950 and 1995. First and foremost, this is a long period historically, starting from just after the end of the Second World War and finishing shortly before the Labour government took office in 1997 and at the point at which the Children (Scotland) 1995 Act came into force. A brief review therefore cannot do justice to what changed and evolved during almost half a century. It can merely highlight developments during this time, emphasising, in retrospect, significant changes.

Such a long time span also requires at least some acknowledgement of what existed before. By starting this review in 1950, it is important to recognise the influence of social policy and attitudes to children in a period stretching back to between the two world wars and to the Victorian period. The importance of this historical perspective cannot be underestimated. In the same way that many of those working in child care and social services today have experiences which stretch back through the second half of the twentieth century, this was also the case for those in the 1950s.

Analysing the experience of children in the past can also be biased by a twenty first century perspective. Improvements in child welfare may appear more insubstantial from a distance than they did at the time. On the other hand, what may have been perceived as a small shift in policy and practice in the past can signal a fundamental change in approach in retrospect.

Finally, there is not a great deal of research which has taken an overarching view of this period in Scotland (Murphy, 1992). There is also, more generally, a paucity of empirical research which has examined the experience of children. This, in turn, impacts on what can be concluded from the information that is available.

2. Methodology

The review touches on significant trends and major changes during the period 1950 to 1995. It has drawn on academic literature, constrained by time and resources from exploring historical accounts or other non academic documents such as central and local government documents which would have added further detail and perspectives.

As there is a very substantial literature that could be explored, this review has focused on a discrete numbers of texts relating to Scotland, the work of social historians, social work, social policy and research which has considered children and childhood. However, this could have been extended to other areas to provide rich sources of additional information. This paper is not an extensive literature review but aims to provide contextual background on the period of the Review.

The focus of this review is Scotland but it is impossible to look at this period without making reference to what happened in the UK generally during this period. Additionally, there are a limited number of academic texts on Scotland and some of the influences during this period were applicable to the whole of the UK.

3. Understanding children's lives

Understanding attitudes to children and childhood over period of time is a complex task (Frost and Stein, 1989; Hendrick, 2003; Hill et al, 1991). A number of particular factors make this particularly difficult.

Firstly, children's situation cannot be considered in isolation from adults, the state and social trends (Foley, 2001). The complexity of 'social, economic, political, biological and ideological factors' must be taken into account in children's welfare (Frost and Stein, 1989, p17). Focusing on improving the practice of those who are directly professionally involved in children in child care is too narrow. Influences on child welfare are therefore diverse and extensive and should not be limited to policies and trends which are solely related to children.

It is hard to define how children are regarded at any point in history. There are few texts which examine the history of children's lives. Sources of material which explored past ideas about children and childhood were not common until recently. In addition, children's lives are not all the same and there is no one single understanding of childhood (Hendrick, 2003). Children's experiences are influenced by their history, gender, class and culture (Frost and Stein, 1989). The evidence from the past is often insubstantial and indirect and those who try to interpret the past can be selective in drawing on evidence to validate their position (Hill et al, 1991). Children's perspectives were rarely sought until more recently (Abrams, 1998; Hendrick, 2003; Hill and Tisdall, 1997).

In spite of the challenges of defining attitudes to children and childhood, the position of children did change during this period (Hendrick, 2003). Shifts in understanding of children and childhood were, however, caught between opposing perspectives which saw children as both innocent and as threats (Cunningham, 2006). Frost and Stein(1989) highlight that children were the object of the 'good intentions' of society but also were an 'oppressed minority' who did not have a voice and were subject to abuse.

4. Scotland's experience

This review focuses on Scotland but also draws on commentary on social policy and child welfare changes in the UK[1] during this period. It is important, therefore, to consider what policies, practices and experiences were similar and where they differed.

Abrams (1998) states that what happened in Scotland in child welfare mirrored that of the rest of the UK, although there was something distinct about Scotland's unique urban and industrial experience. The pattern of religious affiliation and Scotland's education and legal system had a bearing on how children were protected. Murphy (1992) suggests that Scottish attitudes were strongly affected by three main influences; Scotland being a poor country, the dominance of a strong Calvinist religious tradition and an education influenced by both factors. In their study of the war time evacuation in Scotland, Stewart and Welshman (2006) describe how the Scottish experience of evacuation and the condition of children was understood through a structural explanation of poverty and social conditions rather than by blaming the behaviour of individuals.

The experience of Scotland in the Second World War influenced the work of the Clyde Committee which in turn impacted on Scottish child welfare and education policies (Stewart and Welshman, 2006). Murray and Hill (1991) state that although there were areas of common concern between Scotland and the rest of Britain, differences in the implementation of policies could lead to different outcomes.

Similar policies existed in Scotland, England and Wales until the early 1960s when different approaches to juvenile justice evolved and new organisational structures were put in place (Murphy, 1992). Murray and Hill (1991) describe four main trends in welfare in the period up to 1960 which reflect these similarities in policy. These were; linking juvenile offending to child welfare; the increasing role of the state in child protection; more focus on the use of foster care rather than residential care and greater attention to professionalisation and the co-ordination of services.

The picture that emerges is therefore of Scotland, England and Wales confronting similar problems and social trends but adapting policy and practice responses to meet particular cultural and structural differences.

5. Post war Britain

The Second World War was a period of great disruption for families in Britain. Following the war, there was a new sense of optimism and a desire to rebuild Britain social and economically (Lockyer and Stone, 1998). A burst of activity established the foundations for the welfare state with key pieces of legislation introduced in the immediate aftermath of the war: the 1944 Education Act, the 1945 Family Allowances Act, the National Health Service Act 1946, 1946 National Insurance Act and the 1948 National Assistance Act. The period was regarded as a watershed in British social policy with the Second World War stimulating a raft of welfare reforms and an interest in child care (Murphy, 1992; Holman, 1998).

As part of the process of rebuilding Britain, there was a strong focus on families and children (Cunningham, 2006, Heywood, 1959) with children regarded as an investment in the future (Abrams, 1998). This was demonstrated by the government's commitment to families through services for children in health and welfare (Foley, 2001) along with access to education and a range of work opportunities (Abrams, 1998). New collectivist ideas about welfare influenced childcare so that there was a wider concept of state responsibility than in the past with a move by government to have a greater involvement in families (Fox Harding, 1997).

6. Child welfare in 1945

The experience of the war was not the only factor that contributed to the new approach to child welfare. In the period up to the end of the war, there was a view that there needed to be significant changes in the way that services were provided.

The origins of the child welfare systems in 1945 stretched back to the beginning of the Poor Law in the first half of the nineteenth century. The 1908 Children Act was the first significant piece of child centred legislation of the twentieth century and separated the treatment of children who broke the law from adults (Murray and Hill, 1991). Juvenile courts were established in the 1930s which had a stronger focus on the welfare of the child.

The principles of the Poor Law remained intact up to the end of the war with child welfare and child protection responsibilities split between the Poor Law and voluntary organisations (Murray and Hill, 1991). Abrams (1998) views the contribution of the Poor Law and the philanthropic work of the late nineteenth century as providing a firm basis for child welfare which was adapted to meet Scotland's poverty and cultural diversity. However, Holman (1988) states that the central focus of the Poor Law was not on the well being of individual children but aimed to deter dependence.

By the end of the war there were improvements in the previously poor health and well being of Scotland's children. The death rate of children under one had dropped to 40 in 1000 by 1950, down from 77 before the Second World War and 100 before the First World War (Smout, 1987). There still remained major inequalities in society focused around housing, class and where people lived. Since the 1890s, there had been significant developments in early years education, but this was not the case in Scotland where there was not the same commitment to a child centred education. Instead an authoritarian culture remained predominant in the period prior to 1950 (Smout, 1987). In 1945 the school leaving age was raised to 15 years. The extended period that children spent in school was regarded as significant in changing attitudes with children no longer seen to have economic value due to their earning power (Foley, 2001; Cunningham, 2005).

There were a number of events during and immediately after the Second World War which gave additional momentum to the establishment of the 1948 Children Act. The experience of the whole population during the war and in particular the experience of evacuation had had a major impact on politicians, campaigners

---

[1] Most literature refers to Britain rather than the UK in this period

and the public (Cunningham, 2006; Heywood, 2001). The report, 'Our Scottish Towns: Evacuation and the Social Future in Scotland', produced by the Scottish Women's Group on Public Welfare (1944), the Scottish equivalent of the English 'Our Towns' report (Women's Group on Public Welfare, 1943), called for the greater prominence of the family in the rebuilding of the country and asserted the importance of the child guidance movement, nursery schools and closer co operation between home and school.

Concerns about the position of children who were looked after in institutional care had been prominently highlighted by a campaigner for children's welfare, Lady Allen, in 1944 and by the death in foster care of a young boy, Dennis O'Neill. The combination of these events led to the establishment of first the Monckton Inquiry in England, and then the Curtis Committee in England and the Clyde Committee in Scotland which conducted parallel inquiries into the situation of homeless children.

7. 1948 Children Act

The new 1948 Children Act was a response to the poor quality of care revealed by the Clyde Report (1946) and the Curtis Report (1946). The 'best interests' principle was enshrined in the act and indicated a move towards a much more child centred approach with welfare of the child regarded as central (Stewart, 2001; Ball, 1998). Children in care were to be treated as individuals, Packman (1981) states, rather than as a 'category' of young people. The intention was that that they were to have access to the same facilities as other children with provision no longer set at a minimal level. The influence of the new psychological understandings of children was evident with the importance of children's growth and development reflected in the act (Hendrick, 1997).

The 1948 Children Act was regarded as a major step forward for child welfare, paving the way for services through the 1950s and 1960s (Ball, 1998). Although it is generally regarded as an act which gave rise to significant reform, some commentators have questioned whether the act did actually signify a radical period in child welfare. Murphy (1992) states that there was not the same call for post war reform of child care in Scotland as in England and Wales with interest in better family services limited to a small group of professionals and politicians. In addition, the act did not support preventative work with the family. On the other hand, it set the scene for child welfare in Britain up to the early 1970s (Stevenson, 1999).

The Act, which applied in most provisions to Scotland as well as England and Wales, established Children's Committees. Murphy (1992) states that the act was not as fully implemented in Scotland as in England, with only four authorities and two counties meeting the Curtis figure of 400 children which was envisaged as being necessary to justify a children's officer. A part time and piecemeal approach to children's services was therefore adopted. Even where children's officers were appointed, this was sometimes seriously inadequate with the poor development of the structure affecting the service throughout the 1950s. Scotland did not take the opportunity to develop a new professionalism amongst those working with children (Murphy, 1992). Although the Clyde report and the act sought to tighten up the practice of boarding out, there was no attempt to look at the system from the child's point of view (Abrams, 1998).

8. New understandings of children

The two decades preceding the war saw a major growth in pioneering psychological research and practice which informed new understandings of children. These were instrumental in bringing about changes in the ways that children were perceived by adult professionals.

These developments had manifested themselves in a number of ways. Child psychology had begun to influence concepts of childhood and understanding of children's lives through, for example, the work of Cyril Burt on individual differences and Susan Isaacs on child development (Hendrick, 1997).

The new psychological understandings of children were given additional impetus by the establishment of the network of child guidance clinics. These had been set up across England, Scotland and Wales from the 1920s onwards with 13 clinics in place in Scotland prior to the war (Stewart, 2006). The child guidance clinics in Scotland, like the influential Tavistock Clinic in London, were underpinned by psychiatry and medicalised approaches to child mental health and well being. In Scotland, the influence of psychiatry in the child guidance clinics was balanced by its alliance with educational psychology which became stronger after the Second World War (Stewart, 2006). The clinics in Scotland were, according to Stewart (2001), the most significant influence on attitudes to children between the two world wars.

The child guidance clinics emphasised the importance of childhood in the inter-war period which, along with new psychological and medical understandings of children and childhood, meant that there was a greater depth of understanding of children and childhood than at any other time previously (Hendrick, 2003). In spite of this, there was little knowledge or understanding of abuse as a social problem in the early part of the twentieth century (Parton, 1979).

The work that had begun between 1920 and the late 1940s by Burt, Isaacs and others was developed in the 1950s and 1960s by sociologists, psychologists and psychiatrists, contributing to a greater awareness of children's well being and mental health (Hendrick, 1997). This work was influential in child care as well as coming to the attention of the wider public. However, Abrams (1998) indicates that it took until the 1960s for child welfare services to complete a fundamental ideological shift with a greater emphasis on the child's mind.

The contribution of these theories to child welfare was particularly strong in the work of bonding and attachment, drawing on the work of Bowlby (Stevenson, 1998). Where children were removed from home, Bowlby believed that a delay in returning them to their own homes could lead to the permanent separation of parents and children (Bowlby, 1953). He emphasised the importance of training for those working in family and child welfare and the proper care of children who were deprived of a normal home life (Bowlby, 1953). Psychology was the discipline that was used most widely for working with young people who were seen to be delinquent (Murray, 1992). Stevenson (1998), however, in more recent reflections on the influence on social workers of Bowlby and psychoanalysts such as Winnicott in the period from 1948 to 1970, states that skills from this discipline did not percolate through to the wider group of child care social workers. The predominance of psychological approaches also meant that children were seen as immature, requiring interventions which allowed them to grow into mature and competent adults (Heywood, 2001).

New understandings of children therefore made a substantial contribution to child welfare in the 1950s and 1960s, influencing the professional practice of those working with children although there is some question about how much this influenced professionals across the board.

9. Families and parenting

The work of psychologists and behaviourists from the 1920s onwards added to a greater knowledge of the developmental needs of children within the context of parenting. New notions of family rearing were more common in this period but, as Cunningham (2006) states, there was a tension between those who taught the principles of control and others who wanted parents to be aware of their children's feelings.

Family practices of parenting and discipline evolved during the 1950s and 1960s. Newson and Newson's well known work in the 1960s considered parenting practices (1965). They found that material changes of living compared with earlier generations had had an impact on families and that there was a move away from strict discipline practices with parents and children able to communicate much more easily.

In the post war period, the relationship between the state and the family was based on the ideal of a small nuclear family (Parton, 1985). The state took on more responsibilities for individual and family needs across areas of health, education and income. The notion of the 'problem family' who did not fit into the norms of good parenting became more popular after the Second World War (Hendrick, 2003; Welshman, 1999). This in turn had an impact on professionals work with disadvantaged families.

In the 1930s, experts in child care had come to the view that corporal punishment was more likely to do more harm than good (Cunningham, 2006). However, physical punishment was still prevalent in the period after the war with a widely held view that corporal punishment was necessary for the rearing of children. Murphy (1992) highlights that discipline in the home and in schools was frequently harsh and generally supported by society. Lockyer and Stone (1998), in their discussion of the Kilbrandon report and the development of the Children's Hearing System, indicate that discipline in schools was strict with corporal punishment accepted and widely used in Scotland.

Corporal punishment continued to be used in Scottish schools and was not banned until 1986 following a ruling of the European Court. Newson and Newson's 1960s study showed that 95% of parents hit children and 80% thought that they had the right to do so (1965). This study was repeated in the 1980s and it was found that this figure had dropped to 81% of parents hitting children with half thinking that they should not hit children (Newson and Newson, 1989). Families were using physical punishment to discipline their children but more parents were unhappy about this practice.

Physical punishment of children by adults was therefore a continuous backdrop during this period but its use diminished over the decades. Public, legal and political debate about whether parents should hit their children began to explore the possibility of legislative change in the latter part of this period. At the beginning of the 1990s, the Scottish Law Commission's Report on Family Law (1992), which informed the development of the Children (Scotland) Act, made a number of

recommendations on physical punishment which were not taken forward in the Act. The law on physical punishment was amended in the Criminal Justice (Scotland) Act 2003, although the hitting of children by adults was not outlawed by statute.

Parenting practices evolved during this period with more attention paid to the needs and wants of children, influenced by child rearing experts. Children were listened to more. The term 'problem family' was used to define those who did not meet societal norms of parenting. Physical punishment as a method of discipline was used less by parents and was banned in schools.

10. Reform in the 1960s: Kilbrandon and the Social Work (Scotland) Act 1968

During the 1950s, there was a realisation that child welfare was more complex than had been anticipated with the needs of the 'problem family' given higher profile and a rise in juvenile offending (Hendrick, 2003). Prior to social work reform, there were different groups working across child welfare in Scotland (Lockyer and Stone, 1998). These included volunteers in hospitals, a small number of psychiatric social workers, probation officers, welfare officers and a patchwork network of children's officers. There was little integration among these services. Titmuss (1967), writing on welfare in Britain, highlighted that the skills of trained social workers were fragmented and that there needed to be a move to integrated social services.

In response to these different factors, the 1960s saw major administrative reform in child welfare across Britain. The work of the Ingleby committee in England on juvenile justice was followed by the Children and Young Persons Act 1963 which applied to England, Scotland and Wales. This act gave local authorities the duty to provide assistance to families in order to keep children out of care (Murray and Hill, 1991: Titmuss, 1967). The McBoyle committee in its consideration of the prevention of child neglect recommended that a comprehensive social work service should be established in Scotland. However, this work was overtaken by the work of the Kilbrandon committee which in turn led to the Social Work (Scotland) Act 1968. This act brought together services which were previously separate as well as establishing procedures for the Children's Hearings System (Working Party on the Social Work (Scotland) Act 1968, 1969).

The impetus for juvenile justice reform in Britain was the increase in juvenile delinquency after the war, particularly among adolescent boys and young men (Hendrick, 2003, Lockyer and Stone, 1998). This gave rise to greater public concern about crime and young people (Murray and Hill, 1991). These concerns focused on the causes of crime, the appropriate way to assess guilt or innocence and the best approach for dealing with young offenders. On one hand, the young offender was a victim who needed care and treatment. On the other, the young offender was a 'miniature adult' who required to be dealt with through the law (Packman, 1981). In England, there was resistance to proposed changes which were similar to those of Kilbrandon.

A compromise was eventually reached in England with the retention of the juvenile courts with the intention of keeping as many children as possible out of the court system.

Although juvenile delinquency was a pre-occupation of the 1950 and 1960s, there was a more philosophical approach to juvenile delinquency in Scotland than in England (Murphy, 1992). Debate on the balance between welfare and justice had long been an important part of discussion about how to deal with young offenders in Scotland (Murray, 1983). A welfare philosophy was accepted as the framework for dealing with children who committed offences building on new theories of criminality from the early part of the twentieth century which had proposed an emphasis on adverse life experience as predisposing factors for offending ((Asquith, 1983; Murray, 1983).

In 1961, the Kilbrandon Committee was set up to examine measures for dealing with young people who were in need of care and protection. The Kilbrandon Report was published in 1964, followed by a white paper, Social Work and the Community (Scottish Education Department, 1966) which contained a significant number of the recommendations which were outlined in the Kilbrandon Report. Unified social work departments were to be established at local authority level as well as the Children's Hearings System.

The central aim of the new system was to ensure that children and young people did not have to experience the 'rigour' of the adult criminal justice system (Lockyer and Stone, 1998). Views on the response to juvenile offending were divided between 'corrective measures and institutions' and psychological approaches. The Kilbrandon proposals were based on a number of inter-related principles; the best interests welfare principle, the influence of home or wider environments, a central emphasis on family and the principle of prevention (Lockyer and Stone, 1998). The focus was on children in trouble, on their needs not their deeds. The Scottish approach was regarded as more radical than the equivalent changes in England (Asquith, 1983). In England, the report of the Ingleby Committee and Report (Report of the Committee on Children and Young Persons, 1960) had reiterated a view of 1933 legislation which linked neglect and delinquency (Hendrick, 2003). The Kilbrandon recommendations were more child centred and anticipated a future children's rights focus to services although this approach was not prevalent at the time (Lockyer and Stone, 1998).

The development of Children's Hearings System can be viewed as one contribution to an increased recognition of social welfare objectives (Murphy, 1992). The Children's Hearing System has been regarded as a unifying element in Scotland's juvenile justice and care and protection systems (Murphy, 1992; Murray and Hill, 1991. However, Asquith (1983) also warns that the welfare philosophy underpinning the hearings can also mean that children's rights are not adequately protected. When dealing with young people who commit offences, it is complex to reconcile welfare and more legalistic approaches. In addition, Children's Hearings do not have a monopoly over young people who offend. The age of criminal responsibility remains eight years in Scotland in the early part of the twenty first century, children can still be prosecuted and they have to go to court to have facts established.

The setting up of the Children's Hearing System along with the establishment of the social work departments were seen to be radical departures for Scotland's child welfare systems. The new approach to responding to the needs of troubled children was based on a welfare model, moving away from a more punitive approach for those young people who were regarded as delinquent.

11. Rediscovery of poverty

The experience of the Second World War highlighted the extent of poverty and provided an impetus for welfare reform

(Hendrick, 1997, Stewart, 2001). In the 1960s and 70s, poverty was 'rediscovered' as the public perception that poverty had been eliminated after the war was found to be overly optimistic. The work of Abel-Smith and Townsend (1965) highlighted that poverty was about more than a lack of essentials but also was about the extent of social inequalities between sections of society (Holman, 1988). These new perspectives encouraged social workers to look at the relationship between poverty and children going into care (Holman, 1988).

Government itself began to consider again definitions and understandings of poverty. In the early 1970s the Conservative government's Minister for Social Services, Sir Keith Joseph, put forward his notion of the cycle of deprivation, focusing on the failings of families as the problem rather than on a lack of resources and structural inequalities (Holman, 1988, Parton, 1985). Abusing families were therefore seen to have an underlying pathology (Parton, 1985) with parents passing on poor child rearing practices from one generation to another (Holman, 1988).

The renewed political, social and academic interest in poverty was matched by changing social and economic trends with the developing recession of the 1970s. Between the 1970s and 1990s the impact of increased unemployment and changes in family make up had significant implications for society (Fox Harding, 1997).

12. Attitudes to children and childhood

Childhood has been viewed as a period when children are both dependent and powerless (Stein, 1989). This perspective was more prevalent at the beginning of this period, slowly changing during the following decades. In the first part of the twentieth century, children were expected to be silent and did not have a voice (Cunningham, 2006). After the Second World War, children had greater societal importance as citizens as well as members of families (Hendrick, 1997). However, although children were of central concern, this did not necessarily result in a child centred society or mean that children were seen as individuals (Cunningham, 2006). The Curtis Committee, in its report, for example, did not speak out as strongly as it could have about examples of harsh discipline (Hendrick, 2003).

Attitudes did become more liberal as the twentieth century progressed (Hendrick, 2003). This could be attributed to improvements in standards of living, the rise of new psychological understandings and the decline of strict religious views that saw children as being culpable, new approaches to education and increase in respect for children's rights (Hendrick, 2003). Increasing concern for the welfare of young people also meant new approaches to young offenders (Murray, 1983). However, attitudes to children remained torn between different perspectives. On one hand, children are seen as special and the focus of society's energies (Frost and Stein, 1989). On the other they do not have a voice and are subject to exploitation.

Mayall (2007) highlights that there has been a long history of seeing children and childhood as separate from adults and adulthood. She defines children as a minority social group who continue to have low status and are socially excluded. Power inequalities between adults and children remained a potent force during this period with adults using their power to forward their own interests at the expense of children (Abrams, 1998).

There was an ongoing tension between a new and growing

understanding of children and a more longstanding view of the child, linking neglect and deprivation with being depraved. Colton et al (2002), discussing the experiences of victims and survivors of abuse in residential care, highlight that their experience reflected embedded social attitudes to young people who were 'troubled and troublesome' and were seen to be a threat to society. Hendrick (2003) points that much of the social legislation impacting on children characterised the child as helpless and children's presence as threats. Seeing children as threatening has often led to the reality of their experience as victims being disregarded. Stein, drawing on the work of major inquiries into abuse, states that many young people in residential care did not have adults that they could turn to when they were abused (Stein, 2006). There is therefore an inequality in relations between adults and children which is based on age as well as an additional disadvantage for children who are particularly vulnerable through a variety of circumstances.

Cunningham (2006) argues that the modern era of children began in the early 1970s with childhood being prolonged because of the raising of the school leaving age, children being seen as active contributors in family situations and the rights of children coming to be more predominant. Hendrick (1997) states that identifying attitudes to children and children from the 1960s through to the 1980s are more difficult. Although there were media and political concerns about child abuse during this period, these concerns did not necessarily have a central focus on the child.

13. Children's rights

Children's rights were not a new concept post war although there was not a wide understanding of children's rights for the majority of this period. Legislation began to incorporate limited elements of children's rights as far back as the 1908 Children Act. Children's rights had come to prominence in the early twentieth century when the Assembly of the League of Nations passed the Declaration of the Rights of the Child in 1924. In 1959, the United Nations adopted the Declaration of the Rights of the Child. During the 1960s and 1970s there was a growing awareness of children's rights with some arguing for children's liberation and for greater understanding of children's position in society (Archard, 1993; Franklin, 1986; Hendrick, 1997; Hill and Tisdall, 1997). In 1979 the International Year of the Child gave greater prominence to children's rights (Hendrick, 1997). However, it was not until the 1980s that there began to be greater international pressure for the establishment of a UN convention which would lay out children's rights. The UN Convention on the Rights of the Child came into being in 1989 and the UK government ratified the convention in 1991.

This growing awareness of children's rights during the 1960s, 1970s and 1980s did not manifest itself in a child rights approach to services. Instead, a welfare model remained dominant, focusing on the needs rather than the rights of the child (Hill, Murray and Tisdall, 1998). This dominance remained essentially intact in legislation and practice until the Children (Scotland) Act in 1995 which took greater account of children's rights in the principles of the act in a way that had not existed previously. In the period since ratification in 1991 and the Children (Scotland) Act in 1995, there has been a significant increase in the understanding of children's rights at a professional and, more moderately, at a public level. However, ensuring that children's rights are more than a rhetorical commitment has been problematic (Hill, Murray and Tisdall, 1998).

Attention to children's participation rights began to be more common in the late 1970s and 1980s although there was no indication that this had become embedded in professional practice. The lack of a focus on children's rights was highlighted acutely by the findings of the Cleveland inquiry (1988) which stated that children had not been listened to by professionals (Asquith, 1993). In undertaking work for this review it was noted that the literature on social work and child care for this period omits significant mention of children's rights up until the late 1980s and early 1990s, highlighting that a welfare based approach to services remained dominant.

By the late 1970s, new organisations were beginning to emerge which sought to listen to the voices of children such as Childline (Hendrick, 1997). In the 1980s, professionals working with children began to have a greater awareness of children's rights although child abuse inquiry reports showed that greater attention needed to be given to children's views. Abrams (1998) highlights that children in care were not viewed as having rights until the 1980s. This greater visible commitment to the rights of children in care was confirmed by Skinner's report, 'Another Kind of Home' (1992) which emphasised the need for children's rights to be central to their care while they were looked after.

14. Child abuse

One of the most challenging areas in child welfare since the 1948 Act has been the evolving definition of child abuse. During this period understandings of child abuse changed significantly. Child abuse was not a new phenomenon (Archard, 1993, Fox Harding 1997). However, up to the late 1940s, there was little recognition of abuse in the public consciousness (Abrams, 1998). The focus in the early twentieth century was on delinquency, neglect and the problem family rather than on abuse (Parton, 1979).

From the 1960s up to the mid 1980s, understanding about child abuse became more widely known with increased societal awareness of child abuse. 'Battered baby syndrome' was first identified in America at the end of the 1950s and came to prominence during the early 1960s through the work of Kempe and others (Kempe and Helfer, 1980). While interest in 'battered baby syndrome' developed within the medical profession in Britain during the following years, Parton (1979) notes that this interest was not replicated in the social work profession which continued to focus on neglect and casework with the family. Although the term 'battered baby' was emotive, it identified abuse as a medical condition rather than something that was deviant. Dealing with delinquency influenced child and family work in the period after the war but this shifted in the early 1970s to concern about child abuse (Parton, 1985). In Scotland, child abuse was not well developed as a professional concept with the first professional course in child care in Scotland only available in 1960 (Murphy, 1992).

An understanding of emotional, physical or sexual abuse was absent until the 1960s. It was given a particularly high profile by the inquiry into the death of Maria Colwell in the early 1970s (Abrams, 1998; Fox Harding, 1997; Parton, 1979). Fox Harding (1997) identifies that the public and the media became sensitised to child abuse after the 1960s. The publication of the Maria Colwell inquiry report in particular signified a change in child welfare practice and public attitudes and was identified with much wider anxieties about the position of the family, an increase in violence and permissiveness (Stevenson, 1998; Parton, 1985) The discovery of child abuse in the 1980s raised questions about whether child abuse had increased during this period or if there was simply greater awareness of the existence of abuse (Hill et al, 1991).

The Department of Health's summary of child protection research highlights that there are many definitions of abuse and that these often described incidents such as 'beating, sexual interference and neglect' (Department of Health, 1995). However, this summary states that the context in which abuse takes place is likely is to be considered by professionals before these incidents are considered to be abusive. This, of course, emphasises the difficulty of identifying what is child abuse as what is considered 'normal' at one time can be considered 'abnormal' in another (Department of Health, 1995). In parallel to this, parental and societal views of what is good and bad parenting change over time.

Other writers also emphasise that child abuse needs to be understood within historical and social contexts. Jenks (1996), writing about childhood and the battered baby syndrome of the 1960s, says that our tolerance of what could be regarded as abusive conduct has lowered over time. How child abuse and child protection is constructed is a 'selective process' with certain risks seen to be socially problematic while other risks are marginalised (Hill and Tisdall, 1997).

While the inquiry into the death of Maria Colwell focused on physical abuse, inquiries in the 1980s began to focus on sexual abuse with the Cleveland inquiries being most prominent. Scotland found itself having to scrutinise its own practice with regard to child abuse during the Orkney Inquiry into the removal of children from their homes by social workers. The Orkney cases in 1991 raised the profile of child welfare among the public in Scotland in a way that had not happened before (Abrams, 1998).

The many inquiries that characterised the period from 1973 until the late 1980s led to high profile public debate on what was child abuse. However, there was a lack of reliable evidence which could help in defining and diagnosing child abuse and identify what was the most effective form of intervention (Department of Health, 1995). Parton (1985) describes how social workers felt inadequate to the task of dealing with child abuse because there were so many contradictions in determining abuse. Hill (1990) considers a DHSS summary of conclusions from 20 inquiries in the late 70s. He identifies six areas common to the inquiries where particular mistakes had been made. These included social workers not always prioritising their responsibility to the child, risk factors affecting children being overlooked, social workers making mistakes in their interaction with parents, legal procedures not being used appropriately and interagency co-operation not working effectively.

The focus in this period was on the family. Colton et al (2002) state that by the 1990s, awareness of child abuse had moved to the experience of those who had been living in residential care.

Child abuse has therefore proved to be a testing and complex area of child welfare and has been the focus of public and media attention since the early 1970s when child abuse became commonly accepted. Inquiries and research found that there had been failures across a number of areas and that social work staff needed to have better access to evidence, training and education. Inquiry reports began to acknowledge that children's views needed to be heard more.

15. Developments post Social Work (Scotland) Act 1968

The period after 1969 was one of rapid professional reform in Scotland with the percentage of qualified field staff rising from 30% to 97% in 1989 (Murphy, 1992). The Social Work (Scotland) Act 1968 brought together services which were previously separate including probation, child care services and welfare as well as setting up procedures for Children's Hearings. Overall the act was seen as a significant development in child welfare with an attendant significant increase in financial resources (Murphy, 1992). The Children's Hearings System remained in place with essentially the same philosophy and structure as when it was established in the early 1970s (Asquith, 1993).

In Scotland, the implementation of the Social Work (Scotland) Act was followed by local government re-organisation which took place in 1975. This resulted in a two tier system with nine regional and 53 district councils. Services for children were divided up between these two models with regional councils taking on the responsibility for education and social work and district councils responsible for housing and recreation.

Inquiries and concerns about child abuse in the 1980s and early 1990s became levers for exploring policy and practice change. The Cleveland Inquiry (1988) in the late 80s was followed by the Orkney Inquiry (1992) in Scotland. Although the two inquiries had very different contexts, they revealed a number of ongoing difficulties in protecting children's rights at the same time as acknowledging parental rights and responsibilities (Asquith, 1993).The two inquiries added to more longstanding demands for changes in child care law but this was balanced by concern about a growing picture of poor quality care. To undertake changes in law also required changes in services. Asquith (1993) highlights some of the issues where progress was required at this point including improving the knowledge base of professionals in child abuse, exploring the adequacy of training, ensuring parental rights for early appeal against removal of children from home and the need for better inter-agency working.

In England, the Cleveland abuse inquiry was followed quickly by the Children Act (1989). Most of these provisions were relevant to England and Wales with some provisions relating to Scotland around services for younger children. In Scotland, there was a perception that there needed to be a similar overhaul of legislation for children (Hill, Murray and Tisdall, 1998). As a result the Child Care Law Review Group was established in 1988 to consider options for improving child law. The review reported (Scottish Office, 1991), making 95 recommendations but no substantial changes (Hill, Murray and Tisdall, 1998). However, this more muted response was overturned by Scotland's own major child care scandal in Orkney. In the same period, a child care inquiry was undertaken in Fife by Sheriff Kearney (Fife Inquiry, 1992) and the children's reporter system was reviewed. By the early 1990s Scotland was following England in reforming its child care legislation, publishing a white paper, 'Scotland's Children' (Scottish Office Education Department, 1993). The proposals were not necessarily seen as radical but incorporated many of the Child Care Law Review Group's recommendations (Hill, Murray and Tisdall, 1998). The subsequent legislation, the Children (Scotland) Act 1995 signalled a break with previous child care legislation and incorporated children's rights principles.

During the early 1990s, local government re-organisation was once again on the agenda with the abolition of two tier local government and reorganisation into 32 unitary authorities in 1994. By the end of this period, the statutory sector had a central role that would be unrecognisable from the beginning of this period (Murray and Hill, 1991).

16. Conclusions

There are major challenges in undertaking a review of social policy trends and societal attitudes to children and young people in the period 1950 to 1995. First and foremost, this is a long period historically. Those who have explored this period have suggested that there is not a great deal of research which has taken an overarching view of this period in Scotland. There is also, more generally, a paucity of empirical research which has examined the experience of children. This, in turn, impacts on what can be concluded from the information that is available.

Understanding attitudes to children and childhood over period of time is a complex task. Children's situation cannot be considered in isolation from adults, the state and social trends. The influences on child welfare are therefore diverse and extensive.

It is hard to define how children are regarded at any point in history with a lack of texts which examine the history of children's lives. Children's experiences are influenced by a variety of factors. Children's perspectives were rarely recorded in the past with their views not actively sought until more recently.

Substantial changes in social policy and attitudes to children took place in the period 1950 to 1995.In the 1950s, there was a new focus on the family with the development of the welfare state and the development of legislation which sought to secure the social and economic well being of society. Many of these developments focused on the family and, in particular, on children.

The 1948 Children Act was the first significant piece of post war legislation and laid down the foundations for children service departments. This legislation, which also applied to Scotland, did not manifest itself in the same level of children's services developments in Scotland in the 1950s.

Greater understanding of the needs of children developed during the period through the work of psychologists and psychiatrists. This new knowledge influenced professionals as well as parenting practices although physical punishment continued to be used during this period.

During the 1950s there was concern in Britain about the level of juvenile delinquency. This led to the different jurisdictions in Britain exploring how to respond to this trend. In Scotland, the Kilbrandon Report recommended the establishment of the Children's Hearing System, a welfare based approach to responding to the needs of troubled children and young people. The new unified social work departments were set up under the same legislation, the Social Work (Scotland) Act 1968.

The period reflects a growing understanding of the impact of factors on children's lives, particularly those who were most vulnerable. Although the notion of the 'problem family' emerged during the Second World War and was still present as an explanation of both abuse and poverty into the 1970s, the 'rediscovery' of poverty in the 1960s and 1970s increased understanding of the impact of structural factors on children.

Attitudes to children did change with a stronger perspective emerging of children as individuals and greater commitment to their rights towards the end of this period. This was given greater status by the UK government's ratification of the UN Convention on the Rights of the Child in 1991. However, there were conflicting understandings of children and childhood. On the one hand, children's vulnerability, their individual rights and their well being were increasingly recognised. On the other hand, children were seen as depraved and difficult. Although there was inequality between adults and children based on age, children who were vulnerable through a range of circumstances were additionally disadvantaged.

During this period understanding of child abuse developed although commentators highlight that abuse was not a new phenomenon. In the 1960s 'battered baby syndrome' became more known with a greater understanding of child abuse emerging in the 1970s and child sexual abuse in the 1980s. Much of the work on child abuse focused in the 1960s and 1970s on the family. Only in the 1980s did there being to be an acknowledgement of the impact of child abuse on those who lived in institutions.

References

Abel-Smith, B and Townsend, P (1965) *The Poor and the Poorest* London: Bell

Abrams, L (1998) *The Orphan Country: Children of Scotland's Broken Homes from 1845 to the Present Day* Edinburgh: John Donald

Archard, D (1993) *Rights and Childhood* London: Routledge

Asquith, S (1983) *Children and Justice: Decision making in Children's Hearings and Juvenile Courts* Edinburgh: Edinburgh University Press

Asquith, S (ed) (1993) *Protecting Children: Cleveland to Orkney: More Lessons to Learn?* Edinburgh: Children in Scotland

Ball, C (1998) Regulating child care: from the Children Act 1948 to the present day, *Child and Family Social Work*, 1998. 3 pp163-171

Bowlby, J (1953) *Child Care and the Growth of Love*. Pelican, London

Cleveden (1988) *Report of the Inquiry into Child Abuse in Cleveland 1987*. Cm 412. London:HMSO

Clyde (1946) *Report of the Committee on Homeless Children*. Cm.6911. Edinburgh: HMSO

Colton, M, Vanstone, M and Walby, C (2002) Victimization, Care and Justice: Reflections on the Experiences of Victims/Survivors Involved in Large-scale Historical Investigations of Child Sexual Abuse in Residential Institutions. *British Journal of Social Work* 32, 541-551

Cunningham, H (2005) *Children and Childhood in Western Society since 1500*, 2nd ed. Harlow: Pearson Education Ltd

Cunningham, H (2006) *The Invention of Childhood* London: BBC Books

Curtis (1946) *Report of the Care of Children Committee*. CM.6922. London: HMSO

Department of Health (1995) Child Protection: *Messages from Research*. London: HMSO

Fife Inquiry (1992) The Report of the Inquiry into Child Care Policies in Fife. Chaired by Sheriff Kearney. Edinburgh: HMSO

Foley, P (2001) The Development of Child Health and Welfare Services in England (1900-1948) in P Foley, J, Roche and S, Tucker (eds) *Children in Society: Contemporary Theory, Policy and Practice* Basingstoke: Palgrave

Fox Harding, L (1997) *Perspectives in Child Care Policy* London:

Longman

Franklin, B (1986) *Children's Rights* Oxford: Blackwell

Frost, N. and Stein, M. (1989) *The Politics of Child Welfare: Inequality, Power and Change* Hemel Hempstead: Harvestor Wheatsheaf.

Hendrick, H. (1997) *Children, Childhood and English Society* 1880-1990 Cambridge: Cambridge University Press.

Hendrick, H. (2003) *Child Welfare: Historical dimensions, contemporary debate,* Bristol: The Policy Press.

Heywood, C (2001) *A History of Childhood* Cambridge: Polity Press

Heywood, J (1959) *Children in Care: the development of the service for the deprived child* London: Routledge and Kegan Paul

Hill, M (1990) The Manifest and Latent Lessons of Child Abuse Inquiries, *British Journal of Social Work*, 20, 197-213

Hill, M., Murray, K., and Rankin, J (1991) The early history of Scottish child welfare *Children & Society* 5.2, 182-195

Hill, M and Tisdall, K (1997) *Children and Society* Harlow: Addison Wesley Longman Ltd

Hill, M; Murray, K and Tisdall, K (1998) Children and their Families. In English, J (ed) *Social Services in Scotland* Edinburgh: Mercat Press

Holman, R (1988) *Putting Families First: Prevention and Child Care* Basingstoke: Macmillan Education

Holman, B (1998) *Child Care Revisited: The Children's Departments 1948-1971*, London: Institute of Childcare and Social Education UK

Jenks, (1996) *Childhood* London: Routledge

Kempe. C. H and Helfer, R. E (1980) *The Battered Child* Third edition, Chicago: The University of Chicago Press

Kilbrandon Report (1964) *Report of the Committee on Children and Young Persons - Scotland* Edinburgh: HMSO

Lockyer A and Stone F (1998) *Juvenile Justice in Scotland: Twenty-five years of the Welfare Approach* Edinburgh: T & T Clark

Mayall, B (2006) Values and Assumptions Underpinning Policy for Children and Young People in England. *Children's Geographies*, Vol. 4, No. 1, 9-17, April 2006

Murray, K (1983) Children's Hearings. English, J and F.M. Martin (eds) 2nd edn. *Social Services in Scotland*

Murray, K and Hill, M (1991) The recent history of Scottish child welfare, *Children & Society* (1991) 5:3, 266-281

Murphy, J (1992) British Social Services: *The Scottish Dimension*, Edinburgh: Scottish Academic Press

Newson. J and Newson, E (1965) *Patterns of Infant Care in an Urban Community* Harmondsworth: Penguin
Newson, J. & Newson, E (1989) *The extent of parental physical punishment in the UK*. London: Approach

Orkney Inquiry (1992) *The Report of the Inquiry into the Removal of Children from Orkney in February 1991*. Chaired by Lord Clyde. Edinburgh: HMSO
Packman, J (1981) 2nd ed *The Child's Generation: Child Care*

Policy in Britain, 2nd edn. Oxford, Basil Blackwell Ltd

Parton, N (1979) The Natural History of Child Abuse: A Study in Social Problem Definition *British Journal of Social Work* 1979 9: 431-451

Parton, N (1985) *The Politics of Child Abuse* Basingstoke: Macmillan Education

Report of the Committee on Children and Young Persons (1960) (Ingleby Report), London: HMSO

Scottish Education Department (1966) *Social Work and the Community*. Cmnd 3065, Edinburgh: HMSO.

Scottish Law Commission (1992) *Report on Family Law* Edinburgh:HMSO

Scottish Office (1991) *Review of Child Care Law in Scotland* Edinburgh: HMSO

Scottish Office Education Department (1993) *Scotland's Children: Proposals for Child Care Policy and Law, White Paper* Cmnd 2286. Edinburgh: HMSO.

Scottish Women's Group on Public Welfare, (1944) *Our Scottish Towns: Evacuation and the Social Future* Edinburgh: W. Hodge

Skinner, A (1992) *Another Kind of Home*. Edinburgh: The Scottish Office

Smout, T.C (1987) *A Century of the Scottish People* 1830-1950 London: Fontana

Stein, M (2006) Missing years of abuse in children's homes. *Child and Family Social Work 2006*, 11, pp 11-21

Stevenson, O (1998) 'It was more difficult than we thought: a reflection on 50 years of child welfare practice'. *Child and Family Social Work*, 1998, pp 153-161

Stevenson, O. (ed) (1999) *Child Welfare in the United Kingdom* 1948-1998 London, Blackwell Science Ltd

Stewart, J (2001) 'The Most Precious Asset of a Nation is Its Children': The Clyde Committee on Homeless Children in Scotland', *Scottish Economic and Social History*, 21, 1

Stewart, J (2006) Child Guidance in Inter-War Scotland: International Context and Domestic Concerns', *Bulletin of the History of Medicine*, 80, 3, 2006

Stewart, J and Welshman, J (2006) The evacuation of Children in wartime Scotland: Culture, Behaviour and Poverty, *Journal of Scottish Historical Studies*, 26.1+2, 2006, 100-120

Titmuss, R.M (1967) The Welfare Complex in a Changing Society, The Milbank Memorial Fund Quarterly, Vol.45, No.1 (Jan.,1967),pp 9-23

Welshman, J (1999) The Social History of Social Work: The Issue of the 'Problem Family', 1940-70 *British Journal of Social Work* 29, 457-476

Working Party on the Social Work (Scotland) Act 1968 (1969) *Social Work in Scotland* Edinburgh: Department of Social Administration University of Edinburgh

Women's Group on Public Welfare (1943) *Our towns* London: Oxford University Press.

Appendix 2

Historical abuse in residential child care in Scotland 1950 – 1995: A literature review

Robin Sen, Andrew Kendrick,
Ian Milligan and Moyra Hawthorn
October 2007

Scottish Institute for Residential Child Care
University of Strathclyde

Appendix 2

Historical abuse in residential child care in Scotland 1950 – 1995: A literature review

Robin Sen, Andrew Kendrick,
Ian Milligan and Moyra Hawthorn
October 2007

Scottish Institute for Residential Child Care
University of Strathclyde

1. Introduction and Definitions

The issue of the abuse of children and young people in residential child care, both in the past and in the present, continues to be a serious concern. It has been the topic of a number of government enquiries over the past twenty-five years; some of which have focused on particular cases of abuse, others having a more general remit. This literature review has been commissioned for the latest such enquiry in Scotland, the Historic Abuse Systemic Review. However, it is important to state that this continuing focus on the abuse of children and young people in care should not overshadow the positive experiences of children and young people in residential care (Kendrick, 2007; Social Work Inspection Agency, 2006).

It must also be remembered that residential care is not the only public setting in which abuse takes place; Gallagher (2000) highlights that institutional abuse is not just a problem of children's homes, social work or the public sector, but occurs in a wide variety of settings and sectors and is perpetrated by a range of occupational groups. In an analysis of children and young people's calls to Childline about abuse and neglect, abuse by 'teachers or other authority figure' accounted for 138 (3%) of the 3993 calls over a 1-year period (6% of calls relating to sexual abuse only, and 3% of calls relating to physical abuse only). In the majority of calls, the abuser was a parent, step-parent or mother's partner (Vincent and Daniel, 2004).

The Scottish Institute for Residential Child Care was approached to carry out this literature review in June 2007 and agreed to undertake this work between July and September 2007. The focus of literature review will be residential care (residential schools and children's homes) in Scotland over the period from 1950 to 1995. It will identify, as far as is possible from the published literature, evidence of historical abuse and development of child protection policies and practice in relation to residential child care. It will draw on previous work by the authors on this and related topics in residential child care (Kendrick & Fraser, 1992; Kendrick, 1997; 1998; 2003; 2005; 2007; Hawthorn, 2006; Crimmens & Milligan, 2005).

On the one hand, there has been much written about the topic of abuse in residential child care in recent years and references are made to material which covers in depth what must be covered here only in overview; on the other hand, there are significant gaps in the literature, particularly that focused on Scotland until the early 1990s. Therefore, reference will be made to the gaps that exist, and to the wider UK and international context as necessary, although we make no claim to this review being comprehensive. In addition, in order to get an accurate sense of residential provision in 1950, it is also necessary to consider the context of residential care in the years immediately preceding the end of the Second World War.

It is necessary to start with some basic definitions of child abuse and residential care. While both child abuse and residential care are terms which are easily recognisable, what is understood and meant by them may vary considerably. Moreover, in the case of child abuse, what is covered by the term has evolved over time and continues to do so. The Social Work Services Group note that: 'The subject of child abuse is complex and a satisfactory definition of what constitutes child abuse is difficult to frame' (Social Work Services Group, 1985, p. 4). Similarly, in relation to residential child care, Kendrick and Fraser (1992) point out that different authors from differing professional backgrounds have used various terminologies when referring to residential care, making comparison difficult. What is sought here is to establish working definitions for the purpose of this review, which is not to deny that such definitions are problematic and subject to ongoing debate.

Residential schools are relatively easily defined as residential accommodation for children cared for away from home with educational facilities on the premises. The origins of residential schools lay in the combination of the Industrial and Reform schools from the Victorian era into Approved schools. At the start of the period under consideration, 1950, Approved Schools in Scotland, as well as England and Wales, were in existence and under the control of the Home Office. Under the Social Work (Scotland) Act 1968, the Approved Schools in Scotland became 'List D' schools and part of the Scottish Education Department. Subsequently the 'List D' schools were re-classified as residential schools from the mid-1980s when their funding was transferred from the Scottish Office to the Regional Councils.

The term 'children's homes' can refer to a wide range of residential provision for children who are not in the care of their parents and there a number of different classifications within the category of 'children's homes' (Berridge, 1985). Three publications on children's homes from 1960s and 1970s underline some of the different categorisations. Seed and Thomson's (1977) census of day care and residential provision in Highland Region and the Western Isles distinguishes between 'larger' children's homes, 'small' children's homes, 'very small' children's homes and 'family group homes' (they also include education hostels and lodgings as a separate category). Brill and Thomas' (1964) categorisation of different types of residential provision for children in England gives the following categories: 'the receiving home', 'the reception home', 'the observation home', 'the reception nursery', 'the remand home', 'the classifying approved school', 'the intermediate home', 'the short-stay home', 'the mother and baby home', 'the family group home', 'the permanent substitute family in a publicly owned building', 'the larger single home', 'the grouped home', 'the hostel for working boys and girls', 'the adjustment home', 'the long-stay nursery', 'the approved school', 'the hostel for maladjusted children', 'the training home', 'the probation hostel' and 'the probation home'. White's comparative study (1973) of residential provision in Hull and Edinburgh includes five categories of children's residential establishments: 'Small group homes' or 'family group homes', 'large homes', 'nurseries', 'hostels' and 'homes for maladjusted children'.

The term 'children's home' therefore covers a wide range of provision which has been differently described and categorised. The fact that this provision changes and develops over the period from 1950 to 1995 adds to this complexity. This paper includes a review of literature which makes reference to any of the residential care settings for children not in the care of their parents. It does not include settings which are non-residential – playgroups and day centres for example – or residential establishments for children and young people still in the general care of parents or other carers, such as boarding schools and short-stay hospital wards.

If we now turn to definitions of abuse, an early, and generally accepted, definition of child abuse has been provided by Gil:

> Any act of commission or omission by individuals, institutions or society as whole, and any conditions resulting from such acts or inaction, which deprive children of equal rights and liberties, and/or interfere with their optimal development (Gil, 1970, p.16)

More recently, the Scottish Office (1998) produced inter-agency guidance which identified the five categories of child abuse to be used when local authorities place a child on the Child Protection Register. These were:

Physical Injury
Actual or attempted physical injury to a child, including the administration of toxic substances, where there is knowledge, or reasonable suspicion, that the injury was inflicted or knowingly not prevented.

Sexual Abuse
Any child may be deemed to have been sexually abused when any person(s), by design or neglect, exploits the child, directly or indirectly, in any activity intended to lead to the sexual arousal or other forms of gratification of that person or any other person(s) including organised networks. This definition holds whether or not there has been genital contact and whether or not the child is said to have initiated, or consented to, the behaviour.

Non-Organic Failure to Thrive
Children who significantly fail to reach normal growth and developmental milestones (i.e. physical growth, weight, motor, social and intellectual development) where physical and genetic reasons have been medically eliminated and a diagnosis of non-organic failure to thrive has been established.

Emotional Abuse
Failure to provide for the child's basic emotional needs such as to have a severe effect on the behaviour and development of the child.

Physical Neglect
This occurs when a child's essential needs are not met and this is likely to cause impairment to physical health and development. Such needs include food, clothing, cleanliness, shelter and warmth. A lack of appropriate care, including deprivation of access to health care, may result in persistent or severe exposure, through negligence, to circumstances which endanger the child. (Scottish Office 1998, Annex C)

The current literature review is concerned with child abuse in residential child care and acknowledges that while there are some similarities with child abuse in the wider community, there are also important differences (Gallagher, 1999). Rabb and Rindfliesch (1985), for example, point out that some categories of abuse are more applicable to institutional settings than family settings; 'the category of harmful restraint and control has much applicability to institutional care but limited applicability to family settings' (Rabb & Rindfliesch, 1985, p. 287). There continues to be considerable concern about physical restraint practices in residential child care (Steckley & Kendrick, 2007)

The most simple definition of institutional child abuse is any kind of child abuse described in the five categories above, which occurs within an institutional setting. As with the concept of child abuse however, there is debate around the definition of institutional abuse, its indicators and the extent to which neglect constitutes abuse in an institutional setting (Stanley, 1999). Of the various framings of institutional child abuse, one of the most commonly known and used was provided by Gil (1982) which differentiates between:

1. **Overt or direct abuse** of a child by a care worker, which could be physical, emotional or sexual or a combination of them
2. **Programme abuse** of children due to the particular treatment regime
3. **System abuse** of children, where the workings of the child care system fail to meet the needs of children within it and prevent them from reaching their potential

Penhale provides a framework for institutional abuse, more generally, which corresponds to Gil's categories:

Level 1: abuse between individuals within the institutional setting;
Level 2: abuse arising due to the regime of the institution;
Level 3: abuse arising at the system level (broader social structure)
(Penhale, 1999, p. 6)

The concept of 'organised abuse' has also become a focus of discussion in some of the literature. Overt or direct abuse can be committed by an individual or a number of individuals, and may be planned or unplanned. Organised abuse has come into use in both institutional or non-institutional settings to describe a specific form of abuse which can be defined as:

[T]he systematic abuse of children, normally by more than one male. It is characterised by the degree of planning in the purposeful, secret targeting, seduction, hooking and silencing of subjects. Institutional and child abuse are but specialised forms of organised abuse. (Bibby, 1996, pp. 5-6)

The literature review is specifically focussed on historic abuse. Historic abuse refers to allegations of child abuse which occurred in the past. The Lothian and Borders Joint Police/Social Work Protocol states that:

Historic Abuse will include all allegations of maltreatment whether of serious neglect or of a sexual or of a physical nature which took place before the victim(s) was/were 16 years (or aged 18 in some circumstances) and which are made after a significant time has elapsed. Often the complainant will be an adult but some cases will apply to older children making allegations of abuse in early childhood (Lothian and Borders Police et al., 2001, p.5)

However, Hawthorn (2006) notes that the term 'historic abuse' is 'value laden and imprecise' because standards of child care and what constitutes child abuse have changed over time, and also what is publicly acceptable or accepted may differ from what is commonly practiced in the private sphere. The most obvious example of this in the period from 1950 – 1995 concerns changing attitudes towards the corporal punishment and physical chastisement of children. A 1960s survey found that 95 per cent of parents hit their children and 80 per cent of them thought it was right. The survey was repeated in the 1990s when 81 per cent of parents admitted to hitting their children but half of them thought it was wrong (Department of Health, 1995). For those investigating allegations of historic abuse, judgments need to be made as to whether the allegations would be classed as abuse within accepted practice at the time they occurred (Black & Williams, 2005; Hawthorn, 2006). In considering historical abuse in residential care, it is also necessary to recognise the experience of those who were subjected to mistreatment within the residential establishments which were meant to protect and promote their welfare. At the same time it is important not to condemn particular individuals or institutions for practice which worked within and reflected prevailing social attitudes towards child care standards and understanding (or lack of understanding) of child abuse at that time.

2. The Clyde and Curtis Committees: Setting the Context of Residential Child Care from 1950

In 1992 the Directors of Social Work in Scotland, in order to assist the Orkney Inquiry, prepared a report to provide an overview of social work practice in the field of child abuse and child protection. It stated:

An examination of history provides ample evidence that children have been exploited and abused physically and sexually down the centuries...child abuse is not a new problem; what is new is the heightened public awareness. (Directors of Social Work in Scotland, 1992, p.1)

Perhaps reflecting the context for which it was written, the report does not make reference to institutional abuse, focusing only on abuse within the community. Nonetheless, the quotation highlights the importance of placing child abuse within a wider social and cultural context. Social awareness and recognition of child abuse, whether it be within residential care or the community, is not linear but can be awakened and then recede from prominence. In 1857, Tardieu, a French physician published descriptions of thousands of cases of child sexual abuse only for awareness to fall back (Beckett, 2002). In the UK, child cruelty rose to prominence as an issue in the latter part of the nineteenth century in the UK, and this owed much to the philanthropic organisations which were created during the mid-part of the 19th century; for example, the National Society for the Prevention of Cruelty to Children (NSPCC), Barnardo's, NCH, Waifs and Strays (Parker, 1990). In Scotland, the Scottish National Society for the Prevention of Cruelty to Children (SNSPCC) was formed in 1889 following the amalgamation of the Glasgow society with two societies based in Edinburgh, while Quarrier's and Aberlour, the two largest providers of children's homes in Scotland came into being in the 1870s and 1880s (Abrams, 1998).

However, after the First World War:

The issue of child abuse, and indeed of child protection more generally, virtually disappeared from the public agenda, with the exception of a report from a Home Office committee in 1926 on sexual offences against young people. (Parker, 1995, p.7)

Hendrick further comments on the ambivalent attitude towards children during the inter-war years:

Although throughout the period 1918-45 children made guest appearances as 'victims' - usually of poverty, abuse, ignorance or neglect - their regular employment in the theatre of welfare was as threats in various guises: criminal, racial, social, mental and educational, albeit the word was rarely used openly. (Hendrick, 1994, p.207)

The period towards the end of the Second World War saw the re-emergence of child welfare, and to an extent child abuse, as an issue. Significant social changes, not least to the structure and scope of state provision and responsibility for welfare services, were the backdrop to this but there were specific reasons behind the re-emergence of concern for child welfare. Firstly there was the experience of large numbers of evacuee children during the war and the consideration that some of those children may not be able to return to their homes (Hendrick, 1994). This led to consideration of how to provide for these children. Lady Allen of Hurtwood's famous letter to The Times of 15th July, 1944, both reflected and projected growing concerns about the welfare of children looked after away from their families. Lady Allen was the Chairman of the Nursery Schools Association of Great Britain (Magnusson, 1984) and was the widow of a Labour peer, using her political connections to lobby for nursery education during the war years (Holman, 1996). Prior to her letter to The Times, Lady Allen had already written to the Home Secretary and to the Minister of Education about the poor state of residential care and the lack of co-ordination of child care provision (Hendrick, 1994).

Lady Allen's letter suggested there were huge shortcomings in the care system and urged a public inquiry into the care for those looked after outside their families:

> The public are, for the most part, unaware that many thousands of these children are being brought up under repressive conditions that are generations out of date and unworthy of our traditional care of children. Many who are orphaned, destitute or neglected, still live under the chilly stigma of 'charity'; too often they form groups isolated from the main stream of life and education, and few of them know the comfort and security of individual affection (The Times, 15th July, 1944).

In response to Lady Allen's letter, The Times received more letters about deprived children than were generated by any other single subject during the war years (Holman, 1996). Four months after the letter was published, the House of Commons passed a motion calling for an inquiry into conditions in residential homes for children which the Government agreed to in December 1944 (Hendrick, 1994). Two committees were established in 1945, The Committee on Homeless Children (1946) in Scotland, and The Care of Children Committee (1946) in England and Wales (referred to, respectively, as the Clyde and Curtis Committees from now on). While the remit of the two Committees was slightly different, their findings and tone were similar, and both fed into the Children Act 1948 which related to Scotland as well as England and Wales.

Shortly after the establishment of the Committees in 1945, the treatment of children cared for away from home was given added impetus by the death of 13-year-old Dennis O'Neill in foster care in England, and the mistreatment of Norman and Harry Wilson by foster carers in Fife. Dennis, in a state of under-nourishment, died as a result of heart failure after being beaten by his foster parents. He, along with his two younger brothers and sister, had been removed by the NSPCC in 1939 and boarded out to a number of different foster homes before being sent to the care of Reginald and Esther Gough on their Shropshire farm. The Goughs were convicted of neglect and manslaughter and the Monckton Inquiry was established in 1945 to investigate the circumstances of O'Neill's death. It highlighted the lack of co-ordination of child care services, in this case between two separate local authorities and the Education and Public Assistance Committees; the failure to provide adequate supervision of the foster home; and the shortage of appropriately qualified and skilled social workers. Less than six months later John and Margaret Walton of Fife were convicted of wilful mistreatment for severely beating two foster boys in their care, Norman and Harry Wilson, aged 12 and 10 respectively. The treatment of the children in the ensuing criminal cases also underlined the insensitivity of public systems of justice to children who had experienced abuse: Terrence O'Neill, the brother of Dennis, was put on the stand and cross examined for two hours until he broke down in tears. Norman and Harry Wilson were portrayed as out of control by the defence and the former accused of lying in cross examination, despite the clear evidence of their physical abuse - Harry Wilson's headmaster commented that 'it would have been impossible to put a two-shilling pence on a white part of his body so badly discoloured was it' (Glasgow Herald, 2nd August 1945, cited in Abrams, 1998, p.198).

The Clyde and Curtis Committees are important for a number of reasons. They were the first time that the system for the care of children away from home in the UK had been examined systematically, and they provide valuable information regarding the state of residential care at that time. Arguably, they provide a clearer overview of residential child care provision in both England and Scotland than was available for a number of years after. The Committees also laid the groundwork for the Children's Act of 1948 and the operation of the child care system in the initial post-war period. The Committees examined alternatives for children cared for away from their families which were, essentially: 'boarding out' with foster parents; children's homes managed by voluntary organisations; and children's homes managed by the local authority. Children's homes managed by voluntary organisations were by far the more prevalent in Scotland at the time of the Clyde Committee.

Despite the fact that the recent O'Neill and Wilson cases highlighted abuse in foster care, both the Clyde and Curtis Committees were unequivocal in their preference for foster care over residential care. The Curtis Committee reported on children's homes in decaying, damp, neglected buildings which were overcrowded and some children were still, over a hundred years after the 1834 Poor Law reform which set out separate provision for adults and children, living in workhouse accommodation alongside adults. As well as lacking the normality of family life, the Curtis Committee found institutions, particularly the larger ones, were not meeting children's emotional needs:

> The contrast between children in the Homes and the boarded-out children was most marked. The boarded-out children suffered less from segregation, starvation for affection and lack of independence... There was, we thought, much greater happiness for the child integrated by boarding-out into a family of normal size in a normal home. (Curtis Committee, 1946, Para. 370)

The Curtis Report did note disadvantages to fostering in terms of child welfare, but, using a utilitarian argument, recommended it as the preferred option:

> On the whole our judgment is that there is probably a greater risk of acute unhappiness in a foster home, but that a happy foster home is happier than life as generally lived in a large community. (Curtis Committee, 1946, Para. 422)

While the recommendations of the Clyde Committee are in keeping with those of Curtis, in Scotland there were regional differences regarding the care system. Rapid expansion of residential care for children in England took place in the 18th and 19th centuries, whereas in Scotland 'boarding out' was more common and the expansion that there was occurred only after the 19th century. One possible explanation for this was the mistrust of institutions in Scotland: as early as 1868 a report on the Merchant Company Hospitals or Schools criticised the idea of residential care because it removed children from home settings (Tresiliotis, 1988). The differences were reinforced by the different operation of the Poor Law systems in Scotland and England. In Scotland, there was no Poor Law provision for the able-bodied and no consequent need for a workhouse system to assess the suitability of applicants (Parker, 1990). As a consequence, by 1837 when the workhouse system was well established in England, in Scotland it was still confined to Paisley, Glasgow and Edinburgh. There was an expansion of the workhouse system in Scotland after around 1844 (Tresiliotis, 1988), but the preference for boarding out healthy children rather than placing them in workhouse provision distinguished child care policy in Scotland from that in England and Wales.

As a consequence, the Clyde Committee found that in March 1945, of children cared for under Poor Law provision in Scotland, 5,377 were boarded out, 959 were in voluntary homes and 749 in Poor Law institutions. The Committee also found that in addition to these children, there was specific provision for children cared for by the Education Authority under part IV of the Children and Young Persons (Scotland) Act 1937, where 'parents neglect children or are unfit to have control of them'(Clyde Committee, 1946, Para. 22). Children in need of care and protection could be committed to care of a 'fit person' and the Education Authority, under the Act, was deemed to be a 'fit person' while the Public Assistance Authority was not. Of 1,561 children cared for under such provision, 1,077 were boarded out with foster parents, and 484 were in Homes of one kind of another. The Committee further found that 4,788 were cared for in voluntary homes, 3,476 of whom were not the responsibility of any type of public authority. Of those children in public care of some sort in Scotland in March 1945, nearly 65 per cent were in foster care. In England and Wales in 1946, the boarding out proportion was 29 per cent (Frost, Mills & Stein, 1999).

The Clyde Committee was not without some reservations about the fostering system and strongly advised against boarding out to crofts in the Highlands 'where economic conditions are such that the practice of taking children seems to be regarded as an industry… Instances were found where children on crofts were overworked by their foster parents.'
(Clyde Committee, 1946, Para. 73).

The Committee also acknowledged that there had been 'isolated instances of cruelty to children, on which the fierce light of publicity has been brought to bear' (Clyde Committee, 1946, Para. 49), presumably referring to the O'Neill and Wilson cases. However, like the Curtis Committee, the Clyde Committee clearly came out in preference of fostering as the first option for the care of children, and described large institutions as 'an outworn solution':

The uniformity, the repression, the impersonality of these cold and forbidding abodes afford no real consolation to the children who grow up in them, and constitute a sorry preparation for entry into a world where the child must ultimately fend for itself. (Clyde Committee, 1946, Para. 45)

Undoubtedly the solution of the problem is the good foster parent… boarding out with foster parents should remain the principal method of dealing with the homeless child (Clyde Committee, 1946, Para. 46)

The Clyde Committee did acknowledge the need for residential homes in certain circumstances, these being where children were 'specially difficult', they were part of a large family unit too big to place in one foster home or where they had specific care needs. It also included a number of recommendations for improving residential provision. Amongst there were that large institutions should limit the maximum number of children housed in one building to no more than thirty. The Curtis Committee also expressed a preference for small group homes of not more than 12 children of different ages.

It could be argued that Scottish provision was ahead of its time in favouring boarding out, long before the Clyde and Curtis Committees supported fostering as the preferred option. There were other motivations at play in this choice, however, amongst them that boarding out was cost-effective and that there was a desire to 'rescue' poor children by completely removing them from the sphere of their parents (Abrams, 1998). Additionally,

the sense that the Scottish child care system was better could breed complacency about the standards of care it provided to children. When the death of Dennis O'Neill became public knowledge, there was an outcry followed by a public inquiry.

At this time *The Herald* wrote:

Fortunately, Scotland, as in most matters connected to the education and welfare of children, is much in advance of England, and there is little reason to fear that such things as have been called attention to in England could happen this side of the border. (Glasgow Herald, 7th March 1945 quoted in Abrams, p.198)

In July 1945, as we have seen, John and Margaret Walton of Fife appeared in court charged with the ill-treatment of their foster children Norman and Harry Wilson, and were subsequently convicted.

As noted both the Clyde and Curtis committees voiced a number of criticisms of residential care, and while neither identified examples of child abuse as such, they did highlight examples of extremely poor child care practice and institutional insensitivity:

We found no child being cruelly used in the ordinary sense, but that was perhaps not a probable discovery on a casual visit. We did find many establishments under both local authority and voluntary management in which children were being brought up by unimaginative methods, without opportunity for developing their full capabilities and with very little brightness or interest in their surroundings. (Curtis Committee, 1946, Para. 418)

Indeed the Curtis Report simultaneously notes and dismisses the suggestion that there was abuse in children's homes at that time, but also recognises the possibility of abuse in comments that have some prescience:

It is right to say in the first place, as regards Homes for children, that very little evidence, written or oral, has been tendered to us that there are seriously bad conditions in existing Homes in the sense of conditions involving neglect or harsh usage. Some witnesses have come forward to describe to us their own upbringing as inmates of Homes, and in a few instances the picture drawn was a very dark one. Even allowing for some bias and exaggeration, the treatment of these particular children had clearly not been happy or successful. It must be remarked however that the evidence related to a period of ten or more years ago and that there has been much improvement since then in methods of discipline and other conditions…We ourselves have seen excellently conducted Homes run by organisations which have been attacked. We do not therefore feel justified, so far as evidence of this kind is concerned, in forming conclusions adverse to the general administration of child care in any organisation or group of organisations. The witnesses in question did however bring home to us the danger, even in an organisation or under an authority with an enlightened policy, that individuals in charge of groups of children may develop harsh or repressive tendencies or false ideas of discipline, and that the children in their care may suffer without the knowledge of a central authority. A code of rules which sets a proper standard is one necessity but it is plain that no code will suffice without regular inspection and constant watchfulness that the right atmosphere of kindness and sympathy is maintained. (Curtis Committee, 1946, Para. 417)

For Hendrick (2003), the Curtis Report's finding of no evidence of harsh and cruel treatment, and its conclusion that discipline in homes and approved schools was appropriate, lacks credibility.

In Scotland, there have been a number of subsequent allegations of abuse in children's homes, some of which span the time when the Clyde Committee was undertaking its assessment.

One example identified in the published literature concerns the allegations of abuse by former residents at one set of children's homes managed by the Roman Catholic church in Scotland from the 1930s to the 1980s. Amongst the allegations were that children were beaten regularly, children wetting their beds had to walk around wearing their wet sheets and a sign on their backs, children were forced to eat their own vomit and girls on their periods were deprived of sanitary towels and forced to bathe in disinfectant (Abrams, 1998, p.232). Another example cited by Abrams is from 1947 where a housemaster's violent and 'unorthodox' behaviour towards boys in his care at Aberlour orphanage was reported by another member of staff resulting in both of their dismissals (Abrams, 1998).

Magnusson's history of Quarrier's (1984) reported some former residents' statements of abuse. One former resident from 1939-1946 spoke of how her five year old sister was beaten and force fed by a cottage mother for not eating the lumps in her porridge. Other accounts related that some house-mothers forced children wetting their beds to take cold baths. Magnusson notes that:

> The worst thing was that there was little help for it if a child happened to be in a 'bad' cottage. For children under the thumb of a cruel house-mother or father, complaining was out of the question; they would probably be punished for that, too. They were powerless. Besides, the children had virtually no contact with the higher authorities in the Homes, and each cottage could function quite independently inside its four walls. A child could be cruelly mistreated and few outside the cottage would know about it. (Magnusson, 1984, p.109)

A letter from the Chairman of Quarrier's in 1937 to house fathers in charge of boys' cottages highlights that the issue of harsh punishment was a live one at that time. The letter states that three complaints have been received about extreme corporal punishment given to the boys in the cottages. The complaints were from the RSPCC, a donor and a visitor. The Chairman's letter is unequivocally critical about such treatment deeming it counter-productive and 'loathsome'. "Thrashing' is wrong and represents a denial of that which is good in every boy, even the most troublesome' (quoted in Magnusson, 1984, p.109). The letter illustrates that there was a means for outside individuals and agencies to note concerns about the children's treatment and bring them to the attention of the agency's management. It also shows the Chairman's clear desire to stop cruel punishment of the boys, but the incident also demonstrates that such treatment did occur.

Complaints from those outside residential homes were not always addressed sympathetically however. Complaints received about a Barnardo's home in Scotland in 1945 were dismissed by the management there because they had originated from the remarks of the boys themselves (Abrams, 1998).

Further allegations from Quarrier's residents of this era appeared in the Sunday Mail in 1984, the same year as Magnusson's book was first published. In response, a number of other former residents wrote to the letters page, four expressing similar experiences of abuse. Three also wrote noting the happiness of their experiences in Quarrier's village. Magnusson acknowledges the accounts of those who experienced abuse but argues that these 'do not represent the true spirit and quality of life for the great majority of children' at Quarrier's (Magnusson, 1984, p.110).

After 1945, it is acknowledged that there were improvements in the residential child care system. As early as 1945, a Fife children's home stated that it did not allow staff to use corporal punishment of any kind, while in 1947 the Scottish Home Department questioned the use of corporal punishment for girls (Abrams, 1998). Further evidence that the issue of physical abuse in children's homes was live at that time is provided by Councillor Robina Lambie's request to Ayrshire Educational Committee on 14th October, 1947 for an inquiry into Dr Guthrie's School for Boys, an Edinburgh approved school. Cllr. Lambie noted concerns about escapes from the school which the parents knew nothing about until the boys arrived back at their homes, as well as allegations of excessive punishment. 'There are tales of beatings,' stated Cllr. Lambie (The Scotsman, 15th October, 1947)[1]. An inquiry was held and the majority report found that the allegations were unfounded:

> The head master averred that the forms of punishment used in the school were strictly in conformity with the Scottish Education Department rules for approved schools and he produced for inspection the punishment book and other records requiring to be kept in terms of these rules
> (The Scotsman, 10th December, 1947).

Cllr. Lambie however produced her own dissenting minority report:

> Mrs Lambie, in her own report, agreed that as far as she could see the material wants of the boys were well attended to. She said, however, that one of the boys interviewed persisted in his statement that he had been struck across the face, and he did so in front of the head master, which took some courage to do so. Another boy who complained of punishment was not available to them for interview.

> At present, legislation was being brought in for the abolition of whipping in prisons, and steps should be taken to abolish corporal punishment in approved schools. She cited the case of a boy sent to Dr Guthrie's school at the age of eight, and who was now 11. This child was a victim of home circumstances. Why, then, after three years in the school, was he not settling down? Why was he running away at every opportunity? That was not to say, she added, that the school was a bad place.

> Mrs Lambie moved that the Department be asked to hold an inquiry into the system of approved schools. This was seconded by Bailie Mrs Gibson, Kilmarnock.

> The Rev. A. M. Douglas of Maybole, a member of the deputation, said they had made a very thorough investigation, and he was satisfied that there were absolutely no grounds at all for any allegations of cruelty or carelessness on the part of the head master or any officials in the school. The work of approved schools was extraordinarily difficult, he added. They had to deal with a very difficult type of boy. Seventy-five per cent of the boys in the school had an intelligence quota of under 75.

> Mr Sim said the Education Committee could have no alternative but to accept the majority report. They should exonerate Dr Guthrie's school from any blame at all. He

---

[1] Thanks to Roddy Hart for providing the relevant extracts from The Scotsman.

understood that everything possible was done to make boys happy while they were there. Some returned in after years to visit members of staff. The meeting agreed to accept the majority verdict. (The Scotsman, 10th December, 1947)

There is a notable similarity in Rev. Douglas' statement, in the context of allegations of abuse, that approved schools had to deal with 'a very difficult type of boy' and press comments made about Norman and Harry Wilson during reporting of their foster carers' trial.

The Clyde and the Curtis Reports, therefore had highlighted important shortcomings in the provision of residential child care provision but stopped short of identifying abuse in any of the provisions they surveyed. They recommended smaller residential units replace large institutions and emphasised fostering as the preferred method of substitute care.

The resulting 1948 Children Act gave local authorities not only a duty to receive into their care all children who were unable to live with their parents, but to give them facilities and services which they might have had if living at home. It placed a duty on authorities to place such children in foster care wherever possible, and to place them in children's homes only where it were not, and as a temporary measure. The Act clarified the system for providing for children in substitute care by giving the Home Office sole responsibility over this area, and set up two Advisory Councils in Child Care, one for Scotland and one for England and Wales. It stipulated that local authorities had to set up Children's Committees to oversee provision of the children's service in that area, and appoint a Children's Officer who would oversee a team of social workers responsible for children in the Committee's local area. Children's Officers were to be appointed by the local authority but approved by Secretary of State. Finally, the 1948 Act also stipulated that voluntary services were to be integrated into the national child care system through registration and inspection by the local authority and government officials.

3. The Residential Child Care Sector After 1950

The period from 1948 – 1970 saw the 1948 Children Act provisions come into force and then be superseded by the Social Work (Scotland) Act in 1968. Following the report of the Kilbrandon Committee (1964) in Scotland, Social Work Departments replaced Children's Departments and the setting up of the Children's Hearing system.

The presumption against residential care, particularly for babies and young children, was given theoretical underpinning in Bowlby's highly influential publication (1951) on maternal deprivation and mental health. Bowlby was based at the Tavistock clinic in London but his work posited a universal theory of child development. It emphasised the prime significance of a child's earliest attachment to their mother, emotional bonds which formed or failed to form had a profound effect, it was argued, on a child's later emotional and psychological well being. The corollary was to underline the importance of maintaining a child within their family setting, or where this was not possible, in a substitute family setting that replicated this as closely as possible. This therefore supported the preference for fostering over residential care where a child could not be maintained with their birth family. Bowlby himself strongly advocated using familiar people as foster parents and temporary foster parents for short-term, emergency admissions (Packman, 1981).

A Home Office circular in 1948 had already emphasised the importance of preventative work with families to keep children with their parents in the first place and this was underpinned by local policy frameworks. The 'Edinburgh Report' for 1954 states:

The Committee wishes to emphasise that careful investigation takes place before children are separated from their parents – a step which may well lead to the final break-up of a family already unstable. Only when contact with every possible agency with a view to alternative measures has been made and proved fruitless does the Corporation exercise their powers under the Act. (quoted in White, 1973, pp.171 – 172)

The government also sought to regulate Children's Homes more tightly. The Home Office memorandum on The Conduct of Children's Homes in 1952 stipulated, amongst other things, the sort of staff who should be employed, and the decoration and furnishing of the children's living areas (Magnusson, 1984). Regulations for the operation of Children's Homes in Scotland were introduced in 1959, though this was eight years after their introduction in England – it is unclear why this difference in implementation occurred.

Bowlby's work (1951) especially influenced opinion against the idea of residential provision for very young children and resulted in the closure of a large number of residential nurseries, Northumberland County Council being the first to close its provision in favouring of fostering, in 1952. Other authorities followed suit though in 1973 Edinburgh still had some residential nursery provision (White, 1973).

Edwards (1968), a Children's Officer in West Suffolk, reflected the prevailing view of the time in writing:

If children cannot live with their own families, although care in children's homes may be necessary for a time, it is hoped that eventually a more normal substitute home can be provided by ordinary families who are prepared to take them into homes as foster children. (Edwards, 1968, p.40)

There were more pragmatic reasons which favoured foster care as well however. Residential care was up to three times more expensive than foster care (Frost et al., 1999; Kahan, 2000; Crimmens & Milligan, 2005; Parker, 1990). Part of the reason for this was the explicit desire in the Clyde and Curtis Committees to keep fostering allowances down to the minimum needed to maintain children in their care following the baby-farming scandals of the 1870s, and the consequent concern that higher fostering allowances would attract carers with the wrong motives. There was, therefore, a 'happy coincidence', in Parker's words (1990), between financial imperatives and what prevailing public policy deemed to be the best practice for children who were received into public care.

However, whereas in England there was a significant increase in the proportion of children in foster care, (growing from 35 per cent of all children in care provision in 1949 to 45 per cent in 1968), in Scotland the proportion, starting from a higher base, remained roughly constant; falling from 61 per cent of all children in care provision in 1949 to 58 per cent in 1968 (White, 1973). There was also a marked difference in the use of voluntary and local authority home provision in the two countries, with the proportion of local authority provision in Scotland far smaller. In Scotland in 1949, 15 per cent of children in public care were in local authority homes; by 1968 this was 16 per cent. In England in 1949, 44 per cent of children were in local authority homes, by

1968, largely with the increase in fostering, this had fallen to 29 per cent (White, 1973).

Apart from cuts in residential places in the first years after 1948, increasing numbers of children in public care overall meant there was still demand for residential child care provision (Kendrick & Fraser, 1992; Packman, 1981). Moreover, by the early 1960s, placement breakdown rates in foster care, sometimes approaching as high as 50 per cent, resulted in practitioners coming to believe in a need for a better balance between residential and foster care (Kahan, 2000; Tresiliotis, 1988). What did change, was that, in England, Wales and Scotland after 1948, residential care increasingly became used for older children, disabled children and children with severe problems (Tresiliotis, 1988; Frost et al., 1999). The reasons that children were admitted into public care were also changing. At the turn of the 20th century, most children in children's homes in Scotland were orphaned (Abrams, 1998; Magnusson, 1984). Increasingly, however, in the subsequent fifty years, children coming into care had parents who were still living but who were unable, or unwilling, to provide appropriate care for them and this trend continued after 1948. A child's 'illegitimacy' also became a significant reason for children being received into public care in the first decades after 1945, a greater proportion of children being placed in public care for this reason in Scotland than England and Wales (White, 1973).

There were improvements in the residential sector in the period after 1948 in the UK as a whole, as it responded to the observations of the Clyde and Curtis Reports to reduce the size of units and improve both the physical layout of the buildings as well as their furnishing; particularly with the development of the 'family group home' as envisaged in the Curtis Report. Progress was made on the goal of providing children in residential care with food, clothing, activities and facilities comparable to those which children in the community enjoyed, though the goal was far from fully achieved (Berry, 1975; Tresiliotis, 1988). While there is a paucity of information in the literature regarding changes within the residential sector in Scotland as a whole during this period, White's study (1973) shows that developments in the residential sector were subject to considerable regional variation. He notes that, in respect of Edinburgh, the local authority took up to twenty years to respond to the ideas behind the Clyde Report and the 1948 Children Act. The size and use of homes remained the same as before with 'family group homes' planned from 1962 onwards only.

In England, the recommendations of early Children's Committees suggested, amongst other things, 'Aunt and Uncle' befriending schemes to support children's emotional development, and the disapproval of particular punishments such as the denial of food, 'sending to Coventry', shutting children in dark cupboards and sending children to bed in the daytime (Packman, 1981). In 1948, Manchester Children's Department's Children's Committee discussed the draft rules made by the children's home and remand homes sub-committee. They excluded as acceptable punishment the denial of ordinary diet, corporal punishment to girls and infants and any other form of corporal punishment to boys other than four strokes of the tawse. One member of the committee wanted all corporal punishment excluded. After debate, it was agreed that, on trial, no corporal punishment would be allowed for six months (Holman, 1996)[2]. There was also concern about the quality of provision for children and young people in Styal Cottage Homes within the same Children's Department. A number of complaints were raised about staff behaviour, ranging from a member of the public seeing a

housemother hitting a child several times, a relative visiting a child who was shivering after being smacked, and verbal abuse, including some racist abuse, towards children and young people. Holman notes that:

Probably in the past similar complaints had been voiced, but now the difference was that the children's officer took them seriously and insisted on full investigations (Holman, 1996, p.32)

The children's officer, Ian Brown, presented recommendations to the Children's Committee which were accepted. These were for reductions in the numbers of children in each cottage with each having a gender mix of both residents and staff, reductions in domestic duties for the children, improvements in diet and clothing, attendance at outside schools, and that the children should be given bikes with encouragement to make outside visits (Holman, 1996).

Magnusson (1984) documents that Quarrier's held its first Boy's and Girls' Council in 1967 to take on board children's input on the running of the homes in which they stayed. Improvements in the residential child care sector were also reflected in King Raynes and Tizard's (1971) comparison of different forms of residential care. While the description of hospital wards for children with disabilities was resonant of the conditions that Clyde and Curtis had encountered in children's homes over twenty years earlier (Berry, 1975; Packman, 1981), local authority and voluntary children's homes were found to have more child-centred ways of providing care.

The period from 1945 to1970 is widely portrayed in the literature as a 'good' one for the residential child care sector and one of optimism for the child care system generally, with a positive belief in the ability of public intervention to make a positive difference to children's lives (Corby, Doig & Roberts, 2001; Hendrick, 2003; Crimmens & Milligan, 2005; Packman, 1981). Corby et al. (2001) state that: "Arguably the period between 1948 and 1971 was one of the most successful eras in the history of residential care for children." (Corby et al. 2001, p.28). Furthermore, in 1975, Packman wrote:

Now, residential care for children is regarded as both an important and integral part of the service and it covers a wide range of establishments of different size and specialism (Packman, 1981, pp.147-148 [first edition published 1975])

The first half of the 1970s, possibly with a growing awareness of child abuse, saw a steep rise in the number of children in care in both England and Wales, and Scotland, and the numbers remained at that level in the second half of the decade (Abrams, 1998; Corby et al., 2001; Crimmens & Milligan, 2005; Frost et al., 1999). The 'rate per 1000' of children in public care in England and Wales rose from 6.4 per 1000 (87,400 children and young people) to 7.8 per 1000 (100,200) in 1980 (Dingwall & Eekelaar in Corby et al., 2001, p.31). As a result, by 1976 there was the highest ever number of children in residential care in the UK (Crimmens & Milligan, 2005). In Scotland, the numbers in residential care fell steadily from just under 6,000 children and young people in 1954, to under 4,000 by the early 1970s and then peaked at over 6,300 in the mid-1970s. Many of these children remained in residential provisions for substantial portions of their childhoods (Abrams, 1998; Mainey et al., 2006).

However, there was still an underlying concern that residential child care provision was less than satisfactory. In the 1960s the focus on preventative work with families emphasised maintaining children with their families wherever possible while

---

[2] Holman notes that the Committee seem to have overlooked that remand homes and approved schools were managed by the Home Office which did allow use of the cane.

the gathering critique of institutions as places whose mode of working necessarily failed to be responsive to the needs of those living within them (Goffman, 1961; Foucault, 1979), had an effect on the way in which residential homes were viewed. In Scotland, this may have reinforced a pre-existing scepticism regarding residential provision (Tresiliotis, 1988).

While there was an 'unparalleled paucity of research studies focussing either on the ongoing experiences of children [in residential care] or on outcomes, especially the latter' (Tresiliotis, 1988, p.10), the available evidence was not generally positive about residential care. While King et al.'s study (1971) reflected positives about residential children homes, other studies generally did not. Dinnage and Kellmer Pringle (1967) reviewed available research about residential child care in the USA, Western Europe, Israel and the UK 1948-66. They explicitly reject the idea that children are necessarily best placed outwith residential provision:

> There is little basis for such a sweeping rejection of residential homes. On the contrary, there is some evidence that certain children may find it easier to accept, or cope with, a larger, less intimate environment since it is makes less intensive, emotional demands (Dinnage & Kellmer Pringle, 1967, p.37).

They did, however, reject residential nurseries as a suitable long term provision and comment that for older children and young people:

> The two potentially most damaging aspects of residential care are that a psychologically, culturally and educationally restricted, impoverished or, at worst, even depriving substitute environment may unintentionally be provided; secondly that unless special steps are taken, children may grow up without a personal sense of identity, lacking a coherent picture of both their past and their future. (Dinnage & Kellmer Pringle, 1967, p.35)

Berry's (1975) study of 44 children's units in England found that while the care afforded in residential homes had improved since the Curtis Report, not all of its criticisms of residential provision had not been comprehensively addressed. The study found units containing 43 per cent of the children offered 'a mid-point standard of good-enough care', with 17 per cent in more positive units and 40 per cent in more negative units and commented:

> The central, indisputable fact is that a sizeable proportion of children have a comparatively poor experience of daily care in residential life, and this appears to be linked with their care-givers receiving similarly poor experience of ongoing support (Berry, 1975, p.157).

From 1976, the Labour Government began a policy of spending restraint, including the budgets of local authorities. Alongside the questions still being raised about the suitability of residential child care provision and an emphasis on preventative work to keep children with their families, concerns over reducing costs led to a concerted shrinkage in the size of the residential sector (Crimmens & Milligan, 2005). In 1976, almost twice as many children and young people were in residential care compared to those in foster care, whereas in the early 1990s there are more than twice as many children in foster care compared to those in residential care (Skinner, 1992) and by the end of the 1980s the number of children in residential places had fallen to a third from their mid-1970s peak (Kendrick, 2003). This is illustrated in the following table:

Placement in Residential Establishments by sector, 1977 and 1989

	1977	1989
Local authority children's home	2603	1139
Voluntary organisation children's home	170	
List D school (former List D after 1986)	1355	559
Other establishments	921	496
Total Numbers in Residential Establishments	6209	2364

(Kendrick & Fraser, 1992, pp. 14-15)

Kendrick and Fraser (1992) pointed out that this picture of overall decline in the number of children in residential placements masked important differences in the changing role of residential placements for children of different ages. In 1977, 33 per cent of children in care who were aged under five years old were placed in residential care, but this had reduced to four per cent by 1989. For children aged 12 years and older, the reduction in the proportion placed in residential care was much smaller; 34 per cent of 12 to 17 year olds were in residential care in 1977 compared to 30 per cent in 1989.

The 1990s saw a continuing, if slower, reduction in the numbers of children in residential care. Placements were primarily viewed as temporary, pending a return to parental care, foster care or independent living (Mainey et al., 2006).
While the number of children becoming 'looked after' have been increasing gradually in Scotland in recent years, most of the increase has been due to children being looked after at home or with family or friends (Mainey et al., 2006). The average age of children in care, in all types of placement, has also been falling in recent years (Scottish Executive, 2006).
The most recently available figures show that there were just under 13,000 looked after children on 31 March 2006 (Scottish Executive, 2006). Forty-two per cent (5,506) of these were living at home and a further 13 per cent (1,726) were living with friends or relatives. Twenty-nine per cent of children (3,731) were in foster care and 13 per cent (1,638) were placed in in residential care (Scottish Executive, 2006).

The number of residential establishments in Scotland shows a slightly different pattern. In the mid-1970s, there were 288 establishments, and this fell to 158 at the end of the 1980s. However, this had increased to 207 in 2002. This can be explained by the long-term decrease in the size of residential establishments; falling from an average of 25 places in the 1970s to an average of 10 places (Scottish Executive, 2003).

The respective roles of the local authority, voluntary and private sectors in the provision of residential child care remain largely the same as in the early 1980s, albeit on a smaller scale. Nearly all of Scotland's 32 local authorities still directly manage at least one children's home (although two have 'sub-contracted' this task to a major voluntary organisation). There are a small number of private (not-for-profit) providers, though the number of places they provide is growing. Scotland retains a relatively large number of residential schools, which are nearly all run by the voluntary sector. Some of these schools are part of national religious or charitable organisations and some are small, charitable or other not-for-profit organisations. These schools are in the main the successors to the old 'List D' schools and between them they provide about half of the residential places for 'looked after children'.

Scotland also has secure accommodation provision, which is currently expanding from 96 places to a total of 125 places in seven units. Most of these places are also run by the voluntary sector, although two of the city Councils operate their own secure units. Scotland has no equivalent of the 80-bed Secure Training Centres which have been recently established in England, and all secure provision for under-16s remains firmly in the child care sector (Barclay & Hunter, 2007; Smith & Milligan, 2005).

4. Evidence and Awareness of Abuse in Residential Child Care Institutions, 1950 - 1995

There is a distinction to be made between the awareness of the possibility of different forms of abuse in residential child care in the period under consideration and the actual level of abuse which was occurring in the period from 1950 – 1995. There was very little general awareness, public focus or published material regarding child abuse in residential child care in the UK before the mid to late 1980s. Due to this, it is extremely difficult to comment with any certainty on the nature and prevalence of abuse in residential child care in Scotland. Public inquiries into abuse in residential child care since the late 1980s, however, have brought to light a range of abuse in residential units in the UK, some of which dated back to the 1960s. Since the late 1980s there has also been a high level of media and public policy focus on abuse in residential child care in the UK and considerable reference to it in the relevant literature. However, definitive knowledge about the extent and prevalence of abuse in the residential sector remains elusive. The evidence that there is in the UK is primarily based on information from the public inquiries there have been, on research analysing children and young people's own complaints, on surveys regarding abuse of children and young people cared for away from their parents, and abuse identified from more general studies (Kendrick, 1997, 1998). Furthermore, there has been little focus in the published material on abuse in residential child care specifically in Scotland, as opposed to the rest of the UK.

Consequently, this review will firstly consider what awareness there was of abuse within residential child care in Scotland before the mid to late 1980s when child abuse in residential care became a significant public concern. Secondly, the review will then provide an overview of the major inquiries into abuse in residential child care in the UK outside of Scotland. Thirdly, the review will provide an overview of the government requested reviews of residential child care in Scotland, the Skinner (1992) and Kent (1997) Reports, and the two independent inquiries into abuse in residential child care institutions in Scotland, the Edinburgh Inquiry (Marshall, Jamieson & Finlayson, 1999) and Fife Enquiry (Black & Williams, 2002). Finally, the review will provide an overview of the published material currently available, regarding factors underpinning abuse in residential child care in the UK and safeguards to prevent abuse.

5. Awareness of Child Abuse in Residential Child Care before the mid to late 1980s

The 1952 Children and Young Persons (Amendment) Act and Children and Young Persons Act 1963 gave Children's Departments a duty to investigate when informed that a child may be in need of care or protection. The Ingleby Report in England and Wales (1960) also made short reference to the prevention of cruelty to children. We have seen, however, that the public and professional awareness of child abuse has

fluctuated, and this report was set against the absence of child abuse as a predominant public concern during the years from 1948 until the early 1960s (Hendrick, 2003; Parker, 1995).

A significant marker of change was the identification of the 'battered child syndrome'; defined as 'a clinical condition in young children who have received serious physical abuse [and] is a frequent cause of permanent injury or death' (Kempe et al., 1962). While the article resisted giving a narrow social or psychological profile of abusers, they were described as parents or foster parents with poor anger management who may have had experienced similar abuse in their own childhoods. It is notable that the emphasis was on medical identification of the physical abuse to the child and a pathological definition of the abusive parent. The focus flowing from the 'battered child syndrome' was, moreover, young children living in the care of parents in the community, rather than children in residential settings.

In 1963, a year after Kempe and colleagues' paper, two orthopaedic surgeons, claimed that the syndrome was more widespread than believed in the UK and in 1966, the British Paediatric Association stressed the role of hospital casualty doctors in identifying abuse (Parton, 1985). By 1972, many areas had established review and case committees to deal with child abuse in their localities while the DHSS issued evolving guidance on child abuse in 1970, 1974 and 1978 (Parton, 2006) The inquiry into the death of seven year old Maria Colwell marked the emergence of child abuse as a predominant concern in the UK (Butler and Drakeford, 2003; Directors of Social Work in Scotland, 1992; Parton, 1985; 2006). Government guidance on child abuse reflected an evolving public recognition of it: from the initial focus on physical injury to young children, it had referenced the same risk to older children by 1974, acknowledged neglect, failure to thrive and emotional abuse in the early 1980s, and sexual abuse only in 1986 (Directors of Social Work in Scotland, 1992.)

The focus throughout this period however remained on child abuse in the community. In the USA, 1977 marked the public recognition of institutional child abuse as an issue when a major conference on institutional abuse of children was held at Cornell University (Garrett, 1979). Recognition of this issue in the UK was much slower. While there were allegations, evidence of abuse and a number of enquiries in the 1980s, such as those into sexual abuse in Kincora and Leeways homes, see below, the subject of sexual abuse in a residential context did not feature much in professional discourse. The Kincora and Leeways 'scandals' might have been seen as extremely exceptional until the early 1990s when public and professional awareness became more focused on the abuse of children in care following the cases of Frank Beck (Leicestershire) and the 'Pin-down scandal' in Staffordshire (Bibby, 1996; Corby et al., 2001; Kendrick, 1997; Stanley 1999).

In the light of the discussion above, it is not surprising to find that literature written before the 1970s around child care practice and residential practice in the UK makes scarce reference to child abuse in general. As we discuss below, specialist professional literature within the sector prior to the late1980s does make some reference to physical and sexual abuse. However this is not a recognized theme in the professional literature and even where it is acknowledged, it is for the most part perceived as something requiring individual responses rather than the adoption of systemic approaches to safe care and child protection.

We have seen that the Clyde and Curtis Committees identified poor practice in residential care, if not clear cases of abuse.

Other literature did identify specific cases of abuse in residential care. Professional writing in the 1960s, however, did not always acknowledge the potential for abuse in residential care settings. Edwards' (1968), article on residential care makes no reference to institutional abuse but does note the possible reasons why children are in public care to include that they have been adjudged by the courts to be 'neglected and ill-treated' by parents or 'in moral danger' (Edwards, 1968, p.38). Brill and Thomas' (1964) book, focusing on residential chid care in England, demonstrates that there was awareness of the possibility of the sexual abuse of children within the family. Again, however, there is no reference to abuse within an institutional child care setting.

The report of the Kilbrandon Committee (1964) which investigated the Scottish child care system and whose recommendations led to the creation of the Children's Hearing system does not contain any reference to abuse in a residential context but does contain quite a large section on 'residential measures', including detailed consideration of the role of approved schools. It notes a range of criticism of the approved schools but abuse is not one of them. The criticisms are couched in language about there being too many children admitted to facilities and about there being inappropriate admissions due to children being too young, or children having a 'mental handicap'. The Report also notes that the lack of specialist provision in residential child care sector means that children are admitted to approved schools because of the lack of any alternative. Kilbrandon does note that there is a public perception that the schools are 'punitive' but maintains they are not.

While it was not framed as 'abuse', the concern about the use of corporal punishment and harsh punishment was one area were there some focus in residential child care after 1948. As in Cllr. Robina Lambie's minority report into allegations of abuse at Dr Guthrie's Approved School for boys in 1947 (noted above), the use of punishment gave rise to other concerns about the more general treatment of young people in those establishments. The Criminal Justice Act 1948 removed courts' ability to sentence the birch against young people, however corporal punishment remained legal in children's homes in Scotland until The Social Work (Residential Establishments - Child Care) (Scotland) Regulations 1987 came into effect (Black & Williams, 2002).

Holman (1996) notes that the minutes of the children's committee in Manchester from 1948-71, discusses a 'sprinkling' of cases where house parents were severely reprimanded or dismissed for hitting children.

That corporal punishment remained a predominant issue within residential care is also reflected in Berry's (1975) study of daily residential life in England. She notes a headmaster in one of the units studied is reported to have stopped using corporal punishment because the local council had come under Labour Party control. Berry notes that he appeared to be 'motivated less by concern for the boys' skin than for his own' (Berry, 1975, p.150). One community school is also described which had tried to relax its disciplinary policy, but the housemaster believed some staff had responded by using 'unofficial' physical punishment more. He is quoted as saying:

'[T]he boys are hit regularly... hair pulled and heads banged. Boys accept all this as natural.' (Berry, 1975, p.105)

Strathclyde Regional Council's Report 'Room to Grow' (1978/9) investigates all aspects of child care and related wider social policy. It gives emphasis to, amongst many other things, the need to develop fostering and community-based services as much as possible, but also emphasises the continuing need for residential care and for the staff to be properly trained. It contains a substantial critique of the way that homes ran at that time, including criticisms from young people, staff and managers. While there is no mention of abuse at all, there is a section on the use of corporal punishment in residential care and the need to give clear guidance to residential establishments regarding this. The Report recommends against the use of any instrument to give corporal punishment but, reflecting public views of the time, is unsure about 'smacking':

The majority of staff questioned on this stated that some 'smacking' was necessary – but stated that they were against violence to children. (Strathclyde Regional Council, 1978/9, p.36)

Kahan (2000), who worked as a children's officer in Oxfordshire County Council in the 1960s, noted the struggle there was in persuading other professionals that abusive treatment occurred in residential child care settings during the period:

Great difficulty was sometimes experienced in getting doctors, police and lawyers to believe what was happening in group care. I personally had so much unease about the kinds of regimes in approved schools that in the authority I was serving we somehow managed to persuade the courts not to send children to approved schools but to commit them to our care. (Kahan, 2000).

Child sexual abuse did not become recognised as a significant mainstream issue in the UK until the mid-1980s. The Second Report from the House of Commons Social Services Committee 1983-84 noted that:

Most attention hitherto has been focussed on physical cruelty, and specifically on preventing, identifying and treating non-accidental injury to children. Such injuries may at least be visible, however difficult to interpret. Sexual abuse of children can go undetected for long periods. There is now some professional awareness of the extent and effects of sexual abuse. Little thought has been given to its prevention. We recommend that the Department's Child Care Research Liaison Group consider commissioning research into sexual abuse of children (House of Commons Social Services Committee, 1984, Para. 52)

Therefore, as with abuse in residential child care more generally, its lack of coverage in the earlier post-war literature is unsurprising. There are some references to it well before the 1980s, however.

One article (a paper published in 1958, but accessed here from a collection published in 1968) did note the possible sexual attraction of staff to children as a potential issue in a residential setting though some of terminology used is questionable:

There is one feature still to be mentioned which may come as a disquieting discovery: there are no deep taboos or incest barriers to protect other people's children from our sexuality. The child's attractive physical appearance may wake so much response in the worker that he may emotionally seduce the child or, reactively, treat him with special harshness. To this the child may retaliate by becoming more difficult. Childhood feelings towards parents and siblings are transferred with less resistance in the substitute situation. It is one further hazard in child care, and is another example of the way in which children can be made difficult. (Anthony, 1968, p.58)

Another text from 1965, arguing in favour of the employment of single males as housefathers, also notes the possibility of inappropriate sexual attraction between staff and young people in residential settings and the need for safeguards against this:

Not unnaturally in any situation such as a resident community it is inevitable that the climate is likely to be somewhat more erotic than normal. Given adequate safeguards however, there is no reason why this of itself should prohibit the employment of single men. The fact that work in connection with children and young people does from time to time attract persons with abnormal sexual attitudes is no reason for eliminating an important group of potential labour. (Henry, 1965, p.56)

Wills' 'Spare the Child' (1971) reported severe bullying and sexual assault by some young male residents to others in Cotswold Approved school

It was presently discovered that the boys had indeed constructed a kind of parody or caricature of the formal system of discipline, based entirely on the tyranny of a few boys... There were beatings-up which began with a duffle-coat being thrown over the head of the victim so that he could not identify his persecutors. Boys had their hands tied to a hot water pipe just at the point that it left the boiler; boys were made to masturbate themselves or each other for the amusement of bullies; there was a system of homosexual prostitutes; and of course helotry was widespread (Wills, 1971, p.25)

Kahan (2000) recalls that while there was little explicit discussion of child sexual abuse until the late 1970s and early 1980s, there was within residential child care practice in the 1960s 'the occasional knowledge of someone being moved on for sexually inappropriate behaviour to boys or girls' (Kahan, 2000).

Holman (1996) reports that from 1948-71 there were six internal investigations into alleged sexual abuse by Manchester Children's Department. In one incident, in 1951, a deputy superintendent allowed a boy from outside the residential unit to sleep in his room. The matter was investigated by three councillors and the man resigned, with no further action taken as a result. Holman notes that, while incidents were promptly investigated:

This response set the pattern whereby actual or suspected abusers were swiftly pushed out but rarely prosecuted. The reluctance to take the matter to court was justified on grounds that it avoided children having to go through the ordeal of being questioned in court and also that it minimised adverse publicity for the Department. Ken Collis, who spoke as a chairman of both the Children's Committee and the Social Services Committee, said "There was not as much sexual abuse as today but we sacked one man on the spot – he did it elsewhere a year later and was jailed." (Holman, 1996, p.180)

A chapter within a mainstream text book on residential care in the UK from 1980 queries what action should be taken when a young person makes an allegation regarding sexual misconduct towards them from a staff member:

The most difficult statements from adolescents to senior members of staff in institutions must surely be: "Last night when I was ill Mr A. came into my room to take my temperature and put his hand on my breast" or "When were at camp on Saturday Mr Z. came into my tent and played with me." (Davis, 1980, p.269)

The author debates the question of what action should be taken and strongly implies a preference that such allegations should be dealt with within the residential setting as far as possible:

Sometimes, of course, for an officer-in-charge or homes manager not to involve the police means treading on mined ground but I have a feeling that more incidents are being bravely and professionally examined internally, putting into perspective the intensity of sexually based interactions which are bound to happen within the intimacies of group living as the most complicated dyadic and triadic relationships are being worked out (Davis, 1980, p.271)

While the author is clear to state he is not 'suggesting license for free sexual exchanges in residential care' (Davis, 1980, p.269), the article goes on to cite another author on residential care approvingly who had argued that 'a sexual relationship between resident and a worker should not automatically be grounds for automatic dismissal' (Righton[3], 1977 in Davis 1980, p.271).

The above shows even before child sexual abuse became a predominant public concern, there was a clear recognition within residential care that staff could be sexually attracted to children and young people, and that sexual abuse of children and young people (although not termed as such) could occur. Davis' article shows that as late as 1980 there was some questioning within the literature as to whether formal action such as staff dismissal and police involvement were necessarily required when children and young people were sexually abused by staff. By questioning what the best approach was, the article does nevertheless indicate that at least in some cases staff were indeed dismissed and the police notified when sexual misconduct was reported.

In 1975, recognising the need to give children and young people a greater voice over their care the National Children's Bureau organised a national one-day conference for young people living in residential care. Invites were sent to every local authority in England and Wales as well as some voluntary agencies (Scottish agencies were not included). Twenty-eight local authorities and two agencies responded, sending 100 children aged 12-16. Out of this came the 'Who Cares? Young People's Working Group' which met numerous times in the first year and decided to produce a book regarding their experiences in care (Page & Clark, 1977, pp. 9-11).

While the young people's accounts reveal positives about the care they received in residential homes, they also revealed a range of abuse. On discussing what should be included in the book one young person commented: 'If you leave battering out, there's no point in having a book is there?' (Page & Clark, 1977, p.35).

The editors comment on the young people's puzzlement that they could be mistreated in the settings meant to protect them:

Many of the members of our group knew they were in care because they had been ill-treated by their parents. It was a paradox to them to find that they could also be ill-treated in care (Page & Clark, 1977, p.35)

Some of the treatment young people spoke of had resonances of the accounts from those who experienced mistreatment in the 1930s and 1940s. Such treatment included being punished for wetting the bed by being forced to sleep in the soiled bed all night and then being made to sleep on the floor the next night without blankets, having your mouth washed out with carbolic soap for smoking or swearing, and being forced to run down the

---

[3] Peter Righton, was at one time Director of Education at the National Institute for Social Work. He was later convicted and fined for possession of child pornography.

high street in underwear as a punishment.

There were also examples given of forms of physical abuse that were clearly far beyond what, even at the time, might have been considered acceptable forms of corporal punishment. Speaking of a member of staff one young person commented:

> We know she used to get kids in the bathroom and she used to get wooden spoons, massive wooden spoons. Well – this little kid must have been six then – and she used to beat him and he used to get bruises. And you'd wonder why you didn't see him. He was kept in, hidden. Finally she got kicked out, she did get the sack. She must have been mentally disturbed or something. (Page & Clark, 1977, p.36)

Another recalled:

> The housemother hit my little brother across the head and he was half-crying his eyes out when the social worker walked in the door. That time she made out nothing had happened and went all gooey and said, 'Oh, poor dear, did you hit your head?' And he said 'Piss off, you bloody hit me!' Our social worker said, 'Is this true?' and the woman said 'Yes, because he never closed the laundry basket.' They got rid of her after that. (Page & Clark, 1977, p.38)

Both accounts reveal not only abuse but some action regarding the abuse, in terms of staff members being dismissed, though there is no indication that any formal investigation into what had occurred took place or that there was consideration of how to prevent similar incidents re-occurring.

One of the accounts in the book, also strongly implied the risk of sexual abuse from some staff:

> There are good staff and bad staff and then a lot of people in between who don't care what goes on. But the bad ones are right kinky and shouldn't be allowed to look after anybody, not just kids. They should be trained though. But the ones that are bad.. some of them are trained.. and they're still kinky. They shouldn't be in child care then (Page & Clark, 1977, p.36)

Kahan (1975) reported the discussions, in 1970, of ten adults who had been in local authority care in England between1948 and1969. The youngest of the group was 19 at that time, the oldest 34. Again clear positives about time in residential care were revealed but some of the accounts also spoke of mistreatment.

One recalled a young boy who disliked fish so much that he vomited, but was made to eat it every Friday. Another participant described how:

> [The housemother in charge] used to give us malt and cod liver oil, that horrible sticky stuff in a big jar. I didn't mind it but the rest of them hated it and this little boy did. I remember once she forced it down his throat, holding his nose and pulling back his hair back. I was so shocked at what she was doing I just stood up and said 'What do you think you are doing?' He was being sick and everything because he didn't want the stuff. I looked at the others and they were feeling the way I was feeling and we all just stood up and walked out. We didn't speak to her about two hours we were so shocked. (Kahan, 1975, p.65)

One of the adults, Valerie, who had been in a psychiatric hospital as an adolescent reported she was given outdated clothes and was only allowed a bath and clean underwear once a week, and did not see the point in complaining despite having a supportive social worker:

> She had complained to the Sister on the ward, who had said there was no money for luxuries. Valerie claimed her own clothes were in her case locked up in a store room because patients were not allowed to wear their own clothes. (Kahan, 1979, p. 67)

One of the participants did report that when she had complained to her child care officer about the way a member of staff had spoken about her mother, the officer came over to the children's home 'within a short time and talked to me and I felt as though they had done something about it.' (Kahan, 1979, p.67).

Another participant however had received a less satisfactory response:

> Miranda had been more fearless and outspoken than most as a child but as she pointed out to the children's officer, she had not succeeded in persuading her to listen sympathetically enough to her complaints about her boarding school to take action and remove her. Only when external events had indicated clearly that the school was no longer suitable had her social worker and the children's officer brought her back to her long-term home at The Beeches. This was an illustration of how easy it is to ignore the messages children are trying to give. (Kahan, 1979, p.68).

By 1982, there was also a recognition of the rights agenda. Clough's British Association of Social Work text on residential work (which is a general text dealing with all kinds of residential work, not just residential child care), does include some discussion of residents' rights and a section entitled 'protection of rights', implicitly recognising therefore that those rights could be abused:

> In a residential centre people may be managed in a way which denies their rights, and so rights must be specified. (Clough, 1982, p.103)

And:

> [T]he rights of residents need emphasis because they are dependent on staff and are comparatively powerless. (Clough, 1982, p.105)

The author advocates that residents need their rights made explicit and argues that protection of those rights is supported by codes of practice, openness, the involvement of a wide range of staff, administrative and outside management of staff knowing more about the details of daily life in the residential unit, review meetings, consumer participation, the transfer of middle management around large residential institutions, keeping case records, inspection, a complaints procedure and the involvement of an outside person with a resident (Clough, 1982, pp.107-109).

6. Overview of The Major Inquiries into Abuse in Residential Child Care in the UK, excluding Scotland

Corby et al. (2001) estimate that from 1945 – 96 there were 72 public inquiries into child abuse in the UK, all but two of which took place from 1973 onwards. From 1996 – 2000 there were another nine. While only four out of 50 inquiries from 1945 – 1990 concerned residential care, from 1990 onwards they took place in roughly equal numbers to those into abuse in the community. In Scotland, there have only been two major inquiries into abuse in residential child care, both of which have taken place in the last ten years. These are dealt with in the next section.

The first public inquiry in the UK into residential child care after the Clyde and Curtis committees was in 1967 at Court Lees Approved School, Surrey. Following a letter to The Guardian from a staff member which alleged that the headmaster and his deputy had subjected a number of boys in their care to beatings resulting in severe bruising, a Home Office inquiry ensued which found excessive use of corporal punishment and a failure to record all occasions when corporal punishment had been administered, as required by the regulations (Corby et al., 2001). The management committee of the school refused to dismiss the head and his deputy, leading Home Secretary Roy Jenkins, to close the school. However, there was no review of practice in approved schools generally, nor a substantial public response to the findings (Corby et al., 2001).

The awareness of abuse in residential child care in the UK began to grow in the mid-1980s with two major inquiries. The second of the two inquiries concerned abuse at Kincora Boys' Hostel in East Belfast. In December 1981 three residential staff from the hostel were jailed for a series of offences including buggery, gross indecency and indecent assault during the 1960s and 1970s. There were allegations that the abuse at Kincora had involved high ranking officials and there had been an official 'cover-up' (Kelly and Pinkerton, 1996). An internal DHSS investigation was held in 1982 and a Royal Ulster Constabulary investigation the following year. The latter uncovered allegations of sexual abuse in other residential establishments which led to the conviction of four other adults (Hughes, 1986), but failed to quell public concern. In 1986, an inquiry was ordered by the Secretary of State for Northern Ireland, with its focus not to re-open investigation of the allegations of abuse but rather to look at the systems in place for preventing abuse and how to improve them (Corby et al., 2001). The inquiry found no evidence of cover-up but criticised the failure to investigate allegations of abuse and made a number of recommendations for future prevention.

In 1985, the officer in charge of Leeways Children's Home in Lewisham was convicted of indecency after taking obscene pictures of children in the home. An inquiry was set up and, like at Kincora, found that the offences had a long history, in this case dating back to at least 1978 (Corby et al., 2001). Like the Sans Everything Reports and The Ely Hospital Inquiry into the institutional mistreatment of patients the late 1960s, however, Kincora and Leeways seemed to be viewed as one-off cases (Butler & Drakeford 2003; Corby et al, 2001), 'aberrations rather than the tip of the iceberg' (Hopton & Glennister cited in Butler & Drakeford, 2003, p.37).

Child abuse in residential child care had started to gain more attention at the end of the 1980s. The Children Act 1989 in England and Wales was the first legislative provision recognising institutional child abuse in the UK, and the 1991 'Working Together under the Children Act' guidance for England and Wales included sections on the abuse of children living away from home. The previous guidance in 1988 had contained only a sentence about the same subject (Creighton, 1992). However, it was 'Pindown' in 1991 which brought what the Clyde Report had

45 years earlier termed 'the fierce light of publicity' to bear on residential child care.

At least 132 children, the youngest 9 years old, were subjected to the Pindown regime between November 1983 and October 1989 in children's homes in Staffordshire (Levy & Kahan, 1991). 'Pindown' was a form of programme abuse. Levy and Kahan said it had been devised by an area residential manager of Staffordshire Children's Homes, Tony Latham, and openly implemented with the knowledge of senior management. It consisted of punishing children who absconded or refused to attend school by confining them to a sparsely furnished room in night clothes and confiscating all their possessions. The children were deprived of company, any form of entertainment and made to do repetitive copying tasks as homework. They had to knock on the door to pass information to staff members, including the fact that they wished to use the toilet (Levy & Kahan, 1991). The system came under scrutiny after a 15-year-old at one of the homes complained to her solicitor. An inquiry was appointed to investigate Pindown immediately after a Granada television programme publicised the system which had been in use (Stanley, 1999). The inquiry called Pindown 'intrinsically unethical, unprofessional and unacceptable' (Levy & Kahan, 1991, p. 167).

The publication of the Pindown Report led Community Care to publish a series on the 'Crisis in Care' and turned the state of residential child care into an issue of public concern once again.

The Utting Report into residential care in England was requested by the Government as a direct result of the Pindown Report (Utting, 1991). The Report gave some attention to abuse stating that 'Children in residential care are vulnerable to exploitation by adults and to both physical and sexual abuse.'(Utting, 1991, Para. 24) and went on to note that 'Children may need protection from other children as well as from adults. Verbal or physical violence should always be treated seriously, and dealt with under the local child protection procedures.' (Utting, 1991, Para. 26)

The Inquiry into Ty Mawr Community Home, a former approved school in Gwent, Wales in 1992 carried out a review of an unusually high number of suicides, attempted suicides or threats of self-harm. The residents were all adolescent males and there were concerns that they were out of control as well as concerns that residents were being improperly treated. The inquiry found that there was an 'over masculine culture at Ty Mawr" and that there "was a degree of low level physical violence (slapping, cuffing, knuckling, that is striking on the head with the knuckles) by certain members of staff.' (Williams & McCreadie, 1992, p. 33). However it also concluded that due to a lack of structure, planning and resources the institution and its staff were left to cope with young people in impossible circumstances (Williams & McCreadie, 1992, p. 51).

In 1991, Ralph Morris, the Principal and joint owner of Castle Hill Independent Special School for boys with educational and behaviour difficulties, was sentenced to twelve years imprisonment having been charged with sixteen specimen counts of offences ranging from physical assault to indecent assault and buggery (Brannan, Jones & Murch, 1993a, p. 2). Allegations of sexual abuse were made by boys to the local police force in the late 1980s but criminal proceedings were not pursued at that time. It appears that the fact that children were placed at the school by different local authorities prevented any co-ordination of the different allegations until a second boy from the same authority stated he had been abused by Morris (Corby et al., 2001). The inquiry noted that Morris created and exploited a subculture within the school whereby some older and more senior boys were given special privileges and then used to control other pupils. There were many examples of the favoured pupils assaulting other boys at the school at Morris' behest (Brannan et al., 1993a)

The same year as Morris' conviction 1991, Frank Beck, an officer-in-charge of children's homes in Leicestershire, was found guilty on 17 counts involving sexual and physical assault including four offences of buggery and one of rape. Two other children's home staff were convicted of charges of indecent or common assault and a fourth member of staff who was charged died before the case came to trial (Kirkwood, 1993, pp. 1-2). In this case the direct sexual and physical abuse was perpetrated under the cover of Beck's version of 'regression therapy' which was promoted as a treatment of problematic behaviours by young people in the homes run by Beck. The therapy consisted of treating young people as if they were young infants, dressing them in nappies and undertaking personal care tasks for them. It was premised on the grounds it would help them 'regress' in order to deal with previous unresolved emotional issues – including sexual abuse by parents or previous carers. This was in itself a form of programme abuse which the young people found "threatening, violent and humiliating" (Kirkwood, 1993, p. 56). The 'treatment' was, however, used as a front for the physical and sexual abuse of the young people. One 12-year-old, Simon O'Donnell, died after receiving 'regression therapy'. This was found to be a suicide by hanging, however, there has been suggestion that Beck strangled O'Donnell with a towel, trying to restrain him during a sexual assault (Community Care, May 10). Like Pindown, Beck's version of regression therapy was known and sanctioned by management and his work celebrated on TV and in Community Care magazine itself (Stein, 2006). As with Ralph Morris, a number of allegations had been made to the local police force regarding Beck without further action being taken. Following Beck's conviction, as well as the inquiry into Beck's abuse, the Warner Report (1992) investigated recruitment and selection processes for residential staff.

In 1996, the Secretary of State for Wales announced a Tribunal of Inquiry into allegations of abuse in children's homes in the former county council areas of Gwynedd and Clwyd, North Wales, from 1974 onwards. In 1986 and 1987, two staff members had been convicted of sexual offences against young people at a children's home in Clwyd. Around the same time allegations of abuse in a children's home in Gwynedd were made by a former resident and a staff member but did not lead to charges. The staff member involved was subsequently sacked. In 1990, two further staff members from two different residential child care provisions in Clwyd had been convicted of sexual assaults against residents. From 1990-4 there were two Clwyd Social Services inquiries into the abuse and a police inquiry into abuse in both Clwyd and Gwynedd. Concerns were raised that a large proportion of the suspected abusers had a connection to Bryn Estyn Community Home, Clwyd, which closed in 1984. There remained growing concern in the local communities over a cover-up of organised paedophilic abuse. Only six convictions resulted from the police inquiry out of 365 individual reports submitted to the Crown Prosecution Service. Moreover, Clwyd County Council decided not to publish its second inquiry report after their insurers warned that admissions of neglect could invalidate the council's insurance policy (Corby et al., 2001; Parton, 2006; Waterhouse, 2000).

The Tribunal of Inquiry in 1996, under Sir Ronald Waterhouse QC, heard how more than a dozen people who had complained of abuse had met suspicious deaths. During the 18 months that it sat, the tribunal took evidence of 259 complainants, of whom 129 gave oral testimony. It examined the histories of almost 30 residential establishments in Wales and 15 foster homes and investigated the existence of a paedophile ring and allegations of a cover-up. The Inquiry found that there was widespread sexual abuse of young boys in particular in several of the children's residential homes in Wales during the period under review, and other instances of physical abuse. It did not, however, find evidence that there had been a police cover-up about the abuse or establish the existence of a paedophile ring in North Wales children's homes. It did conclude that a number of individual males were targeting teenage males, both within and outside care homes, for paedophilic activities and that:

> Many but not all, of these paedophiles were known to each other and some of them met together frequently, although there were strong antagonisms between individuals from time to time. Inevitably, some information about likely candidates for paedophile activities was shared, expressly and implicitly, and there were occasions when sexual activity occurred in a group. (Waterhouse, 2000, Para. 52.85)

7. Reviews and Independent Inquiries into Residential Child Care in Scotland

'Another Kind of Home' (Skinner, 1992) was the equivalent review in Scotland to the Utting (1991) review in England. Its remit was:

> To examine the current provision of residential child care and the quality of service provided.

> To examine in particular questions of training, control and sanctions, children's rights and inspection.

> To make recommendations for maintaining a service of high quality.

> (Skinner, 1992, p.3).

While therefore the Review did not have a specific focus on abuse in residential child care, it did cover topics which have a connection to abuse and its prevention. It refers to 'complaints of physical or sexual abuse by staff' (Skinner, 1992, Para. 3.2.13) in a section on complaints, and recommends that there is an independent element of any investigation into allegations and that '[t]he police should be informed whenever there is reasonable cause to believe that a child may have been the victim of abuse' (Skinner, 1992, Para 3.2.13). This paragraph also says that:

> Where the allegations are clearly directed at one person some agencies immediately suspend the staff member accused and conduct an investigation. This is not always appropriate, and can lead to staff demoralisation and ineffectiveness if it is an automatic response (Skinner, 1992, Para. 3.2.13)

Recommendation 18 follows on from this paragraph:

> Complaints, allegations or suspicions of physical or sexual abuse of young people or children in residential care, should always be referred to managers, or appointed agents, outwith the home and its management; they should, in every instance

where there is reasonable cause to believe that a child may have been the victim of abuse, inform the police. A record should be kept of any allegations made (Skinner, 1992, p.90).

A reference was also found (Donellan, 1993) to the Brodie Inquiry in Scotland in 1992. This was an investigation by Central Regional Social Work Department into Brodie Youth Centre for 12-16 year olds, near Polmont, prompted by allegations that a form of Pindown technique was regularly being used there, including that children were punished:

> ... by being forced to strip to their underwear, confined for up to 24 hours in rooms with only a bed, and that the centre used two special secure rooms for the isolation punishment. (The Independent, June, 1992, cited in Donellan, 1993 p.5).

The article reports that the inquiry was due to report later in the summer of 1992, however, neither the inquiry itself or any further references were found to it in the published literature.

The Kent Report (1997) and its counterpart in England and Wales (Utting, 1997) were requested following the growing number of established abuse cases in residential child care.

Kent noted that:

> In Scotland we have to face up to the fact that, while perhaps we find smaller numbers and less anxiety about organised abuse, we have since 1990 seen a houseparent in an Edinburgh special boarding school, a nurse in a Glasgow children's hospital, a Lothian residential worker, two foster carers in Tayside, a residential worker in Perth, an officer in charge in Dumfries, another in Strathclyde, and a teacher from a special boarding school in the Old Highland region go to prison for abusing children in their care. Former residential care staff are currently awaiting trial in Edinburgh. (Kent, 1997, Para 3.1)

The Report looked at the dangers faced by children living away from home and evidence of different forms of abuse perpetrated against them in children's homes and residential schools, hospitals, penal institutions and boarding schools, as well as in foster care. It then examined the existing safeguards and made a range of recommendations regarding practice within residential care and foster care, ranging from suggestions about daily operational matters such as the maintenance of complaints logs to be reviewed by external managers (Kent, 1997, p.102), to wider recommendations regarding national policy for monitoring, inspecting and reviewing residential establishments and carers. Kent recommended that national statistics should be gathered from Child Protection Registers, that the Child Protection Committee make an Annual Report to the Secretary of State with specific comment on the situation of children living away from home and that there be research looking into factors underpinning abuse of children living away from home and children in foster care (Kent, 1997, pp. 100-101). There were also specific recommendations that there be an 'Appointed Person' as in England and Wales – an independent outsider – charged with making monthly visits to all Homes and providing a written report of the visit to those responsible for the management of the facility (Kent, 1997, p.122), and that every child living outside of parental care and without immediate access to a parent should have a befriender, independent person or guardian appointed (Kent, 1997, p.123).

The Edinburgh Inquiry (Marshall et al., 1999) was a formal independent inquiry established by Lothian Regional Council following the convictions of Gordon Knott and Brian McLennan in 1997 for serious sexual abuse against children resident in children's homes in Edinburgh Corporation and Lothian Regional Council from 1973 to 1987. Gordon Knott was sentenced to 16 years for abuse committed at Clerwood Children's Home from 1973 to 1977, and at Glenallan Children's Home and various holiday locations from 1978 to 1983. Brian McLennan was sentenced to 11 years for abuse committed at Clerwood Children's Homes from 1977 to 1978 and at Dean House Children's Home from 1978 to 1986. Another former residential worker accused of two charges of abuse was acquitted, while charges against a fourth person were dropped. Knott was found guilty of various charges, including that on "various occasions" he had serious sexually assaulted a boy between the ages of 5 and 9, another boy between the ages of 3 and 7, a third boy between the ages of 11 to 15 and a girl between the ages of 4 and 8. McLennan was found guilty of serious sexually abusing "on various occasions" a girl aged 14 and a girl between the ages of 11 and 17 (Marshall et al., 1999, p.20).

The Inquiry team, had a remit to investigate whether complaints made by victims were properly handled in the past; to investigate the adequacy of the procedures currently in place to protect children against abuse; and to determine what further safeguards might have been needed.

The Inquiry report highlighted the responsibilities of the local authority's Chief Executive in ensuring all Council Departments were aware of their child welfare and child protection responsibilities, and the responsibilities of the Director of Social Work to ensure understandable policy and practice guidance was issued to social workers, residential workers, children in residential care and their parents. Recommendations also emphasised the need for the development of policies and practice regarding recruitment and selection, highlighting the desirability of children and young people in residential care being involved in this process. Training, support and supervision of residential workers were also indicated as issues of importance. The need to give children and young people appropriate feedback on the outcome of allegations and to monitor their satisfaction with the feedback given was stated. The inquiry also made a range of recommendations regarding the monitoring and visiting of residential facilities and the need for the central monitoring of the frequency of the use of restraints. Visits by social workers to children and young people in residential care were highlighted as a key safeguard and it was recommended that the frequency of visits by social workers should be monitored with patterns of visits used to identify if there were any children in residential care who were not receiving appropriate external support and who could benefit from the services of a Children's Rights Officer. Finally, the report recommended that the 'Whistle-blowing' policy within the council be amended to encourage staff to raise concerns about poor management or other practices which could jeopardise the welfare of residents (Marshall et al., 1999).

The Fife Council Independent Inquiry (Black & Williams, 2002) was commissioned by Fife council after the conviction of David Logan Murphy in 2001 on 30 charges of sexual abuse of children who had been in his care as a residential worker. The Inquiry's remit was to consider the lessons Fife Council should take from the experiences of those who had been abused by David Logan Murphy; to review the actions of the former local authorities in Fife; and to advise whether effective safeguards were in place to protect children looked after and accommodated by Fife Council from future abuse.

The Inquiry investigated abuse perpetrated by Murphy between 1959 and 1989. He was employed in St Margaret's Children's Home in Elie from 1959 to 1973 and at Linnwood Hall day and residential school in Leven from 1976 to 1989. The Inquiry found that a former resident of St Margaret's made allegations against Murphy to the Social Work Department in 1970. The Social Work Department decided the allegations were a matter for the police to pursue and notified them, but neither the police nor the Social Work Department took further investigative action regarding the original allegation, and Murphy continued to work at St Margaret's until 1973. In 1973, four young people at St Margaret's made allegations that Murphy had sexually abused them. They were interviewed by the police but no steps were taken to prosecute Murphy and there was little evidence that 'there was collaboration between the police and social work to assess the allegations' (Black & Williams, 2002, p.27). Murphy was suspended from his job at St Margaret's and then moved to work as a Social Work Assistant with older adults in a local Area Social Work Office. In 1976, David Logan Murphy successfully applied for another post as Housefather at Linnwood Hall school. It appears that references were not sought from Murphy's then line manager, or his last line manager in his post at St Margaret's. A senior social work manager informed the Inquiry that they had warned the senior manager in the Education Department who had responsibility for Murphy's appointment about the allegations made against Murphy in 1973. However, it appeared no action had been taken in light of this information. Murphy was left in the sole care of young boys after his appointment and continued to perpetrate further abuse. Two further allegations of abuse from two pupils at the Linnwood Hall school were subsequently made to the Head Teacher against Murphy but to no effect (Black & Williams, 2002).

The Inquiry's Recommendations included a number of measures to make recruitment and selection processes more rigorous, to help children and young people to better express views about their care, to improve and maintain staff awareness on abuse issues and safeguarding, and to improve the inspection and monitoring process of care facilities (Black & Williams, 2002). Like Kent (1997) and Marshall et al. (1999), the Inquiry highlighted the importance of external visitors to children in residential care, but added that notice should be taken of the child's wishes in this regard (Black & Williams, p.49). Like Marshall et al. (1999), the Inquiry also commented on a whistle-blowing policy, in this case recommending that a policy be introduced and monitored (Black & Williams, 2002, p.62), and also highlighted the issue of restraints on children and young people, recommending that Review and Care Plan meetings should consider ways of working with the child or young person to reduce the need for restraint (Black & Williams, 2002 p.63). Black and Williams (2002) also had a strong emphasis on the importance of input from survivors into the Inquiry Report and the recommendations contain a section on what needs survivors have for support. Accordingly, the first part of Recommendation 14 states:

> Wherever the help comes from for survivors the organisations involved need to have the financial backing of the local Council and Health Trust or there needs to be Central Government funding for services for the survivors of abuse across the whole of Scotland. The funding needs to be secure for the future rather than being decided on an annual basis as survivors of historical abuse need long term help. (Black & Williams, 2002, p.54)

While Edinburgh and Fife are the only independent inquiries to be held in Scotland, it should be noted that there have been a number of other allegations of abuse in residential child care institutions in Scotland. Some criminal convictions against residential care staff have resulted from these allegations while some former residents who have reported abuse have claimed, or are still pursuing separate civil claims for compensation. A large number of these are allegations of historic abuse in voluntary sector residential provisions in different areas of the country. There has also been a recent internal inquiry by a Scottish local authority into abuse in a residential school it managed, which has subsequently been closed. None of these allegations or convictions have been the subject of an independent or formal inquiry at the current time.

8. The Safety Of Convictions Of Residential Child Care Workers Found Guilty Of The Abuse Of Children In Their Care

Some of the literature regarding historical abuse in residential child care questions the safety of convictions of residential child care workers (Beckett, 2002; Smith, forthcoming; Webster, 2005). The topic is a hugely sensitive one and there is considerable disagreement regarding it.

There are two broad and interconnected areas of coverage in the literature questioning the safety of convictions: firstly criticisms of the 'trawling' methods used by the police when investigating allegations of historic abuse, which it is argued encourages false allegations of abuse; secondly, corresponding to this, a view that the amount of abuse in residential child care has been greatly overestimated. A common theme in this material is the likening of investigations into abuse in residential child care to a modern day 'witch hunt' (Beckett, 2002; Smith, forthcoming; Webster, 2005).

Beckett (2002), while stressing that he accepts that 'a significant number' of convicted residential child care staff have committed offences against children, states:

> I think that a number of residential social workers are likely to now be serving prison sentences for crimes they did not commit, and there would seem to be a very good case for the evidence in all these cases to be urgently reviewed. (Beckett, 2002, p.628)

Smith goes even further in stating that:

> There is evidence to suggest that many allegations are false, based on the possibility of financial reward, a state of affairs that also diminishes the experiences of genuine victims of abuse (Smith, forthcoming, p.2)

He also questions the evidence base underpinning the view that child abuse in residential child care was 'widespread'.

Webster's (2005) focus is the allegations of abuse in residential care in North Wales which led to the Waterhouse Tribunal of Inquiry Report (2000). While similarly acknowledging the existence of child abuse in residential child care, Webster's analysis questions a large number of the allegations in North Wales and is highly critical of the Waterhouse Inquiry. Webster had previously argued (1998 cited in Beckett, 2002) that one reason for the overestimation of abuse was the use of 'trawling' methods by the police. According to Beckett, Webster argues that former residents of residential child care facilities could be motivated to make false allegations of abuse due to resentment against the 'system', the desire for attention or the wish to claim compensation (Beckett, 2002). Webster (2000) has supported the view that up to 20 innocent care workers have been convicted of abuse in North Wales and the North-West of England.

Corby's review (2006) of Webster is critical of some elements of Webster's (2005) treatment of the events in North Wales and he specifically questions what he sees as one of the implications of Webster's analysis:

> He implies that because unravelling abuse allegations is beset with difficulties, we should return to the status quo where the onus is very much on those making the allegations to prove their accusations beyond doubt. Yet we know that in many circumstances that is not possible and that in such cases those in authority have much greater influence than those in their care. (Corby, 2006, p.287).

Concerns regarding the safety of convictions of former residential child care workers had already resulted in The House of Commons Home Affairs Committee examining the way in which investigations into historic abuse were conducted in 2001-02. The Committee defined 'trawling' in the following way:

> 'Trawling' is not a technical term, rather it is a convenient label used to describe the police practice of making unsolicited approaches to former residents from many of the institutions under investigation. In any investigation, including those into past institutional abuse, the police will contact persons named by the complainant in his or her statement of complaint. Trawling, as we understand it, refers to the process when the police go one step further and contact potential witnesses who have not been named or even mentioned. In a trawl, the police will contact all, or a proportion of, those who were resident at the institution under investigation during the period when the abuse was alleged to have occurred. (House of Commons Home Affairs Committee, 2002, Para.12)

The Committee further noted that:

> The term 'trawling' appears to have become associated with criticism of these investigations. As such, it is not favoured by the police; Chief Superintendent Mike Langdon explained to us that they preferred the word 'dip sampling'. For the sake of convenience, we have used 'trawling'—as we have defined it— rather than 'dip sampling'. (House of Commons Home Affairs Committee, 2002, Para 13)

The Committee voiced significant concerns about the ways that 'trawling' methods had sometimes been used and stated:

> It has been suggested, and we believe it to be so, that a new genre of miscarriages of justice has arisen from the over-enthusiastic pursuit of these allegations. (House of Commons Home Affairs Committee, 2002, Para. 2).

However the Committee also commented that:

> Although we hold some reservations about the conduct of police trawls, we do not accept that trawling should be prohibited. The police have a statutory duty to investigate allegations of child abuse, regardless of whether they relate to contemporary or past events. In general, the longer the delay between the alleged offence and the allegation being made, the more difficult the investigation. We believe that senior officers should retain their discretion to determine the nature

and scale of an investigation, particularly in complex investigations into past institutional abuse. In every case, however, there should be clear justification for the decision to launch a trawl. (House of Commons Home Affairs Committee, 2002, Para. 26).

The Government response to the Committee (House of Commons, 2003) acknowledged the difficulty of investigations into allegations of historic abuse but stated that it did not 'share its [the Committee's] belief in the existence of large numbers of miscarriages of justice.' (House of Commons, 2003, p.4). It further stated that:

> The Committee's conclusions would appear partly to have arisen from a combination of assumptions, which include:
> ■ Significant numbers of complainants make fabricated complaints for dishonest motives;
> ■ They conspire to do so;
> ■ These fabrications remain undetected throughout lengthy inquiries;
> ■ A range of agencies, from the police and CPS [Crown Prosecution Service] to personal injury solicitors, are both unaware of these deceptions and/or unwittingly assist them; or are complicit in their fabrication;
> ■ Significant numbers of complainants are either serving prisoners or ex-offenders;
> ■ They are therefore more likely to be dishonest when making complaints of abuse, (although a different standard is applied and their word is relied upon as significant evidence when they are disclosing details of alleged impropriety in the conduct of investigations); and
> ■ "False allegations" are assumed to have occurred in a whole range of circumstances, from acquittals and cases that do not proceed to occasions when their existence is claimed by either those who claim to have made them or their associates. Rarely is there clear substantiation that these allegations have indeed been deceptions.

The Government sees no evidence to support these assumptions and notes that the Committee have themselves recorded their own reservations in this respect. We are concerned that they have nonetheless relied upon them significantly, without the weight of significant and consistent substantiation to back them up (House of Commons, 2003, p.4).

As the Government response implies, one of the difficulties regarding the issue of the safety of convictions is the lack of clear evidence. This is the case as to both the exact nature and extent of child abuse in residential care and as to false allegations as The Home Affairs Select Committee had themselves noted:

> We recognise that, whilst on the one hand it is difficult to establish the number of false allegations, on the other, it is hard to gauge the true scale of child abuse (House of Commons Home Affairs Committee, 2002, Para. 22).

The Home Affairs Select Committee noted that, in England and Wales, the Crown Prosecution Service had rejected 79 per cent of institutional child abuse cases referred to the police, compared to only 13 per cent for all cases (House of Commons Home Affairs Committee, 2002). However, the Crown Prosecution Service's decision not to proceed with a case does not necessarily mean that the allegations underlying the case were false. The Committee also heard that the police felt confident that false allegations would be discovered, either during the investigative process or trial, and that 'at least three individuals have been prosecuted for perverting the course of justice, on the basis of deliberate fabrication' (House of Commons Home Affairs Committee, 2002, Para, 20). Of the 21 per cent of cases which did proceed to trial, convictions were obtained in 83 per cent of cases, mostly via guilty pleas (House of Commons Home Affairs Committee, 2002). The Government response noted that the Criminal Cases Review Commission (CCRC), set up to investigate possible miscarriages of justice in England and Wales, had received 24 applications of cases of historical abuse between 1997 and 2003. Of these cases, seven had been closed without referral to the Court of Appeal, while the remaining 17 cases were still being dealt with at that time (House of Commons, 2003). In 2004 though, it was reported that, in England and Wales, there were more than 100 cases of convictions of carers and teachers which were being reviewed by the Criminal Cases Review Commission and the solicitors' group, The Historical Abuse Appeal Panel (Community Care, 12 February, 2004) . While some individual convictions against former residential workers carers have been overturned (Hawthorn, 2006), no up to date figures have been found regarding the number of overturned convictions, in Scotland or elsewhere in the UK, including in the literature which questions the safety of convictions or raises concerns about false allegations of abuse. The Home Affairs Select Committee did note that in Scotland, the Scottish Criminal Cases Review Commission has adopted 'a much wider statutory test' (House of Commons Home Affairs Committee, 2002, Para. 134) than the one used by the CCRC in England and Wales to decide whether cases should be sent to the Court of Appeal : the Scottish Commission criterion is whether miscarriage of justice has occurred, while the CCRC criterion is that the Court of Appeal would not uphold a conviction if a case was referred to it . Consequently, the Home Affairs Select Committee recommended the test used by the Scottish commission on the basis that it did not require it 'to predict the views of the appeal court' (House of Commons Home Affairs Committee, 2002)

In respect of the evidence base regarding child abuse in residential child care in the UK, as noted elsewhere in this paper, the continued absence of clear definitions, national data and systematic research studies make conclusive statements about the nature and prevalence of abuse in residential child care difficult (Kendrick, 1997; Gallagher, 1999; 2000; Stanley, 1999; Stein, 2006). This is all the more true in respect of the nature and prevalence of historical abuse in residential care. This should not, however, obscure the fact that the large number of public inquiries into abuse in residential child care since 1985 have documented a range of physical, emotional and sexual abuse in residential child care in the UK, and it should be noted that there have been no legal challenges to the findings of the major abuse inquiries (Stein, 2006).

There is greater consensus within the literature that the focus on abuse within residential child care, as opposed to other care settings, has been unbalanced. For example, despite the lack of evidence to support the view, White (2003) notes that there is a common view that child abuse is mainly associated with residential child care. As we noted in the introduction to this review, Gallagher (1999) states that the findings of his study indicate that:

> Contrary to media representations, the institutional abuse reported here was not just a problem of children's homes, social work or the public sector, but occurred in a wide variety of settings and sectors and was perpetrated by a range of occupational groups. If all children are to be protected, then

policy and practice measures to prevent abuse need to be directed towards a much wider range of institutions. (Gallagher, 1999, p.795)

Several authors have noted the stigma which remains attached to residential child care in the UK since its historical association with Poor Law provision (Abrams, 1998; Tresiliotis, 1988; White, 2003) and the unbalanced focus on residential child care could be seen to both stem from, and reinforce, this stigma.

Colton et al. (2002) considered twenty-four survivors' views of their involvement in large-scale historical investigations of child sexual abuse in residential institutions in the UK. They found that, rather than primarily interested in financial compensation, survivors were motivated to participate in investigations by the desire to see perpetrators brought to justice. The concern to prevent perpetrators committing further abuse against other children was part of this desire. The authors note that while this finding regarding the motivations for participation in historical abuse inquiries 'does not disprove Webster's hypothesis, it does show there are alternative explanations'(Colton et al., 2002, p.544). The study also found there was sometimes a conflict between the desires of large-scale historical investigations to secure convictions against alleged perpetrators, and the needs of survivors for support to process their feelings about what had happened to them. The importance of a public apology from the responsible local authority was highlighted by a number of survivors. The authors note that '[f]or some victims, a public apology by the local authority might well have been more therapeutic in effect than financial compensation' (Colton et al., 2002, p.546). The majority of survivors interviewed also highlighted the importance of skilled long-term counselling and psychiatric help.

9. The Abuse of Child Migrants Sent from Residential Child Care in the UK

The vast majority of emigration of British children to the 'new Dominions' took place from the 1870s until the start of World War I, principally to Canada. Between 80,000 and 100,000 British children were sent there between 1870 and 1930 (Abrams, 1998). Children were also sent to what Britain then called Rhodesia (now Zimbabwe), South Africa, New Zealand and Australia. Around 150,000 British children were sent abroad in total. The exact numbers of children sent from Scottish residential institutions is not known, however 7,000 child emigrants were sent by Quarrier's, 50 from Aberlour Orphanage and 200 from Whinwell Children's Home in Stirling, as well as an unknown number sent from Scottish local authority provisions (Abrams, 1998).

Child emigration continued to Canada, Australia and South Africa in the inter-war years, but at a far slower pace than previously. The post-World War II emigration of children was smaller still but continued until 1967. The most likely destination for children after 1945 was Australia where it is estimated as many as 10,000 children were sent (Bean & Melville, 1989) and it was these children who encountered the greatest abuse. Children were also sent to Canada, Rhodesia and New Zealand in the post-war period. Most child emigrants were sent by voluntary societies in Britain responsible for running residential child care facilities (Bean & Melville, 1989).

While the numbers of children sent in the post-war period were comparatively small, the abuse experienced by some of them was severe. Those sent to Australia encountered a range of physical, emotional and sexual abuse and over and above this the level of care provided to many of them consistently failed to meet basic needs (Australian Senate Community Affairs References Committee, 2001[4]; Bean & Melville, 1989; House of Commons Health Committee, 1998; Humphreys, 1994; Gill, 1998). One of the premises for child emigration in the post-war period was that it would be difficult to find certain children foster families in Britain. This argument had particularly been applied to Roman Catholic children and Glasgow Corporation emigrated a number of Catholic children on this basis (Abrams, 1998).

However emigrant children overwhelmingly swapped institutional care in Britain for institutional care in their country of destination where there were generally fewer safeguards for their welfare than in Britain (Gill, 1987), and despite the public statements that child emigration schemes were for orphaned children for whom there were no chance of a family placement in Britain, most children had at least one living parent (Bean & Melville 1989; BBC Radio 4, 2003a). Children were frequently misled by the staff looking after them both about what emigration entailed and their family circumstances in order to encourage their agreement to leave. One man sent to Australia from Nazareth House (Residential Children's Home) in Lasswade in 1951 commented:

> The nuns told us we were orphans, that we had no family and no future in Scotland. They told us Australia was the Promised Land where we could ride to school on ponies. (quoted in Abrams, 1998, p.143).

It is with good reason that Bean and Melville comment that the 'history of child migration in Australia is in many ways a history of cruelty, lies and deceit' (Bean & Melville, 1989, p.111). Children were informed that parents were dead when this was not the case, family members were not informed children were being sent abroad or misinformed about the nature of the scheme, family members' objections to a child being sent were overridden, contact between the children and family members in Britain was discouraged, with letters censored and sometimes withheld, and siblings sent to Australia together were frequently separated on arrival (Bean & Melville 1989; BBC Radio 4, 2003a).

The emigration of British children from children's homes in Britain began when Maria Susan Rye took 68 children from Liverpool and London to Montreal to Canada in 1869 (Magnusson, 2006). The first children sent from Scotland were 64 boys sent by Quarrier's to Ontario in 1872. Thirty-five were boys from Cessnock Home and 29 were from in orphanages in Maryhill and Edinburgh to Ontario. It was another ten years before Barnardo's sent the first of their children (Magnusson, 2006).

According to Magnusson:

> For Quarrier, emigration was not just a convenient means of clearing Glasgow's streets of waifs and strays; of course it was clear that his Glasgow Homes had limited accommodation but Quarrier also firmly believed that emigration was in the best interests of his children and that Canada was truly a land of opportunity, where boys and girls could make a good fortune for themselves in a new eager country which needed them. (Magnusson, 2006, p.68).

This may have been true, but Hendrick (2003) points towards other motives behind the child migration schemes. First, there was an economic interest as it was cheaper for organisations to maintain children in the Dominions than in Britain. Second, there were political concerns about the numbers of homeless children in cities and how this could affect social order. Third, religious concern within the 'child rescue' movement that children cared for in institutions had to be removed from what was considered the damaging influence of birth family members whose lifestyles were viewed as corrupting and immoral. Finally, imperialism provided a motivation as, from the beginning of the 20th century, child emigrants were seen as a means of solidifying British control of its overseas imperial territories.

While the early emigration schemes received much publicity and large public support, concerns emerged about the welfare of child emigrants soon after they started. In 1875 Andrew Doyle, a former Poor Law Board inspector, visited Canada as part of an investigation of the British emigration bodies and raised concerns from what he had seen that they were poorly run (Magnusson, 2006). The Glasgow Herald had expressed concerns about the emigration schemes in 1883 and the concerns were given strength by the death of Barnardo's boy, George Green, at the hands of his carer, Helen Findlay in 1896. He died as a result of neglect, starvation and violence at the Findlay's farm outside Ontario. Neighbours reported they had frequently seen Findlay hitting George Green. It transpired that George Green had been of weak physique and poor general health, questioning his suitability for this type of emigration in the first place (Magnusson, 2006).

Following this, in Ontario, JJ Kelso initiated The Ontario Act 1897, to provide greater monitoring and regulation of child emigration schemes. By the time of the Act, there were nearly 40,000 British children in Canada, nearly 75 per cent of these on farms in Ontario. William Quarrier stopped the emigration of children from his home in 1897, annoyed by what he saw an unnecessary state interference given that all the feedback he had received about Quarrier's emigrant scheme was positive (Abrams, 1998; Magnusson, 2006).

The year after Quarrier's death, however, in 1904, child emigration from Quarrier's re-started. From 1872 – 1930s 7,000 children went overseas from Quarrier's, which was a small proportion of the total of 100,000 sent from Britain during this time, but 35 per cent of the 20,000 children admitted to Quarrier's Homes during this period (Abrams, 1998).

After World War II British Columbia lifted child migration laws temporarily from 1945 – 8 and Fairbridge Farm School sent children from England to training centres for these three years. (Magnusson 2006). The renewal of the Empire Settlement Acts and the assisted passage agreement with Australia in 1946 facilitated emigration there as well as making emigration possible to New Zealand, Rhodesia and South Africa in the post-war period (Bean & Melville, 1989).

The motives behind the child migration schemes in the post-war period varied according to the country of destination. The Fairbridge scheme to Rhodesia sent children out to become part of the governing white British elite, and was a success in those terms (Bean & Melville, 1989). Those children sent out to Australia on the other hand were earmarked to fill shortages of manual workers in the labour market. As a result of these differential motives for the schemes, the treatment and integration of those children sent to Rhodesia was very much better than that of children sent to Australia (BBC Radio 4, 2003c).

---

[4] Referrred to hereafter as The Australian Senate Inquiry

Within the UK, there were concerns over child migration schemes from the start of the post-war period and whereas the earlier waves of child migration had been greeted with fanfare and publicity, those in the post-war period were undertaken with as little of either as was possible (Abrams, 1998). Due to such concerns, the 1948 Children Act contained specific regulations regarding child emigration. Amongst these were that the Home Secretary had to approve the emigration of each individual child, and be persuaded it was in their best interests; that the parents of the child should be consulted and, where this were not possible, the child themselves had to give clear consent.

The British Federation of Social Workers was one organisation that voiced concerns about child emigration in the immediate post-war period. This initially arose after the Federation was informed that children recruited by Fairbridge Society, London to go to South Rhodesia were not actually orphans but living with both parents. The Federation also expressed concern over the enforced censorship of letters sent between children and their families in Britain and the fact children were encouraged to terminate contact with family members (Bean & Melville, 1989). In response, in 1946, the Federation was assured by the Fairbridge Farm Schools of Australia and Canada that there would not be any large-scale migration of children. The Federation was not satisfied by this, however, and during the passage of the Children's Bill through Parliament lobbied for specific regulation of the activities of voluntary societies involved in emigration schemes. Clause 32 of the bill (section 33 of the Children's Act 1948) stated the Secretary of State 'may by regulations' control emigration arrangements for children cared for by voluntary organisations. The Federation wanted 'may by regulations' to be replaced by 'shall by regulations' (Bean & Melville, 1989). However, it withdrew its insistence after assurances issued by the Lord Chancellor, Viscount Jowitt, during the Parliamentary debate on the bill. Jowitt gave explicit assurances that the Home office would ensure no child would be sent abroad 'unless there is absolute satisfaction that proper arrangements have been made for the care and upbringing of each child'(cited in Bean & Melville, 1989, p.169).

The extent to which this assurance proved hollow is striking. While in Scotland it was the case that the Scottish Office refused permission for a number of children to be sent abroad on the grounds it was it was not in their interests and gave permission for a child to emigrate only once parental consent had been received (Abrams, 1998), the low priority given to ensuring what conditions child migrants were living in Australia is demonstrated by the fact that the first formal government assessment of the conditions for migrant children living in Australia was not undertaken until 1956. The inter-departmental committee on migration policy was highly critical of the care provided to child migrants in Australia, and singled out for particular criticism those institutions, like the Fairbridge Society and organisations managed by the Roman Catholic church, which placed children exclusively in institutional settings (Bean & Melville, 1989) . The report also detailed criticisms about the care provided by a number of residential institutions for child migrants, however these criticisms were contained within a part of the report which was not published (BBC Radio 4, 2003 b). Astonishingly, despite the report, the numbers of children sent to Australia from 1956-66 actually increased (Bean & Melville, 1989). Grier (2002) argues that there was an intentionality to successive British Governments' failure to regulate the actions of voluntary agencies involved in child migration. On the one hand, the lack of direct state involvement in child migration schemes, in most cases, distanced government from responsibility for those children involved in the schemes. On the other hand, successive governments' tacit acceptance of child migration to Australia allowed them to avoid the diplomatic fallout of curtailing, or even stopping, child migration which would have undermined a central plank of post-war Australian immigration policy to attract immigrants of 'good British stock'.

Those child migrants subject to the worst abuse were Roman Catholic boys sent to the Christian Brothers' remote farm schools in Bindoon, Tardun and Clontarf, Western Australia where there was systematic and widespread physical, emotional and sexual abuse (Bean & Melville, 1989). Children as young as eight were forced to engage in construction work at Bindoon (Humphreys, 1994) while the abuse of children at those schools was sometimes so severe that at least half a dozen boys had to have corrective surgery; none of the cases were reported as matters of concern by the medical staff involved (Bean & Melville, 1989).

Former residents of Goodwood Orphanage for girls described treatment from staff characterised by physical cruelty and a lack of emotional warmth. There were also elements of programme abuse that resonated with the Clyde and Curtis Reports' descriptions of the worst residential child care facilities in Britain at the end of World War II, with girls prevented from keeping any personal possessions and having to share items such as toothbrushes and underclothes (Bean & Melville, 1989).

The regimes at Fairbridge Farm schools in Pinjarra, Western Austrailia, and Molong, New South Wales were generally better but as in the case of some institutional abuse in British children's homes, a child's experiences were highly dependent on the cottage parent in charge in a particular cottage (Bean & Melville, 1989).

The Australian Senate Inquiry (2001) found that child migrants were subject to a range of sexual, physical and psychological abuse. Children were beaten with specially made implements designed to cause as much pain as possible, and the severity of some beatings caused physical impairment in later life. While some physical chastisement administered would have been considered legal at that period: 'Brutality was endemic at some institutions and at times descended into what can only be described as torture'(Australian Senate Inquiry, 2001, p.72). The Inquiry found that child migrants were exposed to sexual abuse from a range of individuals including:

> priests at the institution, members of families to whom children were sent on holidays or to work, workers at the institution, regular visitors to the institution, and also in some institutions by other older children.
> (Australian Senate Inquiry, 2001, p.72)

There was also a wider sense in which child migrants were subject to 'programme abuse' and 'system abuse' in that the specific regimes that were inflicted upon children were generally abusive and their wider needs were not met. Children were forced to undertake heavy labouring tasks, provision of basic items such as food and clothing was often inadequate, educational provision was poor and children were sometimes re-named, sometimes referred to by number rather than name, and, in general, deprived of any understanding of their cultural and family history (Australian Senate Inquiry, 2001). On leaving these residential institutions, young people, who had been encouraged to break any contact they may have had with family members in Britain, were very rarely provided with any type of after-care to help them make the transition into wider Australian society, of which they had little knowledge and with which they had no direct ties (Australian Senate Inquiry, 2001; BBC Radio 4, 2003d).

In 1961, the Home office, while allowing the continuation of child emigration, expressed reservations about the work of voluntary societies involved in such schemes, while the Scottish Office expressed its dislike of the fact that voluntary emigration societies' work was only reviewed informally and with their consent (Abrams, 1998). It was not until 1967 that child migration finally stopped. However, it is notable that this was not through any external intervention, but only because the supply of child emigrants to voluntary societies, who were the mainstay of the post-war child emigration schemes, dried up as increasing numbers of British children were placed in local authority care, and because the Australian economy had diminishing need for their labour (Bean & Melville, 1989; BBC Radio 4, 2004d). It was not until 1982, fifteen years after child migration schemes had come to an end, that the British Government made it a legal requirement for any voluntary association to get the consent of the Secretary of State before sending a child abroad (Bean & Melville, 1989).

The House of Commons Health Committee inquiry (1998) on child migration and the Australian Senate Inquiry Report (2001) into the treatment of child migrants in Australia recognised the abuse that many child migrants had suffered. Both inquiries attributed collective responsibility for the abuse to all the governments and agencies which had been involved in the child migration schemes.

10. The Extent of Abuse in Residential Care in the UK

We have stated earlier, that there is limited research evidence about the extent and prevalence of abuse in residential care in the UK, and that definitional issues and absence of national data and systematic research make conclusive statements difficult, particularly in relation to historical abuse (Kendrick, 1997; Stein, 2006). There has been considerably more research carried out in the USA and this has been detailed elsewhere (Kendrick 1997; Gallagher, 1999). The limitations of the research evidence have been a factor in 'alternative' readings of the scale and nature of abuse in residential child care and a questioning of the claims that abuse is widespread (Smith 2007, Webster 2005). Certainly, the particular focus on abuse in residential child care is to be questioned, compared to other institutional settings.

The National Association of Young People in Care (NAYPIC) made an early attempt to highlight abuse in the care system in the UK. They studied the cases of fifty young people who had complained to them in a three month period (Moss, Sharpe & Fay, 1990). NAYPIC found that of the 50 cases '65% of the young people... were sexually abused whilst in care' and '85% of female young people said they had suffered sexual assault' (Moss et al., 1990, pp. 4-5). Over three-quarters of the young people reported that they had been physically abused in care and the 'complaints varied from being hit whilst arguing with staff, up to and including systematic, severe physical abuse' (Moss et al, 1990. p. 5)

A further attempt to provide more detailed information on institutional abuse was carried out by the NSPCC. A survey of NSPCC teams and projects in March 1992 identified 84 cases of alleged abuse in residential or educational settings over the previous year (Westcott & Clement, 1992). The authors

acknowledge that the sample is unrepresentative as it is likely that these are particularly severe cases. Two-thirds of the children involved in the Australian Senate Inquiry, 2001, (63 per cent) were male and one-third were female; 12 per cent of the children were under 10 years; 43 per cent were between 10 and 14 years old; and 45 per cent were between 15 and 17 years of age (Westcott & Clement, 1992, p. 7). A large number of children (42 per cent) had been placed in the residential establishment because of previous abuse. The majority of children (69) suffered sexual abuse; 16 suffered physical abuse; 4 suffered emotional abuse; 6 suffered from inappropriate restraint and 9 suffered other forms of abuse (Westcott & Clement, 1992, p. 11). In half the cases, the perpetrator was a peer, in 43 per cent of cases it was a staff member, and in the other cases it was a sibling. The majority of abusers were male (81 per cent). For the 25 staff perpetrators where their age was known, the majority (19) were aged 40 and above (Westcott & Clement, 1992, p.11).

A more recent account of abuse in residential establishments has been provided by ChildLine (Morris & Wheatley, 1995). They provide an analysis of calls made by 539 children in England and Wales and 137 children in Scotland in 1992/93 over the first six month of the line's operation. Over a quarter of the boys (18) and 11 per cent of the girls (24) from England and Wales and eight callers from Scotland reported bullying and violence from other residents as their main problem. Allegations of current sexual abuse were made by 25 children in England and Wales. In 9 cases, male residents were the perpetrators, in eight cases it was male residential staff and in most of the remainder, the abuse had occurred on home visits (Morris & Wheatley, 1995, p. 54).

Gallagher, Hughes and Parker (1996) carried out a survey of institutional sexual abuse in England and Wales in the context of a national survey of organised sexual abuse. Questionnaires were sent to every police force (N=43), Social Services Department (N=116) and NSPCC team (N=66) in 1992 requesting information on each case of organised, ritual or institutional abuse between January 1988 and December 1991 (Gallagher, Hughes and Parker, 1996, p. 216). Institutional abuse was defined as, 'a case in which an adult has used the institutional framework of an organisation for children to recruit children for sexual abuse' (Gallagher et al., 1996, p. 217). The authors had doubts about the reliability of the findings in that they believed that agencies had reported only a small proportion of high profile cases, 'such as those involving allegations of ritual abuse or large numbers of perpetrators and children' (Gallagher et al., 1996, p. 218). Of the 211 cases reported to the national survey, there were 45 cases of institutional abuse and 16 (8 per cent) were in residential institutions (Gallagher et al., 1996, p. 218).

Research on perpetrators of child sexual abuse has also indicated to some degree the extent of abuse in care settings. A study of social work, criminal justice and health service case files for a sample of 501 child sexual abusers found that '6% of the sample were known to the victim in their capacity as foster or adoptive parent, male residential care-giver or a male who was in care with the victim' (Waterhouse, Dobash & Carnie, 1994, p.16); this is a similar percentage as found in the Childline research in Scotland (Vincent & Daniel, 2004).

Hobbs, Hobbs and Wynne (1999) aimed to determine the frequency and pattern of abuse and neglect of children seen by paediatricians and who were placed in foster or residential homes over a 6-year period. 133 children in foster care were identified following 157 episodes (suspected abuse – 51; probable abuse – 66; confirmed abuse – 40). Foster parents were the perpetrator of physical abuse (28 children) and sexual abuse (22 children); natural parents were perpetrators of sexual abuse in relation to 22 children; and children were perpetrators in 24 cases of sexual abuse (Hobbs et al., 1999). During the same period, 25 children living in residential homes were identified in 34 incidents regarding concerns about physical or sexual abuse. Twelve children were physically abused; six were sexually abused and six were both physically and sexually abused. Eight children were abused by a staff member (all involving physical abuse); four children were abused by another child within the home (two sexual abuse and two physical abuse); and 13 were abused by a child outside the home (nine sexual and four physical). Hobbs et al. (1999) found that there was a higher referral rate for foster care (29.54 per 1,000 placements) than for residential care (23.3 per 1,000 placements); this compares to a referral rate of 3.9 per 1,000 children for the general population.

Gallagher (2000) presents findings from a study of institutional abuse cases referred to social services departments or the police in eight local authority areas from January 1988 to December 1992. A total of 65 substantiated cases of institutional abuse were identified: 'If the findings from the eight areas were typical of the country as a whole, then, in the same five-year period, there would have been between 920 and 930 cases of institutional abuse in England and Wales, or about 185 cases per annum' (Gallagher, 2000, p. 799). Three main types of setting were involved in the identified cases: community-based settings (34 – 52%); foster home (22 – 34%); and residential (9 – 14%).

> From these results it would seem that – contrary to impressions created by media reports – residential institutions, which include children's homes, make up a relatively small proportion of institutional abuse cases (Gallagher, 2000, p. 800)

Gallagher, however, does go on to set out a number of caveats in relation to interpreting these figures.

The Abuse of Young People by other Young People

While much of the focus of historical abuse has been on abuse by members of residential staff, there has been a continuing concern about abuse by other children and young people (Barter, 1997). Abrams (1998) cites an interview with a woman in an orphanage around the end of WWII who speaks of the bullying of children who were different. Wills (1971) noted widespread abuse from some young people to others in Cotswold Approved School.

An early piece of research in Nottinghamshire, found that nearly one third of children placed in care due to sexual abuse were further abused by other residents (Lunn, 1990). Westcott and Clement (1992) found that in a survey of 84 children from 28 teams in the UK, over 50 per cent of abusers in survey were peers of the victim, 42 per cent were below 18, while 43 per cent were staff.

MacLeod (1999) estimated that it is possible that over half the sexual assaults against children and young people in care are committed by other children and young people. The Report of the Committee of Enquiry into Children and Young People Who Sexually Abuse Other Children (NCH, 1992) focussed on the need to place children and young people in appropriate placements where they are not vulnerable to further abuse from other young people. Farmer and Pollock (1999) however found that in fewer than one third of cases, from their interview sample of 40 carers, had the potential risks to or from the child/young person been addressed. In just under 50 per cent of cases no information regarding the child or young person's previous

history of abuse or being abused was given to carers at the start of the placement.

Sinclair and Gibbs (1998) found that nearly half (44 per cent) of the 223 young people in their study, stated they had been bullied during their stay in the children's home. Further, 23 per cent of females and 7 per cent of males reported that someone had tried 'to take sexual advantage' of them, with peers rather than staff being responsible.

The most detailed piece of research on this was conducted by Barter and her colleagues (Barter, 2007; Barter et al., 2004). This research took place in 14 English children's homes and 71 young people between the ages of 8 and 17 were interviewed, as well as 71 residential staff members. The aim of the research was to clarify the context within which particular types of violence occur, rather than measure the frequency of violent incidents. Four different forms of peer violence were derived from young people's accounts:
- Direct physical assault – e.g. punching, grabbing hair, beatings.
- Physical 'non-contact' attacks which harmed young people emotionally rather than physically – e.g. destruction of personal belongings.
- Verbal abuse
- Unwelcome sexual behaviours – e.g. flashing, inappropriate touching, rape.
(Barter, 2007, p. 141)

Three-quarters of young people experienced physical assault, mainly as victims (40) but also as perpetrators (25), and this ranged from low-level physical violence to high-level violence such as knife attacks and severe beatings. Non-contact violence was experienced by nearly half the young people, generally as part of a wider cycle of peer violence. Low-level verbal insults seem to be a common aspect of residential life. High-level verbal attacks which contravened boundaries of acceptability, were considered to be more damaging than some forms of high-level physical attacks. Sexual violence was reported the least often; girls were three times more likely to report this than boys, highlighting the issue of gender, sexuality and abuse (O'Neill, 2007). All the incidents involved some degree of coercion and most perpetrators were male (Barter, 2007)

11. Factors in Abuse in Residential Care

Enquires into the abuse of children and young people in residential child care and the broader literature have identified a number of factors which contribute to the potential for abuse. The identification of these factors also suggests the issues which need to be addressed in order to safeguard children and young people in residential care. Colton (2002), for example, identifies the main factors as including: the training and education of caregivers; the management and organisation of residential care; the culture of residential institutions; the status of children in public care; and issues concerning masculinity and sexuality (Colton, 2002, p. 34)

Denial of Abuse

Bloom (1992) suggests that the single greatest impediment to adequately protecting residential clients from sexual abuse is the attitude that 'it can't happen here' (Bloom, 1992, p. 133). Brannan, Jones and Murch (1993a; 1993b) highlighted that a significant feature in the investigation of abuse at Castle Hill School was the 'disbelief of other professionals and parents and their initial inability to accept and comprehend the sheer volume and extent of the abuse' (Brannen et al. 1993b, p.273).

In relation to Scotland, Black and Williams (2002) state:

> Public attitudes to care staff in these years was very positive. Staff would be seen as devoting their time and life to children in need. There would have been total disbelief at any hint of abuse by staff to gratify their own sexual needs. A former member of the social work management team recalls that in the 1960's and 1970's there was a lot of scepticism by the police about allegations of sexual abuse by girls against their fathers. As young people in care were already seen as having problems and as being trouble makers, the likelihood of being believed when making an allegation about a respected member of staff, would be very low. (Black & Williams, 2002, p.19)

Research in the USA has highlighted that residential establishments may be reluctant to report incidents of abuse because they fear damaging their reputation, and the possible loss of their credibility, referrals and licence (Durkin, 1982a; 1982b; Gil & Baxter, 1979; Harrell & Orem, 1980; Powers, Mooney & Nunno, 1990). Colton (2002) highlights the 'cult of silence' which is 'a common characteristic of enclosed, inward looking, organisations which reject criticism, are unreceptive to new ideas, and encourage routines and patterns of practice that are rigid and conservative' (Colton, 2002, p. 37). This leads us into another important factor in abuse of children and young people in care.

Isolation and Vulnerability of Children in Residential Placements

A significant feature of residential child care, particularly in the past, concerns its physical and social isolation. Wardhaugh and Wilding (1993) state that:

> The corruption of care is more likely in enclosed, inward-looking organisations (Wardhaugh & Wilding, 1993, p. 21; see also Colton, 2002).

Berridge and Brodie's (1996) comparison of the Pindown, Ty Mawr and Leicestershire homes (Frank Beck) cases found that the social isolation of the units in the latter two cases reduced the chance of identifying the abuse. They are unclear as to whether social isolation was a factor in the 'Pindown' case, however the inquiry report into Pindown noted 'the resistance to experiences and ideas from the outside' (Levy & Kahan, 1991, p.154).

In 1973, White's study of residential child care in England and Scotland noted that:

> The staff (mainly those who live in) clearly felt isolated in more than one way in nearly all the homes... Apart from this almost physical isolation it may be that the isolation from decision-making and from an overall view of what is happening, takes its toll too. This is a persistent and inherent problem in residential care. (White, 1973, p. 442)

Doran and Brannan comment that the likelihood of abuse is increased by: 'the isolation of the institution from the wider network of care. This isolation can be exacerbated by geographical considerations' (Doran & Brannan, 1996, p.158). Inquiry reports have also highlighted children's isolation as a factor inhibiting their reporting of abuse (Hughes, 1986; Levy & Kahan, 1991, Kirkwood, 1993; Marshall et al., 1999; Black & Williams, 2002). The physical and geographical isolation of residential establishments is likely to have the effect of reduced visits by professionals and families.

Children and young people in residential establishments are also isolated by the social and political processes which bring them in to care. It can be argued that all children are socially excluded. Hill, Davis, Prout and Tisdall (2004) highlight the fact that while children are one of the most governed groups in society, and some of the highest users of state services (health, education and social security), they 'traditionally have had little or no input into national and local policies' (Hill et al., 2004, p. 78). Stein highlights, however, that these were not just any children but children in care:

> They were children and young people who, in the main, came from very poor families and neighbourhoods (Bebbington & Miles 1989), who had experienced neglect, physical or sexual abuse... Many had difficulties within their families, which often manifested itself in problems such as not going to school, running away from home or getting into trouble, and some were children with physical disabilities or emotional and behavioural difficulties whose families were unable to care (Stein, 2006, pp. 12-13)

Kendrick (2005) stresses that not only the prior experience of children and young people children in residential care, but the very process of entering residential care reinforces their social exclusion. Entering residential care is likely to be a stressful time for children and young people because of feelings of displacement, loss and lack of control (Hayden et al., 1999). The social stigma related to residential child care has also been emphasised by children and young people themselves (Polat & Farrell, 2002; Ridge & Millar, 2000; Who Cares? Scotland, 2004).

Discussing the care system as whole, White (1999) writes:

> They are different (socially excluded) from other children by virtue of a number of different labelling processes which make themselves felt at school, in the neighbourhood, in relation to the 'public' world of social services – and, of course, because they are palpably not included physically or psychologically in their own families (White, 1999, p. 73)

Colton (2002) stresses the 'indifference' and 'ambivalence' of public attitudes to children in care. While every major review of residential care (Wagner, 1988; Utting, 1991;1997; Skinner, 1992; Kent, 1997) has underlined the need for the existence of residential child care sector, the stigma attached to residential care is highlighted in much of the literature. Abrams (1998) notes that: 'Girls and boys sent to a children's home are Scotland's forgotten children... Since Scotland had rejected the poorhouse for its needy children, it was widely assumed that only 'problem' children were sent to an institution' (Abrams, 1998, p.78). A number of other authors have commented on the continued existing connection made between residential institutions and the stigma of poor law aid (Corby et al., 2001; Kendrick & Fraser, 1992).

The power imbalance between adults and children can be exacerbated by the residential environment:

> Children in institutions are frequently described as a 'voiceless' population, having no control over decisions affecting their current and future placements, and no influence over the quality of care they receive (Westcott, 1991, pp. 12-13; see also Nunno & Motz, 1988; Stein, 2006; Wardhaugh & Wilding, 1993)

This is a crucial factor in preventing children from reporting abuse and has been highlighted in a number of Inquiry reports (Hughes, 1986; Levy & Kahan, 1991, Kirkwood, 1993; Waterhouse, 2000).

Siskind stresses that children in institutions are often particularly vulnerable to sexual abuse 'because of their developmental lags and insecurities and their increased reliance on adults' (Siskind, 1986, p. 15). The particular vulnerability of disabled children to abuse in residential settings has been noted in this regard (Doran & Brannan 1996; Kendrick, 1997; Oosterhoorn & Kendrick, 2001; Stein, 2006; Westcott, 1991b).

Management and Organisation

Wardhaugh and Wilding (1993) identify both management failure and the absence of clear lines of accountability as factors in institutional abuse, while Colton (2002) notes that the Waterhouse Report 'reveals a complete failure of management and accountability at every level' (Colton, 2002, p.35). Berridge and Brodie, in their comparison of cases of abuse in residential care in the UK identify three common features:

> … management of facilities and heads of homes tended to be ineffective or non-existent. Line managers also had minimal, if any, direct contact with units and so were in no position to observe malpractice, assuming of course that they would have recognised it. Adequate complaints systems were not in place (Berridge & Brodie, 1996, p. 184)

Wardhaugh and Wilding stress the 'absence of clear lines and mechanisms of accountability' as a factor in institutional abuse (Wardhaugh & Wilding, 1993). Stein (2006) also sees the failure of managerial, organizational and inspection systems as central to the abuse of children in residential care. He stresses the role of management in suppressing complaints and 'whistle blowing' by individual members of residential staff.

Siskind discusses a number of 'administrative styles' which have been identified with patterns of institutional sexual abuse: an autocratic director, protected by strong political and administrative networks, discourages participation by staff and residents in shared decision-making; emphasis is placed on the difficulty of handling residents and on control; reliance is placed on theoretical or ideological models which tend to distance and dehumanize relationships with residents; and an oppressor mentality promotes hostility toward females, children or minorities (Siskind, 1986, p. 20; see also Wardaugh &Wilding, 1993). Colton (2002) and Stein (2006) also identify the way in which institutional cultures can develop to deprive children and young people of their 'humanity'.

Training and Conditions of Residential Staff

The Curtis Committee (1946) viewed the training of child care staff as of such importance to improving the quality or residential care that it released an interim report urging the creation of a new body to manage new training courses in England. The first priority was training for staff in children's homes. This focus on the training of residential child care staff has been repeated in each and every inquiry report since. Despite this, there continues to be major concerns about the rate of progress in training residential staff (Colton, 2002), and ensuring that they have attained the qualifications necessary for registration. Recent cross-national, comparative research clearly links the level of qualification of residential child care staff, with the outcomes and well-being of children and young people in residential care (Cameron and Boddy, 2007)

Durkin (1982a) stresses the fact that institutional work brings out the worst in child care workers. Baldwin cites research which showed how the attitudes of child care workers on the causes

and handling of delinquency changed from being 'quite enlightened and permissive' when they started working in residential care to being 'much less permissive', and showing 'punitive, unenlightened views, shared with other personnel' (Baldwin, 1990, p. 150) when they had done the job for some time. Residential workers are often overworked and underpaid and they have little say in decision-making (Baldwin, 1990; Gil & Baxter, 1979; Nunno & Rindfleisch, 1991; Wardhaugh & Wilding, 1993). Tired caregivers suffering from burnout may abuse children, and a number of authors have identified the way in which burnout is characterised by increasing negative attitudes towards clients or children including depersonalisation and dehumanisation (Edwards & Miltenberger, 1991; Maslach & Jackson, 1981; Mattingly, 1981; Stein 2006).

Sexuality, Gender and the 'Targeting' of Residential Care

The lack of a focus on gender and sexuality in relation to the abuse of children and young people in residential care has been highlighted by a number of authors (Green, 2005; O'Neill, 2007).

> Gender inequalities in residential children's homes need to be illuminated and challenged, and more recognition given to the impact of gender on workers' relationships and attitudes, management practices, the abuse and exploitation of children and ultimately on the quality of the residential experience and outcomes for girls and boys (O'Neill, 2007, p. 102)

The anxieties of residential child care staff in dealing with sexuality have been highlighted and the implications of this for practice in terms of denial, uncertainty, reactive, punitive and inappropriate responses, particularly in relation to 'peer sexual abuse' (O'Neill, 2007; Green & Masson, 2002; Kendrick, 1997)

Pringle discusses the broader issues of abuse by men and he argues that 'if the male potential for abuse is so organically linked to both masculinity and entrenched patriarchal structures as suggested in this paper' (Pringle, 1993, p. 16), then the role of men in care services must be questioned. Berridge and Brodie (1996) found a 'macho' or masculine culture to be a factor in the three inquiry reports they examined.

Wolmar (2000 in Colton, 2002) has argued that the increase in male staff in residential establishments after the 1960s has been, given that the vast majority of perpetrators are male, a major factor in abuse in residential child care. Wolmar does not argue against the employment of males however, noting that children, particularly males, need good male role models. He however does articulate the need for greater safeguards against abuse where men are employed.

The literature stresses that paedophiles target work settings and activities which will give them access to children whom they can abuse (Gallagher, 2000; Sullivan & Beech, 2002). Colton and Vanstone (1996) conducted in-depth interviews with seven men who worked with children and who sexually abused them. They found choice of career as a motive for abuse varied from individual to individual, but could include purposive selection of both particular job types and duties within the job role that could provide opportunity for abuse, as well as underlying motivations that were not clear to the individuals themselves at the time.

Brannan et al. comment that: 'the control and seduction of a great number of young boys proved to be an underlying motivation for the conception and growth of Castle Hill School' (Brannan et al., 1993a, p. 6).

A number of inquiries (Hughes, 1986; Kirkwood, 1993; Waterhouse, 2000) have considered whether paedophile rings existed around residential care facilities. Kirkwood identified other cases of sexual abuse in children's homes and while concluding that the evidence did not tend to support that a paedophile ring was operating noted that: 'during the period 1973 to 1986 there was an alarmingly high number of child sexual abusers at work in Leicestershire Children's Homes' (Kirkwood, 1993, pp. 295-296). As noted above, Waterhouse (2000) did not find the existence of a paedophile ring in North Wales but did comment that many of those adults involved in abusing children in care homes knew each other and shared information about possible targets for abuse.

These issues highlight that the importance of addressing issues of gender and sexuality in residential child care, particularly in relation to the abuse of children and young people.

12. Conclusion

This literature review has aimed to draw together published material on the historical abuse of children and young people in residential child care in Scotland. We have been conscious while doing this that there has been an inevitable focus on the negative experiences of children and young people. Briefly, in this conclusion, we hope to highlight the lessons learnt from such negative experiences so that in the future children and young people can be sure to experience the very best that residential child care and the staff members who work in the sector can offer. There are three crucial aspects in safeguarding children from abuse. Staff and carers must be of the highest quality which demands rigorous procedures in selection and assessment, and ongoing training and support. There must be an open culture and environment in residential care. Finally, listening to children and young people is absolutely central to safeguarding them from abuse and harm.

Staff members themselves are central to safeguarding children and young people in residential care. Recruitment and selection practices must be improved to ensure that the best candidates are selected, and dangerous candidates are deterred. Staff members must be trained and qualified to an appropriate level in order to undertake the complex task of residential child care to the best of their ability. They must receive regular supervision and be supported by management, both within the residential establishment and by external management and leadership. They must be supported by other professionals and consultancy to deal with the multitude of difficult issues that they will face in working with the children and young people in their care. Through such efforts residential child care will be staffed by confident, autonomous individuals responsible for the delivery of a professional quality and calibre of nurture and care.

There must be a concerted effort to improve the status of residential child care and reduce the stigma linked with the sector. This involves improved resources at a number of different levels: in the quality and design of buildings; in the pay and conditions of staff members; and in the range of residential provision in order to afford choice and the availability of the most appropriate placements.

Residential child care must provide an open environment and culture so that staff members can reflect on their practice, identify concerns, give feedback and access complaints systems. They must be aware of the mechanisms for 'whistleblowing',

although this should not be viewed as a substitute for an open culture. Inspection and the monitoring of standards is part of this open culture, as is involvement of families and communities in the day-to-day activities of residential care.

Listening to children and young people must be central to this open culture. It must provide an environment which nurtures their self-esteem, and provides them with a range of opportunities to have their voice heard and, when necessary, to complain. There must be complaints systems which children and young people feel confident in using; and which they consider will be effective. Children and young people must also be involved in the decision-making which affects their lives; rights of participation are closely linked to rights of protection. They should have access to independent advocacy services. A focus on the rights of children and young people is essential to prevent further abuse of children and young people and to promote children's safety.

In acknowledging the abuse and neglect suffered by children and young people in residential care in the past, the future safety of children and young people must be ensured.

References

Abrams, L (1998). *The orphan country*. Edinburgh: John Donald Publishers.

Anthony, J. (1968). Other People's Children [first published in 1958], In Tod, R.J.N. (1968) *Children in care*. London: Longmans.

Australian Senate Community Affairs References Committee (2001). *Lost innocents: Righting the record - Report on child migration*. Accessed at:http://www.aph.gov.au/senate/committee/clac_ctte/completed_ inquiries/1999-02/child_migrat/report/index.htm, on 5th September 2007.

Baldwin, N. (1990). *The power to care in children's homes*. Aldershot: Avebury.

Barclay, A. and Hunter, L. (2007). Blurring the Boundaries: The Relationship Between Secure Accommodation and 'alternatives' in Scotland. In A. Kendrick (Ed.), *Residential child care: Prospects and challenges. Research Highlights Series* (pp. 166-180). London: Jessica Kingsley.

Barter, C (1999). Practitioners' experiences and perceptions: Investigating allegations of institutional abuse. *Child Abuse Review.* 8(6), 392-404.

Barter, C. (2007). Prioritising Young People's Concerns in Residential care: Responding to peer violence. In Kendrick, A. (ed.) *Residential child care: Prospects and challenges.* London: Jessica Kingsley Publishers.

Barter, C., Renold, E., Berridge, D. and Cawson, P. (2004). *Peer violence in children's residential care.* Basingstoke: Palgrave Macmillan.

BBC Radio 4 (2003a). *Children of the empire: Child migrants programme 1*, broadcast 15 September 2003.

BBC Radio 4 (2003b). *Good British stock: Child migrants programme 2*, broadcast 22 September 2003.

BBC Radio 4 (2003c). *Nobody to trust: Child migrants programme 3*, broadcast 29 September 2003.

BBC Radio 4 (2003d). *Children of the empire: Child migrants programme 1*, broadcast 6 October 2003.[5]

Bean P. and Melville J. (1989). *Lost children of the empire*. London: Unwin Hyman.

Beckett, C. (2002). The witch-hunt metaphor (and accusations against residential care workers), *British Journal of Social Work*, 32(5), 621-628.

Berridge, D. (1985). *Children's homes*. Basil Blackwell: Oxford.

Berridge, D and Brodie, I. (1996). Residential Child Care in England and Wales: The Inquiries and After. In Hill, M. and Aldgate, J. (eds) *Child welfare services: Developments in law, policy, practice and research* (pp. 180-195). London: Jessica Kingsley Publishers.

Berridge, D. and Brodie, I. (1998). *Children's homes revisited*. London: Jessica Kingsley Publishers.

Bibby, P. (ed.) (1996). *Organised abuse: The current debate*. Aldershot: Arena.

Berry, J. (1975). *Daily experience in residential life: A study of children and their care-givers*. London: Routledge and Keegan Paul.

Black, A. and Williams, C. (2002). *Fife Council independent enquiry established by the Chief Executive following the conviction of David Logan Murphy for the sexual abuse of children*. Kirkcaldy: Fife Council.

Bloom, R.B. (1992). When staff members sexually abuse children in residential care, *Child Welfare*, 71(2), 131 – 145.

Bowlby, J. (1951). *Maternal care and mental health*. Geneva: World Health Organisation.

Brannan, C., Jones, J.R. and Murch, J.D. (1993a). *Castle Hill report: Practice guide*. Shrewsbury: Shropshire County Council.

Brannan, C., Jones, J.R., and Murch, J.D. (1993b). Lessons from a residential special school enquiry: Reflections on the Castle Hill Report, *Child Abuse Review*, 2, 271-275.

Brill, K. and Thomas, R. (1964). *Children in homes*. London: Victor Gollanz.

Butler I. and Drakeford, M. (2005). *Scandal, social policy and social welfare* (2nd edition). Bristol: Policy.

Cameron, C. and Boddy, J. (2007). Staffing, Training and Recruitment: Outcomes for Young People in Residential Care in Three Countries. In A. Kendrick (ed), *Residential child care: Prospects and challenges*, (pp. 210-225). London: Jessica Kingsley Publishers.

Clough, R. (1982). *Residential work*. London: Macmillan.

Clyde Committee (1946). *Report of the committee on homeless children*. Cmd. 6911. Edinburgh: HMSO.

Colton, M. (2002). Factors associated with abuse in residential child care institutions, *Children & Society*, 16(1), 33-44.

Colton, M, Vanstone M and Walby C (2002). Victimization, care and justice: Reflections on the experience of victims/survivors involved in large-scale historical investigations of child sexual abuse in residential institutions, *British Journal of Social Work*, 32(5), pp. 541-552.

Community Care, May 10th, 2000, The Truth They Didn't Want to Hear, Accessed at: http://www.communitycare.co.uk/Articles/2000/05/10/21472/the-truth-they-didnt-want tohear.html?key=REGRESSION%20THERAPY, on 3rd September, 2007.

Community Care, 12 February, 2004, Abuse Reviews Need Balance Not Panic, Accessed at: http://www.communitycare.co.uk/Articles/2004/02/12/43771/abuse-reviews-need-balance-not-panic.html, 3rd September, 2007.

Corby, B. (2006). Book Review : The Secret of Bryn Estyn : The Making of a Modern Witch Hunt, *Child Abuse Review*, 15, 219-220.

Corby, B., Doig, A. and Roberts, V. (2001). *Public inquiries into abuse of children in residential care*. London: Jessica Kingsley Publishers.

Creighton, S.J. (1992). *Child abuse trends in England and Wales 1988 – 90*, London: NSPCC.

Crimmens, D. and Milligan, I. (2005). Residential Child Care : Becoming a Postive Choice. In Crimmens, D and Milligan, I. (eds.) (2005) *Facing forward: Residential child care in the 21st Century* (pp. 19-28). Lyme Regis: Russell House Publishing.

Curtis Committee (1946). *Report of the care of children committee*. Cmd. 6922. London: HMSO.

Davis, L.F. (1980). Sex and the Residential Setting. In Walton, R.G. and Elliott, D. (eds) *Residential care: A reader in current theory and practice*. Oxford: Pergamon.

Department of Health (1995). *Child protection: Messages from research*. London: HMSO.

Dinnage R. and Kellmer Pringle, M.L. (1967). *Residential care: Facts and fallacies*. London: Longmans.

Directors of Social Work in Scotland (1992). *Child protection policy, practice and procedure: An overview of child abuse issues and practice in social work departments in Scotland*. Edinburgh: HMSO.

Donnellan, C. (ed) (1993). *Children in care: Issues for the nineties*. Independence: Cambridge.

Doran, C. and Brannan, C. (1996). Institutional Abuse. In Bibby, P. (ed) *Organised abuse: The current debate* (pp. 155-166). Aldershot: Arena.

Durkin, R. (1982a). Institutional child abuse from a family systems perspective: a working paper, *Child & Youth Services*, 4, 15 – 22.

Durkin, R. (1982b). No one will thank you: first thoughts on reporting institutional abuse, *Child & Youth Services*, 4(1-2), 109-113.

Edwards D.M. (1968). Children at Risk and the Child Care Service. In Deeney, A.H. (ed.) *Children at risk*. London: Church Information Office.

Edwards, P. and Miltenberger, R. (1991). Burnout among staff members at community residential facilities for persons with mental retardation. *Mental Retardation*, 29(3), 125 - 128.

Farmer E and Pollock S (1999). Mix and match: Planning to keep looked after children safe, *Child Abuse Review*, 8(6), 377-391.

Foucault, M. (1979). *Discipline and punish: The birth of the prison*. Harmondsworth: Penguin.

[5] Thanks to SIRCC Library for sourcing this material

Frost, N., Mills, S. and Stein, M. (1999). *Understanding residential child care*. Aldershot: Ashgate.

Gallagher, B. (1999). The abuse of children in public care. Child Abuse Review. 8(6), 357-365.

Gallagher, B. (2000). The extent and nature of known cases of institutional child sexual abuse, *British Journal of Social Work*, 30, 795-817.

Gallagher, B., Hughes, B. and Parker, H. (1996) The Nature and Extent of Known Cases of Organised Child Sexual Abuse in England and Wales. In Bibby, P. (ed) *Organised abuse: The current debate* (pp. 215-230). Aldershot: Arena.

Garrett, J.R. (1979). Institutional maltreatment of children: An emerging public issue, *Residential and Community Child Care Administration*, 1, 57-68.

Gil, D.G. (1970). *Violence against children: Physical child abuse in the United States*. Cambridge, Mass.: Harvard University Press.

Gil, E. (1982). Institutional abuse of children in out-of-home care, *Child & Youth Services*, 4(1-2), 7-13.

Gil, E. and Baxter, K. (1979). Abuse of children in institutions, *Child Abuse & Neglect*, 3, 693-698.

Gill, A. (1998). *Orphans of the empire: The shocking story of child migration to Australia*. Sydney: Random House.

Goffman, E. (1961). *Asylums: Essays on the social situation of mental patients and other inmates*. New York: Doubleday.

Green, L. (2005) Theorizing sexuality, sexual abuse and residential children's homes: Adding gender to the equation. *British Journal of Social Work*, 35, 453-481.

Green, L. and Masson, H. (2002) Adolescents who sexually abuse and residential accommodation: Issues of risk and vulnerability, *British Journal of Social Work*, 32(2), 149-168.

Grier, J. (2002). Voluntary rights and statutory wrongs: The case of child migration, 1948-67. *History of Education*, 31(3), 263-280.

Harrell, S.A. and Orem, R.C. (1980). *Preventing child abuse and neglect: A guide for staff in residential institutions*. Washington: U.S. Department of Health and Human Services.

Hawthorn, M. (2006). Historic abuse in residential care: Sharing good practice, *In Residence No 4*. Glasgow: Scottish Institute for Residential Child Care.

Hayden, C., Goddard, J., Gorin, S. and Van Der Spek, K. (1999). *State child care: Looking after children?* London: Jessica Kingsley Publishers.

Hendrick, H. (1994). *Child welfare: England 1872 – 1989*. London: Routledge.

Hendrick, H. (2003). *Child welfare: Historical dimensions, contemporary debate*. Bristol : Policy Press.

Henry, R. (1965). The Man in Residential Care. In Lambert, D. (ed) *Change and the child in care*, Annual Review of the Residential Child Care Association. Harpenden: National Children's Home.

Hill, M., Davis, J., Prout, A. and Tisdall, K. (2004). Moving the participation agenda forward. Children & Society, 18, 77-96.

Hobbs, G., Hobbs, C.J. and Wynne J.M. (1999). Abuse of children in foster and residential care, *Child Abuse & Neglect*, 23(12), 1239-1252.

Holman, B. (1988). *Putting families first: Prevention and child care*. Basingstoke: Macmillan.

Holman, B. (1996). *The corporate parent, Manchester Children's Department 1948-1971*. London: National Institute for Social Work.

House of Commons (2003). *The Government reply to the Fourth Report from the Home Affairs Committee Session 2002-2003 HC 836 The conduct of investigations into past cases of abuse in children's homes*. Cm 5799, London: HMSO.

House of Commons Health Committee, (1998). *The welfare of former British child migrants*. HC 755, Session 1997-98. London: Stationery Office.

House of Commons Home Affairs Committee (2002). *The conduct of investigations into past cases of abuse in children's homes*. Fourth Report, Accessed at: http://www.publications.parliament.uk/pa/cm200102/cmselect/cm haff/836/83603.htm on 3rd September, 2007

House of Commons Social Services Committee (1984). *Children in care, Government response to the Second Report from the Social Services Committee*, Session 1983-4. London: HMSO.

Hughes, W.H. (1986). *Report of the inquiry into children's homes and hostels*. Belfast: HMSO.

Humphreys, M. (1994). *Empty cradles*. London: Transworld.

Kahan, B. (1979). *Growing up in care: Ten people talking*. Oxford: Blackwell.

Kahan, B. (2000). "Residential Child Care After Waterhouse", Accessed at http://www.childrenuk.co.uk/chukmar/mar2000/bkspeech.htm on 6 July, 2007.

Kelly, G. and Pinkerton, J. (1996). The Children (Northern Ireland) Order 1995: Prospects for Progress? In Hill, M. and Aldgate, J. (eds) *Child welfare services: Developments in law, policy, practice and research* (pp. 40-55). London: Jessica Kingsley Publishers. Kempe, C.H., Silverman, F., Steele, B., Droegmueller, W. and Silver, H. (1962). Battered-child syndrome, Journal of the American Medical Association, 181, p. 17-24.

Kendrick, A. and Fraser, A. (1992). *The Review of Residential Child Care in Scotland: A Literature Review. In The review of residential child care in Scotland: The three supporting research studies*. Central Research Unit Papers, Edinburgh: Scottish Office.

Kendrick, A. (1997). Safeguarding Children Living Away from Home from Abuse: A Literature Review. In Kent, R., *Children's safeguards review*, Edinburgh: HMSO.

Kendrick, A. (1998). In their best interest? Protecting children from abuse in residential and foster care, *International Journal of Child & Family Welfare*, 3(2), 169-185.

Kendrick, A. (2003). Children Looked After in Residential and Foster Care.In Baillie, D., Cameron, K., Cull, L-A., Roche, J. and West, J. (eds) *Social work and the law in Scotland* (pp. 135-146). London: Palgrave/Open University Press.

Kendrick, A. (2005). Social Exclusion and Social Inclusion: Themes and Issues in Residential Child Care. In Crimmens, D. and Milligan, I. (eds) *Facing forward: Residential child care in the 21st century* (pp. 7-18). Lyme Regis: Russell House Publishing.

Kendrick, A. (ed). (2007) *Residential child care: Prospects and challenges*. London: Jessica Kingsley Publishers.

Kent, R. (1997). *Children's safeguards review*. Edinburgh: HMSO.

Kilbrandon Committee (1964) *Children and young persons Scotland: Report By the committee appointed by the Secretary of State for Scotland*, Cmnd. 2306. Edinburgh: HMSO.

King, R., Raynes, N.V. and Tizard, J. (1971). *Patterns of residential care: Sociological studies in institutions for handicapped children*. London: Routledge and Keegan Paul.

Kirkwood, A. (1993). *The Leicestershire Inquiry 1992*. Leicester: Leicestershire County Council.

Levy, A. and Kahan, B. (1991). *The pindown experience and the protection of children: The Report of the Staffordshire Child Care Inquiry*. Stafford: Staffordshire County Council.

Lindsay, M. (1999). The neglected priority: Sexual abuse in the context of residential child care. *Child Abuse Review*, 8(6), 405 – 418.

Lothian and Borders Police, The City of Edinburgh Council, West Lothian Council, East Lothian Council, Midlothian Council, Scottish Borders Council (2001). *Joint police/social work protocol on the management and conduct of enquiries into allegations of historic abuse*. Edinburgh: The City of Edinburgh Council.

Macleod, M. (1999). The Abuse of Children in Institutional Settings: Children's Perspectives. In Stanley, N, Manthorpe, J. and Penhale, B. (eds) *Institutional abuse: Perspectives across the life course* (pp. 44-49). London: Routledge.

Magnusson, A. (1984). *The village: A history of Quarrier's*. Bridge of Weir: Quarrier's Homes.

Magnusson, A. (2006). *The Quarriers story : A history of the Quarriers*. Edinburgh: Birlinn.

Mainey, A., Milligan, I., Campbell, A., Colton, M., Roberts, S. and Crimmens, D. (2006). The Context of Residential Care in the United Kingdom. In Mainey, A. and Crimmens, D. (eds) (2006), *Fit for the future: Residential child care in the United Kingdom* (pp. 6-22). London: National Children's Bureau.

Marshall, K., Jamieson, C. and Finlayson, A. (1999). *Edinburgh's children: The report of the Edinburgh inquiry into abuse and protection of children in care*. Edinburgh: City of Edinburgh Council.

Maslach, C. and Jackson, S.E. (1981). *Maslach Burnout Inventory*. California: Consulting Lists Press.

Mattingly, M.A. (1981). Occupational Stress for Group Care Personnel. In Ainsworth, F. and Fulcher, L.C. (eds) *Group care for children: Concept and issues*. London: Tavistock Publications.

Morris, S. and Wheatley, H. (1994). *Time to listen: The experiences of young people in foster and residential care*. London: Childline.

Moss, M., Sharpe, S. and Fay, C. (1990). *Abuse in the care system: A pilot study by the National Association of Young People in Care*. London, National Association of Young People in Care (NAYPIC).

NCH (1992). *The Report of the committee of inquiry into children and young people who sexually abuse other children*. London: National Children's Home.

Nunno, M. and Motz, J.R. (1988). The development of an effective response to the abuse of children in out-of-home care, *Child Abuse and Neglect*, 12, 521 - 528.

Nunno, M. and Rindfleisch, N. (1991). The abuse of children in out of home care, *Children & Society*, 5(4), 295 – 305.

O'Neill, T. (2007). Gender Matters in Residential Child Care. In Kendrick, A. (ed.) *Residential child care: Prospects and challenges* (pp. 93-106). London: Jessica Kingsley Publishers.

Oosterhoorn, R. and Kendrick, A. (2001). No sign of harm: Issues for disabled children communicating about abuse, *Child Abuse Review*, 10, 243-253.

Packman, J. (1981). *The child's generation: Child care policy in Britain* (2nd ed). Oxford: Basil Blackwell. [first published in 1975]

Page, R. and Clark, G.A. (eds) (1977). *Who cares? Young people in care speak out*. London: National Children's Bureau.

Parker, R (1990). *Away from home: A history of childcare*. Ilford: Barnardo's.

Parker, R. (1995). A Brief History of Child Protection. In Farmer, E. and Owen, M. *Child protection practice: Private risk and public remedies*. London: HMSO.

Parton, N. (1985). *The politics of child abuse*. Basingstoke: MacMillan.

Parton, N (2006). *Safeguarding childhood: Early intervention and surveillance in a late modern society*. Basingstoke: Palgrave Macmillan.

Penhale, B. (1999). Introduction. In Stanley, N, Manthorpe, J. and Penhale, B. (eds) *Institutional abuse: Perspectives across the life course* (pp. 1-15). London: Routledge.

Polat, F. and Farrell, P. (2002). What was it like for you? Former pupils' reflections on their placement at a residential school for pupils with emotional and behavioural difficulties, *Emotional and Behavioural Difficulties*, 7(20), 97-108.

Powers, J., Mooney, A. and Nunno, M. (1990). Institutional abuse: A review of the literature, *Journal of Child and Youth Care*, 4(6), 81-95.

Pringle, K. (1993). Child sexual abuse perpetrated by welfare personnel and the problem of men. *Critical Social Policy*, 36, 4 - 19.

Rabb, J. and Rindfliesch, N. (1985). A study to define and assess severity of institutional abuse/neglect, *Child Abuse & Neglect*, 9, 285-294.

Ridge, T. and Millar, J. (2000). Excluding children: Autonomy, friendship and the experience of the care system. *Social Policy & Administration*, 34(2), pp. 160-175.

Scottish Executive. (2003). *Children in residential accommodation 2001 - 2002*. Edinburgh: Scottish Executive.

Scottish Executive (2006). *Looked after children 2005-2006*. Edinburgh: Scottish Executive.

Scottish Office (1998). *Protecting children - a shared responsibility: Guidance on inter-agency co-operation.* Edinburgh: The Scottish Office.

Seed, P. and Thomson, M. (1977). *All kinds of care: An investigation into the use of residential and day care facilities for children in the Highlands and Western Isles of Scotland.* Aberdeen: University of Aberdeen.

Sinclair and Gibbs (1998). *Children's homes: A study in diversity.* Chichester: Wiley.

Siskind, A.B. (1986). Issues in institutional child sexual abuse: The abused, the abuser and the system. *Residential Treatment for Children & Youth*, 4, 9-30.

Skinner, A. (1992). *Another kind of home: A review of residential child care.* Edinburgh: The Scottish Office.

Smith, M and Milligan, I. (2005). The expansion of secure accommodation in Scotland: In the best interests of the child? *Youth Justice*, 4(3), 178-191.

Smith, M. (forthcoming). Historical abuse in residential child care: An alternative view, *Practice*.

Social Work Inspection Agency (2006). *Extraordinary lives: Creating a positive future for looked after children and young people in Scotland.* Edinburgh: Social Work Inspection Agency.

Social Work Services Group (1985). *Child abuse: Report of the working group on social work issues in child abuse.* Edinburgh: Scottish Education Department.

Stanley N. (1999). The Institutional Abuse of Children: An Overview of Policy and Practice. In Stanley, N, Manthorpe J and Penhale B (eds) (1999) *Institutional abuse: Perspectives across the life course* (pp. 16-43). London : Routledge.

Stanley, N. (2004). A year on from the Climbié Inquiry. *Child Abuse Review*, 13, 75-79.

Steckley, L. and Kendrick, A. (2007). Hold on: Physical restraint in residential child care. In Kendrick, A. (ed) *Residential child care: Prospects and challenges* (pp. 152-165). London: Jessica Kingsley Publishers.

Stein, M. (2006). Missing years of abuse in children's homes. *Child and Family Social Work*, 11, 11-21.

Strathclyde Regional Council (1978/9). *Room to grow.* Glasgow: Strathclyde Regional Council.

Stuart, M. and Baines, C. (2004). *Progress on safeguards for children living away from home.* York: Joseph Rowntree Foundation.

Sullivan, J. and Beech, A. (2002). Professional perpetrators: Sex offenders who use their employment to target and sexually abuse the children with whom they work. *Child Abuse Review*, 11, 153-167.

Thomas, T. (2001). Preventing unsuitable people from working with children – the Criminal Justice and Court Services Bill, *Child Abuse Review*, 10, 60-69.

Triseliotis J. (1988). Residential Care From a Historical and Research Perspective. In Wilkinson J.E. and O'Hara G. (eds) *Our children: Residential and community care.* London: National Children's Bureau Scottish Group.

Utting, W. (1991). *Children in the public care: A review of residential child care.* London: HMSO.

Utting, W. (1997). *People like us: The report of the review of the safeguards for children living away from home.* London: Stationery Office.

Vincent, S. and Daniel, B. (2004). An analysis of children and young people's calls to ChildLine about abuse and neglect: A study for the Scottish Child Protection Review, *Child Abuse Review*, 13, 158 – 171.

Wagner, G. (1988). *Residential care: A positive choice, Report of the Independent Review of Residential Care.* National Institute for Social Work. London: HMSO.

Wardhaugh, J. and Wilding, P. (1993). Towards an explanation of the corruption of care, *Critical Social Policy*, 37, 4-31.

Warner, N. (1992). *Choosing with care: The report of the committee of inquiry into the selection, development and management of staff in children's homes*, London: HMSO.

Waterhouse, L., Dobash, R.P. and Carnie, J. (1994). *Child sexual abusers.* Central Research Unit Papers, Edinburgh: Scottish Office.

Waterhouse, R. (2000). *Report of the Tribunal of Enquiry into the abuse of children in care in the former county council areas of Gwynedd and Clwyd since 1974*, London: HMSO.

Webster, R. (2000). Do you care to go to jail?, *Professional Social Work*, June.

Webster, R. (2005). *The secret of Bryn Estyn: The making of a modern witch hunt.* Oxford: Orwell Press.

Westcott, H. (1991a). *Institutional abuse of children - From research to policy: A review.* London: NSPCC.

Westcott, H.L. (1991b). The abuse of disabled children: a review of the literature, *Child: Care, Health and Development*, 17(4), 243-258.

Westcott, H. and Clement, M. (1992). *NSPCC experience of child abuse in residential care and educational placements: Results of a survey*, London: NSPCC.

White, K. (1973). *Residential child care past and present.* Unpublished MPhil Thesis, University of Edinburgh

White, K. (1999). Children and Foster Care: Inclusion, Exclusion and Life Chances. In White, K. (ed.) *Children and social exclusion* (pp. 71-80). London: NCVCCO.

White, K. (2003). The Ideology of Residential Care and Fostering, In White, K. (ed.) *Reframing children's services.* London: NCVCCO.

Who Cares? Scotland (2004). *Lets face it! Care 2003: Young people tell us how it is.* Glasgow: Who Cares? Scotland.

Williams of Mostyn (1996). *Childhood matters: Report of the National Commission of Inquiry into the Prevention of Child Abuse*, London: HMSO.

Williams, G. and McCreadie, J. (1992). *Ty Mawr Community Home Inquiry.* Gwent County Council.

Wills, D.W. (1971). *Spare the child: The story of an experimental approved school.* Harmondsworth: Penguin.

Appendix 3

Children's residential services: Learning through records

Nancy Bell, Researcher
Historical Abuse Systemic Review
November 2007

Appendix 3

Children's residential services: Learning through records

Nancy Bell, Researcher
November 2007

Contents

Acknowledgments

I would like to thank the many individuals who contributed to this report. In particular, I am grateful to former residents for offering their expert contributions under difficult emotional circumstances, allowing me insights into the many challenges they faced in trying to learn more about who they are and "what happened" many years ago in places where they spent their childhood.

I would also like to thank those individuals working for voluntary and religious organisations; local authorities; universities and archives who displayed a genuine and heartfelt understanding about why records are important and why significant records associated with children's residential establishments, such as children's files, must be preserved and made accessible.

Last, but not least, thank you to the Historical Abuse Systemic Review's legal researcher, administrative assistant, other researchers and various individuals who contributed their expertise to this report.

Nancy Bell
Researcher
November 2007

Executive Summary

The Historical Abuse Systemic Review remit began with the words "...against the background of the abuse suffered by children up to the age of 16 in residential schools and children's homes in Scotland...". The review intended to learn from a systemic perspective – that is, from an overall service provision viewpoint – how abuse was allowed to happen in children's residential establishments throughout Scotland between 1950 and 1995.

This report on records highlights the important insights we gained into the challenges of locating and accessing records associated with children's residential services. Secondly, the report also illustrates records' importance and the complexities associated with children's residential services records, which are an essential component to monitoring children's safety and ensuring accountability.

The content of the report focuses primarily upon:

■ Issues associated with records and the review's remit
■ Why children's residential services records are important and to whom
■ Former residents' experiences of locating and accessing records
■ The legal context for children's residential establishment records
■ The review's search for information and what we found

By focusing on these we hope to contribute to a better understanding of the importance of children's residential establishment records and the need to ensure their preservation and accessibility.

The **conclusions** in the report are as follows:

Chapter 1: The review's remit specifically refers to records, a topic addressed during the 2004 parliamentary debate on child abuse in institutions. However, the remit is based on numerous assumptions about records that do not take account of the realities of locating and accessing records associated with children's residential services. Various issues arose, making information-gathering and locating and accessing records extremely challenging:

Central databases: None exist for children's residential services that cover the 45 year period under review.
Definitions for "residential schools" and "children's homes": Many terms have been used throughout the years to describe residential settings for children.
Service provision: Residential services have been varied, extensive and changing from 1950 to 1995.
Existence of records: There have been no records retention and disposal schedules for records associated with children's residential establishments; therefore, it is impossible to know what records should or do exist without laborious searching.
'Public records' definition: This definition is unclear and access to records held by private bodies, providing public services, depends upon their goodwill.
Records location, volume and types: There are large numbers of different record types in many locations and not all records have been put into records management systems, archived or both of these.

Access to records: It is complicated to access records, due to legal restrictions and the lack of standardised access to records policies.
Records as 'relevant': Determining record relevancy is subjective and difficult to assess without examining records, a time-consuming task requiring adequate resources.
Attitudes: Some helpful and some poor attitudes may determine access to relevant information.

While records were essential to the work of the review, we learned that records are also very important to many individuals for many reasons. Organisations and government depend on records, while records are also necessary for future research. Records have particular significance to former residents for several reasons such as their search for identity, establishing a historical account, practical administrative challenges in daily life, their sense of belonging and general interest. Records also ensure that former residents' rights are realised, specifically their rights under human rights, freedom of information and data protection legislation.

Many children's residential establishment records appear to be missing, but there is evidence that these records may exist in far greater numbers than is known. It is critical that the importance of records – which is apparent to former residents, archivists and others – is known by people responsible for generating and managing records to ensure that significant records for children's residential establishments are preserved and made accessible.

Chapter 2: Former residents who lived in children's residential establishments have rights associated with records. These include the legal entitlement to view records associated with their childhood experiences in residential placements. Some former residents contacting the review, however, found that locating and accessing records associated with children's residential establishments is fraught with challenges. There is no central tracing database, for example, to assist former residents seeking information about their experiences, their family history and children's residential establishments in general.

The described experiences of former residents contacting the review illustrate the many difficulties former residents encountered when trying to locate information they expected to be available to them. Located records often don't contain the information former residents expected, or hoped, to see. Some residents are upset when they read certain information in their records for the first time as elderly adults. Some records are missing. Poor records management in the past has meant that some former residents are unable to realise their legal entitlements to access records.

The challenges faced by former residents contacting the review are consistent with experiences highlighted in other inquiries, such as those into child migration and institutional child abuse.[1] Some key aspects include:

Locating records: Records may be located in several locations and information may be in many types of records, unknown and unidentified to former residents. These records may also exist in places at considerable geographical distance from where former residents live, requiring them to incur significant costs to access records.
Missing records: Records may be missing for various reasons, such as inadequate searching, the misplacement of records or because records have been destroyed.
Support to view records: Former residents may be prevented from gaining access to their records without agreeing to support services from organisations and local authorities

concerned about the possible effects that reading file contents may have on former residents.
Information within records: Once former residents have gained access to their records, they're often disappointed or distressed by what isn't in their records or by what they learn for the first time in their lives.
Record quality: Former residents described their difficulty in reading photocopied records and in reading incomplete information that had pages missing or information blocked from view.

One critical lesson we learned is how the search for records and records content affect the lives of children as adults in later years. Through the experiences of former residents with records, it is possible to see what must be done to make the future experiences of children in state care, who seek information about their childhood experiences, less traumatic. It is also possible to see what issues need to be addressed to meet the current needs of former residents trying to locate and access records. From a broader perspective, society benefits when we are able to gain insights into past practices through personal records associated with children's residential services.

Chapter 3: The regulatory framework for children's residential services shows how **children's residential establishments** needed to generate more records in later years. At the same time, this regulatory framework does not take account of all the records generated in association with **children's residential services**. From 1950 to 1995, the law specified what records needed to be generated within approved schools, children's homes, residential placements for children with 'mental disorders' and remand homes, for example. The law outlined managers' and the Secretary of State's duties and powers relating to records, imposing an oversight responsibility for individual children's welfare and children's residential establishments facilitated through records.

As an illustration, the 1933 law required managers for approved schools to ensure proper record keeping, which included 'punishment books', and to review the records, possibly to monitor children's safety and quality of service provision. The 1961 rules included additional requirements such as keeping records of children's progress and absconding. Approved school managers, who had an obligation to manage '...the school in the interests of the welfare, development and rehabilitation of the pupils', were also required to read the log book, keep meeting minutes, report to the Secretary of State and make records available to inspectors. The 1952 and 1959 regulations for children's homes show the association between records and the duties of managers, inspectors and the Secretary of State, who was to receive 'punishment returns'.

The 1987 regulations[2] continued to place duties on managers for proper record generation and required managers to prepare a statement of functions and objectives for their establishment[3]. In particular, managers had responsibility for ensuring children's records, including 'health particulars', were kept along with a log book registering important events, such as 'discipline' administered. The language in the 1987 regulations changed to 'discipline' from 'punishment' used in earlier legislation, which coincided with the banning of corporal punishment in schools. In the 1980s, new regulations for secure accommodation also demanded records for children placed there and access to those records by inspectors. The Secretary of State could request individual records for children placed in secure accommodation.

---

[1] see British House of Commons Health Select Committee Report (1998); Parliament of Australia Senate Report (2001); and Parliament of Australia Senate Report (2004).
[2] 1987/2233. In force from 1 June 1988. Superseded by the Residential Establishments – Child Care (Scotland) Regulations 1996 (SI 1996/3256) and the Arrangements to Look After Children (Scotland) Regulations 1996 (SI 1996/3262)
[3] ibid paragraph 5

Then, the Children's (Scotland) Act 1995 and other regulations, including those for secure accommodation, followed. The legal provisions for records associated with children's residential establishments changed once again and became more expansive, suggesting a growing reliance on records as a method for monitoring and improving services to children. Managers of children's residential establishments continued to have responsibility for records, including detailed statements of function and objectives. The law introduced statements on 'children's rights and responsibilities' to be given to children along with information about complaints procedures. The requirement to generate personal records for children in children's residential establishments continued although the requirements for what those records must contain developed further under the 1995 Act.

Chapter 4: In our review of public records legislation, it became apparent that the Public Records Act 1937 is the main legislation responsible for ensuring the preservation of public records, which include records for children's residential services. According to public records experts, however, this law is significantly outdated and needs reform. Notably, there is no adequate definition of 'public record' and no duty imposed on local authorities to transfer their public records to archives for preservation. There is also no legal specification about how records generated by private bodies receiving public funding must be preserved and made accessible.

The public records legislation sits alongside other law. The Local Government etc (Scotland) Act 1994, for example, provided for the transfer of records between the old and new authorities. While the law said local authorities should make "proper arrangements" for the "preservation and management" of their records, it did not require them to do so. Furthermore, the 1994 Act allowed local authorities to dispose of any records it did not consider "worthy of preservation", which meant that individuals within local authority departments – who may have been unskilled as records managers and archivists – were making decisions about what records were destroyed.

Current freedom of information and data protection law depends upon records existence to ensure that individuals' realise their legal entitlements to access records. There is an urgent need, therefore, to review all public records legislation to make certain that it is coordinated and facilitates access to records. Legal authority, reflected in standards and guidance, is also needed to guide the proper management of records. Inadequate legislation leads to poor records management practices which, in turn, have significant implications for records associated children's residential establishments, affecting what is preserved, destroyed and made accessible.

In recent years significant initiatives have attempted to address gaps in records legislation. These include the Archival Mapping Project (1999), the Public Records Strategy (2003-2004) and the Code of Practice on Records Management (2003) – all of which relate to record preservation and access. We found, however, that despite these important initiatives, several outstanding issues remain including the need to:

■ Reform public records legislation;
■ Clarify what happens to records held by private bodies that receive public funds;
■ Address variations in records access policies and the lack of records access policies, in some places; and
■ Coordinate public records legislation to ensure individuals' are not being denied their legal entitlement to access records.

And, within this context, special consideration needs to be given to the records of children's residential establishments - the 'homes' where adults lived as children, away from their families.

Chapter 5: Major local government reorganisations and changes to children's services legislation in 1968 occurred during the period 1950 to 1995. These factors would have impacted on the generation and preservation of records associated, directly or indirectly, with central government as well as local authorities and organisations. The reporting and policy relationship between organisations and central government would have changed throughout the years, with significant implications for records. The absence of appropriate records legislation would also have impacted on record preservation at all levels.

The former Scottish Executive Education Department ('SEED') made records available for us to consider during the review. Prior to these records being made available, the Scottish Information Commissioner had examined SEED's process of gathering records relating to historical abuse in residential schools and children's homes. The ensuing report (Scottish Information Commissioner, 2005) identified many issues that arose for us and we concur with several findings in that report. The report identifies the challenges associated with SEED's search for records, such as the large numbers of existing records and the nature of unstructured information. Some findings from the Scottish Information Commissioner's report are as follows:

■ Past records management practices were not as robust as current practices.
■ What records exist today depends upon the quality of record-keeping in the past.
■ Most SEED records contain policy information and, for example, inspection reports.
■ Titles can be misleading and there are inconsistencies and gaps in the records (Scottish Information Commissioner, 2005).

In our search for central government records, like the Scottish Information Commissioner, we learned about the existence of records not identified on SEED's list – records potentially relevant to the review. This factor made the task of reviewing all possibly relevant SEED records very time-consuming and beyond the review's resources. It was difficult to determine from the record names, for example, what information the records held and – without reviewing the records – whether the information in the records was relevant. In many of the records we reviewed, however, we identified important information germane to our understanding about children's residential services.

Chapters 6 and 7: We relied on information located within records held by voluntary organisations, religious organisations and local authorities to fulfil our remit. Our information-gathering process shows how difficult, if not impossible, it is to gain insights into systemic factors contributing to children's abuse within residential establishments without the existence of records. In general, our search for information revealed that local authorities, voluntary organisations and religious organisations all faced similar challenges when trying to locate records, making accessibility difficult. We found that it was impossible to determine where all 'relevant' records for children's residential establishments are held, and this situation will remain until all significant records for children's residential services are identified, located and catalogued.

Locating records associated with children's residential services is an enormous and daunting task. We learned, for example, that

management records relating to the same topic may be located in many locations. We also found that the lack of records in one location, for example, didn't mean that those records, or records relating to the same topic, don't exist. We discovered that many children's residential establishments changed function, ownership and closed, making the ownership of records, such as children's files and management records, and what happened to those records somewhat unclear. The local authorities, voluntary and religious organisations were reorganised or relocated, which led to massive uncertainty about what happened to records through transitions. Employees with corporate memory left their employment, taking their memory of where records are located with them.

When children left their residential placements, various unregulated approaches guided what happened to **children's records.** These approaches were complicated by the possible existence of several children's records for one child depending on what services were involved. Children's records may have existed within the children's residential establishments, local authority social work or children's departments, local authority education departments or education authorities, health boards and voluntary or religious organisations. For children placed outwith their own local authorities, it was reported that children's records returned to the child's originating authority and were dispersed to central offices. It's not clear what happened to the records of Scottish children placed in children's residential establishments in England.

Our information gathering, however, depended upon organisations and local authorities having located and identified all "relevant" records together with their ability to make those records immediately accessible. As our search for information shows, two large government reorganisations, major legislative changes and changes within organisations throughout a 45 year period led to challenges in the search for information:

■ Poor records management practices in the past mean that records are missing, have been destroyed or were not generated in the first instance.
■ Corporate memory was held by individuals who have retired or died.
■ There was no legislation requiring sound records management, such as schedules of records that had been retained and destroyed.
■ Organisations have changed locations or experienced fires or floods, causing damage to records.
■ Children's residential establishments closed or changed management and their records locations are unknown.
■ Few general records are easily accessible and specific to children's residential services.
■ The labelling of records is poor and the records' catalogues inadequate.
■ It was very time-consuming and costly to search for information.

A number of voluntary and religious organisations, while committed to better records management, lacked, and continue to lack, a proper records management system and full-time archivists. Not all local authorities currently employ archivists and records managers and some did not adequately support their existing archival services.

Voluntary organisations, religious organisations and local authorities found it difficult, and at times impossible, to respond to our queries about past management policies and practices, including policies that relate to monitoring children's well-being and keeping children safe. For those organisations and local authorities that did respond, the information they provided

suggests that records have become increasingly relied upon for monitoring children's safety, promoting their well-being and evaluating the quality of services provided to children.

The poor overall state of records, however, raises important issues about how voluntary organisations, religious organisations and local authorities that provided children's residential services are held accountable to children, former residents and others, for the services they provided.

Concluding remarks: We depended upon records to gain insights into past experiences within children's residential services and, in doing so, we learned invaluable lessons about records associated with children's residential establishments and children's services in general. We've identified reasons why records are important, to whom and for what reasons. We've developed awareness about the many challenges facing individuals who seek and work with records. And, we now recognise the significant costs – personal, historical, and social - for survivors of institutional child abuse, others who lived in children's residential establishments and society when records cannot be located and accessed. There are economic benefits to proper records management – now and in the future. For children living away from home and in state care today, records are essential for monitoring their safety, promoting their well-being and holding children's services accountable for what they offer children.

Poor recording keeping practices have, and continue to have, many implications:

■ This review experienced difficulty in addressing its remit due to the poor state of records associated with children's residential services. Future inquiries[4] will also be affected unless proper records management practices are universally adopted;
■ Challenges exist for local and central governments, religious organisations and voluntary organisations needing to respond to inquiries about past management policy and practices.
■ Former residents of children's residential establishments may be unable to realise their legal entitlements to access personal information and information about children's residential services.
■ Individuals may be denied access to justice that depends upon the collaboration of records;
■ It is difficult to develop a full historical account of children's residential services in Scotland without records.
■ There are risks to children in care today as records play an essential role in monitoring children's safety and well-being.
■ There is the potential lack of accountability by organisations and government who are responsible for their services to children.
■ Future research that could contribute to a better understanding of Scotland's social history may be hindered.

The establishment of 'historical accounts', in particular, is important to former residents. Records play a critical role in establishing accounts about what happened in children's residential establishments throughout Scotland and what contributed to children's abuse. Records may complement the oral histories of people who lived in children's residential establishments and those who worked in children's services. Records add to our understanding about how those establishments, and children's services in general, are situated within Scotland's wider social fabric.

Records are vital to ensuring '...that past experiences and lessons are not lost'. It was within the spirit of learning lessons that this report was written. From the knowledge we have gained, we would like to encourage all those individuals who found it difficult to place importance on records to learn more about

---

⁴ 'Future inquiries': May include public or judicial inquiries; inspections; police investigations; audits and any other processes inquiring into matters relating to children's services.

records – to see beyond records as administrative inconveniences to how records connect to the humanity of children living away from home and in state care. Records have significance beyond the immediate, they have importance in perpetuity.

We are extremely grateful to former residents for their sharing their expertise and their experiences about records, as it was apparent that their contributions were accompanied by an emotional cost to them. We appreciate, as well, the support, enthusiasm and passion shared by many people who believe in the importance of preserving records that allow us to better understand people's experiences, the provision of children's residential services and their interrelationship with Scotland's social history. Lessons that we learn from records allow us to better meet the needs of children living away from home and in state care today.

It is not too late to make important changes to address critical and outstanding issues identified within the report.

Chapter 1: Records and children's residential services

Introduction

> "Children are at once the most vulnerable citizens in any society and the greatest of our treasures[5]."

Children in residential establishments, living away from home, are among the most vulnerable, yet abuse has occurred in the very places where children should have been safe and nurtured. The remit for the Historical Abuse Systemic Review begins with the words "…against the background of the abuse suffered by children up to the age of 16 in residential schools and children's homes in Scotland…". The review intended to learn from a systemic perspective – that is, from an overall service provision viewpoint – how abuse was allowed to happen in children's residential establishments throughout Scotland between 1950 and 1995.

Our review, like all inquiries, depended on records[6] to meet its remit objectives. In our search for records, and information within, we learned about important issues associated with our search. This special report on records, therefore, emerged for two primary reasons. First, we believe it is necessary to highlight the significant insights we gained from our experiences, and the experiences of others, in the search for information about children's residential services. Records, and access to information within them, are fundamental to helping us understand what has happened in the past. Secondly, 'monitoring' is a key aspect of the review's remit with children's services records playing a crucial role in monitoring children's safety and ensuring accountability - it is a role that is not always valued. For these reasons, we concluded that records merit special consideration.

Society depends on records, which are important for countless reasons and in all spheres of life. Records associated with children's residential services have been, and continue to be, an essential part of ensuring children's safety and well-being. Records have a significant meaning to people who lived in children's residential establishments – they're essential to their sense of identity. These, and other factors, are important for understanding adult survivor experiences of childhood abuse, for responding to their needs and for developing better ways of taking care of children who live in residential establishments today.

This first chapter considers the assumptions that our remit was based on. It reports on the parliamentary discussion in which records featured and the challenges we faced when we began gathering information. It examines why records are important, to whom and why. Finally, it reports on myths and realities linked to records that were, supposedly, missing.

The assumptions behind the remit of the review

The review's remit states:

> "4. For the purposes of his investigation the Independent Expert will, in addition to information that is publicly available: (1) have access to all documentary records of the former Scottish Office in so far as in the possession of Scottish Ministers from the period under consideration and in so far as relating to residential schools and children's homes which will be subject to redaction[7] to ensure that no individual can be identified; (2) be expected to seek the cooperation of local authorities and other organisations with responsibility for the management and administration of residential schools and children's homes in making available to him such documentary records and explanation of such records as he considers to be necessary for his purposes.

> "5. Except in so far as provided above the Independent Expert is not expected to consider material or submissions from individuals or from local authorities or such organisations except to the extent that he may consider it necessary for the purposes of his investigation to obtain information from organisations representing the interests of the survivors of abuse."

The remit is based on the assumption that all relevant information would be found within the "documentary records of the former Scottish Office…subject to redaction" in addition to information "publicly available". It suggests that we should seek the co-operation of local authorities, voluntary and religious organisation that may hold information of potential use, which is not "publicly available". There was no legal requirement for local authorities and organisations to assist us by granting access to information. While the former Minister of Education and Young People had encouraged organisations to "open their files" during the 2004 parliamentary debate, we relied on local authorities and organisations to help us within the spirit of co-operation.

The remit didn't anticipate that we'd "…consider material or submissions from individuals…local authorities or…organisations…" We depended on former residents and others, on the other hand, to tell us where potentially relevant information might be located. Many people made invaluable contributions to our search for records. They added immensely to our understanding of the general state of children's residential services' records, during the period when we, and others, encountered many complications associated with identifying, locating and accessing such records. We also learned, through discussions with former residents of children's residential establishments, about the challenges they faced finding and accessing records.

We're extremely grateful to everyone who made extraordinary efforts to locate information and to tell us about existing records that might help us to understand how abuse was allowed in children's residential establishments. It was evident that many recognised the valuable contribution children's residential services records make to our understanding of historical childcare services in Scotland – a vital component of Scotland's social

---

[5] Acceptance Speech of the President of the African National Congress, Nelson Mandela, at the Nobel Peace Prize Award Ceremony: Oslo, Norway. December 10, 1993.

[6] 'Records' refers to paper files, photographs, videotapes, databases and electronic files whereas 'files' are considered hard copy documentation or electronic versions of recordings. 'Information' includes records, files and verbal evidence.

[7] 'Redaction': The process of blocking out or deleting specific information from records.

history. We also learned about records' importance to former residents of children's residential establishments, as those records are often the only tangible connection former residents have to their childhood experiences.

Despite the contributions many individuals made to our search for information, however, it became apparent that poor records management practices have led to poor outcomes from personal, historical and social perspectives, as this report illustrates. From the viewpoint of this review, our work was seriously hampered by the dire state of records associated with children's residential services. Preserving records and making them accessible, we learned, is critical to ensuring that we respect the needs of individuals who lived, and live, in residential placements. Records are vital to making certain that we learn important lessons about what happened in children's residential establishments.

Background: the parliamentary discussion

The Scottish Parliament recognised the significance of records, and making them available, during its debate about institutional child abuse held on 1 December 2004[8]. The then Minister for Education and Young People, Peter Peacock, (the Scottish Executive, now Scottish Government)[9], spoke about "opening a new chapter" on historical abuse in institutional care. He announced that the Scottish Executive was "...working to open all files that are relevant to people seeking insights into what has happened in residential establishments in which they lived", confirming that the Scottish Executive was involved in a process to ensure that sensitive personal information was not released.

The Minister also indicated that the Public Petitions Committee had raised the issue of contact with organisations that held "relevant" information. He stated that he wrote to various organisations to request that they open their files, commenting that he had received positive responses. In noting that he wanted "relevant files" to be identified and made public, the Minister stated that these were "exceptional circumstances" requiring the involvement of the Keeper of the Records[10]. The Minister further announced that he had asked the Freedom of Information Commissioner to examine the Scottish Executive's own process of tracing and opening their records. It was reported that the Public Petitions Committee welcomed the involvement of the Freedom of Information Commissioner "...in the investigations into abuse"'.

> "I want him to verify that we have been taking all reasonable steps to be open and, if he finds deficiencies in any actions, I want him to highlight those so that I may rectify the situation. I hope that those actions will reassure Parliament and the survivors of abuse that we are being as open as possible."

Some MSPs commented about the need for transparent records, such as those held by the Scottish Executive and other organisations stating, for example, that "it is vital that all relevant and available paperwork is out in the open". During the debate, one MSP raised the topic of "missing records", indicating it was important to know why records are missing. This MSP described the importance of locating and preserving records associated with children who were in care, and the need for former residents' support to enable access. In stating that no destruction of records should be allowed, this member also recommended a "register of those records"

to assist former residents to access their records:

> "The individual record of a young person will indicate where they were, but there will not necessarily be a collective record for an institution of who was there at a particular time. Ironically, one of the ways in which many of the adults were traced during the [local authority] experience was through a pocket-money book that turned up, which contained the children's names; it was only through that document that people were able to go back and look for individual child care records. One lesson for the future is that we must ensure that there is better record keeping. Separate records must be kept for child and family social work files and there must be better collation of records on institutions."

In his closing statement, the Minister stated: "I want to make it clear that the Executive is absolutely determined to bring to the surface all the information and knowledge about what has happened that are in our possession and we encourage others to do exactly the same."

The challenges arising for the review

The review's remit is set against a "...background of abuse" and the 2004 parliamentary discussion revealed the importance MSPs placed on records to provide insights into how that abuse was allowed to happen. The parliamentary discussions, however, were based on assumptions about records, including the assumption that records can be located and that they're accessible. We met several challenges, however, at the beginning of our search for information, as described below.

Centralised databases
No existing information provided a detailed overview of the regulatory framework for children's residential services between 1950 and 1995, which made the search for related policy, guidance and standards difficult. No central database records the names of children's residential establishments, their location, dates of operation, their purpose or their management structures for the entire period under review. No central database identifies what records are associated with children's residential services and where they are located.

Defining "residential schools" and "children's homes"
Many formal and informal terms were used to describe residential settings where children lived without parental care, making it challenging to define "residential schools" and "children's homes". The imprecise definitions, which altered in meaning throughout the review period, had implications for our search for records (see Appendix A).

Range of service provision
We found the range of residential services provided to children between 1950 and 1995 was extensive and extremely complex. Hundreds of children's residential establishments existed, with many places changing function, location and management or closing down. Wide-ranging, complicated and changing policy structures guided decisions about which services were provided. Central government, local government, voluntary and religious organisations all provided guidance and direction to individual children's residential establishments. Psychological, health, judicial, religious and education services intersected, at times, with direct services to children in residential places. Various professional associations provided guidance and direction within specialised

---

[8] This section is drawn from The Scottish Parliament Official Report 1 December 2004. See at: http://www.scottish.parliament.uk/business/officialReports/meetingsParliament/or-04/sor1201-01.htm

[9] The term 'Scottish Executive' was changed to Scottish Government after the Historical Abuse Systemic Review began its work. As 'Scottish Executive' was used predominantly throughout our review, it is mainly used in this report although 'Scottish Government' may also be referred to.

[10] 'Keeper of the Records': The National Archives of Scotland ('NAS') is headed by the Keeper of the Records of Scotland, who is responsible to the Scottish Ministers for the management of the NAS and to the Lord President of the Court of Session for the efficient management of the court and other legal records in Scotland. The office of Keeper of the Records of Scotland was created in 1949, although its antecedents date back to the 13th century. See: http://www.nas.gov.uk/about/keeper.asp

areas. Because of this complex picture, it was impossible to identify all records that might have existed and relate to children's residential services during a 45-year period within the constraints of our review.

Determining whether records existed

It was necessary to determine what records might have existed, in various locations, and to distinguish them from those records that actually do exist. We learned it was also possible that many records relating to the same topic were generated in different locations, such as children's residential establishments, social work and education departments. Record-keeping practices varied immensely from establishment to establishment, within organisations and local authorities and at central government level. Many records would have been generated in association with professional services to children. Throughout the years large volumes of policy papers, special reports, investigation reports and other such documents were generated throughout Scotland. Poor records retention policies have meant that not all essential records were managed properly and archived.

"Public" records and accessibility

During the 2004 parliamentary debate, the Minister indicated that he wanted to make certain that everything was being done "...to identify and make public relevant files" as "...these are exceptional circumstances..." Under the terms of the remit of the review, we sought the co-operation of local authorities and organisations in making records available. The term "public records", however, has particular meaning under the Public (Scotland) Records 1937 Act (see Chapter 3). Any public disclosure of records, as well, is subject to the Freedom of Information (Scotland) Act 2002 and the Data Protection 1998 Act. From beginning of our review, therefore, these laws made it difficult for organisations and local authorities to comply with the proposed spirit of opening up their records and to grant us unfettered access to all records relating to children's residential services.

We faced many challenges in accessing records. Some potentially significant records in archives are designated as 'closed', which means they can't be viewed by the public. Records are owned by voluntary, private and religious organisations, which had no legal obligation to grant us access. There were also geographical problems in accessing records, as they are stored throughout Scotland and England.

While MSPs called for records relating to children's residential establishments to be opened and made transparent, it was a request with complex implications. Records needed to be located before they could be accessed and records disclosure needed to be made within the context of legislative requirements. Records couldn't be made accessible to us, and to the public, until it was clear what was "relevant", to whom and for what purpose. The task of determining relevancy was fraught with difficulties (see below). Furthermore, as there are no clear, standardised access policies in all records locations, we had to learn about a multitude of access requirements in a multitude of locations (see Appendix B).

Location and volume of records

The 2004 parliamentary debate made clear that the Scottish Executive possessed records which it intended to make publicly available to those with an interest in determining how abuse was allowed to happen. The Minister reported to Parliament that he had written to certain organisations about their records. In his report, the Scottish Information Commissioner (2005) identified the difficult process facing the Scottish Executive. As the

Commissioner's report stated, it took approximately two years with dedicated resources for the Scottish Executive to locate and catalogue information, a process made challenging for many reasons identified in this report.

We learned that there are many locations where records may be found throughout Scotland and England (see Appendix B). Records relating to one children's residential establishment, for example, may be in several locations such as central offices; local authority departments; regional, local, national or university archives; private storage facilities; museums and libraries. Records have shifted from place to place due to relocations; reorganisations; closing of children's residential establishments; changes in management; lack of storage and for many other reasons. Often the transfer of records wasn't tracked, making it difficult, if not impossible, to find out where records were sent.

Vast numbers of records relate to children's residential services due to the extent of the services provided and the years involved. As organisations, local authorities and central government found records as a result of our inquiries, it became clear that not all records have been identified, located or archived. We also learned that some records are at varying stages of discovery. Some were found in boxes in basements or other unidentified locations. Some remain in a records management process while others have been archived. It is apparent, however, that far more records exist than is currently known, as many records have not been properly identified and put into records managements systems for transfer to archives.

Type of records held

It was apparent from our information-gathering that it was extremely difficult, if not impossible, for various organisations, central and local government to locate, identify and make accessible records without guiding criteria such as a records retention schedule. (This is a system that makes clear what records must be retained and disposed). In our search for information, we learned about the many record types (see Appendix C) that might be relevant to our understanding of institutional child abuse. Unlike the health profession, however, there is no records retention schedule for social services and, in particular, children's residential services that make clear to organisations, local authorities and central government what records must be retained or destroyed.

Determining what was relevant

Records relating to children's residential services are crucial for allowing insights into how abuse was allowed to happen within children's residential establishments. These records are particularly important because there is an absence of empirical research (research that draws from observation and experience) throughout the UK, relating to child institutional abuse for the period under review (see Kendrick, 2007; Elsley, 2007; Stein, 2006; Barter, 2003).

> "It is now evident that there are missing years from our history of child welfare. Recent inquiry reports have documented the years of physical, sexual and emotional abuse of children and young people who were living in children's homes, particularly between the mid-1960s and mid-1980s – although contemporary historical research, derived from the accounts of adults who were in care earlier, suggest a longer missing history of abuse (Rafferty & O'Sullivan 1999 in Stein 2006: 11)....we do not have a detailed picture of the prevalence or type of abuse."

Our work depended on the existence of records without which it was impossible to seek insights and to develop a better understanding about what happened in children's residential establishments. It also relied on organisations and local authorities acknowledging the significance of records for helping society to better understand children's residential services and what happened within places where children lived. Assessing what are relevant records and what was recorded was challenging work that involved working in stages. The following points emerged:

■ We had to identify local authorities and organisations associated with children's residential service provision over a 45 year period.

■ We had to identify what records might be held by local authorities, organisations and central government and where those records might be located. This was extremely time-consuming.

■ It was impossible to determine relevancy without examining the records. This was a monumental task for us, organisations and local authorities working with limited time and resources.

■ Relevant has different meanings to different people. When asked for information by the review, local authorities, organisations and central government had to make their own individualised and varying interpretations about what might be relevant and helpful to the review.

■ The issue of what and who determined record significance in the past has had significant implications for what records have been retained and for what records can be accessed. This is the case for records relating to children living in residential environments, individual children's residential establishments and children's services in general.

Our preliminary work has revealed that some records contain vast amounts of information important to the remit while other records contained little, or no, relevant information. Significant information was often buried within records relating to non-relevant matters. The task of identifying, locating and determining "relevant" information for the review, therefore, was extremely difficult for us and for the many people working for organisations and local authorities who contributed to the review.

Attitudes toward records
We found that many individuals in organisations recognised the importance of records associated with children's residential services although organisational policies did not always reflect that significance. At the same time, we also found that negative attitudes and misunderstandings about the significance of records prevailed, sometimes held by those in senior positions. These negative attitudes appeared at odds with the attitudes of others providing information to the review.

Many of the people who helped us recognised the value of records, particularly the role of records in providing insights into how abuse might have occurred within children's residential establishments. Some commented that not all lessons from the past had been learned. Several mentioned the significant historical place held by children's residential establishments and their links to other parts of Scottish society. Some remarked on the lack of historical knowledge about children's residential services and the importance of records to help society understand. The many people working in organisations and local authorities who valued the preservation of records, however, were often constrained in their attempts to locate and preserve records due to insufficient funds, lack of staff, low value placed on such records and legal concerns. According to some, for example, advice they received from solicitors and insurance companies, concerned about litigation, inhibited their ability to make records more accessible.

We found that some individuals in key positions, such as senior managers, didn't understand the significance of records. They lacked sufficient knowledge about what records existed and where such records were, or might be, located. One local authority, for example, was unable (or unwilling) to tell us where records – such as inspection reports for children's residential establishments in its area – were located. A religious organisation was unwilling to help us find out where historical records for their children's residential establishment might be found. The voluntary organisations expressed a guarded willingness, at times, to provide information, often constrained by legal and other concerns.

We were told that senior people working in social work departments had ordered records associated with children's residential services to be destroyed. These included children's files and management records. According to some archivists, the reasons for this destruction were not apparent as retention and disposal schedules were not kept and made available to them. Many records managers and archivists expressed concern about these types of decisions being made by unqualified people and the poor attitudes demonstrated by some record holders toward preserving valuable records specific to children's residential services. Some archivists also reported that they had attempted to obtain historical records for children's residential services but that senior managers in local authorities and organisations had not provided the requested information or allowed for the inspection or transfer of such records.

Former residents reported that they often faced poor attitudes from staff managing records, finding some unhelpful, lacking in empathy and understanding about records. Their experiences parallel the findings in the Australian Parliament Senate Report on Australians who experienced institutional or out-of-home care as children. This report identified that carer leavers found some people with responsibility for locating records in Australia "unsympathetic and unemphathetic" as well as "lacking in understanding, capacity or willingness to provide assistance" (Parliament of Australia Senate Report, 2004).

The poor attitudes demonstrated by some staff working in key areas relating to children's residential services made identifying, locating and accessing records more difficult. At the same time, we learned that many people had a specific interest in preserving such records and who have contributed significantly in recent years to protecting such records from destruction.

Records: why are they important?

Records are important for many reasons. In its work, the Scottish Executive's Public Records Strategy (2004) examined what makes records significant, to whom and for what purpose. The strategy identified that one possible answer was "...to ensure that past experiences and lessons are not lost". Parliamentarians expressed this same opinion during their December 2004 discussion when they placed importance on records for providing insights into how abuse was allowed to happen in residential schools and children's homes between 1950 and 1995.

The Public Records Strategy identified other reasons why records are important, such as "public accountability", "to provide background and context to current and future work" and public access to information. During the workshops associated with the strategy's consultation, participants identified other purposes, such as: corporate memory, protecting rights and interests of individuals and authorities, research to produce change, legal knowledge, individual and family identity and the importance of documenting society for current and future use. "Historical interest of future generations" and "assisting social inclusion" were also identified as reasons why records should be preserved.

Drawing from the Public Records Strategy's work, the following section highlights why records are important to this review and other inquiries, organisations, local authorities and central government, future research and former residents.

Why records are important to this review and other inquiries

Fundamental to our work, as the Public Records Strategy identifies, is ensuring "...that past experiences and lessons are not lost". Past experiences, we suggest, begin yesterday and extend back throughout the centuries. Our work and other inquiries into the past could not proceed without the existence and proper preservation of records. They're essential to ensuring that we, as a society, gain insights into past experiences and learn valuable lessons as we continue to search for ways to improve the well-being of children's lives, such as those children living without parental care and in vulnerable situations.

In today's world, there are preventative, monitoring and responsive approaches taken to keeping children safe in residential care – all of which rely on current and past records. Preventative and monitoring approaches rely upon suitably generated records, such as those created through assessments, reviews, incidents, complaints and inspections. Responsive approaches, often taking the form of investigations and inquiries, also rely upon properly maintained records - past and present - to review current and historical practices possibly harmful to children. By analysing information within records, inspections and inquiries can reveal what has happened and what can be improved upon "...to ensure that past experiences and lessons are not lost". In other words, records are extremely important for contributing to informed decision-making about keeping children safe and responding to claims of abuse.

The Bichard Inquiry (2004) into the deaths of two children in England who were killed by someone known to them, examined record-keeping practices to learn about whether these might have contributed to, or prevented, the children's deaths. The inquiry found there were many problems with the review, retention and deletion of records, leading to confusion and poor decision-making by the police and social services. These conclusions led the Bichard Inquiry to make many recommendations for changes in current records practices that will ultimately determine, as well, what historical records will exist for the future.

In Scotland, one independent review examined services provided to the families of children neglected and abused within their community. This review included investigators from police, health, education and social work inspectorate services (Social Work Inspection Agency, 2005). The final report stated that the review depended upon local authority, agency and health records to make certain that the "...life stories of the three children...were at the centre of our investigation". The fact that these records existed and could be examined meant that the investigators were able to establish important facts about the children's lives, conduct "...an analysis of practice, policy and management of all agencies involved", and make key recommendations for improving their child protection services. From a systemic perspective, investigators depended on records for providing insights into what happened to the children that led to their abuse.

Records were important to fulfilling our mandate. They're also essential to other inquiry processes investigating, from historical and contemporary perspectives, matters relating to children, their welfare and their protection.

Children's residential establishments, voluntary and religious organisations, local authorities and central government

Individual residential establishments, voluntary and religious organisations, local authorities and central government have a vested interest in ensuring that records are generated, properly managed and preserved. This is also a legal obligation. Contemporary records in these locations are needed to evaluate, monitor and respond to children's entitlements to excellent quality care. Various records types, such as personal files, incident reports, complaints records and logs, are relied upon for monitoring children's safety and responding to concerns, while records are also associated with organisations being held accountable.

Historical records are important because they embody corporate memory: they make sure that when individuals leave work, the information they've gleaned through their careers is retained. Available and properly generated records also make possible contemporary and historical analyses, investigations, monitoring and audits – internal and external. All of these hold organisations, local authorities and central government accountable for the quality of their services, while possibly contributing to a better understanding of residential childcare services.

Further research

There is a growing interest in Scotland's social history and childhood, as evidenced by the proliferation of research about adults' childhood experiences as well as other experiences associated with, for example, life in inner-city tenements, shipyards, coal mines and during the slave trade era. There is a gap in the empirical research (research that draws from observation and experience) about children's experiences in children's residential establishments in Scotland between 1950 and 1995. Research into children's residential services, particularly for the earlier years, could be enhanced by further study.

Records for children's residential services make that research possible while allowing, as well, for an exploration into the relationship between children's residential services, children's experiences and other sectors of society. Some suggest it is important to acknowledge that children who lived in children's residential establishments are the same people who fought for Scotland during the wars, contributed to society's betterment and, in particular, worked to enhance the well-being of young people growing up a generation later. Research into the childhood experiences of children in children's residential establishments in Scotland can establish those links.

There is a lack of research into historical abuse in children's residential establishments. Records should be identified, located and made accessible to researchers who can add to a body of historical knowledge about childhood experiences relating to abuse. Social research can improve our understanding about what happened in children's residential establishments and influence what needs to change to improve the lives of children in care today.

Former residents of children's residential establishments

Former residents (see also Appendix D) told us that records about their lives and children's residential establishments have great significance to them for many reasons, which follow.

Historical accounts:

Advocates focusing upon reparation for survivors of abuse suggest that developing accurate historical accounts is necessary to help survivors heal from injustices[11]. Developing historical accounts takes many forms, including an analysis of records that must be located and made accessible. Historical accounts can contribute to reconciliation arising from human rights abuses. This is exemplified in South Africa by the work of its Truth and Reconciliation Commission.

"I hope that the work of the Commission, by opening wounds to cleanse them, will thereby stop them from festering. We cannot be facile and say bygones will be bygones, because they will not be bygones and will return to haunt us. True reconciliation is never cheap, for it is based on forgiveness which is costly. Forgiveness in turn depends on repentance, which has to be based on an acknowledgement of what was done wrong, and therefore on disclosure of the truth. You cannot forgive what you do not know...[12]"

Bishop Tutu, as Chairperson of the Truth and Reconciliation Commission, argued that learning about past events through historical accounts and disclosure of truth is an essential component to reconciling past abuses. In Scotland, former residents indicated that they want a historical account of their experiences in children's residential establishments to emerge. Survivors of institutional child abuse place huge importance upon records for insights into their circumstances, for informing any legal proceeding they're involved in and for helping them to heal from the long-lasting effects of child abuse. The 1998 Law Commission of Canada discussion paper on institutional child abuse reveals that through their research survivors of institutional child abuse identified, among their various needs, the "need for establishing the historical record":

"Many survivors have expressed the need to have a permanent, physical reminder to memorialise the fact of their abuse and to establish an archive of their experiences...[they] also need to ensure that history will not be written or rewritten as continuing denial" (Law Commission of Canada, 1998).

Former residents' rights:

Former residents have legal rights, including human rights entitlements under the Human Rights Act 1998 which stipulates that "...[e]veryone has the right to respect for his private and family life, his home and his correspondence...[13]. Records associated with children's residential establishments – the homes where former residents' lived as children – play a critical role in the interpretation of what respect means to former residents for their private and family life, their homes and their correspondence. Former residents state that those records are important in terms of what they reveal – and don't reveal – about them as individuals, and about their experiences.

In particular, records are important to ensure that former residents realise their entitlements under freedom of information and data protection legislation, which grant former residents the right to view records associated with their experiences. Records are critical for ensuring that former residents experience their right to justice and to fair and proper legal or administrative proceedings. It is important that former residents aren't denied these entitlements because significant records cannot be located.

Search for identity:

Some former residents lacking basic information about their lives reported that they don't have a sense of belonging or identity. They described how they're responding to a basic human need to better understand who they are and who they are associated with.

Searching for identity is often associated with general interest in family history and social background. This has become a burgeoning area, with archivists reporting unprecedented requests from adults for records about their past. Hundreds of thousands of orphans, for example, separated from their parents during the Holocaust are searching for information about their families after nearly 60 years. An international tracing centre established after the war forwarded approximately 12 million files to a museum in Jerusalem, the first batch of 50 million files to be released after government and Jewish organisation lobbying (Scotland on Sunday, 2007).

Child migrants' search for information in records is linked to their search for an identity that derives from "...certainty about individual circumstances and knowing about oneself" (Parliament of Australia Senate, 2004). Many child migrants reported to an Australian Senate committee that they found their loss of identity a great hardship. Former residents contacting this review told about experiences similar to those reported by child migrants, with some former residents indicating that they have siblings who were child migrants. An Australian report on those who experienced institutional or out-of-home care as children states that:

"People who make the decision to apply for their records are on a journey of self discovery. They are dealing with the unfinished business of their childhood. People searching want to understand more about the circumstances that led to their placement in care, who their parents were and whether or not they have brothers or sisters. In addition some people have recollections about their time in care, and are keen to see if there is any verification of the experiences they remember. We have an obligation to assist in this journey and to help these adults complete what has been unfinished for them, often for many years" (Parliament of Australia Senate, 2004).

There are many reasons why former residents as children may not have learned information important to them as adults. There is evidence to suggest that, in the earlier years under review, adults responsible for children in residential establishments placed little value on providing information to children. In turn children were often silent, afraid to ask questions and express their concerns. Many children were isolated from or had little contact with siblings, families and friends. Children removed from families experienced trauma that inhibited learning and focusing on information that they now realise, as adults, is important to their sense of belonging and identity.

There is evidence that authorities placed restrictions on family members who were trying to contact children. Children weren't informed about their family members' inquiries about them. Former residents say that, as a result, they have gaps in knowledge about their families and their circumstances. At the same time, some former residents report vivid memories of some childhood experiences, which they want to verify in some tangible and physical way.

Many former residents reported that they had, and continue to have, no understanding about why they were placed in children's residential establishments away from their family. Some want to

---

[11] See Centre for Conflict Resolution and Human Rights, Tufts University at http://fletcher.tufts.edu/chrcr/.

[12] Response by Archbishop Tutu on his appointment as Chairperson of the Truth and Reconciliation Commission, November 30 1995. http://www.wits.ac.za/histp/tutu_quotes_by.htm.

[13] See Human Rights Act 1998 at http://www.opsi.gov.uk/ACTS/acts1998/19980042.htm.

trace other family members, as they were often separated from siblings and parents at a young age. Many reported that they didn't know why they were denied contact with their family members. Others said they were searching for confirmation of their birth names (which may have been changed on placement), birthdates, birthplace, educational background, medical histories, family members' names and family histories. Some former residents are searching for information about other child residents, employees and key adult figures in their lives.

The British House of Commons Health Select Committee Report (1998) on the welfare of former British child migrants highlights that many report similar experiences to those living in children's residential establishments in Scotland. In that report, the Committee recognised the need for former child migrants to have and to access their individual records:

> "This is of great importance to them as a means of coming to terms with their past experiences, achieving a fuller sense of personal identity, and (in some cases) making contact with surviving relatives in the UK and elsewhere. In addition, health difficulties may be caused by the absence of complete medical records" (British House of Commons Health Select Committee Report,1998).

Former residents stated that they were often provided with erroneous information about their family lives, for example, that they were orphans when one or both parents were alive. Some believed their families had abandoned them or didn't want them. For those people in both groups who assumed they had no family ties, many reported that they didn't look for family members until years later when they requested their records and learned that other family members existed:

> "Their lies prevented me from searching for my family after I had left the home. I had been told I had no family...I was told there was nobody to look for. Their deception cost me my identity and any chance at a family life, I had to invent myself and then live with confusion for decades" (Parliament of Australia Senate Report, 2001).

Some former residents in Scotland have discovered that parents contributed to their upkeep when they lived as children in children's residential establishments – a fact they didn't know until they saw their records as older adults. Former residents say this knowledge is important because it reflects their parents' concern for their welfare.

Practical implications:
There are practical implications for former residents who lack basic information about their lives in that they may find it difficult to obtain passports, birth certificates before marriage and gather their medical histories. The personal details known to most of us , including birth names, birthdates, nationality, mother's maiden name and so on, may be unknown to former residents making it difficult, if not impossible, for them to complete questionnaires "...and so there is a tendency to avoid any situation that requires this kind of information...We have become invisible citizens" (Parliament of Australia Senate Report, 2001).

A sense of belonging:
Some former residents told us that for many years they felt socially excluded from those who grew up in family homes, knowing their parents, siblings and other family members. Records may permit former residents to trace their family connections and to move towards a sense of belonging to family

and community. Families and descendants of former residents may also want to know about their family members as there are historical associations that are important to families and their descendants.

Many years ago children who died in large children's homes, for example, were buried at the back of graveyards in large unmarked graves. These children were the daughters, sons, siblings and relatives of people today who are searching for verification of family experiences and family identity, both of which contribute to feelings of belonging to societies that value family life.

General interest:
Former residents' interest extends beyond their own circumstances and placements. Some said that, as children, they didn't know that other children's residential establishments existed throughout Scotland. As a result, they've developed an interest as adults in learning more about the widespread institutionalisation of children. Some have visited the locations of former large children's homes. Former residents have searched in museums, libraries and archives for records and discovered photographs of earlier children's residential establishments. What former residents have learned, however, is that it's difficult to find records as no central system for children's residential services identifies where records are held.

Missing historical records: myths and realities

It was evident from the beginning of our information-gathering that records were missing from various locations although it wasn't evident why. Former residents, parliamentarians, the courts and the Scottish Information Commissioner have all questioned why records relating to children's residential establishments appear to be missing. Organisations and local authorities may not know why records can't be located. While it's often assumed that, when records are missing, they don't exist, we found that this wasn't always the case.

The Scottish Information Commissioner (SIC) addressed the topic of missing records in his report ('the SIC report')about the Scottish Executive Education Department's (SEED) search for records:

> "The issue of missing records or gaps in records was raised by several Members of the Scottish Parliament during the course of their debate on institutional child abuse in December. The tracing of relevant records has also been a considerable practical issue in the action currently being considered by the Court of Session. The availability of records has been continuing concern of members of INCAS...the definition of 'missing' is clearly important and I have given much consideration to this matter" (Scottish Information Commissioners Report, 2005).

The SIC report indicated that "missing" may imply that records existed in the first instance and that they've been lost or destroyed. The SIC report found that the existing SEED records contained "gaps" and lacked consistency, although it noted that records were very much "of their time".

> "They contain large amounts of miscellaneous information and there are gaps in the series of documents within them. It is also not clear what they ought to contain beyond reports of statutory inspections and even the timescales for these are not clear" (Scottish Information Commissioners Report, 2005).

The Australian Senate Report (2001) into child migration found that various factors impacted the source of available information to child migrants about what information they could locate. Examples included the volume of information initially available, record-keeping practices and the survival of physical records throughout the years. The report noted that other factors made records difficult to locate, including the imprecise requirements about what information to record and other details about what must or must not be kept and by whom. As later chapters identify, these factors had an impact on record-keeping in Scotland as well.

In our search for information, we found that certain records that were believed to be missing may not have been generated in the first place, or had been destroyed. We also found, however, that adequate searching for records associated with children's residential services has not taken place throughout Scotland. During our review, for example, organisations and local authorities located records that had previously been unidentified. It also became apparent that records thought to be missing may exist in unknown locations. With the passage of time, individuals with corporate memories of records have left their employment and knowledge about what records exist and where left with them. As information about the transfer of records often went unrecorded, it was, and can be, difficult for organisations and government to locate existing records. This work has been made difficult, in part, because legislation has not required proper records management (see Chapter 3).

In general, we found that records about children's residential services in Scotland may exist in larger numbers than is realised and in previously undisclosed locations. While many records from the past appear to be missing, it is too early to conclude that missing records associated with children's residential services do not exist or cannot be located.

Conclusion

The remit of the review specifically refers to records. However, the remit is based on numerous assumptions about records that do not take account of the realities of locating and accessing records associated with children's residential services. Various issues arose for us, making information-gathering and locating and accessing records extremely challenging:

Central databases: None exist for children's residential services that cover the 45 period under review.
Definitions for "residential schools" and "children's homes": Many terms have been used throughout the years to describe residential settings for children.
Service provision: Residential services have been varied, extensive and changing services from 1950 to 1995.
Existence of records: There have been no records retention and disposal schedules for records associated with children's residential establishments, therefore, it is impossible to know what records should or do exist without laborious searching.
'Public records' definition: This definition is unclear and access to records held by private bodies, providing public services, depends upon their goodwill.
Records location, volume and types: There are large numbers of different record types in many locations and not all records have been put into records management systems, archived or both of these.
Access to records: It is complicated to access records, due to legal restrictions and the lack of standardised access to records policies.
Records as 'relevant': Determining record relevancy is subjective and difficult to assess without examining records, a time-

consuming task requiring adequate resources.
Attitudes: Some helpful and some poor attitudes may determine access to relevant information.

While records were essential to our work, we learned that records are also very important to many individuals for many reasons. Organisations and government depend on records, while records are also necessary for future research. Records have particular significance to former residents for several reasons such as their search for identity, establishing a historical account, practical administrative challenges in daily life, their sense of belonging and general interest. Records also ensure that former residents' rights are realised, specifically their rights under human rights, freedom of information and data protection legislation.

Many children's residential establishment records appear to be missing, but there is evidence that these records may exist in far greater numbers than is known. It is critical that the importance of records – which is apparent to former residents, archivists and others – is known by people responsible for generating and managing records to ensure that significant records for children's residential establishments are preserved and made accessible.

Chapter 2: Former residents' experiences

Introduction

This chapter reports on the challenges faced by former residents contacting us with identifying, locating and accessing records associated with children's residential services. Records, as noted in the previous chapter, are extremely important to former residents. They're also relevant to inquiries such as this review. They can offer substantial insights into approaches to keeping children safe in residential placements and, in particular, monitoring practices related to individual children. The legacy of good and bad practices in the past may be illustrated in records. Records may also reflect attitudes towards children and whether children are valued. The records important to former residents, therefore, are important to us all.

We've appreciated the willingness of former residents to share their very difficult experiences relating to records and what their individual records show. This has allowed us to better understand the importance of records, how abuse can happen in children's residential establishments and how records continue to impact on people's lives many years after they leave an establishment. By examining information within individuals' records, for example, it was possible to see how the social and geographical isolation of some children in residential placements put them at serious risk. The records for many older former residents show a dearth of information about family contact and relationships with outside professionals, which created additional vulnerability in children already vulnerable due to their out-of-home placements.

Former residents lived in children's residential establishments managed by local authorities, voluntary and religious organisations with direct and indirect central government involvement. They were placed as children for many reasons, often related to inadequate social conditions such as poverty, poor health and lack of family support. Many crave insights into their childhood experiences, which they hope to gain by locating and accessing records associated with their experiences in residential establishments. As the following shows, however, it was extremely difficult for some former residents to find information about the past.

Former residents' experiences with records

Visits to graveyards showed that children who died in children's residential establishments are buried there although it is unknown how many due to poor record practices. Some children lie in unmarked graves. Former residents who lived in one children's home described their attempts to find records for children who died while they'd lived in that same home. These deceased children are buried in a large area within a local graveyard. While some organisations have kept records identifying the children who died in their establishments, the former residents found there were few records identifying the deceased children and few records about their deaths.

Some former residents believe that society may never know how many children died in residential establishments, who the children were, where they're buried and the reasons for their deaths. What their experience suggests, however, is that their difficulty in locating information reveals the low importance placed on the children's identity and the children's value to their extended families and others. Some former residents believe it is essential to identify those children and acknowledge them in a humane, caring way that reflects the equal importance of those children to others.

Archivists described their experiences with former residents searching for records. An archivist working for a religious organisation, for example, told about a former resident who, as a 63-year-old, wanted to know why he went into their children's home. The archivist said the organisation didn't have all their children's records (and many records they held contained scant information). In this situation, however, the archivist was able to locate this man's record. In it, the archivist discovered very many letters that the children's home manager had exchanged with this man's mother throughout the numerous years he spent in the children's home. The man had never seen the letters.

Another archivist working for a religious organisation described how he had received a visit from an elderly man looking for information about his stay in its children's residential establishment. While the organisation had no children's record for this former resident, it had a children's register that listed all the children and provided details about their admission. According to the archivist, the man looking for information about his childhood wanted to hold the register as it was the only tangible evidence existing that confirmed he had stayed in the children's home.

Former residents, in their 40s, 50s and 60s told us that they had difficulty locating and accessing their individual records and other information. They also said how disappointed they were to find such little information and how distressed they became at reading some information for the first time once they'd obtained their records. Some older former residents had seen their individual records while others were still trying to locate their records and other information. Archivists reported that family members and generations of families were also requesting information about family members and ancestors. The former residents of children's residential establishments who were seeking records and who contacted us were older adults. This pattern is consistent with a wider population of adults who often begin their family history searches in their later years. The following describes some former residents' experiences, as told to us.

"Mr C"

Mr C lived in a large children's home for 18 years. In January 2007 he requested his personal records from the organisation responsible for managing the home, receiving his records in May 2007 with a letter explaining their contents. When he reviewed his records, he was surprised at how little information they contained after spending such a long time at the home. Despite spending time at the local hospital and receiving medical examinations, for example, he said there was no medical information. Mr C said his records contained "a spattering of details about family", "entry" into the children's home, "some school reports" and "written home parents' reports". Mr C said that "...all the records lack detail or sufficient information to provide a true reflection..." of his stay at the children's home or "...to allow any evaluation of abuse or abnormal behaviour within a child under care. Actually I would go so far to say that the record seemed to be doctored and do not reflect a complete picture of my stay..." at the home.

Until Mr C received his records in May 2007, he believed he was an only child with no family. When he read his records, however, he learned that he had a "...half brother, many aunts and uncles together with extended family of cousins and nieces." Mr C says he was able to locate his family easily despite his records stating that there was a lack of information about his father. Mr C says his records identify the ship his father served on and the period he served in the Navy, making it possible for him to identify his father's position in the Navy and to possibly make contact with him. Mr C thinks it's possible that the children's home could have contacted the Navy to see if it was possible for him to have some contact with his father. Mr C would like to know "...what information has been deleted" from his records and "...what criminal acts have been covered up..."

Mr C has typed his records and put them into a timeline "...to determine some history of [the children's home] not only for my own peace of mind but also because I was abused (physical and sexual) at this home... I know that abuse has been covered up and the record certainly show that cover up with missing medical records... Having written to [the children's home] to enquire about the missing records medical records there seems to be a complete blank as to what happened to all medical records health and dental when all health and dental matters were handled through the [children's home's] hospital and dental surgery."

"Mrs E"

The circumstances in which Mrs E received her personal records from the children's home began with an article published in a national newspaper about her experiences. The children's home staff member visited her at her home after reading the article, saying the information in the article "had come to them completely out of the blue". He told Mrs E he would get someone to access information about her from the children's home. At the time, Mrs E was 62 years old. She expected records to be the reports about the children that went every month to the children's home central office from the places where the children lived. An after-care worker then visited her home, leaving documents for her to read. These, she found, were records about her placement.

Mrs E lived in a large children's home for 16 years. While living there, she says, she was told she "was an orphan from the gutter". During her time at the home, Mrs E says she never saw another person she knew. Later, when reading her records as an elderly person, she learned she had a twin brother who also stayed at the children's home and a father who contributed a weekly sum to her care. Mrs E said there was a man named in her file, as she read the information in it, but he wasn't identified as her father (which he was) and the man who contributed to her care.

In the years Mrs E lived in the children's home, she was unaware that she had other relatives in her children's home. Reading through her records, she was shocked to discover she had three cousins, two boys and a girl, living there. She became very upset reading her record information when she learned that they were orphans as her father's older brother, their father, had died very suddenly. She also learned information about the children that she believed should not have been in her own records.

When reading through her records, Mrs E saw that the girl named in her file – her cousin – lived in the same cottage as she had as a small girl. Mrs E knew her as a "big girl", who was beaten. Whenever this girl was beaten, Mrs E says she was taken by the hand and told that would happen to her one day. Mrs E says she can still hear her screams and that the shock and horror of knowing that this girl was related to her haunts her today. She also read in her records that she had an older brother who had looked after her and her twin brother. Years later, when Mrs E was looking for her twin brother she discovered that she also had a mother who was still alive, who had a twin sister with children.

Mrs E says she found the experience of accessing her personal records, at 62 years of age, extremely distressing. She said that the process left her without a sense of belonging to a family and without a sense of identity as she had never known her family while she lived in the children's home and for many years thereafter.

"Mr. G"

As a 10-year old, Mr G, who lived in one local authority, was placed at an approved school in another local authority in the late 1950s. He said that he came from a "loving home". Prior to his placement, his father had died at 42 years and his mother had difficulty coping with a large family while living in impoverished circumstances. When Mr G was discharged from the approved school after three years, he described how he was called to the clothing store, given a set of clothes, put on a bus and told that his mother would meet him at the bus station in his home local authority. Throughout his time at the approved school, Mr G said he received little information about his family circumstances and about why he continued to reside at the approved school for a three-year period.

Mr G told us that he'd been trying to locate his personal records, particularly his record about his approved school experience, since January 2003. In 2007 he was still trying to locate information about the approved school and his individual records. During this search, he said he'd learned that records for him should have been held by the placing local authority's social work department while the approved school should also have had them. As he was placed through the court system, with Department of Education involvement, he said he believed it was possible that the related departments had records as well. He added that he'd learned that approved school management records should have existed as well – records generated at the approved school, by the approved school's external managers, by social work departments and at central government level.

In January 2003, Mr G said he began by contacting the Information Commissioner, asking for information about where he might locate his records for his time at the approved school. In response, the Commissioner's office referred him to the Scottish Executive Education Department ('SEED'). After receiving the Information Commission office's letter, in July 2003 Mr G wrote to SEED providing information about the approved school and asking for access to any related records held by SEED. In February 2005, he received a reply in which SEED said they had spent the "...last 6 months identifying the files we hold on residential establishments in order that we can make these available to view to anyone with an interest. We do not hold any personal files but do have files which relate to the management, running and inspection of some establishments. These files are now available to view."

The letter added that general files for "some establishments" were available to view at the National Archives of Scotland (NAS) and provided contact details for NAS, indicating that information could be viewed there unless it was exempted under the Freedom of Information legislation. Mr G, who lives in England, was told that SEED had redacted (removed information, such as personal details) from some files to make them publicly accessible and that his name did not appear in any redacted files. SEED said it held files relating to the approved school that Mr G had attended and for the period he attended. If he wanted to see these files he should contact a named person at SEED, and to do so with another person if he wanted someone to accompany him.

In October 2005 Mr G also wrote to a local authority's children's services division to ask about where he might get information about his school records for the period he attended the approved school. He wrote to the local authority where the approved school was located. A response in October 2005 said that "pupil records" follow children from establishment to establishment and that, when a pupil leaves full-time education, the last establishment to provide education is required to retain the pupil record for five years. The officer who wrote the letter said the local authority had adopted a policy of sending all records "...for confidential destruction after five years" and, when an establishment managed by the authority closed, the records were "held centrally" for five years. The officer advised Mr G that the approved school wasn't managed by the local authority he had written to and that he should contact the last school he attended. The officer added: "I appreciate your desire to track your school records, but from previous experience obtaining records from this period is extremely difficult."

In February 2006, the same local authority officer wrote to Mr G stating that as the approved school he attended wasn't a local authority school, they didn't hold any related pupil records. The officer said, however, that he had forwarded Mr G's inquiries to the local authorities' archivist to see if any records were held there and that if information was found Mr G would be told. The following month, Mr G received a letter from the local authority's archives services stating that they didn't hold any records for the approved school. Mr G was advised to contact the archivist for the religious order at the approved school G had attended.

Mr G also wrote to another local authority's social work services department to ask for any records they may have relating to his placement at the approved school, as he had lived in that local authority before his placement. In March 2006, he received a letter from a senior child protection officer who asked him to outline the steps he had taken in his search for records and to provide his full name and address.

In the meantime, following the local authority's archivist's advice, Mr G wrote to the religious order's archivist to ask if the religious order had any records about his stay at the approved school. In April 2006, Mr G received a letter from the religious order's solicitors in which they indicated that the religious order "did not run Schools in Scotland. The Schools were run by a Board of Managers", who were the employers of the members of staff which included members of the religious order. The solicitor told Mr G that, for those reasons, the religious order "...do not hold the school records and they have never done so". The solicitors also stated that the School closed in the 1980s and that the National Archives in Scotland may hold documentation relating to the school.

Mr G wrote to the religious order again and asked about the school managers who appointed the religious order. The religious order's solicitors responded in a June 2006 letter by stating that the board of managers did not "appoint" the order members but rather the order members were "employed" by the managers. The letter continued: "In law there is a substantial difference between the Order running a school and members of the Order being employed at the school." The solicitors also told Mr G that the religious order had no contact details for the approved school managers for the 1950s. A subsequent letter from the religious order's solicitors in July 2006 stated that Mr G's letter to the religious order's provincial office had been forwarded to them. They reiterated that the religious order had no "details of the Board of Managers" who employed members of the religious order in the late 1950s, also stating that the religious order "...would have had no reason to hold such information".

After reviewing a management file for the approved school (held by SEED), Mr G wrote to the solicitors stating that he had seen a report in which it stated that the approved school "...is owned and administered..." by the religious order. The solicitors replied that the report was incorrect and that the religious order never owned or administered the approved school. In their letter, the solicitors quoted the Approved Schools (Scotland) Rules 1961 (Statutory Instrument 1961) which provided for "...Managers to determine the number, type and qualifications of staff to be employed by them. The same statutory instruments also provided for disciplinary action against members of staff." The letter added that the "...contention in the final paragraph of your letter can also be readily explained. However, there is little point in doing so as you clearly do not accept what can be checked from other sources...we do not propose to enter into a wider dialogue at our clients expense".

In September 2006, Mr G received another letter from the local authority's social work services department, senior child protection officer who said she was still trying to trace his social work records. She wrote: "To date I have had no success but I have again contacted the City Council Archivist to request their assistance." She added that she would keep him informed of her progress. Mr G wrote to a city council archivist to ask if the archives held his individual records but received no reply. In our general inquiries, we were unable to determine where Mr G's records might be located.

In October 2007, almost five years later, G hasn't found any records that verify he spent three years at an approved school in Scotland. He's been unable to locate and access any personal information about his childhood for that period of time, including information about his family, placement, education and health.

"Mr. J"

Mr J and his siblings were placed in a large children's home in the 1950s after their father died during the Second World War,

his mother developed tuberculosis and his extended family was unable to care for them. Mr J, who describes his home as a "good home", says his mother had to "work hard" to have her children returned to her after she recovered from her illness.

In 1998, he began his search for records relating to his experiences at the children's home and in 2007 he still hadn't found them. Mr. J stated that, on the other hand, he has received his complete records from the army. He wrote an initial letter to his local authority social work department requesting his children's home records. Mr J says he received a response from a social worker in the department stating that they couldn't find any record of his time spent there. According to Mr J, the social worker said that she'd written to another local authority to request information about records they might possibly hold, but they held no records relating to Mr J or the children's home.

Mr J then wrote to the religious organisation that had responsibility for the children's home to ask for information about his records. The organisation's archivist responded and, in her letter, provided information about Mr J gleaned from the children's home registers held at the organisation's provincial house. This information included Mr. J's date of admission, his father's name and the date he was killed in active service, his mother's name and her address. The letter stated that Mr J's mother, during his admission, was staying in a sanatorium. The religious organisation's archives held no other information about Mr J's experiences in the children's home.

In 2005, Mr J wrote to the local authority where the children's home was located asking for information about the home under freedom of information legislation. The reply, from the local authority's "directorate policy and support officer", told Mr J that he could not seek "personal information" under the freedom of information legislation as those requests fell under data protection legislation. However the letter said that the officer would consider his request under both sets of legislation and provide him with any "general information" about the children's home. The officer indicated that she would also check the records "once again" for any possible "personal data" they might hold although she indicated it was unlikely she would find any information.

In response to Mr J's request in 2005 to access his records, a local authority administrative assistant working in the social work department wrote to him that she had forwarded his request to the head of child and family services "for consideration" and that the head of service or a member of her team would contact him. He received a letter dated November 2005 from a social work department fieldwork manager, stating that he had requested an archival search and would get back to Mr J with information. In January 2006 Mr J received a letter from the manager stating that after further archival searching, "...no record of your period at [the children's home] can be found".

Further to a telephone conversation, Mr J received a letter from the fieldwork manager stating that he had submitted another archival search for Mr J's records and providing the address for the religious organisation running the children's home during Mr J's placement. As Mr J had already contacted the religious organisation and learned they had no records for him, he did not follow this up. In February, 2006 Mr J received a letter from the fieldwork manager stating: "...there is no trace of any files relating to you or other family members for whom you provided details".

In addition to writing letters, M J told us, he made numerous phone calls and visited the regional archive where social work departments from various local authorities had deposited records. He said he'd attended the regional archive because another former resident, who lived in the same children's home during the same year, had located his records there. However when he visited the archive, the archivist told him he wasn't allowed to see his records. Rather, the archivist needed to inform the appropriate local authority social work department about his request and send his record to that department to be reviewed by a social worker before Mr J could see them. Mr J later learned that he could see his records but the archivist was unable to locate them. The local authority social work department had no recording to show what had happened to the records.

Mr J told us that in February 2007 he visited the regional archives for a second time to ask if his file was found. He left information for the archivist to contact him but didn't hear from her, which he described as "bad manners". At the time of this report Mr J still hadn't located his personal records or other pertinent information relating to his childhood experiences in a large children's home.

"Ms Y"
In the late 1960s and early 1970s, Ms Y lived as a young child, together with her siblings, in a large children's home. When she requested her personal records some time ago, she was told they had been lost in a fire in the 1980s. Ms Y said that in recent months, her brother asked for and received his records from the organisations responsible for the children's home. Her brother's records contained personal information about her, however, and she said she was "disgusted" with the organisation for passing on the information without her consent. She reported that it also concerned her that the information was sent by "everyday post".

Also in recent months, when Ms Y's sister requested her records, Ms Y said that she had accompanied her sister to the organisation where the records were held. She learned that her own records still existed and she was able to obtain them. When she reviewed her records she didn't see certain information she expected the records to contain and noticed that the date for her mother's death was inaccurate. When she asked the organisation where her mother was buried, she was told that her mother had not died and that she was living in England after remarrying. Ms Y told us that she was "devastated" and waited two weeks for the organisation to contact her mother after they said they'd try to reach her. Eventually the organisation contacted Ms Y to say that they had "made a mistake" and her mother was dead, although they didn't know where she was buried. She told them that they had recorded the wrong date for her mother's death in the record and told them where her mother was buried – information the organisation put into the record.

It is her understanding that the house parents and social work department kept records about the children at the children's home but she described the records as a "complete joke". Her sister didn't get the same background information about their family as she did and the information in her brother's records wasn't the same as the information in her and her sister's records. Ms Y said there were "things in the files that aren't true", which she wanted removed from the records. She said the organisation took the information out and burned it.

Ms Y had the impression that the organisation decided what information from the records they would give to Ms Y and her sister before they could see the records. She did not see information recorded about the concerns that led to her placement but she did see information like "attention seeker", "she tells lies" and "psychiatric referral". Ms Y said this type of labelling concerned her, describing how, at eight years old, she was taken from her family when her mother died and, when placed in the children's home, she was told to "dry her face and get on with it". She was initially separated from all her siblings except her oldest sister, who was "made to beat [her] up". She said the children's home staff did not demonstrate any empathy or understanding about the effects of death, her removal from her family and the damage to her sibling and family relationships. Ms Y told us there was no documentation in her records about the "punishments", "the cold baths", putting her in a shed or giving her a toothbrush to scrub walls.

She said the organisation offered no counselling services to people who access their records: services she thinks are very important.

Challenges for former residents: locating and accessing records

Some former residents (see also Appendix E) reported that it was difficult to return to the organisation responsible for managing the establishment where they lived because of unhappy memories associated with their experiences. Former residents also said they were told that the interests of third parties needed to be protected. It appeared to them that organisations and local authorities treated the records of former residents as institutional property that former residents did not have an entitlement to see. In their opinion, data protection and freedom of information legislation appeared to make certain records less accessible to them.

Several former residents in the 1950s and 1960s stated that they were refused access to their records because they were told they needed to be "protected" from information that other adults, such as social workers, determined might have been "traumatic" for them to read. These former residents were told that they had to access their records through a social work department, if the records were held by local authorities. They couldn't access their records unless the social work department requested the records on their behalf, reviewed the records and then appointed a social worker to sit with them while the former residents reviewed the records.

Some former residents said they were opposed to this approach. They also believed it was possible that employees in social work departments and organisations would remove information from records if those employees perceived it as damaging to their institutions. While some former residents understood the importance of counselling support, they wanted a choice about whom and under what circumstances such support was offered. Some indicated they didn't want support from people working for the local authority or organisation responsible for the children's residential establishment where they had lived. Some stated they interpreted some access records policies as "paternalistic".

Some former residents who accessed their records indicated that their disappointment at the poor quality of record-keeping, lack of record completeness (particularly relating to education and medical information), inaccuracy and missing pages. In some instances, their names had been changed, family names were spelled incorrectly and dates of birth were altered. Some former residents indicated that they wanted the opportunity to add information to their records – setting the record straight. Some thought certain information was not properly recorded, had been withheld inappropriately, falsified or lost. Others were unable to locate any record about their time in an establishment. In their search for family information, some former residents learned that they had siblings who died in children's residential establishments or parents who died shortly before or after their placement.

Former residents' experiences parallel challenges arising for former child migrants who wanted to locate and access records about their experiences. Some former residents had siblings who were sent abroad through child migration schemes. In their investigation into child migration, the British House of Commons Health Select Committee (1998) published a report that recognised the need for former child migrants to have access to their records. The report also stated that, in Australia, freedom of information fees were waived for child migrants who wanted to see their records. The report concluded that the "...overall picture remains one of unnecessary delays and difficulties being put in the way of former child migrants seeking to locate and retrieve information about their past and their birth-families."

> "We recommend that sending and receiving agencies, local authorities and governments should accept the principle that all relevant information held on former child migrants should be passed on, with due sensitivity, to those concerned, their descendants or representatives, on request" (British House of Commons Health Select Committee, 1998).

The Australian Parliament Senate Report (2001) into child migration states that "there is very little information available" about the childhoods of child migrants, which may be held by a number of different organisations. The report found that while children's records, for example, should have contained certain information, such as birth certificates, baptismal certificates, health reports and school reports, the records did not contain this information. Some people reported that their records did not contain the name of a mother or father, place of birth or their birth date was incorrect.

The report also found that family background information was scant and non-existent in some instances. It found, however, that practices on personal records varied from organisation to organisation. Some had scant or no information while others had more substantial information. The report discussed the poor attitudes towards making children's records and other information accessible to child migrants, which, in turn, made it difficult for child migrants to reunite with their families. These findings, and others in the report, are similar to what former residents describe as their experiences in Scotland.
In summary, former residents identified numerous barriers in trying to locate and access records relating to children's residential establishments. These barriers included:

- the state of records thought to be missing;
- lack of a central location where people can request information and receive advocacy support about where and how to search for records;
- lack of a central location that has details about what records exist;
- lack of a central location that provides specialised guidance on records management and access policies;
- unfamiliarity with the extent of locations where records may be located;
- unfamiliarity with the types of records that may be available;
- lack of clear, consistent and supported access to records policies;
- lack of knowledge about record-keeping requirements;
- expense;
- distance required to travel to locations where records are held;
- lack of computer access and literacy;

- poor attitudes, such as little understanding about records' significance, resistance to disclosure and a patronising approach to making records available;
- confusion about records control and ownership;
- litigation concerns;
- incomplete records;
- poor quality of information photocopied;
- considerable time and perseverance required to locate records;
- delays in responding to requests for information about records;
- former residents' mistrust of keepers of records;
- lack of consistent records management and archival practice; and
- inadequacies in legislation to ensure records are preserved within archives.

Conclusion

Former residents who lived in children's residential establishments have rights associated with records. These include the legal entitlement to view records associated with their childhood experiences in residential placements. Some former residents contacting the review, however, found that locating and accessing records associated with children's residential establishments is fraught with challenges. There is no central tracing database, for example, to assist former residents seeking information about their experiences, their family history and children's residential establishments in general.

The described experiences of former residents contacting the review illustrate the many difficulties former residents encountered when trying to locate information they expected to be available to them. Located records often don't contain the information former residents expected, or hoped, to see. Some residents are upset when they read certain information in their records for the first time as elderly adults. Some records are missing. Poor records management in the past has meant that some former residents are unable to realise their legal entitlements to access records.

The challenges faced by former residents contacting our review are consistent with experiences highlighted in other inquiries, such as those into child migration and institutional child abuse.[14] Some key aspects include:

Locating records: Records may be located in several locations and information in many types of records, unknown and unidentified to former residents. These records may also exist in places at considerable geographical distance from where former residents live, requiring them to incur significant costs to access records.
Missing records: Records may be missing for various reasons, such as inadequate searching, the misplacement of records or because records have been destroyed.
Support to view records: Former residents may be prevented from gaining access to their records without agreeing to support services from organisations and local authorities concerned about the possible effects that reading file contents may have on former residents.
Information within records: Once former residents have gained access to their records, they're often disappointed or distressed by what isn't in their records or by what they learn for the first time in their lives.
Record quality: Former residents described their difficulty in reading photocopied records and in reading incomplete information that had pages missing or information blocked from view.

---

[14] see British House of Commons Health Select Committee Report (1998); Parliament of Australia Senate Report (2001); and Parliament of Australia Senate Report (2004).

One critical lesson we learned is how the search for records and records content affect the lives of children as adults in later years. Through the experiences of former residents with records, it is possible to see what must be done to make the future experiences of children in state care, who seek information about their childhood experiences, less traumatic. It is also possible to see what issues need to be addressed to meet the current needs of former residents trying to locate and access records. From a broader perspective, society benefits when we are able to gain insights into past practices through personal records associated with children's residential services.

Chapter 3: Generating records for children's residential establishments – the legal framework 1933-1995

Introduction

Fundamental questions arose during our research into records. What did the law say about the generation and maintenance of records within the complex environment of children's residential services from 1950 to 1995? This chapter outlines the general laws, rules and regulations for the legal framework that provided for records generation within children's residential establishments from 1950 to 1995.

Records linked to children's residential services were, and continue to be, produced by organisations that included children's residential establishments, local authorities, voluntary organisations, religious organisations, professional bodies, the children's hearing system, justice, education and health care systems, inspection agencies and central government. In some cases, laws specified which records had to be generated within children's residential services while other records came into existence through localised policies and practice. It's not possible within the scope of this chapter to review all of these.

It is possible, however, to identify specific regulations for generating records within children's residential establishments from 1950 to 1995, which are highlighted in the following summary. (While evidence suggests that many establishments adopted individualised record-keeping systems as well, those approaches are not detailed in this chapter). The summary doesn't cover all the records associated with children's residential services that may have been generated. It does, however, offer an insight into the types of records specific establishments needed to create to comply with the law[15].

Generating records in children's residential establishments: 1933-1968

This section summarises key legal references to records for approved schools, children's homes, homes for children with 'mental disorders' and remand homes.

Approved schools

In 1933, the **Children and Young Persons (Scotland) Care and Training Regulations 1933**[16] required the headmaster or headmistress to keep records "as may be required". Paragraph 23 required:

- a general record of all admissions, licences and discharges;
- individual records of all children in the care of the managers;
- a log book recording any written report on the school communicated to the managers, visits of any managers, and all events connected with the school that "deserve to be recorded";
- a punishment book[17]; and
- a separate register of children attending the school-room for instruction.

Also under the 1933 regulations, children were allowed to receive letters (and visits) from their parent or guardians. Any letters should have been placed on children's files[18].

The **Approved Schools (Scotland) Rules 1961**[19] confirmed these requirements, with the added requirement to keep "an adequate record of the progress of each individual pupil" and a record of every time a pupil absconded from the school[20]. Other records required under these rules related to after-care services, although it is notable that this requirement was omitted under the Approved Schools (Scotland) Amendment Rules 1963[21].

The 1961 rules ensured that the records were available to the management at all times, with the log book put before them at each meeting and the chairman certifying that he or she had read the items recorded since the last meeting[22]. The managers were responsible for making certain that all necessary records were generated and maintained to ensure proper reporting to the Secretary of State:

"The Managers shall manage the school in the interests of the welfare, development and rehabilitation of the pupils and for this purpose they shall take into consideration any report which may be communicated to them by or on behalf of the Secretary of State[23]."

These rules also required the managers and any committee they appointed to keep minutes of their proceedings and to make these available to an inspector[24]. Children also retained the right to receive letters with the added stipulation that they should be actively "…encouraged to write to their parents at least once a week"[25]. Every letter to or from the child could be read by a staff member deputed by the Headmaster or Headmistress, and "reasonably" withheld if appropriate (although the facts and circumstances of any letter withheld was to be noted in the log book, and the letter preserved for at least a year)[26]. Any letter to one of the managers, or to the Secretary of State or any of his officers or departments, could not be withheld[27]. These letters should have been placed within children's and organisational records.

---

[15] This section is informed by the Historical Abuse Systemic Review report chapter 2 on the regulatory framework.

[16] SI 1933/1006. Revoked by the Approved Schools (Scotland) Rules 1961 (SI 1961/2243)

[17] See also SI 1933/1006.

[18] See also SI 1933/1006.

[19] SI 1961/2243. Brought in under the Children and Young Persons (Scotland) Act 1937, s83 and Schedule 2, paragraph 1(1). Amended by the Approved Schools (Scotland) Amendment Rules 1963 (SI 1963/1756)

[20] SI 1961/2243 paragraph 11(1)(b) and (f). The details to be shown in the punishment book were outlined under paragraph 32

[21] SI 1963/1756

[22] ibid paragraph 3

[23] ibid paragraph 4

[24] ibid paragraph 1(3)

[25] ibid paragraph paragraph 35. For this purpose postage stamps were to be provided free, once a week, by the managers.

[26] Ibid

[27] Ibid

Children's homes

The Voluntary Homes (Return of Particulars) (Scotland) Regulations 1952[28] required that the Secretary of State should receive certain details relating to a 'voluntary home', which term included children's homes . These details included:

- the home's name and address;
- the name of the person in charge;
- the number of boys and girls in the home according to age;
- the number of boys and girls in the home who were receiving education, training or employment in the home and outside it;
- the name of any government department or departments, other than the Scottish Home Department, that inspected the home; and
- the date of the last inspection by each such government department[29].

The **Administration of Children's Homes (Scotland) Regulations 1959**[30] contained provisions on generating records in local authority and voluntary children's homes[31]. Schedule 2 required the following records to be kept:

"1. A register in which shall be entered the date of admission and the date of discharge of every child accommodated in the home.

"2. A log book in which shall be recorded every event of importance connected with the home, including visits and inspections, every punishment administered to a child in the home, and every fire drill or practice, a note of the fire precautions recommended to the administering authority…and of the extent to which these recommendations have been implemented.

"3. Records of food provided for the children accommodated in the home in sufficient detail to enable any person inspecting the records to judge whether the dietary is satisfactory.

"4. A personal history of each child in the home. This shall include his medical history; a note of the circumstances in which he was admitted to the home; and in the case of a child in the care of a local authority of the circumstances which made it impracticable or undesirable to board him out; a record of the progress made during his stay in the home (in which it shall be noted…visits received from parents, relatives or friends…and any emotional or other difficulties experienced by the child); and a note of his destination when discharged from the home."

The person in charge of the home was responsible for compiling the records, which were to be open to inspection by anyone

visiting the home under the powers granted to the Secretary of State or the requirements placed on the administering authority[32]. Similarly, the person in charge of the home was required to maintain the medical record of each child accommodated in the home, making such records available at all times to the medical officer and to any person authorised by the Secretary of State or the administering authority to inspect them[33].

Homes for children with 'mental disorders'
The Secretary of State had the power to make regulations under section 40 of the **National Assistance Act 1948** about the conduct of residential homes for persons suffering from what was called "mental disorder". This power included making regulations about what records had to be kept. The Secretary of State could also require notices to be given about persons received in such homes[34]. Additional powers of inspection under section 39 included the power to inspect any records and to interview any person resident in the home in private[35].

Remand homes
Under the **Remand Home (Scotland) Rules 1946**[36] the superintendent was required to keep a register of admissions and discharges, and a log book in which "every event of importance connected with the remand home" was to be entered[37]. The log book had to contain details of all visits, dates of inspection and all punishments. This latter obligation was reinforced by the requirement to immediately record all punishments in the log book and send, every quarter to the Secretary of State a return, or record, of corporal punishment administered. This 'return' had to be sent in the form he or she required[38]. In general the books – the log book and register of admissions and discharges – were to be open to inspection by or on behalf of the council or by an inspector and inspected at regular intervals not exceeding three months[39].

Generating records in children's residential establishments: 1969 - 1995

The Social Work (Scotland) Act 1968 made provision for children's residential establishments throughout Scotland. The **Social Work (Residential Establishments – Child Care) (Scotland) Regulations 1987**[40] ('the 1987 Regulations') were introduced to revoke the 1959 Regulations and 1961 Rules. They addressed general residential care for children for whom local authorities and voluntary organisations were responsible under the Social Work (Scotland) Act 1968. The 1987 Regulations applied[41] to **any** residential establishment providing residential accommodation for children which was either controlled or managed by a local

[28] (SI 1952/1836). Exercised under section 97 of the Children and Young Persons (Scotland) Act 1937, revoking the Children and Young Persons (Voluntary Homes) Regulations (Scotland) 1933 (SI 1933/923)

[29] ibid Schedule 1 and paragraph 11

[30] SI 1959/834. Revoked by the Social Work (Residential Establishments-Child Care) (Scotland) Regulations 1987

[31] SI 1959/834 paragraph 14

[32] ibid

[33] ibid paragraph 15

[34] ibid s21(1) (repealed by the Social Work (Scotland) Act 1968, Sch 9)

[35] ibid s21(2) (repealed by the Social Work (Scotland) Act 1968, Sch 9)

[36] SI 1946/693

[37] ibid paragraph 20

[38] ibid paragraph 17(b)

[39] ibid paragraph 20

[40] 1987/2233. In force from 1 June 1988. Superseded by the Residential Establishments – Child Care (Scotland) Regulations 1996 (SI 1996/3256) and the Arrangements to Look After Children (Scotland) Regulations 1996 (SI 1996/3262)

[41] As determined by paragraph 3 of the Regulations (1987/2233)

authority, one required to be registered under section 61 of the 1968 Act[42], or a school voluntarily registered in accordance with section 61A of the 1968 Act[43]. It was considered to be the duty of the managers[44] of any such establishment to provide for "the care, development and control of each child resident there as shall be conducive to the best interests of the child"[45].

A requirement was placed on the managers under the regulations to prepare a "statement of functions and objectives" for that establishment[46], including details specified in Schedule 1 stipulating:

"6. Arrangements for record keeping in accordance with regulation 14, including:
(a) procedures for the selection of children to be admitted to the establishment;
(b) details of admissions and discharges from the establishment;
(c) procedures for access to records for staff, children and parents; and
(d) records regarding any involvement of children and parents in relation to decisions taken about the child's welfare while resident in the establishment."

The basic provisions of the 1987 Regulations required managers (in consultation with the person in charge) to ensure that all necessary records, including health particulars, were properly maintained for each child resident in an establishment[47]. Managers also had a duty (again in consultation with the relevant person in charge) to ensure that a "log book of day to day events of importance or an official nature" was kept and maintained; this would include "details of disciplinary measures imposed"[48].

Secure accommodation
After amendments to the Social Work (Scotland) Act 1968 by the Health and Social Services and Social Security Adjudications Act 1983[49], specific regulations were made about the provision and use of secure accommodation in Scotland. The **Secure Accommodation (Scotland) Regulations 1983**[50] placed a duty on the person in charge to keep a record of the child's placement, including details of what supervision was required and any reviews of the placement by virtue of the 1968 Act[51]. Such records were to be open at all times to inspection by the Secretary of State who could request copies[52]. The **Secure Accommodation (Scotland) Amendment Regulations 1988**[53] required that the newly defined managers of such establishments should consult with the person in charge about the need to keep records[54].

More legal provisions were needed to govern secure accommodation for children detained, under court order, in residential care under section 413 of the **Criminal Procedure (Scotland) Act 1975**[55]. In response, The **Residential Care Order (Secure Accommodation) (Scotland) Regulations 1988**[56] were introduced. These regulations provided for record-keeping, requiring that the person in charge maintain a record of the child's placement in secure accommodation including:
■ details of any reviews undertaken in accordance with the Regulations;
■ the date and time of the child's placement, release or both of these; and
■ the child's full name, sex and date of birth[57].

These records were to be available for inspection by the Secretary of State who could require that copies of them be sent to him[58].

Generating records: The Children (Scotland) Act 1995

The legal provision for generating records in children's residential establishments changed with the Children (Scotland) 1995 Act. With this Act, it is possible to see that certain legislative improvements to generating records within children's residential services were made. The regulations and guidance for the Children (Scotland) Act 1995, applicable today, contain specific provisions on records for children's residential establishments, including secure accommodation.

For example, managers must consult with the person in charge and prepare a statement of functions and objectives for the establishment.[59] The person in charge must report to the managers within 12-month intervals on how the statement is being implemented and its progress. Managers must also visit the establishments within six-month intervals and prepare a comprehensive report on the statement's implementation. The Act adds:

"Managers may, in consultation with the person in charge, make appropriate amendments to the statement. Copies of the statement (or amended versions) should be made available to children and parents. The managers should also make the statement available, on request, to any local authority or children's hearing considering placing a child in such an establishment.

"The statement should provide the establishment with an overall sense of direction. It should describe what the home sets out to do for children; the types of service which it seeks

---

[42] As amended by section 1 of the Registered Establishments (Scotland) Act 1987

[43] Inserted by section 2 of the Registered Establishments (Scotland) Act 1987

[44] Meaning "(a) in the case of a voluntary organisation, the management committee to whom powers are delegated within the organisation for management of the residential establishment; (b) in the case of a local authority, those officers having delegated powers under section 2 of the Act, as read with section 56 of the Local Government (Scotland) Act 1973, for the management of the residential establishment: The Social Work (Residential Establishments – Child Care) (Scotland) Regulations 1987 (1987/2233), paragraph 2(1)

[45] ibid paragraph 4

[46] ibid paragraph 5

[47] ibid paragraph 14

[48] ibid paragraph 15

[49] Section 8 inserted the new sections 58A to 58G into the 1968 Act

[50] SI 1983/1912. Paragraph 19 revoked rules 33 and 34 of the Approved Schools (Scotland) Rules 1961

[51] ibid paragraph 16(1)

[52] ibid paragraph 16(2)

[53] SI 1988/841

[54] ibid paragraph 11 (amending paragraph 16 of the 1983 Regulations)

[55] Section 413(1), as substituted by section 59(1) of the Criminal Justice (Scotland) Act 1987

[56] SI 1988/294

[57] ibid paragraph 7(1)

[58] ibid paragraph 7(2)

[59] see Children (Scotland) Act 1995, Regulations and Guidance, Volume 2, Chapter 4.

to provide directly or in association with other agencies; the outcomes it seeks to achieve and the timescales. The statement might be organised around the eight principles set out in the report "Another Kind of Home" (HMSO, 1992)[1][60]"

Under the regulations and guidance for the Children (Scotland) 1995 Act, the statement of functions and objectives (see Appendix F) should detail the arrangements for children's residential establishments[61]. Additional records, however, must be generated within children's residential establishments. The establishment, for example "...should produce a statement of the rights and responsibilities of children residing in their establishments..." with children and their parents being given such a statement[62]:

"Each establishment must have a formal complaints procedure which is part of the responsible agency's procedures. The procedure should be easily understood and readily accessible to the children and staff. This procedure should include provision for children to gain access, by such means as private use of a telephone, to a person independent of the establishment, for instance a complaints officer. Complaints should be followed up promptly and thoroughly. The child should be informed, usually in writing, of the outcome. A record should be maintained of the complaint, follow-up and outcome. Staff should receive training to familiarise them with procedures. It is also helpful to review the number and characteristics of complaints on an annual basis to identify any wider implications for practice and management in the establishment[63]."

There are also detailed provisions for personal records (see Appendix G) for children residing within children's residential establishments. Under the regulations and guidance, children's records should be comprehensive and up-to-date, with cross-references to other records with more detailed information. Records should be checked regularly by the person in charge and be available to the social worker for the responsible local authority[64].

Introduced under the Children (Scotland) 1995 Act, the **Arrangements to Look After Children (Scotland) Regulations 1996** were intended to work alongside the Residential Establishments - Child Care (Scotland) Regulations 1996 (which superseded the Social Work (Residential Establishments - Child Care) (Scotland) Regulations 1987). These additional regulations required local authorities to make a care plan "to address the immediate and longer-term needs of the child with a view to safeguarding and promoting his welfare[65]" immediately when the child became looked-after by a local authority. Local authorities were obliged to conduct stringent reviews of the child's placement and the care plan at frequent intervals[66] and to make a record of such review information[67].

The **Residential Establishments - Child Care (Scotland) Regulations 1996**[68] were introduced to provide for children's placements in residential establishments under the Children (Scotland) 1995 Act[69]. Again, managers were required to prepare a statement of functions and objectives setting out their responsibilities[70], subjecting them to periods of review to ensure they implemented their obligations properly[71]. Minimum requirements (again almost identical to those contained in the 1987 Regulations) were specified about the need to keep log books and personal records[72].

Keeping proper records was emphasised by the provision requiring local authorities to establish written case records for children looked after by their authority. These records needed to include:
- the care plan;
- any report in their possession concerning the child's welfare;
- review documents; and
- details of any arrangements whereby another person acted for the placing local authority[73].

Personal records had to retained until the 75th birthday of the person it related to or, if the child died before reaching the age of 18, for 25 years from the date of death[74]. The local authority was required to ensure the safe-keeping of such case records and keep them confidential, subject only to any legal provision or court order[75].

---

[60] Ibid

[61] The eight principles in 'Another Kind of Home' are individuality and development; rights; good basic care; education; health; partnerships with parents; child centred collaboration and a feeling of safety.

[62] See Children (Scotland) Act 1995, Regulations and Guidance, Volume 2, Chapter 4.

[63] Ibid

[64] Ibid

[65] S.I. 1996/3262 paragraph 3

[66] ibid paragraphs 8 and 9, namely 6 weeks within the date of first placement, 3 months within the date of the first review and thereafter periods of 6 months within the date of the previous review

[67] S.I. 1996/3262 paragraph 10

[68] S.I. 1996/3256. Superseded themselves by the Regulation of Care (Requirements as to Care Services) (Scotland) Regulations 2002 No 114

[69] Applying to any residential establishment controlled or managed by a local authority, one which required registration under s61 of the 1968 Act, or a school voluntarily registered in accordance with s61A of the 1968 Act: S.I. 1996/3256, paragraph 3

[70] ibid paragraph 5(1) and the Schedule to the Regulations

[71] ibid paragraph 5(2) and (3)

[72] ibid paragraphs 12 and 13

[73] ibid paragraph 11

[74] ibid paragraph 12(1), the requirements being met by either retaining the original written record or a copy of it, or in some other accessible form (such as a computer record): S.I. 1996/3262 paragraph 12(2)

[75] ibid paragraph 12(3)

New regulations were also introduced to govern secure accommodation in residential accommodation, replacing the previous sets of secure accommodation regulations[76]. The **Secure Accommodation (Scotland) Regulations 1996**[77] applied to the use of secure accommodation for any child looked after by a local authority or for whom the local authority was responsible under criminal procedure legislation. These regulations consolidated the main provisions of the previous legislation. The requirement to keep a record of the child's placement in such accommodation was maintained, including obligations to hold details of the child and any reviews undertaken of the placement by virtue of section 73 of the 1995 Act[78].

Conclusion

The regulatory framework for children's residential services shows how **children's residential establishments** needed to generate more records in later years. At the same time, this regulatory framework does not take account of all the records generated in association with **children's residential services**. From 1950 to 1995, the law specified what records needed to be generated within approved schools, children's homes, residential placements for children with 'mental disorders' and remand homes, for example. The law outlined managers' and the Secretary of State's duties and powers relating to records, imposing an oversight responsibility for individual children's welfare and children's residential establishments facilitated through records.

As an illustration, the 1933 law required managers for approved schools to ensure proper record keeping, which included 'punishment books', and to review the records, possibly to monitor children's safety and quality of service provision. The 1961 rules included additional requirements such as keeping records of children's progress and absconding. Approved school managers, who had an obligation to manage '...the school in the interests of the welfare, development and rehabilitation of the pupils', were also required to read the log book, keep meeting minutes, report to the Secretary of State and make records available to inspectors. The 1952 and 1959 regulations for children's homes show the association between records and the duties of managers, inspectors and the Secretary of State, who was to receive 'punishment returns'.

The 1987 regulations[79] continued to place duties on managers for proper record generation and required managers to prepare a statement of functions and objectives for their establishment[80]. In particular, managers had responsibility for ensuring children's records, including 'health particulars', were kept along with a log book registering important events, such as 'discipline' administered. The language in the 1987 regulations changed to 'discipline' from 'punishment' used in earlier legislation, which coincided with the banning of corporal punishment in schools. In the 1980s, new regulations for secure accommodation also demanded records for children placed there and access to those records by inspectors. The Secretary of State could request individual records for children placed in secure accommodation.

Then, the Children's (Scotland) Act 1995 and other regulations, including those for secure accommodation, followed. The legal provisions for records associated with children's residential establishments changed once again and became more expansive, suggesting a growing reliance on records as a method for monitoring and improving services to children. Managers of children's residential establishments continued to have responsibility for records, including detailed statements of function and objectives. The law introduced statements on 'children's rights and responsibilities' to be given to children along with information about complaints procedures. The requirement to generate personal records for children in children's residential establishments continued although the requirements for what those records must contain developed further under the 1995 Act.

---

[76] Chiefly, The Secure Accommodation (Scotland) Regulations 1983 (SI 1983/1912); The Secure Accommodation (Scotland) Amendment Regulations 1988 (SI 1988/841); The Residential Care Order (Secure Accommodation) (Scotland) Amendment Regulations 1988 (S.I. 1988/1092)

[77] S.I. 1996/3255

[78] ibid paragraph 16

[79] 1987/2233. In force from 1 June 1988. Superseded by the Residential Establishments – Child Care (Scotland) Regulations 1996 (SI 1996/3256) and the Arrangements to Look After Children (Scotland) Regulations 1996 (SI 1996/3262)

[80] ibid paragraph 5

Chapter 4: An overview of records law and key initiatives after 1995

Introduction

This chapter provides an overview of general records legislation. It also highlights significant records developments in recent years and legal issues arising that remain today.

Between 1950 and 1995, thousands of records specific to children's residential services were generated. While today the importance of preserving such records, and making them accessible, is recognised, the law has not always provided for records to be preserved and made accessible. As a consequence, it was extremely difficult for us, former residents and others to identify and locate significant historical records – despite how critical it is, from an individual and society's perspective, to protect such records. The Scottish National Archives Policy (1999)[81] states that:

> "…a civilised society, concerned to uphold the rights of the citizen, to encourage efficient administration and to ensure that its history is accessible to all, should make provision for its archives to be preserved and made available for consultation."

These provisions for records, however, must be considered within their broader context of public records and other records-related legislation. Several key initiatives have been associated with the public records legislation as some legal issues associated with records are outstanding, such as issues related to preservation and access. These issues may have particular implications for records associated with children's residential services.

Records legislation: overview

The **Public Records (Scotland) Act 1937 ('the 1937 Act')** was the primary legislation in place during the period of our review (see specialist legislation above) for ensuring preservation and access to public records. It remains as the main legislation governing the work of the National Archives of Scotland (NAS), along with the Public Registers and Records (Scotland) Act 1948, and some parts of the Public Records Act 1958, as amended by the Public Records Act 1967[82]. The 1937 Act, which still applies to this day in amended form, was introduced with the intention of making "better provision for the preservation, care and custody of the Public Records of Scotland"[83], but was chiefly concerned with providing for the transfer of records of central and local Scottish courts to the Keeper[84] of the Records of Scotland.

The Act is notable in that, along with government departments, agencies, non-departmental public bodies, and statutory bodies[85], it allowed local authorities to transfer their records to the Keeper[86] but did not require them to do so. The 1937 Act also outlined the Keeper's powers over and duties to records, permitting him or her to take whatever steps considered necessary for cleaning, preserving, repairing and arranging of any records sent to the Keeper under the Act[87]. The Keeper also had the power to issue extracts or certified copies of any records sent to him under the Act[88]. And the Keeper could dispose of records he or she decided had no long-term value, although this provision applied mainly to court records.

Finally, the 1937 Act was significant in creating the **Scottish Records Advisory Council,** which was eligible to "submit proposals or make representations to the Secretary of State, the Lord Justice General, or the Lord President on questions relating to the public records of Scotland", and in particular, to "the custody, preservation, indexing, and cataloguing of those records, and to facilities for access to and examination of them by members of the public"[89].

The 1937 Act was, and remains, the main primary legislation governing the creation and maintenance of public records, although other developments had an impact on the requirement to keep records. The **Public Registers and Records (Scotland) Act 1948**, for example, recognised the need for creating two positions: a Keeper of the General Register of Sasines and a Keeper of the Records of Scotland. In England and Wales, the **Public Records Act 1958** departs from the 1937 Act in placing a **duty** on every person who is responsible for public records to make arrangements to select the records which ought to be permanently preserved.

Since 1962, some aspects of the 1958 Act have been applied in Scotland by agreement between the UK and Scottish Keepers. With this agreement, UK public bodies operating wholly or mainly in Scotland could transfer their records to the National Archives of Scotland rather than to the National Archives (London)[90]. In 1962, the Scottish Office adopted the arrangements for access to government records set out in the 1958 Act and also adopted similar arrangements for selecting, transferring and preserving government records. Similarly, although the **Public Records Act 1967** did not apply to Scotland, its provision reducing the standard closure period for UK government records from 50 years to 30 years (the "30-year rule") was adopted.

Previous regulations were introduced under the 1937 Act's section 12 to govern the rules for disposing of records other than court records[91], but the provisions were consolidated under **The Disposal of Records (Scotland) Regulations 1992**[92]. These provisions provided that the Keeper could authorise the destruction of any such records (other than a record of an older date than the year 1707) where they had no sufficient value to justify their preservation[93]. The provisions also allowed the Keeper to dispose of any records that should be held by any

---

[81] See reference at: http://www.dundee.ac.uk/archives/SAL-october1999summary.htm

[82] No legislation mentions the National Archives of Scotland by name, as all rights and responsibilities are vested personally in the Keeper of the Records of Scotland

[83] The Public Records (Scotland) Act 1937, c.43 introductory note

[84] The Public Records (Scotland) Act 1937, c.43 s1 – 3, subsequently amended by the Law Reform (Miscellaneous Provisions) (Scotland) Act 1966 (c. 19), s. 8(4). See also footnote 8.

[85] ibid Part II, as amended by the Statute Law (Repeals) Act 1981 (c. 19), Sch.1 Pt. XII, and the Public Records Act 1958 (c. 51), Sch. 4

[86] ibid s5

[87] ibid s8

[88] ibid s9, restricted by Abolition of Domestic Rates Etc. (Scotland) Act 1987 (c. 47), ss. 20(11)(b)

[89] ibid s7(3)

[90] Made possible by an interaction between section 3(8) of the 1958 Act and section 5(1) of the Public Records (Scotland) Act 1937

[91] S.R & O. 1940/2107 (Rev XIX p 846: 1940 I, p917). These regulations were revoked in part by S.I. 1969/1756 and S.I. 1990/106. The rules for disposal of court records is governed by The Disposal of Court Records (Scotland) Regulations 1990 No 106

[92] 1992 No 3247

[93] ibid reg. 3(a)

person, body or institution other than the Keeper by transferring them to that person, body or institution[94]. Before the disposal of any records, however, the Keeper was required to obtain the consent of the Scottish Records Advisory Council and, in relation to particular records, certain other persons or bodies. For example, when local authority records in the possession of the Keeper were authorised for destruction, the local authority was required to give consent[95]. These regulations still apply today. They've been amended by the **Disposal of Records (Scotland) Amendment Regulations 2003**[96], which required the consent of Scottish Ministers and the Scottish Parliamentary Corporate Body for destruction of Scottish Administration and Scottish Parliament records.

The **Freedom of Information (Scotland) Act 2002**, put fully into force on 1 January 2005, introduced a statutory right of access to all types of recorded information of any age held by Scottish public authorities, subject to certain conditions and exemptions. It was designed to be promoted and enforced by a fully independent Scottish Information Commissioner. In amendments to the Public Records (Scotland) Act 1937, the 2002 Act allowed for the matters on which the Scottish Records Advisory Council could advise Scottish Ministers to include those relating to the application of that Act to information contained in records held by the Keeper[97].

The **Human Rights Act 1998** and the **Data Protection Act 1998** exist as other key legislation relating to records. The Human Rights Act 1998, for example, effectively incorporates the rights and freedoms guaranteed by the European Convention on Human Rights, with implications for what records are created, maintained and accessed.

The **Data Protection Act 1998** intends to ensure the fair and lawful processing of the personal data of living individuals, obliging organisations to provide a reasonable degree of confidentiality for information about people, and to respect their privacy. Based on eight fundamental right-based principles, the Act requires that:
- data is obtained fairly and lawfully;
- the "data subject" is informed about who the "data controller" is (that is, the institution);
- the purpose or purposes for which the data held will be used;
- who will receive the data held will be disclosed;
- personal data is kept accurate and up to date;
- personal data is not kept for longer than necessary.

The Act also gives significant rights to individuals about personal data held about them by institutions, including the right to request access to data and to be supplied with a copy of all personal data held. The Act came into force by degrees and initially related only to personal data held on computer systems, but now also applies to personal data held in paper-based files.

Records legislation: local authority records

In addition to the chief provisions governing public records in the 1937 Act, several local government acts included requirements affecting records. The **Local Government (Scotland) Act 1973** introduced a two-tier system of local government comprising nine regional authorities, 53 district councils and three unitary island councils. This took effect in 1974 and survived until 1995. The Act included several sections with a bearing on recording and publishing information and on rights of access to records. However Section 200, which governed the transfer of records between the old and new authorities and required the new authorities to make "proper arrangements" for their records, was repealed by the **Environment Act 1995**[98].

Later, the **Local Government (Access to Information) Act 1985** focused largely on establishing the rights of access to information held by local authorities[99]. The **Local Government etc (Scotland) Act 1994** replaced the two-tier system of Scottish local government with 32 unitary authorities, taking effect in 1995. This Act provided for the transfer of property, including records, between the old and new authorities[100]. It also obliged local authorities to make "proper arrangements" for the "preservation and management" of any records that had been transferred to them under the Act, created or acquired by them in the exercise of their functions, or otherwise placed in their custody after consulting the Keeper of the Records of Scotland[101]. The Act allowed for a local authority to dispose of any records it didn't consider "worthy of preservation"[102]. Furthermore, local authorities could determine what was appropriate for enabling proper use of their records and could make provision for enabling people to inspect their records and to make or obtain copies[103].

Historical records and children's residential establishments: significant developments

It is evident that there are significant weaknesses in Scotland's archival legislation as the Public Records Act 1937 is limited in its scope and outdated. Other countries, such as New Zealand, updated their archival legislation to reflect "...changes in technology, legislation and record-keeping practices that have occurred in the past 47 years".[104] Their legislation objectives are to:
- promote accountability between the Crown, the public, and Government agencies;
- enhance public confidence in the integrity of public records;
- enhance and promote...historical and cultural heritage; and
- encourage partnership and goodwill envisaged by the Treaty of Waitangi in relation to public records.

In England, there are existing proposals to change current legislative provisions for records management and archives, partially in recognition of the vast numbers of people who have

---

[94] ibid reg. 3(b)

[95] ibid reg. 4(b)

[96] 2003 No.522

[97] The Public Records (Scotland) Act 1937, s7 (3A), as inserted by the Freedom of Information (Scotland) Act (2002 ASP.13), Pt 7 s 70 (2)

[98] This information is taken directly from the NAS website: http://www.nas.gov.uk/.

[99] Inserting Sch 7A into the Local Government (Scotland) Act 1973, access to certain information was exempted, including: "Information relating to the adoption, care, fostering or education of any particular child or relating to the supervision or residence of any particular child in accordance with a supervision requirement made in respect of that child under the Social Work (Scotland) Act 1968"

[100] The Local Government etc (Scotland) Act 1994, s15

[101] ibid s53(1)

[102] ibid s53(2), "records" being defined as including charters, deeds, minutes, accounts and other documents, and any other records, of whatever form and in whatever medium, which convey information, but not including records which are the property of the Registrar General of Births, Deaths and Marriages for Scotland

[103] ibid s54(1)

[104] see New Zealand Public Records Act (2005) see at: http://gpacts.knowledge-basket.co.nz/gpacts/public/text/2005/an/040.html

developed an interest in historical records. Scotland's own records legislation, as evidenced above, does not adequately ensure the preservation and accessibility of records although within the last 10 years there have been significant initiatives to address the apparent weaknesses in Scotland's archival legislation. Several of these are described below.

Archival mapping project (1999)

In 1999, the National Archives of Scotland managed a Scottish archive services mapping project that followed earlier pilot projects in England and Wales. The Scottish project was designed to allow for strategic approaches to funding initiatives for public and private sector archive services. During 1998, the project sent questionnaires to local authorities, health boards, universities, national institutions and specialist repositories[105]. The results showed "...a wholly unacceptable level of development...the picture of inadequate staffing, seriously unsatisfactory buildings, and administrative neglect is not one of which the country can be proud" suggesting, as well, that the overall picture of archives in Scotland at that time was "grim". The project concluded that there was significant need for archival storage and accommodation:

> "The emergence of purpose-built local archive repositories as separate physical entities in Scotland's major cities would be a major advance, bringing automatic recognition of the value of archives as an essential component of our heritage and society.

> "If the complexities of the funding gap both outside and within parent organisations could be bridged to begin this absolutely fundamental process, there is a better likelihood of development in all other aspects of archives provision; especially if neighbouring archive offices existing in close proximity can find ways of adopting a collaborative approach to, for example, conservation needs or development of automated cross-institutional finding aids."

The mapping project report also identified the need for more staffing, with the mapping project report stating that a Scottish Records Archives Council could be the "...natural vehicle to achieve the provision of proper resources for archives throughout the country":

> "[Scotland's archivists'] collective achievements, especially over the last two decades in the face of huge difficulties, should not be underestimated. Without their services the nation would have lost great chunks of its collective memory. How valuable is that memory to the people of Scotland? It is nothing less than the written record of the Scottish identity upon which our very way of life is based. We already have a 'Scottish National Archives Policy'. A Scottish Archives Act may well translate its nine broad principles into law in the next millennium. Our archives must also then find the resources they so richly deserve."

Public Records Strategy (2003-2004)

The Scottish Executive recognised that Scottish public records legislation, such as the Public Records (Scotland) Act 1937, needed to be reviewed and established a Public Records

Strategy[106]. This awareness followed the introduction of the Freedom of Information (Scotland) Act 2002 and the Data Protection Act 1998. New technological developments, such as electronic and digital records, also highlighted the importance this Strategy had.

> "The purpose of this project is to examine existing legislation, guidance, standards and practices relating to Scottish public records and archives, together with the roles and functions of the key stakeholders in relation to those records, and to consider whether these need to be amended or updated to, for example:
> - "take account of recent legislation (such as the Freedom of Information (Scotland) Act 2002 and the Data Protection Act 1998);
> - "take account of developments in technology (such as electronic records), developments in records management practices, devolution, and any other relevant issues;
> - "improve the quality and consistency of records management and archive arrangements across the Scottish public sector; and
> - "promote the use of archives and improve their accessibility."

While the Strategy "...would cover private archives held by Scottish public authorities, it will not be designed to apply to the archives of private organisations or individuals, although they may choose to adopt elements of it. Representatives of private archives will be included in the consultation process for their general interest and expertise in records and archives." The Strategy's stated overall goal was "...to develop measures for managing Scottish public records in the 21st century, ensuring that the appropriate records are kept, maintained, preserved and accessible to the public". The Strategy intended to include:

- "a clear description of the purposes and benefits of maintaining properly managed public records and archives;
- "outline proposals for a Scottish Public Records Bill, if considered appropriate;
- "outline proposals for guidance and standards designed to improve the quality and consistency of records management and archive arrangements across the Scottish public sector;
- "consideration of the need for arrangements to enforce records management requirements and standards;
- "a list of the Scottish public authorities which should be subject to the Strategy;
- "proposals for the future roles/functions of existing public records stakeholders (including the Keeper, NAS, SRAC and Scottish public authorities) and of any proposed new stakeholders;
- "a description of the "public records" which should be covered by the Strategy and, if considered appropriate, proposals for a statutory definition;
- "proposals for the management of non-paper records, particularly records kept in electronic form;
- "proposals to promote and improve accessibility of archives;
- "consideration of the scope for increased cross-sectoral working, for example between archives and museums, galleries & libraries;
- "a suggested timetable for implementation of the Strategy; and
- "any other issues which are relevant to the purpose of the Strategy."

---

[105] This section draws from: Archive Services in Scotland Mapping Project Board (2000). An Archival Account of Scotland, Public and Private Sector Archive Services in Scotland: Funding Opportunities and Development Needs Report. See at: http://www.archives.org.uk/sca/anarchiv.pdf

[106] This section draws from: The Scottish Government Public Records Strategy (2004).

The ensuing consultation process involved a range of interested groups, such various Scottish public authorities, archivists, records managers and users of records, with an 'Issues for Discussion' paper preceding seven workshops. These workshops addressed many key themes considered important, including:

- what public records are and why we keep them;
- which Scottish public authorities should be covered by any future legislation;
- what aspects of record keeping should be legislated for;
- what standards and guidance might be required;
- how requirements could be enforced and by whom; and
- the future of relevant institutions such as the National Archives of Scotland and the Scottish Records Advisory Council (MacQueen 2005).

While the workshops resulted in considerable feedback, there was no resulting consultation document as proposed.

Code of Practice on Records Management (2003)

The Code of Practice on Records Management (2003) is also known as the Section 61 Code, in reference to the Freedom of Information (Scotland) Act 2002. Prepared in consultation with the Scottish Information Commissioner and the Keeper of the Records in Scotland, it provides guidance to all public authorities for practice in keeping, managing and disposing of records. The code also provides instructions about records transfer to the National Archives of Scotland and other public archives. It's based on the premise that freedom of information legislation needs to be compatible with the creation of reliable records, being able to locate records and proper archival and disposal arrangements.

The code states that all public authorities must manage their records "effectively", led by senior managers and that such an approach may require a change in culture. The Scottish Information Commissioner is responsible for promoting "observance with the Code", which also states that if authorities fail to observe the Code "…they may be failing in their duty under the Act".

Historical records and children's residential services: Current legal issues

The Public Records Strategy consultation process highlighted that public and private sector archive services need to be developed and properly funded to ensure that "history is accessible to all". Survivors of historical child abuse have identified that establishing the historical record of their experiences is important to them. The identification of significant records needs to be coordinated with the preservation and access to records generated in association with those experiences. As indicated in an earlier chapter, however, the preservation of records relating to children's residential services is important to former residents, and others, for many reasons.

Current legal issues make preserving children's residential services' records, and their accessibility, extremely challenging. The following section examines key issues that need to be addressed to:

- protect former residents' and the public's legal entitlement to records;
- preserve records for research; and
- make certain that future inquiries into what happened in children's residential establishments can proceed.

Definitional challenges: "Public" and "Private"

A complication arising when searching for records relating to children's residential services is that The Public Records (Scotland) Act 1937 doesn't define "public records". It can be difficult to understand the distinction between public and private records, for example, which has serious implications for people responsible for preserving records and for people entitled to access these records.

Organisations, local authorities and central government provided children's residential services between 1950 and 1995. Assessing who owns records can be challenging, particularly in circumstances where private enterprises provided public statutory services on a contractual basis. These factors have implications for the preservation and accessibility of records without which it is difficult, if not impossible, to understand what happened in children's residential establishments. Once public records are defined, however, complications remain:

> "[The **Public Records (Scotland) Act 1937**] applies only to the Courts and to government departments, boards of trustees, or other bodies or persons holding records which belong to Her Majesty and related exclusively or mainly to Scotland. So, although the courts, the Scottish Parliament, the Scottish Executive and its agencies, and the NHS are covered, many other public bodies are not: for example, local authorities, NHS trusts, and universities" (MacQueen 2005).

The Scottish Records Advisory Council has proposed that "public records" are records created or received by a public body. Voluntary and religious organisations that provided residential services to children, however, are not covered under the Public Records (Scotland) Act 1937 and may not be covered under any reformed legislation unless there is clarification about how to define those records the organisations generated when providing children's residential services.

In October 2007, the Scottish Information Commissioner called on the Scottish Executive to protect the freedom of information rights of individuals. He claimed that those rights are being lost when public services are managed by private or charitable bodies[107]. It is important, therefore, to clarify the distinction between "public" and "private" records for children's residential services to ensure that all significant records associated with children's residential services are preserved and made accessible.

Reforming archive legislation

There is an urgent need to reform the current Public Records Act 1937 in Scotland. In doing so, this initiative would complement the current Freedom of Information (Scotland) Act 2002, which makes records accessible. Despite recent improvements that this Act makes, the legal provision for maintaining and preserving public records in Scotland is still viewed by many as inconsistent and incomplete[108], operating through outmoded legal provisions such as those in the UK Public Records Acts of 1958 and 1967.

As far back as 1974 it was recognised that "…modern practice has largely outstripped the Public Records (Scotland) Act 1937 and new legislation will soon be required to provide a more satisfactory basis for the preservation of records in Scotland" (Imrie 1974). Indeed, the 1937 Act is viewed as basic legislation limited in its scope. The Freedom of Information Act 2002, however, recognises the need for, and depends on, solid

---

[107] Freedom of Information Conference, October 25, 2007, 'A Culture of Openness: Freedom of Information moving into a new era'.

[108] MacQueen also recognises that there is no legal obligation on any other Scottish public authorities, such as higher and further education institutions, police authorities, etc to manage their records or to maintain archives (although many do so anyway, to highly variable degrees of quality).

legislative authority for archives housing any information relating to organisations responsible for public services. There are significant limitations to the current Public Records (Scotland) Act 1937. It doesn't define "public records". It's limited in its application to public bodies. It imposes no obligation on public bodies to manage their current records properly (only courts are required to transmit their records to the Keeper). And it provides little definition of the powers and functions of the Keeper (MacQueen 2005).

Furthermore, although local authorities are required to make proper arrangements for preserving and managing their records in separate legislation[109], such a requirement is undefined and lacks any sanctions to enforce it. Indeed, this provision was late in coming[110], and records were therefore kept and handed over to the Keeper almost entirely on a voluntary and customary basis: the inadequacy of this system has also been heavily criticised by archivists' groups[111].

Inadequate public records legislation means that local authorities don't take consistent approaches to their archives, with some local authorities not appointing records managers and archivists to ensure proper preservation of their records. While many local authorities have archives, archivists have commented on the lack of funding, staff and storage facilities and the lack of value placed upon their work. Archivists, and others participating in the Public Records Strategy, have stressed that there is an urgent need for a strong regulatory framework for archival work relating to records. Current weaknesses in public records legislation remain until new archive legislation is passed.

A response to the Public Records Strategy notes that there is consensus that "...all public authorities should be subject to a statutory obligation to carry out 'effective and efficient records management'" (MacQueen, 2005). According to the Strategy, primary legislation should impose on Scottish public authorities general statutory requirements to:
- create, manage, store, preserve and properly dispose of their records;
- keep track of their records, including any transmission, lending and destruction;
- prepare and publish indices, lists, guides, calendars and summaries of their records;
- review their records and provide for archiving records that merit permanent preservation;
- provide public access to their archives; and
- consult the appropriate body or office-holder before destroying any records.

MacQueen, 2005 notes that '[t]hese general statutory requirements should be complemented by sector-specific codes of practice or guidance setting out in detail how these requirements should be met. Such codes or guidance should be enforceable in the same way as the over-arching legislation". Clearly, there is a need to introduce new public records legislation to ensure the preservation and accessibility of records and to develop a specific approach to children's residential services records.

Records management

Statutory authority is needed to guide the proper management of records, such as their identification, keeping and destruction. Records management has implications for records associated with children's residential establishments, in deciding what is preserved, what is destroyed and what is made accessible.

"Any freedom of information legislation is only as good as the quality of the records to which it provides a right of access. Such rights are of limited use if reliable records are not created in the first place, if they cannot be found when needed, or if the arrangements for their eventual archiving or destruction are inadequate" (Code of Practice on Records Management , 2003).

Significantly, there are no legal obligations on various Scottish public authorities (and private organisations holding records generated when providing publicly funded services) to manage their records or to maintain archives (MacQueen 2005). Because there is "incomplete and inconsistent legal provision for Scottish public records and archives"(ibid:8), this state of affairs has an impact on children's residential services' records. This inconsistency also extends to private archives that hold similar types of records.

While existing public records legislation is inadequate, the Code of Practice on Records Management (2003) attempts to fill the gap by providing guidance to Scottish public authorities on managing how records are kept and destroyed (see Appendix H). This code arose from requirements in the Freedom of Information (Scotland) 2002 Act. These stated that Scottish Ministers should publish a code that provides: "...guidance to Scottish public authorities as to the practice which it would...be **desirable** for them to follow in connection with the keeping management and destruction" (Code of Practice on Records Management, 2003) of their records. The word 'desirable' means that there is no statutory requirement for public authorities (or private organisations) to employ record management practices consistent with the Code.

Deficiencies in the current records legislation have serious consequences for significant children's residential services records and all such records for child care services. Important records that aren't subject to strict records management procedures may be destroyed, lost or damaged, with the result that access to those records is denied to many people with rights to access under current legislation. There is a need, therefore, to ensure that new archive legislation includes proper records management to protect legal entitlements and to make certain those entitlements are realised.

Access to records

Freedom of information and data protection laws grant access to records. But many barriers remain to people accessing records they are legally entitled to view.

"What should members of the public be entitled to expect from [public] archives, in terms of not only freedom of information, but also of the other uses – historical, cultural, genealogical – to which the public may wish to put the material? Access has to be considered in all its aspects: for example, physical location and condition (especially in relation to disability discrimination laws), cataloguing and indexing, and online facilities. There is also the danger of providing useless access, such as putting information on a website without a search facility or facilities for blind users" (MacQueen, 2005).

While archives are viewed as depositories of records, they are "...also disseminators, of material of historical, genealogical, social and political interest at many different levels" (MacQueen, 2005). Archives cannot exist as disseminators of material, however, unless access is subject to standards and regulation that address the current barriers to access that many people encounter today.

---

[109] The Local Government (Scotland) Act 1994, s53

[110] Section 200 of the Local Government (Scotland) Act 1974 (repealed by the Environment Act 1995) appears to be the first to highlight the need to maintain records, but this was more clearly pronounced under the (albeit limited) terms of the Local Government (Scotland) Act 1994

[111] See for example the reports by the Archive Services in Scotland Mapping Project Board, An Archival Account of Scotland (2000); and by the Archives Task Force, Listening to the Past, Speaking to the Future (2004), as cited in Hector L MacQueen, "Reform of Archival Legislation: a Scots Perspective" Journal of the Society of Archivists vol 26 (2005) 201-214.

Our review identified barriers making it difficult for former residents and others to access records held by local authorities, organisations and central government. The Scottish Government has its own Code of Practice on Access to Scottish Executive Information (1999)[112] and more precise information about how former residents, and others, may access specific information held on residential schools and children's homes. But former residents still reported difficulties in gaining access to information held by central government. The Scottish Information Commissioner Report (2005) identified that the Scottish Executive Education Department ('SEED') had formalised its arrangements for giving access to 'List D' schools (name given to Approved Schools in the early 70s) and children's homes. However it indicated that it would be helpful if SEED provided a list full list of records found in their searches, including their reference, title and location. By identifying that SEED's access information on the web was difficult to locate, the SIC recommended making other forms available to individuals with no computer access or computer skills.

Our review found that several organisations with private archives located within their organisations had access policies in place. We learned, however, that there are huge variations in access policies, with some local authorities and organisations having no proper access policy in place. The universities' archives and the National Archives of Scotland have access policies, which apply to all records held in their archives. Former residents reported that they found inconsistencies in policies confusing which, in turn, limited their ability to gain access to records they're legally entitled to view.

There is evidence, as well, of existing records that may not be accessible because they aren't being managed properly or they haven't been archived. Local authorities, in particular, have records in a myriad of locations, many of which have not been archived. We learned that local authorities, for example, have used private storage companies at significant cost to store records and there are no schedules of records with the effect that local authorities may not know what is there, making some records inaccessible.

There is evidence that some current access to records approaches, and policies, are creating barriers for people wishing to exercise their legal entitlement to view public records. As a result, we identified an immediate need for standard model access-to-records policies that recognise special needs, such as advocacy and counselling services, associated with accessing children's residential services records.

Co-ordinating the legislation: Public Records Act 1937, Freedom of Information Act 2002, Data Protection Act 1998 and the Human Rights Act 1998

The Freedom of Information (Scotland) Act 2002 and the Data Protection Act (1998) depend on strong archival legislation to ensure that records are properly managed and preserved so records can be made accessible. In addition, there is an obvious overlap between the operation of the Data Protection Act 1998 and the Freedom of Information (Scotland) Act 2002. At times, for example, there can be tension between the rights of an individual under the Data Protection Act and the duties of a public authority to disclose information under the Freedom of Information Act. There is a need to coordinate this legislation with the Human Rights Act 1998 and public records legislation to ensure that former residents, and the public, are not denied access to records they're legally entitled to view.

There were indications in Australia that people who had lived as children in institutions were having difficulty gaining full access to records under that country's freedom of information legislation:

"Freedom of Information (FoI) legislation has been passed in all Australian jurisdictions. The legislation covers personal information compiled by government agencies. The Committee heard evidence that some care leavers have experienced difficulty in accessing information under FoI procedures. There were cases where information was provided only after persistent efforts to pursue records and instances where large amounts of information were withheld. Care leavers were particularly angry that the material on files, even if years old, was still withheld" (Parliament of Australia Senate Report, 2004).

The Data Protection Act 1998 in Scotland requires that personal data is kept accurate and up to date and not kept for longer than necessary[113]. This Act, together with other legislation, needs to ensure that important records associated with people's experiences in children's residential establishments are preserved and its legal requirements, conversely, do not result in the destruction of significant records. Without adequate safeguards, this provision of the Act may result in the legal destruction of personal information that individuals who lived in or had some association with children's residential establishments may want to access.

Special considerations

During the parliamentary debate in December 2004, the Minister stated that he wanted "relevant files" to be identified and made public, noting that these are "exceptional circumstances" requiring the involvement of the Keeper of the Records. Special considerations must be given to children's residential establishments' records, because the places where adults lived as children, away from their families, constituted their homes. Children did not choose to live in these homes – institutions for many children – but were placed there, often under state guardianship. The state and other responsible organisations, former residents suggest, have an ongoing duty of care to them as adults, particularly those adults who were abused as children while living in residential placements. It is a duty that includes making it possible to establish historical accounts and learn about what happened in children's residential establishments through accessible records.

There is an urgent need, therefore, to recognise records for children's residential services, and child care services in general, as "exceptional". This requires new archive legislation and associated standards and guidance affecting significant children's residential services records. There is an urgent need to encourage good records management practices to protect signficant records associated with children's residential services and to see those records as associated with "exceptional circumstances".

Records for children's residential services may serve two purposes: evidence for legal purposes and memory that has personal, cultural, and social historical significance. A specific records retention schedule is needed, taking account of these purposes and with legal authority. This is necessary for guiding organisations, local authorities and central government in their records management practices.

---

[112] See http://www.scotland.gov.uk/Resource/Doc/158138/0042787.pdf
[113] See Data Protection Act 1998 at http://www.opsi.gov.uk/ACTS/acts1998/19980029.htm

Conclusion

In our review of public records legislation, it became apparent that the Public Records Act 1937 is the main legislation responsible for ensuring the preservation of public records, which include records for children's residential services. According to public records experts, however, this law is significantly outdated and needs reform. Notably, there is no adequate definition of 'public record' and no duty imposed on local authorities to transfer their public records to archives for preservation. There is also no legal specification about how records generated by private bodies receiving public funding must be preserved and made accessible.

The public records legislation sits alongside other law. The Local Government etc (Scotland) Act 1994, for example, provided for the transfer of records between the old and new authorities. While the law said local authorities should make "proper arrangements" for the "preservation and management" of their records, it did not require them to do so. Furthermore, the 1994 Act allowed local authorities to dispose of any records it did not consider "worthy of preservation", which meant that individuals within local authority departments – who may have been unskilled as records managers and archivists – were making decisions about what records were destroyed.

Current freedom of information and data protection law depends upon records existence to ensure that individuals' realise their legal entitlements to access records. There is an urgent need, therefore, to review all public records legislation to make certain that it is coordinated and facilitates access to records. Legal authority, reflected in standards and guidance, is also needed to guide the proper management of records. Inadequate legislation leads to poor records management practices which, in turn, have significant implications for records associated children's residential establishments, affecting what is preserved, destroyed and made accessible.

In recent years significant initiatives have attempted to address gaps in records legislation. These include the Archival Mapping Project (1999), the Public Records Strategy (2003-2004) and the Code of Practice on Records Management (2003) – all of which relate to record preservation and access. We found, however, that despite these important initiatives, several outstanding issues remain including the need to:
- Reform public records legislation;
- Clarify what happens to records held by private bodies that receive public funds;
- Address variations in records access policies and the lack of records access policies, in some places; and
- Coordinate public records legislation to ensure individuals' are not being denied their legal entitlement to access records.

And, within this context, special consideration needs to be given to the records of children's residential establishments - the 'homes' where adults lived as children, away from their families.

Chapter 5: Searching for information: Major changes and Scottish Government records

Introduction

The chapter begins by examining the contextual legal background directly or indirectly affecting central government, local authorities and organisations. It also highlights key aspects of the Scottish Information Commissioner report entitled 'Examination of the Scottish Executive Education Department's Procedures for the Identification and Provision of Access to Records related to Children's Homes and Residential Schools' (2005). This report is significant in that it addresses the issue of the former Scottish Executive (now Scottish Government's) records made available to our review. The chapter also describes some of the challenges accompanying these records.

Contextual legal background

Many factors affected the generation, preservation and accessibility of records at all levels of government and within organisations. While undoubtedly many poor records management practices existed, they did so within a context of inadequate statutory records regulation, standards and guidance. The previous chapter highlighted inadequacies in public records legislation, dating back to 1937, and the current issues that remain outstanding. This prevailing legal context would have seriously impacted the preservation of public records generated by central government, local governments and organisations.

Additional legislative changes, reorganisations and new policy initiatives would have had direct, and indirect, implications for central government records. Voluntary and religious organisations providing children's residential services needed to comply with legal requirements and with their own internal, and changing, organisational structures and requirements. Local authorities with responsibilities for children's residential services experienced major upheavals, such as the introduction of the Social Work (Scotland) Act 1968 and two major local government reorganisations.

The regulatory framework within the review's report (chapter 2) illustrates major changes to children's services, for example, when the Social Work (Scotland) Act 1968 was introduced, bringing together probation, childcare, welfare and mental health officers in one department. These responsibilities became wider as several functions of the local health authorities were also transferred to social work departments[114]. The new departments carrying out social work functions were based initially on 52 counties, cities and large burghs[115] until the local government reorganisation in the 1970s reorganised social work services on the basis of regional and islands councils[116].

[114] SW(S)A 1968, s 1(4). Amended by the National Health Service and Community Care Act 1990 (c 19), s 66(2), Sch 10, and by the Mental Health (Care and Treatment) (Scotland) Act 2003 (Modification of Enactments) Order 2005, SSI 2005/465, art 2, Sch 1, para 4(2).

[115] SW(S)A 1968, s1 (as originally enacted)

[116] SW(S)A 1968, s1. Amended by the Local Government (Scotland) Act 1973 (c 65), ss 161, 214(2), Sch 20, Sch 27, Pt II, para 183). For the regional and islands councils, see SW(S)A 1968, Sch 1, Pt I. Also amended by the Children Act 1989 (c 41), s 108(7), Sch 15, the Local Government etc (Scotland) Act 1994 (c 39), s 180(1), Sch 13, para 76(2); the Children (Scotland) Act 1995 (c 36), s 105(4), Sch 4, para 15(2). Local Government (Scotland) Act 1973, ss 1, 161, Schs 1, 20 repealed. Regional and islands councils are replaced by unitary councils constituted under LG(S)A 1994, s 2; as to such councils, see LG(S)A 1994, s 1, Sch 1.

Under the new 1968 Act, social work committees and sub-committees were appointed to address all functions carried out by social work departments[117]. As social work departments had such extensive areas of duties and responsibilities and such wide interests, major social work committees formed sub-committees and delegated various functions[118]. This new 1968 Act, which took effect in 1971, led to major changes within local authorities, therefore, which changes had significant implications for records associated with children's residential services.

The establishment of new social work departments occurred slightly before the Local Government (Scotland) Act 1973 established the two-tier system of local government in Scotland from 1975 to 1996[119] leading, once again, to major reorganisation and consequences for records. Years later, when the Local Government etc (Scotland) Act 1994 abolished the two-tier system of local government and replaced it with 32 unitary authorities, records associated with children's residential services would have been affected.

Changes to local government and the law would also have impacted in records associated with central government, voluntary and religious organisations. The organisations had contractual arrangements with local authorities while central government continued to have oversight and policy responsibilities for local authorities' children's residential services. The lack of regulations, standards and guidance for records management would have presented major challenges for central government, local authorities, voluntary and religious organisations in managing their records.

Searching for information: SEED and NAS

Before our review, the former Scottish Executive Education Department ('SEED') had gathered records it considered important to the issue of historical abuse in List D schools and children's homes[120]. SEED's initiative led to a list of records made publicly available and accessible to us. As we found, however, large volumes of records existed and more central government records were possibly relevant to our review than the SEED list identified. Given our staffing and time constraints, the scrutiny of these records was restricted to a select number of records among the vast numbers of potentially significant central government records available.

We began our search by identifying the most obvious places where records may be located. These included SEED and National Archives of Scotland ('NAS'), in addition to voluntary organisations, religious organisations and local authorities. Before the review began, SEED had begun a search for records relating to residential schools and children's homes, which resulted in a list of disclosed records for public access. According to SEED, these records were held in two locations: their central offices in Edinburgh and NAS. The SEED redacted (edited) records are held in its central offices while other records are located at NAS.

We examined some SEED records to find out what records might be relevant to our work. As this involved reading considerable numbers of records, time limitations and lack of staff made it impossible to consider all records on the SEED list. From those examined, however, it was possible to identify that these records contained significant information. We also learned that many other records not on SEED's list also exist within NAS, making the task of reviewing SEED records far more labour-intensive than anticipated. As some records located at NAS were closed, SEED began a process in which department officials reviewed these

records at their central offices before granting us access. This process, again, made locating relevant information cumbersome and time-consuming.

Background: SEED and Scottish Information Commissioner report

This section provides the background to SEED's initiative to gather its records. This initiative was announced by the Minister of Education and Young People in the Scottish Parliament in December 2004 and was intended to make records associated with residential schools and children's homes publicly accessible. The Scottish Information Commissioner report ('SIC Report 2005')[121] is significant in that it encapsulates many of our findings and provides excellent insight into similar issues arising for local authorities, voluntary and religious organisations attempting to locate records for the review. For those reasons, this section highlights related information from that report.

In the SIC Report 2005 states that the SIC's records examination focused upon whether the Scottish Executive took "reasonable" action to locate and make accessible "...all historical records relating to institutional children's homes and residential schools in Scotland". This approach involved generating an audit trail for the SEED search and considering records management practices over certain decades. The SIC Report 2005 shows investigators reviewed Scottish Executive records management policy and "examined and tested the measures introduced by the Scottish Executive to open these records to the public". During the initial stages, the SIC's process included interviewing survivors of abuse about their information needs.

The SIC Report 2005 states that interest in records relating to children's residential establishments had been generated by individual information requests, court actions and the media. In response to individual information requests, the SIC report notes that SEED wrote to each individual confirming "...that the Executive held no personal records relating to the applicant but that it did hold records which relate to the management, running and inspection of some institutions". In the letters sent, the SIC Report 2005 notes that SEED identified records that may interest each applicant and offered to make them available for inspection at SEED's offices. The SIC Report 2005 stated that the "...full response to the applicants making requests for information about residential childcare and education took as long as 22 months to provide" despite the existence of the Code of Practice on Access to Scottish Executive Information (1999) that responses should occur within 20 working days.

In reference to the court cases, the SIC Report 2005 notes that the "[l]ack of access to records about the pursuer's school record and information about the running of the school has proved a significant difficulty in the conduct of the case" although SEED provided records to the pursuer's (persons instigating court action) agents and assisted the court commissioner in trying to locate records:

"The issue then of what records were held, what they contained and who could access them is an important part of establishing what is known and can be known about the experience of those in institutional childcare and education.

"What is clear to me as will be seen in subsequent sections of this report, is that when questions were raised about records and requests were received about specific institutions and their residents, the Executive did not know what information

---

[117] SW(S)A 1968, s 2(1). Repealed by LG(S)A 1994, Sch 14.

[118] Local Government (Scotland) Act 1973, Sch 20, para 2. Repealed by LG(S)A 1994, Sch 14.

[119] Local Government (Scotland) Act 1973 (c 65), Pt I (ss 1-11) (repealed)

[120] See http://www.scotland.gov.uk/Topics/Education/accesstoinfo/residentialestablishments

[121] Scottish Information Commissioner (2005). Examination of the Scottish Executive Education's Procedures for the identification and Provision of Access to Records related to Children's Homes and Residential Schools

it held. In response, it undertook a lengthy programme of research to identify what might be available."

The SIC Report 2005 concluded that "past records management practices were less robust than the current system, particularly in the maintenance of records registers. The information held on the IMPReS database for old records is entirely dependent on the quality of the information that was available at the department level at the time. In turn, NAS is entirely dependent on the quality of the records which are submitted to it."

"The Scottish Executives records for institutional care and education are not about individuals, but tend to be policy papers and inspection reports...the existence of such information in records appears to be due to the decision-making of individual record holders...these records are very much of their time and that the existence of apparently unrelated material in historical records is often what gives insight to the cultural and social values of the period in question...they contain what they contain. However, it is important to note that the contents are not focused in the way that might be desired by an individual searching for information about their own education or care."

The SIC Report 2005 noted that the titles of records could be misleading and that the search was hampered by the "lack of clarity" about what people were looking for:

"The greatest single obstacle encountered in the Scottish Executive's search, however, was the mismatch between expectations, the volume of records available and their actual contents."

The SIC report also observed that in their sample check of redacted records, resulting from a NAS search, that no records contained "structured personal records for individual children...":

"Most records, however, contain some personal information relating to individual pupils or members of staff. Such information appears to have been recorded by Her Majesty's Inspectors of Schools in relation to specific incidents that were brought to their attention in the course of their work...these records are very much 'of their time' and it is clear that information about individual children did pass freely between the institutions and the inspectors...

"[some records contain]...quarterly punishment returns records submitted by headmasters of the approved schools to the Education Department. These documents are countersigned by the school's senior management and record the names of pupils, method of corporal punishment, reasons for the punishment and the names of staff administering and witnessing it...

"...record titles do not always reflect the range of the contents', which may be attributable to the '...particular shortcomings and inconsistencies of past records management policies and practices...

"Although the records contain much that will be of importance to researchers in the future, the variety of the record contents presents potential problems for anyone who intends to conduct a search for evidence of institutional child abuse. It means that there can be no substitute for a thorough examination of record contents, an extremely time consuming exercise."

The SIC Report 2005 noted "there are inconsistencies in the time series of documents within the records" and "apparent gaps in the records" which may be due to "deficiencies of the records management practices, changes in the frequency of inspections and destruction or loss of parts of the records over time'".

In conclusion, the SIC Report 2005 determined that SEED's search for records was challenging because SEED officers had to deal with large volumes of records containing unstructured information. The SIC Report 2005 stated that it found files in their review "...which should have been identified and recovered by SEED". As the process for searching for information was undocumented, the SCI Report 2005 indicated it wasn't possible to determine how efficient the process for looking for information had been. It also stated that "over 2 years of systematic searching has gone on and the task is not yet concluded" and that while certain files were not recovered by SEED, "such instances should not detract from the considerable success in recovering relevant records from millions of files stored over the past 60 years."

According to the SIC Report 2005, a key question arose as to what the records ought to have contained. "The answer to this may rely on interpretation of the responsibilities of different public authorities for the care of the children and for the management of the institutions", noting that these responsibilities were unclear:

"What is apparent from this examination is that there is very little evidence that the records held by the Scottish Executive contain the information that would meet the hopes and expectations of members of INCAS and their helpline users. However, the scraps of personal information held in government records may be all that is available and therefore they assume a great importance to individuals."

Review search outcome: SEED and NAS records

We concur with several findings and conclusions in the SIC report 2005. In our review of SEED's disclosed records, for example, we found it was impossible to know from the records' names what information the records held and whether they contained relevant information. We found that many records contained varying degrees of significant information, making it an extremely time-consuming undertaking to assess relevancy given the large numbers of records that contained potentially important information. Similar to the SIC report's finding, we found additional open records in the NAS catalogue, not on SEED's disclosed list, that we considered relevant to our review. We also examined a small number of records at NAS that were 'closed' after gaining permission from SEED; we found that they contained potentially significant information.

Overall, we determined that SEED and NAS records contain considerable information that was potentially necessary to fulfilling the review's remit. As lack of time and staff made it impossible to examine those records thoroughly, however, the report's findings are limited by these factors.

Conclusion

Major local government reorganisations and changes to children's services legislation in 1968 occurred during the period 1950 to 1995. These factors would have impacted the generation and preservation of records associated, directly or indirectly, with central government as well as local authorities and organisations. Changes in legislation and local government structure meant the reporting and policy relationship between organisations and central government changed, as well, throughout the years. Those factors, together with the absence of appropriate records legislation, likely had significant implications for records management practices at all levels.

The former Scottish Executive Education Department ('SEED') made records available for us to consider during the review. Prior to these records being made available, the Scottish Information Commissioner had examined SEED's process of gathering records relating to historical abuse in residential schools and children's homes. The ensuing report (Scottish Information Commissioner, 2005) identified many issues that arose for us and we concur with several findings in that report. The report identifies the challenges associated with SEED's search for records, such as the large numbers of existing records and the nature of unstructured information. Some findings from the Scottish Information Commissioner's report are as follows:

■ Past records management practices were not as robust as current practices.
■ What records exist today depends upon the quality of record-keeping in the past.
■ Most SEED records contain policy information and, for example, inspection reports.
■ Titles can be misleading and there are inconsistencies and gaps in the records (Scottish Information Commissioner, 2005).

In our search for central government records, like the Scottish Information Commissioner, we learned about the existence of records not identified on SEED's list – records potentially relevant to the review. This factor made the task of reviewing all possibly relevant SEED records very time-consuming and limited due to lack of resources. It was difficult to determine from the record names, for example, what information the records held and – without reviewing the records – whether the information in the records was relevant. In many of the records we reviewed, however, we identified important information germane to our understanding about children's residential services.

Chapter 6: Searching for information: Voluntary organisations and religious organisations

Introduction

We depended on information located within records held by voluntary organisations, religious organisations and local authorities. The following two **chapters** report on the process we used to gather information; they describe the challenges organisations and local authorities encountered in their search for information and what this meant to our review.

As no central database identifies local authorities and organisations responsible for managing children's residential establishments between 1950 and 1995, we began gathering information by trying to find what organisations had management responsibilities. We then circulated questionnaires to local authorities and organisations and, later, sent surveys to local authority archivists. One response reflected assumptions that information was readily available and in specified locations:

"As we have discussed with the Executive, they are likely to hold most of the information that you require and an approach via the archives of ex-Regional Councils is likely to provide much of the other information. In addition there have

already been enquiries into historical abuse which have gathered much of the information you are requesting."

As the following chapter demonstrates, however, we learned that there was no detailed regulatory framework publication for children's residential services covering the period 1950 to 1995. We identified that records containing information about children's residential services are held in multiple locations and in large volume throughout Scotland and England (see Appendix B). No central database identifies where these records are, which made it extremely difficult to identify what records existed. And, while there have been previous inquiries into child abuse within residential settings in Scotland, we were unable to identify any public inquiries with a similar remit or that covered a 45-year time frame from 1950.

We distinguished between information held in people's memories and information in records, although the two are invariably intertwined. Some individuals associated with children's residential services could recall what records existed, identifying possible locations and making it possible to glean information from them. On the other hand, many individuals with knowledge about the early years under review have retired or are deceased, taking their corporate memory with them.

Our task of obtaining significant information, therefore, could not be easily accommodated by local authorities and organisations as their information-searching process was a resource-intensive task. Deciding what information was relevant to the review, was difficult, if not impossible, for organisations and local authorities to decide without viewing all their available records. Despite the challenges, however, many individuals and organisations recognised the importance of records and made considerable efforts to assist us.

These chapters represent a preliminary, mapping introduction to records associated with children's residential services and held by voluntary organisations, religious organisations and local authorities. The search for information entailed circulating questionnaires and surveys, interviewing and making site visits to places throughout Scotland and England. However our work doesn't set out to represent an exhaustive information-gathering process. Rather, this preliminary introduction illustrates the need for further investigation.

Searching for information: general approach

We began by assessing which voluntary and religious organisations had provided children's residential services throughout Scotland so that we could ask whether those organisations held records. We learned that local authorities had sometimes assumed responsibility for residential establishments managed by voluntary and religious organisations, complicating our search for information. Our search didn't include contact with private trusts, specialised service providers of residential establishments for children with disabilities or individual providers of children's residential services, such as small children's homes.

We circulated a questionnaire to 32 local authorities to identify information about past children's residential establishments falling within current local authority boundaries, record locations and management policies. We also forwarded questionnaires to 11 voluntary and religious organisations, in a staged process as new information came to light about what organisations might have provided children's residential services. We obtained information about records through letters and interviews with those who had some association with records, including designated persons responsible for responding to our questionnaire; archivists; librarians; records managers; service providers and various other people with historical knowledge about children's services.

After sending the questionnaires, we met with archivists to discuss various issues about information-gathering. With expert help from a local authority archivist, we also developed and forwarded a survey to all local authority archivists to establish what children's residential services' records, and related information, might be in their records management systems and archives.

Questionnaire

At the outset we considered what information might be relevant based upon what is known today. As there was no existing regulatory framework for the early years of the review, it was not possible to be guided by statutory references to records. It was also impossible to anticipate what information existed within records and what information might be relevant without thoroughly examining various records relating to children's residential services. To acquire general information about such services and past management policies, therefore, we circulated questionnaires to local authorities and organisations.

One local authority representative noted that the questionnaire reflected "modern practices and protocols that were not the subject of good practice guidelines over the past 50 years", stating that "...we could not expect to find examples in place". This statement, however, presumed a linear progression from poor practice to good practice, which we didn't want to assume. Relatively little is known about children's residential services in Scotland, particularly for the early years under review.

As a result, the questionnaire was designed to give local authorities and organisations the opportunity to inform us about what management approaches existed, to confirm what didn't exist and to report on what isn't known. In our own review of records, we found examples from the 1950s of good practice by today's standards, suggesting that research into this area might result in challenges to those assumptions that good practice examples didn't exist.

The questionnaire, divided into three time periods to reflect key legislation and policy developments, requested information for the period 1950-1995 as follows:
- Types of children's residential services provided, whether those services were directly or indirectly managed
- Whether external monitoring or self-monitoring structures were used when providing children's residential services and details about inspection responsibilities in particular
- Whether local authorities and organisations held general and specific records for children's residential services such as: general management records, policy and practice guidelines, inspection reports, records for individual children's establishments, individuals records (for former residents) and other unspecified records
- Whether local authorities and organisations held specific policy and practice guidelines about employee recruitment and training, child protection, children's rights, whistleblowing, formal complaint processes, bullying, grievances, incident reports, advocacy services, records management and inspections
- Whether local authorities and organisations had records for children's residential services that are no longer available and, if so, what records are no longer accessible

The questionnaire also attempted to determine specific details about children's residential establishments in Scotland between 1950 and 1995, requesting the following information:
- Names of children's residential establishments
- Dates opened
- Locations
- Purposes
- Young people attending (age, gender, needs)
- Dates closed (if applicable)
- Dates reopened (if applicable)
- Current status
- Types of service monitoring
- Other relevant details

Survey

We circulated surveys to all archivists in Scotland after learning about the significance of their role in locating and preserving records. We met local authority and NAS archivists several times for their expert input and guidance on important issues about records associated with children's residential services. The survey requested the following information:
- Overview of holdings in archives and records management systems
- General local authority department records pertaining to children's residential establishments (that is, policy and practice guidelines, annual reports, committee reports to council, senior management reports, organisational and structural reviews and minutes of committee meetings)
- Specific records from various sources (that is, inspection reports, children's officer and director reports, investigation reports, audit reports on local authority departments and residential establishments)
- Special reports on children's residential establishments
- Children's residential establishment records generated on-site (that is, log books, punishment books, visitor's books and individual case files)
- Names of children's residential establishments
- Voluntary and church organisation records
- Access to records policies

Search outcome: Voluntary organisations and religious organisations

The following section summarises the responses submitted by voluntary organisations and religious organisations to the questionnaire. These responses took various forms; some voluntary and religious organisations completed the questionnaire while others provided information in other forms, such as through interviews and detailed correspondence.

Voluntary organisations

We began with little information about what voluntary organisations in Scotland provided residential services to children from 1950 to 1995. There was, and remains, no central database with that information. The complex nature of children's services exacerbated this issue, further complicated by how children's residential establishments were defined and the magnitude of managerial structures in place. The review contacted six known voluntary organisations providing residential services to children from 1950 to 1995; however, we don't purport to have identified all voluntary organisations responsible for children's residential services during this period. The varying descriptions of children's residential establishments, for example, reveals the extent to which many voluntary organisations may have been involved in service provision (see Appendix A).

Some voluntary organisations operated strictly as children's charities while others provided various services to children, their families and other adults with specialised needs. Some organisations provided services in Scotland while others offered services throughout the United Kingdom. These factors made identifying, locating and accessing records specific to children's residential services extremely challenging for us and for the voluntary organisations helping us.

All the voluntary organisations contacted submitted the questionnaire in full or provided information in detailed form, which included outlining the difficulties those organisations had locating and making information available. We visited locations where voluntary organisations kept records and interviewed people responsible for managing their records. All the voluntary organisations had attempted to locate and archive their records or were in varying stages of developing their archives to ensure important records were preserved. Individuals working in voluntary organisations make decisions about what records to preserve, although not all individuals are trained in records management or as archivists. Some voluntary organisations have placed certain records in university archives, where the records are managed by trained records managers and archivists. No regulatory framework exists, however, to ensure statutory compliance and consistent practices among all the voluntary organisations holding children's residential services records.

Children's residential establishments

Most voluntary organisations were able to provide names and details relating to the children's residential establishments they were responsible for, although the lack of a centralised database made it difficult for the voluntary organisations to trace the history of the services they provided. Most voluntary organisations, however, found it difficult to locate significant information relating to each establishment.

Challenges to locating records

Like religious organisations and local authorities, voluntary organisations have been in existence for many years and throughout that time many changes have affected their record-keeping practices. Their records, located in places throughout Scotland and England, are found within one, two or more locations (such as various organisation locations and university archives).

One voluntary organisation reported that it was challenging to find information for the questionnaire because they were working on their archive, it was work that required substantial hours and "there is no person around with that kind of time". This organisation said they were deciding what records to keep and to not keep, although they said this was a "big job" partly because the records were split between two locations. Another organisation said that they couldn't answer many questions in the questionnaire due to the extensive time period of 45 years. The organisation said that, while children's records were held for their children's homes, "...there are no general records which are easily accessible due to there being a large number of documents, with information that is difficult to search by type..."

One voluntary organisation reported great difficulty in responding to the questionnaire. They said that although they had an extensive archive dating back to the mid-19th century, "this archive consists almost entirely of the records of individual children who spent varying lengths of time at [the voluntary organisation]..." and not management records. The organisation said it had an access to historical records policy that was affected by confidentiality rules and data protection laws.

Another voluntary organisation reported that, after consulting their insurers and solicitors, they were able to provide certain information in response to our questionnaire. In attempting to locate information, this organisation had sought assistance from their after-care department staff, library staff and properties department while also searching library card indexes held in two locations. The organisation said it was difficult to decide relevancy, the reasons for retaining and destroying of historical information and "the balance of the documentation", such as whether it provided a "balanced historical viewpoint".

In identifying the challenges involved in searching for information about children's residential services, including the cost and personnel implications, one organisation also said their library card system "...is not sophisticated and although it is possible to identify some homes, it is impossible to review the relevance of material without the material being accessed and reviewed". The library card system "...did not highlight generic questions such as 'complaints' and, as a result, the information cannot be systematically traced". The organisation said that the university libraries index was similar:

> "A reference to a home may state that numerous pages are available, sometimes 100 or more, but the relevance of these pages is again impossible to judge without access and review. The material held on microfiche is again poorly labelled and difficult to access making any search extremely difficult and time-consuming and the relevance of material identified unclear."

As to policy and guidance to 1955, this organisation said they were unable to find out if their historical information was complete or whether guidance was located elsewhere. For the period after 1955, it had "...no consistent and detailed record of policy changes". The organisation said it was difficult "for practical reasons" to complete the questionnaire.

Another voluntary organisation said that a residential school under their management had undergone a major review during the latter review period. In relation to both care and education records, the review noted inadequacies in the early '90s:

> "The standard of filing and recording in [the residential school] falls below reasonable expectation. Currently two sets of files exist. The main files...contain only admission papers, review reports and correspondence. They do not contain any ongoing assessment or record of key events and developments in children's lives. The other set of files are the Family Counsellors' files and these are only a record of their home visits and contacts with the family. They are not files on children.

> "No files for individual children are kept by the care staff in the units so there is no chronicling of developments in children's care and changing perceptions of their needs and worries. One result of this is that when it is necessary to write review reports there is no record to refer to and reliance has to be placed on subjective memory, undue emphasis inevitably falling on recent events and perceptions.

"Log books meet minimum statutory requirements to keep a record of all major and minor incidents which happen in the school but do no more than that. Reading them gives an overall impression of life in each of the Units but their value is limited to a chronological record of events and a means of communication and update between shifts.

"The level of recording by class teachers was uneven and there was no uniform system. With the removal of the former Headmaster's managerial overview established systems of central form filing had fallen into disuse..."

A voluntary organisation identified the potential location of relevant information when they reported that the chair of its management committee submitted written reports to the Scottish Council. According to the organisation, copies of these reports were also sent to their head office. The former Scottish Office and the immediate local authority were represented on the residential establishment's management committee, making it possible that similar records with relevant information existed in these locations as well.

One voluntary organisation conducting a residential school review in the early 1990s found that "children's records are fragmented and inadequate" and "log books are of limited value because their content is largely routine." The review also found that as there was no complaints system at the school for parents or children, there was no record of complaints. Another voluntary organisation said their archive of management records remained at a residential school that's open today, while additional records were held in the organisation's local and head offices. "It has not been possible to access all of these files within the time frame for this exercise." While the early years records had not been reviewed, this organisation said "...it seems unlikely that review of these files will add substantially to this report..."

Another voluntary organisation referred to a "Professional Advisory Panel" established to advise the residential school's principal and managers "...on policy and practice issues". This showed another possible location where significant information might be located. As the various groups on this panel were representatives from the voluntary organisation, the residential school, the local authority social work and education departments and an educational psychologist, it is possible that each person represented on the panel generated records now held in various locations. This complexity shows the massive challenge faced by voluntary organisations and by us when trying to locate information about children's residential services.

Records: Locations and types

The records for children's residential services provided by voluntary organisations are located within individual residential establishments, individual voluntary organisations, libraries, museums and various archives located in Scotland and England[122].

One voluntary organisation reported that "[a]part from the individual children's records our archive is very slim", although they indicated that the archive did contain a range of records: annual reports, narratives of fact, register of staff, visual material (including photographs, films, videotapes), letters and artefacts. The organisation speculated that the lack of records may be due to the "different standard of record-keeping prevailing at that time."

Another voluntary organisation said they didn't hold "relevant" records, although it was possible significant records remained

with the residential school archive, as the school remained open. One voluntary organisation reported that their library held annual reports and publications, which included "books about the changes and developments in residential care" and a university archive held various records specific and non-specific to children's residential services. Most voluntary organisations, however, reported that policy and procedural records were most difficult to locate. Some said that certain records were lost during moves and changes to services:

"Whilst we have records for individual young people we have little else...Each move/opening/closure appears to have been accompanied by a clear out of old records...We do respond regularly to former residents who wish for copies of their files, but there appears to be little else still in existence."

One voluntary organisation said they held some admission books, "minute books", organisation magazines and annual reports, adding, however, that they didn't hold any log books, punishment books or medical records. It said the card index for the library/archive was "not reliable". Another voluntary organisation stated that records in their two local archives consisted primarily of management committee minutes, associated correspondence and reports dating from 1955, although other records existed in England.

Most voluntary organisations hold children's files for the children living in residential establishments managed by their organisation. On the other hand, management records specific to children's residential services were difficult for voluntary organisations to locate, held in small numbers or did not exist at all. The voluntary organisations reported that some general information about children's residential services did exist. But they added that it was difficult, if not impossible, for them to assess what might be relevant to us because possibly significant information was held within other records.

As there was no systematic or consistent record-keeping in earlier years, voluntary organisations indicated that their held records are difficult to catalogue, affecting the search for particular types of information. Like local authorities and religious organisations, corporate memory that might help to locate information for early years, was often held by people who no longer worked for them, adding to the complexity of locating information.

Religious organisations[123]

Our review began with little information about the religious organisations in Scotland providing residential services to children from 1950 to 1995. Like the voluntary organisations and local authorities, the religious organisations have no central database with specific information about children's residential establishments and no other central system exists within Scotland. As we've indicated, this issue is complicated by the diverse nature of the services provided to children in residential establishments in general.

As a consequence, we found it extremely difficult to determine which religious organisations had provided children's residential services and which held relevant records. We contacted 16 religious organisations to ask whether and what services they provided; and 11 religious organisations advised they had some involvement. This association, particularly during the early years, was extensive and complex. Some organisations only provided children's residential services in Scotland while others provided

---

[122] See Appendices B and C.

[123] Religious organisations: Protestant and Catholic, including orders, conferences and congregations.

extensive services to children and adults throughout the UK. These factors made it difficult for them to identify, locate and access significant records.

According to archivists for the religious organisations, some individuals within religious organisations have been slow to recognise the importance of records. Many religious organisations do not employ full time archivists or records managers, making it difficult for the organisations to respond to requests for information. This situation, however, is beginning to change. In growing recognition of the importance of its history, one religious organisation has employed an archivist to write their history. The archivist indicated the task has taken him on a search for historical records in many places including Europe and America. Several religious organisations, while recognising the importance of preserving their records, stated there are resource constraints that made it difficult to address record preservation in a timely way.

Children's residential establishments

We requested information from religious organisations about their children's residential establishments and met with varied responses. Some organisations had specific, detailed information about what children's residential establishments they'd managed while others had little or no information. We found that it was difficult for the religious organisations to determine where relevant information relating to their children's residential establishments might be located and what records might exist.

Challenges to locating historical records

We found that, similar to the voluntary organisations and local authorities, religious organisations faced many challenges in locating records. One archivist reported that "...time is taken up by going through minutes of various committees to find exactly where various parts of the organisation fitted into the organisation" while another archivist reported that "...archives are slowly and painfully being reorganised but there is a big task still to be done as I am only part-time archivist". Some, but not all, religious organisations contacted had archivists although many were employed part-time, making the task of locating information more difficult for them. Like local authorities and voluntary organisations, the religious organisations said that people who know, or knew, about records were no longer employed or associated with them adding to the archivists challenges as well.

Some religious organisations, under the guidance of an archivist, had formally moved their records into a records management system to be archived later. Some organisations said it had been, and remained, expensive and time-consuming to employ records managers and archivists. This was particularly the case for children's residential services' records when that service was relatively small compared with other services they provided. One religious organisation said they had no archivist at their on-site location and many records sat uncatalogued in boxes. However there was an archivist at the college location where various other records belonging to the religious organisation were stored.

One organisation reported that they had been in existence throughout the UK for 100 years and beyond, generating thousands of records. Some organisations said that they had provided, and continue to provide, various services to children and adults; as a consequence there are large numbers of records for religious organisations. These records, which are in different

places throughout the UK, incorporate information beyond what is specific to children's residential services, making it challenging to trace particular types of information.

Religious organisations said that, like local authorities and voluntary organisations, they had changed offices and regions so that it was often unclear what happened to the records. Some noted that reorganisations and moves had resulted in the dispersal and disposal of certain records. Others found their records in boxes in basements after contact from us; others had records on shelves waiting to be reviewed and catalogued.

Religious organisations also stated that records relating to children's residential services and management policies, for example, had been merged with other less relevant records. The religious organisations reported that it was impractical to keep old policies and other related information and that locating records specific to Scotland for those organisations with projects throughout the UK was difficult. Some religious organisations also noted that there was no previous requirement to keep management records relating to their children's residential services.

Some religious organisations reported that records tended to remain in the residential schools and children's homes until these closed. As there was no clear policy about records transfer, many of those records went missing and they are hard to locate today. One religious organisation said their records in Scotland were scarce as they had a policy of destroying records after seven years (although this organisation said they followed a different policy in England).

Religious organisations said that labelling records had been problematic; it wasn't always apparent from labels what the records contained. Labelling had been inconsistent, haphazard and depended on individual judgement. These particular challenges made records managers and archivists work difficult and time-consuming.

While some religious organisations acknowledged that their record management practices were poor in the past, they also indicated that those practices had improved in recent years. Some organisations said their present practices were influenced by records guidance issued by the government. One organisation said they consulted with voluntary organisations for guidance on preserving their records relating to children's residential services as part of their growing initiative to archive related material. The large numbers of records that have not been put into records management systems or archived, however, made it challenging for religious organisations to locate and provide information to us.

Historical records: General locations

Children's residential services records, and other related childcare service information, belonging to religious organisations may be located in centralised archives, diocesan archives, archdiocesan archives, individual church archives, museums and various other archives, including the National Archives of Scotland. Their records may also be found in local authority archives, social work departments, libraries, museums, the former Scottish Executive Education Department and other non-religious archives.

One religious organisation based throughout the United Kingdom said that their records specific to Scotland may be integrated with other records and located in various locations as they had many projects throughout England and Scotland. They said their records tended to remain in project locations until the project closed, when the records were sent to a centralised location; they remained there until it was possible to review the records for archiving.

Some large religious organisations are very complex, making it difficult for people within and outwith the organisation to locate records associated with particular topics. When boards of managers managed approved schools, for example, they were often associated with religious organisations operating as autonomous entities that may, or may not, have deposited boards of managers' records with religious archives existing throughout the United Kingdom.

Some religious organisations said they gave their children's residential establishment records, including children's files, to local authorities when the organisations ceased to be involved with children's residential services. Others said that management records generated on-site often remained in the establishment when religious organisations ceased to be involved with it. Various religious organisations, however, also operated child guidance clinics and managed childcare committees, with some records deposited in archives and others not.

Locating records within individual religious organisations

The religious organisations have taken various approaches to their records, with many placing greater significance on preserving records than in earlier years. Like voluntary organisations and local authorities, some religious organisations' records – and the information in the records – are sparse. One archivist, who described past record-keeping practices as "haphazard", said that records management needed to be considered within the context of the time:

"It was difficult to determine what records should have been kept, what might be missing and what wasn't required at various points time."

One international religious organisation said they had no "official" archivist although someone was responsible for managing their records. When we contacted this organisation they found boxes of records relating to children's residential services in their basement, providing us with a list of all records held and access to those records. Another religious organisation said that records for one children's residential establishment were dispersed to two locations: the organisation's central location and an education authority.

Another international religious organisation said they had no archivist, making it difficult for them to locate records. The organisation said that, while they were looking for information, they didn't expect to find much: "Our headquarters have moved four times during the period you mention, and have been subject to a fire and a flood! I have not found any records relating to management policies guiding work in providing residential care services to children and doubt that such exists."

The solicitors for another religious organisation stated that people associated with the religious organisation were employed at various residential schools during the review's period:

"[The religious organisation] did not own, manage or run schools in Scotland. A small number of the [religious organisation] were individually employed by the then Managers of schools in various capacities including Head Master, Deputy Master and as teachers in certain schools...."

"...the [religious organisation] did not provide – nor was the [religious organisation] contracted to provide – residential care for children and young people in Scotland in the period 1950-1995. It also follows that our clients hold no records relating to the pupils, staff or the running of the establishments in Scotland, other than a community book."

We asked if we could see this community book. The solicitors replied:

"The community book is unlikely to be of any relevance to your enquiry....the book holds records of members of [the religious organisation] who were employed at the Schools but also members of [religious organisation] who were not. Some of those members were employed at Schools. However, the community book was not held for, or on behalf of, any given School."

The solicitors added that "...our clients are under no obligation to allow your researcher unfettered access to their archives simply to confirm what has been stated".

In contrast, other religious organisations told us about more extensive records that they held. However all religious organisations acknowledged that poor record keeping practices in the past had led to incomplete records associated with their children's residential services. One religious organisation's part-time archivist indicated that their archives in England contained some records "...of the various residential services..." that the organisation provided. Another archivist said that their organisation held management administration records, providing us with a schedule of what records were held. The archivist said their record-keeping requirements had changed over the years and information they didn't keep, with hindsight, was information they should have kept and would keep today.

Another religious organisation said it was challenging to locate records as one children's home, for example, had changed its purpose "...many times over the years" while other children's homes transferred from one organisational responsibility to another, or had changed functions – or both of these. This organisation stated, however, that some records did exist. Another religious organisation said that all their records, managed by a part-time archivist, were in a central location in England. One religious organisation said all the records from their hospital for children with mental disabilities went to the Scottish Mental Health Office in Edinburgh when the hospital closed, while other management records were held in their own archives or went to local religious organisation archives.

One archivist said that when their organisation's children's homes closed throughout the UK, all their registers had been put in the cellars of the main organisation so the archivist could review what needed to be archived. The archivist said that records were requested from various locations, with the result that some records were sent and some weren't. According to the archivist, all children's records went to the local authorities although the archivist realised "too late" that those children's records shouldn't have been sent to the local authorities as the organisation now believed they have an after-care responsibility to former residents. The archivist said that senior people within the organisation recognised the value of keeping historical records and regretted that so many records had been destroyed, lost or not properly maintained.

Historical records: Types and other information

One religious organisation said they held some general management records, individual files, registers of admissions and discharges and log books for 1950-1969, for example. They don't hold specific policy and practice guidelines for this period (although they indicated that Social Work Services Group circulars would have covered this time period). This organisation said they had records that were no longer accessible, such as general management records, policy and practice guidelines, inspection reports, and individual files on former residents.

Drawing from organisational information, another religious organisation said that between 1950 and 1969 formal complaint processes, inspection processes and managerial reporting existed. They said that there were regular inspections of their children's residential establishments through external management and financial auditing processes during this period. This religious organisation indicated that regular inspections by Social Work Services Group and HMI took place, but they had no knowledge about whether the local authorities had inspection processes in place. The organisation couldn't determine from their records if policy and practice guidelines existed for the following: employee recruitment and training, child protection, whistleblowing, formal complaint process, bullying, grievances, incident reports, advocacy support, records and information management and inspections.

For the period 1970 to 1985, this organisation said they had used formal complaint processes, inspections, external visitors, audit reports and managerial reporting to monitor their children's residential services. The organisation said their work was subject to annual external scrutiny of management, financial audits and "dialogue with user authority" while other outside agencies inspected their children's residential establishments on an annual or regular basis. The organisation said these agencies were local authority education departments inspecting the residential schools and social work departments inspecting children's homes and residential care for children with disabilities. The organisation said that central government's Social Work Services Group's work largely set the policy and practice guidelines for this period.

This organisation said they had records for the period 1970 to 1985 that were no longer accessible, such as some general management records, all policy and practice guidelines, some inspection reports, and some individual children's records. They said they had policies and procedures for employee recruitment and training, formal complaint process, grievances and inspections. On the other hand, they said there were no policies and procedures for whistleblowing, bullying, advocacy support and records and information management. They were unable to determine whether policies existed for child protection and incident reports.

For the period 1986 to 1995, the organisation said they had used formal complaint processes, advocacy services, inspections, external visitors, audit reports, managerial reporting, incident reports and care plan reviews to monitor their children's residential services. The organisation said their work was subject to external scrutiny of management annually, financial audits and strategic review while other outside agencies inspected their children's residential establishments annually or regularly. The organisation said these these agencies consisted of HMIe, a local authority inspection unit, Social Work Services Group, Registration and Inspection and the Care Commission. The organisation said that the local authority education department inspected residential schools every year and the social work department inspected the

residential schools and residential care for children with disabilities.

The organisation said that for the period 1986 to 1995 they had some general management records, policy and practice guidelines, inspection reports and individual records for former residents. They also had policy and practice guidelines for this period related to employee recruitment and training, child protection, formal complaint process, bullying, grievances, incident reports, advocacy support. But they had no policy and practice guidelines for children's rights, records information and management or inspections. The organisation said they'd had records that were no longer available, such as some general management records, policy and practice guidelines, inspection reports, individual children's residential establishment records and individual records. For this period, the organisation said they had policies and procedures for employee recruitment and training, child protection, children's rights, whistleblowing, formal complaint process, bullying, grievances, incident reports and inspections. There were no policies and procedures on inspections, records and information management or advocacy support.

Another religious organisation had responsibility for several children's residential establishments between 1950 and 1995. For the period 1950-1985 they didn't know if the organisation monitored their children's residential establishments in any form or whether, as an organisation, they monitored their own work. This organisation said they couldn't determine from their records whether local authorities or their own organisation inspected their children's residential establishments or if outside agencies had that responsibility. They also found it difficult to find records relating to their children's residential establishments, including specific policy and procedure records for this period, and were unable to find out if those records ever existed.

The organisation told us that for the period 1986 to 1995 they monitored their children's residential establishments through formal complaint processes, advocacy services, children's rights services, inspections, external visitors, audit reports, managerial reporting, child protection reports, incident reports, care plan reviews and whistleblowing reports. They used internal inspections and internal audits to monitor their own work. They reported that local authorities inspected their residential services on an annual basis. The organisation said there were no other inspection processes although they added that it was possible that local authority social work inspected one of their children's residential establishments every year.

This organisation had some records for this period relating to children's residential establishments. These included inspection reports and some individual records which were held in archives. The organisation couldn't find specific policy and practice guidelines for the period 1986 to 1995. It said that it had records for this period that were no longer available as "most records were destroyed", although the organisation didn't know specifically what records existed before their destruction. The organisation said that between 1986 and 1995, however, there were no policies and procedures on inspections, records and information management or advocacy support.

Another religious organisation provided names of children's residential establishments and details relating to several residential establishments in operation during the period under review. They said they had started services to children in the 19th century following a request from the government of the day. This religious said they held some admissions registers, management administration files, memoranda, guidelines, and handbooks which, they said, tended to be general in nature. One religious organisation provided a list of all children's homes and centres they operated throughout a 100-year period, including details such as the children's residential establishment's name, location, governing body and whether records existed for the places identified. In some instances, the organisation said it was unable to find records for particular children's residential establishments although their archives held some records for other places.

One religious organisation said they operated several children's homes and residential nurseries, visited by members of the organisation's central administration every two or three years between 1950 and 1969. The organisation said they used this process to monitor their work and that they didn't know if other inspections occurred. Their records for this time period consisted of a few individual records, admission registers and visitation reports (prepared by members of the congregation's central administration). The organisation couldn't say if they had – or had in the past – specific policies and practices relating to children's residential services for the period 1950 to 1995. They did, however, have a directory that covered some related policy information in general terms. The organisation said it held registers, including children's registers, account books and staffing records:

> "The main body of records for this period comprise the admission register for each [children's residential establishment] – it is a complete series. These usually contain a record of discharge as well. There are supporting records of observations, discharge, and some after-care but these are not so complete as the admissions register.

> "It was not common during this period to open individual case files. Such as there [were] may have been destroyed somewhere at some stage and not deposited in the central archive, or they were transferred to local authorities."

The organisation said that during the period 1970 to 1985 senior managers visited their children's residential establishments every two or three years and that the organisation used this process to monitor their own work. The organisation couldn't determine from their records whether other inspections occurred. They said their records consisted of few individual records, admission registers and visitation reports prepared by senior managers. They couldn't find out from their records whether they had – or ever did have – management policies and practices relating to children's residential services for this time period. However they said there were records that contained some information in general terms. They'd had records for this period but these were no longer available. They no longer had individual records except a "residual few":

> "The main body of records for this period comprise the admission register for each [children's residential establishment] – it is a complete series, supplemented by a complete series of observations, discharge, and some after-care records. During the 70s, the use of individual case files developed rapidly & was virtually standard practice by 1985. When children were discharged or transferred or when houses were closed, the case files were routinely transferred to local authority or other appropriate agencies. The few files remaining in the archive were probably overlooked.

> "The Directory gives advice/instructions on the general life of the [religious organisation] and there is some reference to records and to child care & education. What 'policy

statements' there are would be very general and included in various communications of the [senior manager], and sometimes in response to developing legislation and practice."

Another religious organisation said they held various records in their archives relating to children's residential establishments, such as log books, registers (account books, staffing records, children's registers), visitor logs, the "odd" accident book and children's record. They said the children's registers contained: name of child, birth date, parents, baptism, parents' occupation, person recommending their care, date of discharge and "observations". They said they had "disposal books" which indicated where children went, what happened to them, and possibly some information about the children's mothers. They said they had some inspection reports, some house meeting reports, correspondence, financial information, miscellaneous papers, council minute books, and visitation reports by the senior managers. They added that the visitation reports might have included references to children. They said their children's files went to the local authorities, were destroyed or possibly went to their archives "by accident".

The archivist for another religious organisation reported attempts to gather historical records by writing and visiting various to obtain what was available. According to this archivist, some records obtained included children's files although the archivist reported that not many files existed if there were no "significant events" in the children's lives or the children "didn't cause any trouble". The archivist said the organisation created children's files if, for example, social services were involved. The archivist mentioned that social services would also have children's files. The archivist noted that the organisation had few children's files for the period before 1970; after 1970 the organisation generated a larger number of files.

One religious organisation said they were responsible for several children's residential establishments that were during the period under review. This organisation said they withdrew their children's residential services when Scottish Office funding stopped in 1983 and that new management assumed responsibility for one of their children's residential establishments. The organisation provided us with a complete list of all records held and directly associated with their children's residential establishments.

Chapter 7: Searching for information: Local Authorities

Introduction

This chapter reports on our information-gathering specific to local authorities.

As indicated earlier, during the period under review local authorities went through many policy changes and two major government reorganisations. What happened in one local authority exemplifies the upheaval these caused, and their potential effect on records. This local authority, formed in 1996, had existed within a larger regional council between 1975 and 1996. Between 1950 and 1975, however, it had consisted of three county councils with only a portion of each council falling within the boundaries of the current local authority. This situation was replicated across much of Scotland, requiring local authorities to manage complicated records transfers. Inevitably, records have been dispersed to various locations not always known, misplaced, or destroyed although there are also significant records in existence and accessible.

General challenges to locating information

Local authorities, like the voluntary and religious organisations, found it challenging to locate and provide information relating to children's residential services (see Appendix I). In our request for information, we anticipated that local authorities would inform us about children's residential establishments within their current geographical boundaries and that details about children's residential services would be taken from records located within their departments and archives. Responses by local authorities, and individuals within those local authorities, however, reveal how many local authorities found it difficult to provide information about children's residential services because their corresponding records have not been adequately managed and archived. In the absence of records, and the information within them, corporate memory relies on individuals, many of whom, for the earlier years in particular, have left their employment, taking that memory with them.

Some local authority representatives speculated that few records were available. Others made considerable efforts to locate records and information in them. One local authority reported that their council solicitor in charge of their archives was checking to see what materials the local authority possessed. This local authority, and another local authority, had no employed, trained archivist at the time. They reported, however, that they held records for children's residential services' staff, "significant events" in residential schools, such as incident reports, and punishment logs.

Many individuals commissioned by their local authorities to locate records and information were industrious and creative in their search for information. One local authority person contacted local volunteer-led history societies and local libraries, both of which he identified as possible sources of records relating to children's residential establishments. He contacted voluntary organisations, spoke to long-serving colleagues, met with retired colleagues and contacted local residential establishments for older people to see if anyone could remember children's residential establishments in the area. He visited his local authority archives to see how the records were catalogued and stored.

He found photographs of older children's residential establishments (that is, children's homes) in files in the local authority department offices. These photographs included pictures of children from the home going on adventure trips and adults working with children at that time. He referred to these photographs as "social documentation" that would likely have some relevance to people who lived and worked in children's residential establishments. He suggested that many records relating to children's residential establishments provided "fabulous insight" into the social history of child protection and child care services in Scotland in the earlier years.

Our request for information highlighted the nature of relationships between local authority departments and the local authority archives. Some local authority people working in departments worked closely with their local authority archivists to find information for us. Others didn't contact their archivist for help or resisted getting the archivist involved. One local authority had established an archival working group, which decided to prioritise the development of archival practices relating to children's residential services' records after contact from us. Their work included examining their record retention and disposal approaches, developing a system of coding and identifying what records the local authority possessed. We learned, however, that there are no consistent, standardised records management and archival practices throughout Scotland to ensure significant records are preserved in every local authority.

Questionnaire

Many factors had an impact on the local authorities' ability, or willingness, to locate information for us and respond to the questionnaire (see Appendix I). Some responded to the challenges they met by contacting us to discuss how to approach their work, given the difficulties they faced; they also said they realised the work's importance. Others, as indicated above, adopted an approach that best suited their circumstances, while some local authorities resisted involvement with searching for information. We recognised that the questionnaire was an imposition and we found it extremely helpful to receive information from local authorities about the challenges they faced when trying to locate records.

Seventeen local authorities returned the questionnaire, while 11 provided summarised information gleaned from information they were able to locate. Some local authorities didn't have, or didn't use, archivists. While we didn't receive questionnaire responses from all local authorities, it's possible to speculate that all local authorities faced similar challenges in locating information, particularly for the earlier periods under review.

Our information-gathering was also hampered when a professional association questioned our remit and its information requirements. This led to misinformation circulating about the review and resulted in some local authorities, which had demonstrated a willingness to help us, deciding not to continue with their search for information. It is difficult to know how much the involvement of this association affected the local authorities' co-operation in working with the review.

Children's residential establishments

No central database that we could locate identifies what children's residential establishments existed in Scotland, and where, during the period 1950 to 1995. Local authorities said that certain children's residential establishments known to them changed function, management or place, making it difficult to determine if and where related information might be. As many local authorities were unable to locate management records and children's files from closed children's residential establishments, it was sometimes difficult for them to identify what places had existed and to provide any related details.

Two councils commissioned a retired social worker with management experience to report on children's residential establishments run by the former corporation to 1975 and by the regional council from 1975 to 1995. This researcher examined council records such as "…minutes of the Children's Committee, the Education Committee, the Health and Welfare Committee and the Probation Committee. The sub-committee minutes of each of these have also been read." With the assistance of his local authority archivists, he was able to identify the children's residential establishments, including those establishments located outwith Scotland, where children from the local area were placed.

From scrutinising the minutes, this researcher learned that the detailing of children's officers' and probation officers' expenses prior to the early 1970s illustrated the places visited and how frequently officers made visits, for example, to approved schools. According to this research, these reporting practices changed when social work departments were introduced. This research led to a compilation of details about various children's residential establishments, including residential schools and children's homes, where children were placed by their home authority. This research also shows how it was possible to gain insights into monitoring practices by examining council minutes and reported financial information.

One local authority individual developed two lists of children's residential establishments: one of "confirmed existence" and one of "non-confirmed existence". He said he'd contacted two voluntary organisations with children's residential establishments within their boundaries. One voluntary organisation responded with detailed information about their children's home while the other "seemed surprised" that they had responsibility for a children's home that had been open within the local authority's boundaries. This shows the confusion that exists about what children's residential establishments existed throughout Scotland and what management structures governed the services they provided.

Records: Locations, types and general information

Local authorities' departments may or may not have preserved children and management records; transferred records or put records in local authority archives. We found that large volumes of records for children's residential services were situated in many locations throughout Scotland and England (see Appendix B). One local authority person reported that their records are held in regional archives, corporate archives, the local authority's social work and education departments, and in various storage centres. This person said local government reorganisations and the establishment of social work departments in the 1970s, led to confusion about where records were sent and what records existed. It appeared that many local authorities didn't know where all records associated with children's residential establishments might be located, what records should exist or what records were destroyed.

Local authorities' contacts reported that during local government and policy changes records went missing or may have been destroyed. Other local authorities' representatives said that records about children's residential services may be buried among other records as there was no clear, well-established cataloguing system for existing records. They said there were no consistent records management and archival practices among the local authorities, leading to potential difficulties in determining what types of records are held today and where, although it was apparent that many record types exist that have potential relevance to children's residential services (see Appendix C).

Records and policies: 1950 to 1969

Most local authorities indicated that they didn't know if they had any records relating to children's residential services for this period. Two said they did have such records, such as general management records, policy and practice guidelines, individual residential service provider records, and individual files for former residents. All local authorities said they had no inspection reports for children's residential services or their own departments for this time frame.

Many local authorities didn't know if they had specific policy and practice guidelines for the period before 1969, such as those relating to employee recruitment and training, child protection,

children's rights, whistleblowing, formal complaint processes, bullying, grievances, incident reports, advocacy services, records and information management or inspections. All said they didn't know if they had those specific policy and practice guidelines.

Some local authorities reported that they'd had general records relating to children's residential services while others said they didn't know if they had such records. The records identified as no longer accessible included all or some of the following: general management records, policy and practice guidelines, inspection reports, individual residential services provider records, and individual files on former residents.

Records and policies: 1970 – 1985

Some local authorities had records relating to children's residential services for this period while other local authorities responded that they didn't or didn't know. Those with records said they had some general management records, policy and practice guidelines, individual residential service provider records, and individual files for former residents. All the local authorities said they had no inspection reports for children's residential services or their local authority departments.

Some local authorities had specific policy and practice guidelines for this period relating to child protection, formal complaint processes, grievances, incident reports and records and information management. None had, or knew if they had, specific policy and practice guidelines for employee training and recruitment, children's rights, whistleblowing, bullying, advocacy support or inspections.

Some local authorities had general records relating to children's residential services that were no longer accessible, while others said they didn't know. The records that were no longer available included some or all of the following: general management records, policy and practice guidelines, inspection reports, individual residential service provider records, and individual files on former residents.

Some local authorities had had specific policy and procedure guidelines, relating to this time frame, for employee recruitment and training, child protection, children's rights, bullying, grievances, incident reports and records and information management. Others said they didn't know if they had any specific policy and procedure guidelines or didn't have guidelines for whistleblowing, formal complaint processes, advocacy support or inspections.

Records and policies: 1986 – 1995

Most local authorities indicated that they had records relating to children's residential services for this time frame. A small number said they didn't have such records or didn't know. Records held were some or all of the following: general management records, with some policy and practice guidelines, inspection reports for residential services, inspection reports for local authority services, individual service provider records, and individual files for former residents.

Some local authorities reported that they had specific policy and procedure guidelines for employee recruitment and training, child protection, children's rights, whistleblowing, formal complaint processes, bullying, grievances, incident reports, advocacy support, records and information management and inspections. Others said they didn't have these specific policy and procedure guidelines; some said they didn't don't know if such guidelines existed or not.

Some local authorities reported they'd had general records that were no longer accessible while others said they didn't know if they had such records. One local authority indicated that their general records remained accessible. The records some local authorities reported as no longer accessible included some general management records, policy and practice guidelines, inspection reports, individual service provider records, and individual files on former residents.

Some local authorities said they'd had specific policy and procedure guidelines for employee recruitment and training, child protection, children's rights, whistleblowing, formal complaints processes, bullying, grievances, incident reports, advocacy support, records and information management and inspections. Some reported that they didn't have these specific policy and procedure guidelines while others said they didn't know if they had specific guidelines for employee recruitment and training, children's rights, whistleblowing, bullying, grievances, incident reports, advocacy support or records and information management.

Monitoring: 1950 to 1969

While one local authority said they directly monitored children's residential establishments, most local authorities said they didn't or didn't know if the local authority directly or indirectly monitored children's residential services between 1950 and 1969. One local authority stated that managerial reporting was used as a monitoring approach when providing direct children's residential services and incident reports were used to monitor indirect provision of children's residential services. Most local authorities, however, said that no monitoring approaches were used or they didn't know if particular monitoring approaches, such as child protection reports, incident reports, complaint processes or inspection services were used to monitor direct or indirect provision of residential services. All local authorities indicated they didn't know if their own work was monitored during this time frame or said that it wasn't.

In response to particular questions about inspection services for this period, all local authorities reported that they didn't know if their local authorities or other agencies had responsibility for inspecting children's residential establishments during this time frame. All local authorities reported that other agencies didn't have – or they didn't know if other agencies had – responsibility for inspecting the local authority departments.

Monitoring: 1970 to 1985

Many local authorities reported that they directly monitored their own children's residential establishments between 1970 and 1985 while several indicated that they didn't or didn't know. Most, however, said they didn't know if the local authority had monitored contracted children's residential services, while a few said that they did or did not. Some local authorities said they used monitoring approaches for children's residential establishments such as formal complaint processes, children's rights services, external visitors (that is, outside professionals providing services), managerial reporting, child protection reports, incident reports and care plan reviews. Some local authorities reported they did not use any monitoring approaches or they didn't know if any monitoring approaches were used during this time frame.

Some local authorities said they used certain monitoring approaches for contracted children's residential services; these approaches included managerial reporting, child protection reports, incident reports and care plan reviews. Other local authorities stated that they didn't use any monitoring approach or didn't know what, if any, monitoring took place. One said it monitored its own work in providing children's residential services, but most local authorities said they didn't or didn't know.

All local authorities responded that they did not have or didn't know if the local authority had responsibility for inspecting children's residential services during this period. Some reported that other agencies were directly responsible for inspecting children's residential establishments, while most local authorities replied that no agency had responsibility or they didn't know. The Scottish Office, Social Work Services Group and the Social Work Services Inspectorate were named as entities with inspection responsibilities.

All local authorities responded that other agencies had no responsibility for inspecting their local authority departments or they didn't know if any agency had such responsibility during this time period.

Monitoring: 1986 - 1995

Most local authorities responded that they directly monitored children's residential establishments. Two local authorities reported they didn't or they didn't know if monitoring took place. Some local authorities reported that they monitored contracted children's residential establishments while other local authorities reported that they didn't or didn't know.

The local authorities that directly monitored children's residential establishments said they used monitoring approaches such as formal complaint processes, advocacy services, children's rights services, inspections, external visitors, audit reports, managerial reporting, child protection reports, incident reports, care plan reviews and whistleblowing reports. One reported they didn't use any of these. While local authorities indicated they used the same monitoring approaches for indirect children's residential services, a few didn't know what monitoring approaches were used and one replied that none was used.

Several local authorities reported using monitoring approaches to inform their own work while a smaller number stated that they didn't monitor their own work or they didn't know if such monitoring occurred. Most responded that they had responsibility for inspecting children's residential services while some replied they did not. A small number reported that other agencies had responsibility while most said other agencies didn't have responsibility; one didn't know. Local authorities that reported inspection responsibilities indicated that education and social work departments had responsibility along with the Social Work Inspection Group.

A small number reported that other agencies had responsibility for inspecting their local authority while most replied that no other agency had responsibility and two local authorities reported they didn't know.

Local authorities: archivists survey

The following information represents general comments received from archivists in responses to the survey. At the time, five local authorities had no archivists in post. We received 19 completed surveys, with several archivists submitting a joint survey and two archivists providing information in another form. A summary of the records held within the archives can be found in Appendix C.

According to archivists, records were transferred from council to council during local government reorganisations, which seriously affected records' availability and preservation. They reported that some NHS records relating to children's homes were held in their archives. One said their archival holdings were small due to a lack of storage space, indicating that most of their pre-1975 archives relating to the county council and the former burgh councils were held by the National Archives of Scotland. Another archivist said the minutes for their district council, in existence from 1975 to 1995, were held by their legal department.

One archivist said their archive didn't hold specific records relating to children's residential establishments although the archivist tried to locate this information from local authority departments without success. Another reported being "instructed to destroy all Senior Management team records in 2004". The archivist noted that all records after 1996 were on recycled paper and were unlikely to survive in the long-term. One archivist reported no knowledge of the use of any electronic storage systems. Archivists also reported that committee files pertaining to children's residential services weren't kept and that archivists were "not consulted in respect of widespread retention changes to [local authority] records".

One archivist reported that a local authority had appointed its first professional archivist in 1996 as the regional authority had chosen "not to make any archival provision. Consequently until 1996 the [current] archives had neither custody nor responsibility for these records". Before the formation of the current council in 1996, the city archives tried to address these issues with some success but the present archive held "almost no Education or Social Work records; the responsible departments choosing to make their own arrangements. We are however aware that a very considerable volume of records no longer survive." One archivist gave us a list of 82 children's homes and residential schools, but said their archives held very few records for these establishments.

Archivists reported that records might be held in unknown private storage companies subcontracted by departments; the Scottish Adoption Agency; National Archives of Scotland; health archives; university archives; the national libraries; Care Scotland and other health boards. One local authority archive holds records for a former orphanage. We were told:

"Some Archive records are held elsewhere in Libraries and Museums, or still with the Service that created them. (The Town Council records for the [current council] are held in [x] University Library.

"The records of the [x] Orphanage...are held at [x] Museum. The collection includes lists of children in the orphanage, trustees minutes, inventories, correspondence, and accounts, 1790s – 1980s.

"It is not possible to determine the contents of the archives relating to children's residential establishments. The archives are only partially listed, and while items such as the main minute books are mostly identified and available, the wider scope of records are not so accessible, or readily identifiable. Items may still be in the possession of the individual homes."

One archivist reported that their archival records "...mainly contain correspondence and product sales literature regarding the ordering of equipment" for children's residential establishments. According to the archivist, the records included some information about children's homes. One archivist indicated that their archive held records such as "...a register of punishment for the period 1919-1977, relating to certain residential school and reference to a register of [x schools] for the period1964-1968 as being in the possession of the headmaster at the school".

"There is very little within the records we hold... We do not hold any Social Work client files or registers here at the Archive Centre...certain files can be identified but it is not possible to state these are the only records, as they only reflect those transferred..."

The archivists identified that the search for information relating to children's residential establishments relied on clear naming and listing of records. They said that, in some instances, the records made very vague references to their contents.

They made particular remarks about **records management**.

The archivists said that not all local authorities had records managers in post or records management systems. Some archivists reported that "individual departments are responsible for managing and storing their own records". The "...archive service currently provides records management storage for some [emphasis added] council departments ..." Archivists said that various departments made their own arrangements for past and current records. Some archivists said they provided guidance and advice to council departments on how to manage their records.

Some archivists reported that their law and administration council section was evaluating records management procedures. Other archivists stated that "...records management is dealt with by the council's standards and compliance unit" and, within some local authorities, the social work department does their own records management.

Conclusion

We relied on information located within records held by voluntary organisations, religious organisations and local authorities to fulfil our remit. Our information-gathering process shows how difficult, if not impossible, it is to gain insights into systemic factors contributing to children's abuse within residential establishments without the existence of records. In general, our search for information revealed that local authorities, voluntary organisations and religious organisations all faced similar challenges when trying to locate records, making accessibility difficult. We found that it was impossible to determine where all 'relevant' records for children's residential establishments are held, and this situation will remain until all significant records for children's residential services are identified, located and catalogued.

Locating records associated with children's residential services is an enormous and daunting task. We learned, for example, that management records relating to the same topic may be located in many locations. We also found that the lack of records in one location, for example, didn't mean that those records, or records relating to the same topic, don't exist. We discovered that many children's residential establishments changed function, ownership and closed, making the ownership of records, such as children's files and management records, and what happened to those records somewhat unclear. The local authorities, voluntary and religious organisations were reorganised or relocated, which led to massive uncertainty about what happened to records through transitions. Employees with corporate memory left their employment, taking their memory of where records are located with them.

When children left their residential placements, various unregulated approaches guided what happened to children's records. These approaches were complicated by the possible existence of several children's records for one child depending on what services were involved. Children's records may have existed within the children's residential establishments, local authority social work or children's departments, local authority education departments or education authorities, health boards and voluntary or religious organisations. For children placed outwith their own local authorities, it was reported that children's records returned to the child's originating authority and were dispersed to central offices. It's not clear what happened to the records of Scottish children placed in children's residential establishments in England.

Our information gathering, however, depended upon organisations and local authorities having located and identified all "relevant" records together with their ability to make those records immediately accessible. As our search for information shows, two large government reorganisations, major legislative changes and changes within organisations throughout a 45 year period led to challenges in the search for information:

■ Poor records management practices in the past mean that records are missing, have been destroyed or were not generated in the first instance.
■ Corporate memory was held by individuals who have retired or died.
■ There was no legislation requiring sound records management, such as schedules of records that had been retained and destroyed.
■ Organisations have changed locations or experienced fires or floods, causing damage to records.
■ Children's residential establishments closed or changed management and their records locations are unknown.
■ Few general records are easily accessible and specific to children's residential services.
■ The labelling of records is poor and the records' catalogues inadequate.
■ It was very time-consuming and costly to search for information.

A number of voluntary and religious organisations, while committed to better records management, lacked, and continue to lack, a proper records management system and full-time archivists. Not all local authorities currently employ archivists and records managers and some did not adequately support their existing archival services.

Voluntary organisations, religious organisations and local authorities found it difficult, and at times impossible, to respond to our queries about past management policies and practices, including policies that relate to monitoring children's well-being and keeping children safe. For those organisations and local authorities that did respond, the information they provided suggests that records have become increasingly relied upon for monitoring children's safety, promoting their well-being and evaluating the quality of services provided to children.

The poor overall state of records, however, raises important issues about how voluntary organisations, religious organisations and local authorities that provided children's residential services are held accountable to children, former residents and others, for the services they provided.

Chapter 8: Concluding remarks

We depended upon records to gain insights into past experiences within children's residential services and, in doing so, we learned invaluable lessons about records associated with children's residential establishments and children's services in general. We've identified reasons why records are important, to whom and for what reasons. We've developed awareness about the many challenges facing individuals who seek and work with records. And, we now recognise the significant costs – personal, historical, and social - for survivors of institutional child abuse, others who lived in children's residential establishments and society when records cannot be located and accessed. There are economic benefits to proper records management – now and in the future. For children living away from home and in state care today, records are essential for monitoring their safety, promoting their well-being and holding children's services accountable for what they offer children.

Poor recording keeping practices have, and continue to have, many implications:
■ This review experienced difficulty in addressing its remit due to the poor state of records associated with children's residential services. Future inquiries[124] will also be affected unless proper records management practices are universally adopted;
■ Challenges exist for local and central government, religious organisations and voluntary organisations needing to respond to inquiries about past management policy and practices;
■ Former residents of children's residential establishments may be unable to realise their legal entitlements to access personal information and information about children's residential services;
■ Individuals may be denied access to justice that depends upon the collaboration of records;
■ It is difficult to develop a full historical account of children's residential services in Scotland without records;
■ There are risks to children in care today as records play an essential role in monitoring children's safety and well-being;
■ There is the potential lack of accountability by organisations and government who are responsible for their services to children;
■ Future research that could contribute to a better understanding of Scotland's social history may be hindered.

The establishment of 'historical accounts', in particular, is important to former residents. Records play a critical role in establishing accounts about what happened in children's residential establishments throughout Scotland and what contributed to children's abuse. Records may complement the oral histories of people who lived in children's residential establishments and those who worked in children's services. Records add to our understanding about how those establishments, and children's services in general, are situated within Scotland's wider social fabric.

Records are vital to ensuring '...that past experiences and lessons are not lost'. It was within the spirit of learning lessons that this report was written. From the knowledge we have gained, we would like to encourage all those individuals who found it difficult to place importance on records to learn more about records – to see beyond records as administrative inconveniences to how records connect to the humanity of children living away from home and in state care. Records have significance beyond the immediate, they have importance in perpetuity.

We are extremely grateful to former residents for their sharing their expertise and their experiences about records, as it was apparent that their contributions were accompanied by an

---

[124] 'Future inquiries': May include public or judicial inquiries; inspections; police investigations; audits and any other processes inquiring into matters relating to children's services.

emotional cost to them. We appreciate, as well, the support, enthusiasm and passion shared by many people who believe in the importance of preserving records that allow us to better understand people's experiences, the provision of children's residential services and their interrelationship with Scotland's social history. Lessons that we learn from records allow us to better meet the needs of children living away from home and in state care today.

It is not too late to make important changes to address critical and outstanding issues identified within the report.

References

Archive Services in Scotland Mapping Project Board (2000). An Archival Account of Scotland, Public and Private Sector Archive Services in Scotland: Funding Opportunities and Development Needs Report.
See at: http://www.archives.org.uk/sca/anarchiv.pdf

Barter, Christine; Abuse of Children in Residential Care; NSPCC Information Briefings; 2003; available from www.nspcc.org.uk/infom accessed on 31.10.2007

Bichard Inquiry Report (2004). House of Commons. London: The Stationary Office. See at: http://www.bichardinquiry.org.uk/report/

Elsley, Susan (2007). Attitudes to children and social policy changes. Literature review prepared for Historical Abuse Systemic Review.

House of Commons: The British Parliament Select Committee on Health – Third Report (1998). The Welfare of Former British Child Migrants. See at: http://www.parliament.the-stationery-office.co.uk/pa/cm199798/cmselect/cmhealth/755/75502.htm

Imrie, John, "The modern Scottish Record Office", Scottish Historical Review 53 (1974), 198-9, 201, 202, 205-6, as cited in Hector L MacQueen, "Reform of Archival Legislation: a Scots Perspective" Journal of the Society of Archivists vol 26 (2005) 201-214.

Law Commission of Canada (1998). Institutional Child Abuse Research Paper. Available at www.lcc.gc.ca/research_project/98_abuse_3-en.asp accessed on 01.09.2007

MacQueen, H.L. (2005). Reform of Archival Legislation: a Scots Perspective" Journal of the Society of Archivists vol 26. pp 201-214. Parliament of Senate (2001). Lost Innocents: Righting the Record - Report on child migration. See at: http://www.aph.gov.au/senate/committee/clac_ctte/completed_in quiries/1999-02/child_migrat/report/index.htm

Parliament of Australia Senate (2004) Forgotten Australians: A report on Australians who experienced institutional or out-of-home care as children. See at: http://www.aph.gov.au/Senate/committee/clac_ctte/inst_care/report/

Scotland on Sunday; September 9 2007; Files Put Faces To Millions; Annette Young.

Scottish Information Commissioner and National Archives of Scotland (2003). Code of Practice on Records Management. See at: http://www.scotland.gov.uk/Resource/Doc/1066/0003775.pdf

Scottish Information Commissioner (2005). Examination of the Scottish Executive Education's Procedures for the Identification and Provision of Access to Records related to Children's Homes and Residential Schools. http://www.itspublicknowledge.info/home/ScottishInformation Commissioner.asp

Scottish Government (2003) The Scottish Public Records Strategy. See at: http://www.scotland.gov.uk/About/FOI/18593/13851

Sen, R., Kendrick, A., Milligan, I., Hawthorn, M. (2007). Historical Abuse in Residential Child Care in Scotland 1950 – 1995: A Literature Review. Scottish Institute for Residential Child Care, University of Strathclyde.

Skinner, A. (1992). Another Kind of Home. Edinburgh: The Scottish Office.

Social Work Inspection Agency (2005). An Inspection into the Care and Protection of Children in Eilean Siar. Scottish Executive. See at: http://www.swia.gov.uk.

Stein, M. (2006). Missing years of abuse in children's homes. Child and Family Social Work 2006, 11, pp 11-21.

Appendices

Appendices D, E, J and K present information submitted by survivors. They contain the comments and opinions of the authors and not those of the review.

Appendix A

Children's residential establishments 1950-1995 Examples of related terms

Schools
1. List D schools
2. Residential special schools
3. Independent schools for children with functional difficulties and special needs

4. Approved schools
5. Boarding schools
6. Residential schools
7. List G schools

Children's homes

1. General care long & short term
2. Remand homes
3. Assessment centres
4. Reception homes/centres for emergency and short term care
5. Home for children nearing independence
6. Boys home
7. Children's home
8. Home for maladjusted children
9. Day and residential resource centre
10. Residential child care unit
11. Voluntary home/ working boys' home
12. Home for girls under a court order
13. Voluntary girls training home/ hostel
14. Teenage short stay refuge
15. Children's unit
16. Orphanage
17. Residential and outreach resource
18. Young persons unit
19. Young people's units
20. Children's shelter
21. Residential unit
22. Long term home
23. Short stay home
24. Teenage transitional unit
25. Widower's children's homes

Residential Places for Children with Special Needs

1. Special care homes and schools for children with functional difficulties and special needs
2. Homes for 'mentally handicapped'
3. Intermediate treatment homes for children requiring short training and supervision away from home
4. Residential homes for young people with complex physical and learning disabilities
5. Respite resources for children with disabilities
6. Residential respite units for children with severe learning difficulties

Secure accommodation
Probation home
Family group homes
Holiday homes

Hostels

1. Hostels with care and supervision.
2. Children's hostels
3. Voluntary home/ working boys' home or hostel
4. Youth hostel
5. Hostel for homeless young women
6. Hostels with care and supervision generally for older children who cannot follow normal family life
7. Voluntary girls training home/ hostel
8. Hostel for mothers with children and children and babies in need of fostering
9. Hostels for working children
10. Probation hostel

Appendix B

Children's residential services: Possible records locations
Basements and other storage areas
Children's residential establishments
Individual possession
Local authority departments: Social work, education, legal
Local authority archives
Local authority councils (general locations)
Local authority libraries
Local history societies
National Archives of Scotland
National Library of Scotland
Museums
Placing agencies
    Local authority education committees, regional hospital
    boards, educational authorities, juvenile courts, local
    authorities children's departments, national child care
    committees (associated with religious organisations).
Private storage facilities[125]
Professional associations' archives
Property departments
Regional NHS health boards
    Religious organisations (Scotland and England)
    Central offices, religious organisation archives, university
    archives, provincial houses, diocese and archdiocese archives
Scottish Government education, health, legal services
departments
Scottish Government Library
Scottish Mental Health Office
Specialist libraries
Solicitors' offices
University archives (Scotland and England)
Voluntary organisations (Scotland and England)
    Organisation archives, university archives
Unknown and undisclosed locations[126]

Appendix C[127]

Children's residential services: Possible records

Voluntary organisation records
Abstract of accounts
Admission books/papers
Annual reports
Artefacts
Children's records
Cottage industrial school punishment registers
Family counsellor files
Industrial schools society minute books
Institution minute books
Letters
Log books
Minute book of general committee
Narratives of fact
Orphanage, logbooks and admission registers
Orphanage applications
Orphanage minute books
Orphanage magazines
Papers concerning closure
Residential school log books
Residential school admission registers
Residential school admission registers

---

[125] Private storage: We've learned that local authority departments, for example, have stored records in private storage facilities and that it is possible that no list exists for what is stored there.

[126] Many 'children's agencies' associated with children's residential establishments included: child care offices, adoption societies, guidance clinics, enquiry centres, social services centres, youth advisory services and so on. Also, other places associated with committees responsible for children's services, regional hospital boards, educational authorities, inspection bodies, juvenile courts, national child care committees, assessment centres, remand homes and intermediate training schemes may have records pertaining to children placed and possibly relating to those establishments as well.

[127] These are record types that voluntary organisations, religious organisations and local authorities identified as examples of some of their held records. These examples do not represent all records types that may contain information relating to children's residential services.

Registers of staff
Review reports
Society minute books
Visual material (photographs, films, videotapes)
Working boys' home minute books

Religious organisations
Accident books
Account books
After-care records
Audit reports
Children's records
Children's registers (name, DOB, parents, baptism etc)
Council minute books
Desk diaries
General management records
Handbooks
House meeting reports
Individual children's records
Inspection reports
Letters
Log books
Managerial reports
Meal books
Memoranda
Minutes of manager meetings
Observation records
Photographs
Policy and practise papers/guidelines/statements
Punishment books
Record books
Register of admissions/discharges
Register of cooperators and benefactors
Rules of punishment
School logs
Staffing records
Visitor books/logs
Visitation reports
Whistleblowing reports

Local authorities: General
Action plans (resulting from reports)
Annual reports
Applications for admittance to children's homes
Audit reports
Care plan reviews
Cash books
Child abuse registers
Child protection reports
Children and young people admitted to care registers
Children's committee member reports
Children's department records
Children's director reports
Children's officer reports
Circulars
Committee reports to councils
Department reports
Donations and gifts records
General management and policy records
General social welfare registers
Health authority records
Immunisation records
Incident report records

Individual residential services provider records
Individual children's records
Inspection reports (children's residential establishments or
    departments)
Investigation reports
Ledgers for children's homes that show when children were
    placed in or discharged from residential establishments
Log books
Medical reports
Medical officer reports
Minutes of council meetings
Minutes of council children's committee meetings
Minutes of council committee meetings
Minutes of professional associations meetings e.g. Approved
    school managers and educational psychologists
Organisational/structural reviews
Papers on closure of establishments
Papers relating to children's hearings
Photographs and memorabilia
Pocket money registers
Policy and strategy papers
Punishment books
Punishment returns
Register of clothing given to children
Register of guardians
Register of presents given to children
Reports on residential establishments
Reports on local authority departments
Senior management reports
Some policy and practice guidelines
Special reports
Staff registers
Visitor books

Local authorities: Archives

Corporate records
Records - Poor Relief and 'care issues'
Parochial boards and parish councils records
Former burgh records
Town council minutes
Town council committee files
Parish council files

County council
County council minutes
Minutes of children's committees
County clerk's correspondence files re: 'setting up child care
    establishments'
County council children's panel advisory committee reports
County council children's officer annual reports
County council index to social work cases
Sub-committee education reports
County council residential education institutions: financial
    records and annual reports
Social work committee papers
Education committee minutes
Children's committee minutes
Reports and notes from committees
Health circulars
Minutes of the County Council, Committees and Sub-Committees
Subject files of County Council (Children's Officer/Social Work
    Department)

Minute books with general references to childcare

Corporation records
Annual Reports (Children's department)
Annual Reports (Education department)
Education department file on residential schools
Social Work journal for residential services
Education ie file on residential schools for children with mental
   disabilities
Reports to children's committees
Report on use of remand homes for pre-trial investigations
Residential special schools records
Residential school records ie teaching staff
HM inspectors of schools reports
Correspondence file on residential education
Correspondence on residential schools for children
   . with mental disabilities
Residential special school statistics
Review of children's department: Organisation & methods
Review of social work department
City corporation records

District Council
District Council Minutes
District sub-committee minutes
District council committee papers
District files ie Questions of management:
   Residential Homes for Children

Division Records
Residential homes
Social work records ie Social needs and social work resources
Overview of Division Social Work record ie Social Needs and
   Social Work Reports
Social work department correspondence on Children's Act 1975
Social work department ie List D hearings and headquarter
   meetings
Draft reports re: social needs and social work resources
Restructuring of social work department record
Questions of management of residential homes for children
   report
Child care section record
Child Care Act 1975 record
Residential homes record
Social work group for children records
Child care review group records
Correspondence on national children's homes

Regional councils
Regional council minutes
Committee papers for regional councils, including major reports
Records for regional council and predecessor authorities and of
   businesses, families and organizations within [the council area]
Social work file on council children's centres and homes
Law and administration department social work records
Annual reports for child guidance service
Social work committee officer/member group child care reports
Social work committee officer/member group general reports
Records on registration of residential establishments
Child guidance service annual reports
Files on registration of residential establishments
Social Work Committee Officer/Member Group reports
   on child care
Social Work file on residential establishments
Social Work official opening of establishments
   (residential and daycare) report

Social Work – practice guidelines for residential workers
Social Work – working party reports on residential care matters
Children's residential establishment registration records

General records
NHS records
Family and estate collections
Business archives
Church records
Solicitor records
Records of societies and associations
Social work department files
Education department files
Social Work (Scotland) Act 1968 ie setting up social work
   department
Records 'deposited by other organizations and individuals'
Committee papers (including major reports)
Mental Welfare Register – names, addresses, dates, tick columns
   regarding 'mental illness' and 'mental deficiency'
Certificates with name of child, information of who/where child
   received from.
Visiting committee reports
Fieldwork and general services sub-committee minutes
Legislation relating to children

Reports
Corporation annual reports, children
Corporation annual reports, education
Alternatives to Substitute Care, Adoption, Fostering and After
   Care; Quality of Substitute Residential Care: Towards a Social
   Policy for Children
Report by Director of Social Work on Residential Child Care
Report by Children's Officer. Costs of prevention
   following the act
Annual Report of the County Medical Officer
'The Residential Story: A possible approach for teachers
   in special schools'
"Residential Child Care Strategy for the Eighties:
   Home or Away?"
Response to Home and Away
Report by the Needs and Resources Group on the Form
   and Content of the 1982 Report
Social Work department – Social Needs and Social Work
   Resources amended reports

Specific records
One local authority social work department holds various records
related to children's residential establishments going back to
1953 and holds a register of children boarded out, for example,
between 1959-1978, 1966-1974 and placements made 1958-1985
and 1972-1995. This local authority also has a register for
children in foster homes[128].

Children's residential establishments (local government records)
Children's separate register
Minutes of House Committee of children's home
Records for:
■ children's home for "mentally disabled"
■ boarded-out children
■ family group home
■ special school
■ children's home
Accident reports
Residential nursery records – admissions and discharges
General records for farm school accession, including a visitors book.

---

[128] Some children in children's residential establishments also spent time in foster care.

Children's residential establishments (generated on-site)
Admission register
Attendance registers and summaries
Application forms for post of houseparents
Applications for admittance
Cash book and pocket money register
Correspondence files
Diaries
Daybooks
Education files
General files
Incidents files
Log books
Memorabilia
Minutes, photographs, videos
Night diary
Night logbooks
Pupil testing materials
Photographs
Postcards
Register of students
Register of admission and discharge
Register of attendance
Report books
Visitors books

Appendix D

Survivor's organisation submission

A **survivors' organisation**, representing the views of adults abused as children in residential establishments, submitted the following information to the Historical Abuse Systemic Review about **why records are important** to them:

1. "Many children who were in-care are not aware even today the possible reasons and circumstances why they were put into care. It is a record of particular importance to a group of vulnerable adults."
2. "In some cases care organisations and its employees...were not truthful in providing the factual and actual reasons and circumstances why a particular child was in its care at the time."
3. "Former children have gained this information concerning their families and other circumstances previously withheld from them as children in-care which is different to what they had been initially informed i.e. That they were an orphan yet years later in some cases 30 odd years + later after they have left the home they were to learn that in fact they had parents & siblings and were in fact not an Orphan. In many cases these siblings and parents were still alive. Also in a few cases parents had remarried and so had other children."
4. "It is perhaps the only record that may exist for that particular individual and as such holds particular importance to former children who are now adults."
5. "It is perhaps the only record that may assist in tracing other members of a family such as siblings and parents that they were unaware existed if the care organisation had not informed them."
6. "The Historical records may be of particular importance in assisting to prosecute the law with regards to allegations being made by former children. They can be part of a trail in establishing the truth."
7. "If the Historical records are inaccurate or not complete it raises serious concerns and issues for all parties especially so

in prosecuting the law. It begs the Question WHY are they not accurate or complete."
8. "For ex-employees of institutions it may help verify accurately their view and uphold accounts of a child's time in-care and may support the case that abuse did not in fact take place or otherwise if the records are a true and accurate account."
9. "For children in care it may reinforce the case that abuse took place or otherwise."
10. "In some cases we understand that Historical case records which are not complete or inaccurate may not in fact be of no or little value to the Police authorities investigation allegations of historical misconduct or abuse."
11. "In other cases the records may contain references to police reports or issues pertaining to the police visits or contacts with the care home such as when former children absconded from its care at the time."

The **survivors' organisation** also identified the **types of records** it considers important to people who lived as children in children's residential establishments. The submission states that "...all Historical records should have been kept in there entirety by all care institutions and other such entities and are all relevant".

"These historical children's records are protected in LAW and as such should have been treated accordingly down the generations by all institutions and care organisations regardless and in that priority with regards collating, archiving, retention and storage of all files and records held by all institutional & organisations. Legislation and relevant children's Acts were in place to protect children in care such 1948 Children's Act and other such legislation. Policies within care institutions should have reflected and abided by this legislation and the relevant Children's Acts."

"Given that Institutional organisations such as [a particular children's home] have not retained ALL relevant records of a particular child. The following in our view are of particular importance and extremely relevant in providing a record and accurate account of a child's time in-care. We do not list these in and particular importance order and this list in not exhaustive."

1. "Medical records/history and all medical entries concerning each individual child while in-care in [children's home]. Immunisation and admissions to hospital."
2. "All previous family history and why a child was placed in care. Throughout the process."
3. "All School records/reports."
4. "All recorded entries by all the care employees. (In chronology of date within each Institution or within that organisation such as different households within an organisation date of entry and exit.)"
5. "All Social work or-Welfare records pertaining to the child in-care and their immediate family and siblings before and during in-care. Entered into all records."
6. "All visits by outside investigative bodies or individuals sent. All other visits."
7. "Audit trail of Social work-Welfare dept within all care organisations. Any and all Access given to Children's files by employees and senior management and why (signed and dated)."
8. "All police visits and reports concerning children absconding etc."

Appendix E

Survivor's organisation submission

A **survivor's organisation**, representing the views of adults abused as children in residential establishments, made the following submission to the Historical Abuse Systemic Review about **former residents' experiences with locating and accessing records.**

1. "Local Authority records are particularly difficult to locate as there has been numerous changes in structures down the years such as [local council]. These records are stored and retained at various area control social work centres across Scotland such in my own case [town in Scotland]."

2. "In my own case there were five [name] siblings all in-care through [city council social work dept] yet there are no files or records for any of us. Despite me taking up the issues concerning my siblings files and my own directly with [name] the director of Social work, [city council]."

3. "There appears to be no sense of urgency by the Local Authority to help locate files/records of a historical nature for Survivors. As in my particular case no one wrote back to me until I raised the issue again despite filling out the relevant form it took a year for a formal response and another to inform me that there was no records or files."

4. "To date there are no [city council] Social work records for any of the [name] siblings despite the fact that I was able to provide them with documentation from my [name] children's file with regards correspondence written at the time by a [city council] Social worker at the [city council] with regards my family and admissions into [children's home]."

5. "[Children's home] current staff are insensitive about the needs and issues of former children who request their records or files especially those involved in the recent court cases. We also have others former children who have made this claim to us."

6. "The current [children's home] organisation and management is more concerned about limiting any fallout or potential complaint from those requesting their records. The current system is purely designed and there to minimise the issues and keep a tight lid on them. It's a typical stance by [children's home] to be fully in control of all the issues."

7. "Current [children's home] employees (aftercare workers) are making disparaging comments concerning other children who have had their cases upheld in the Courts to other former residents verbally and in emails. (we can provide the emails and testimony to the systemic review team)."

What works for people who want to locate and access their Historical records files.

1. "That it is provided within the time allowed for in Law which is 40 days under the Data Protection Act 1998 all care institutions and organisations should abide fully by the law."

2. "That the process is explained fully in writing to the applicant (former resident) when they first make contact with the former care home, organisation or Local Authority including any costs."

3. "That it is done independently outwith the organisation i.e. another social work dept and former children are offered independent support and help such as counselling provided and offered beforehand. As in our experience for many former children it can be very traumatic experience when they access their past histories and records for the first time ever in many cases."

Appendix F

Children (Scotland) Act 1995 Regulations and Guidance, Children Looked After by Local Authorities, Volume 2, Chapter 4 (residential care): Excerpt

Personal records

50. The managers in consultation with the person in charge should ensure that all necessary records, including where necessary health particulars, are maintained in respect of each child accommodated in the establishment. A child's personal record provides a common understanding of the plan for him or her, arrangements made, agreements and decisions which have been reached and the reasons for them. It also enables the implementation of planning decisions to be kept under review.

51. The record should include all the information about family history, involvement with the authority and progress which is set out in guidance on children who are looked after by a local authority. The record maintained by the residential establishment should include:
   - date of the placement
   - the supervision requirement or provision by reference to which the placement was made
   - the views of the child and his or her parents about the placement
   - reasons for the placement
   - persons notified about the placement
   - reports of visits by the child's social worker
   - date of termination of the placement
   - reasons for ending the placement
   - persons notified about the termination of the placement
   - arrangements for providing the child with continuing support.

52. Personal records should be comprehensive and up-to-date. They should also include cross-references to other records where more detailed information is held. Records should be checked regularly by the person in charge of the establishment. In addition they should be accessible to the responsible social worker. Arrangements for access to personal records by children under sixteen have been modified by the Age of Legal Capacity (Scotland) Act 1991 as explained in the guidance on children looked after by a local authority.

53. The managers in consultation with the person in charge of the establishment should ensure that a log book is maintained of day-to-day events, particularly concerns about individual children. References to individual children entered in this log will be detailed in personal records. In addition other entries such as the use of measures of control, complaints or accidents will be entered in separate logs dedicated to those respective purposes. In order to avoid unnecessary duplication and to facilitate rapid access it is helpful if entries in different logs about the same event are cross-referenced.[129]

The regulations and guidance for the Children (Scotland) Act 1995 make certain provisions relating to records for secure accommodation.

9. The managers, in consultation with the person in charge of the secure establishment in which the child is placed, must keep a record of the child's placement in such accommodation. This should clearly distinguish between placement in secure

accommodation and placement in open accommodation in the same establishment. The record must include

- the child's full name, sex and date of birth
- the supervision requirement, order or provision by reference to which the placement was made
- the date and time of the placement, reasons for and persons authorising the placement, and the child's previous address
- the name and address of each person notified about the placement
- the outcomes of the placement
- the date and time of the child's discharge, the name of the person authorising his or her discharge and his or her subsequent address.

These records should be available for inspection by the Secretary of State and, where relevant, by the local inspection unit.

10. Good practice would require that the following information is also recorded
   - characteristics of the child
   - previous involvement of the local authority
   - reasons for admission
   - assessment of needs, with reference to development, education and health, and behaviour
   - care plan and programmes of intervention
   - summary notes of medical examinations, ongoing health problems, routine medication, diagnosis and treatment for episodes of acute injury or illness, referral to specialists
   - psychological and psychiatric reports
   - accidents
   - education reports
   - social work reports
   - mobility and leave arrangements
   - complaints and their outcome
   - use of measures of control (including the use of a single locked room)
   - arrangements for throughcare and aftercare
   - reasons for discharge
   - place to which discharged.

Appendix G

Children (Scotland) Act 1995 Regulations and Guidance, Children Looked After by Local Authorities, Volume 2, Chapter 4 (Residential Care): Excerpt

Annex: Statement of functions and objectives should detail the following arrangements for children's residential establishments:

- providing information about life in the establishment to children and parents prior to admission or as soon as possible following admission
- defining the child's rights and responsibilities
- identifying appropriate relationships between children and staff
- taking account of the needs, including any special needs, and wishes of each child
- safeguarding the physical care of children
- education and healthcare, including the provision of a healthy lifestyle
- assisting each child to develop their potential
- involving children and parents in decisions about the child's future

- reviewing and evaluating the support and development of children within the establishment
- ensuring that each child's religious persuasion, racial origins, cultural and linguistic background are given proper regard
- sanctions relating to the control of children
- protecting children
- dealing with unauthorised absences
- involving children in decisions about daily living
- creating opportunities for children to use local community facilities
- dealing with complaints from children and parents
- record keeping
- visits by relatives and friends
- recruiting, supervising and training staff
- deploying and using staff to fulfil the responsibilities of the establishment effectively and efficiently
- fire precautions and alarm tests
- meeting health and safety requirements
- throughcare, including aftercare
- consulting children and staff in preparing and reviewing the statement of functions and objectives
- identifying the functions and role of external managers.

Appendix H

Code of Practice on Records Management (2003) Excerpt[130]

What is records management?
Records management is the systematic control of an organisation's records, throughout their life cycle, in order to meet operational business needs, statutory and fiscal requirements, and community expectations. Effective management of corporate information allows fast, accurate and reliable access to records, ensuring the timely destruction of redundant information and the identification and protection of vital and historically important records.

Why is records management necessary?
Information is every organisation's most basic and essential asset, and in common with any other business asset, recorded information requires effective management. Records management ensures information can be accessed easily, can be destroyed routinely when no longer needed, and enables organisations not only to function on a day to day basis, but also to fulfil legal and financial requirements. The preservation of the records of government for example, ensures it can be held accountable for its actions, that society can trace the evolution of policy in historical terms, and allows access to an important resource for future decision making.

Legislation is increasingly underlining the importance of good records management, in addition to being sound business practice. Compliance with Acts such as Freedom of Information and Data Protection is underpinned by effective records management: without properly organised and retrievable records, requests for information governed by statutory response timescales will be impossible to service. Indeed, section 61 of the Freedom of Information (Scotland) Act 2002 is the 'Code of practice as to the keeping, management and destruction of records'.

Organisations are also producing increasingly large amounts of information and consequently greater volumes of records, in both paper and electronic form. It is essential that information is

---

captured, managed and preserved in an organised system that maintains its integrity and authenticity. Records management facilitates control over the volume of records produced through the use of disposal schedules, which detail the time period for which different types of record should be retained by an organisation.

The growth in electronic communications and data, from emails to databases, presents new challenges, but can be managed by the same records management principles that are applied to paper documents. Sound records management is also an essential basis for the transition to EDRM (Electronic Document and Records Management) that many organisations are embracing. In the public sector this has been driven in part by E-government targets, where public services are to be made available electronically. Where existing paper based systems are poorly managed, current problems will simply be migrated to a new electronic system unless they are addressed in the preparations for EDRM.

Modern society has rising expectations concerning the accessibility of information. People now expect efficient and speedy responses to requests for information, and a policy of 'open government' has been followed and developed by several successive governments.

The benefits of records management
Systematic management of records allows organisations to:
- know what records they have, and locate them easily
- increase efficiency and effectiveness
- make savings in administration costs, both in staff time and storage
- support decision making
- be accountable
- achieve business objectives and targets
- provide continuity in the event of a disaster
- meet legislative and regulatory requirements, particularly as laid down by the Freedom of Information (Scotland) Act and the Data Protection Act
- protect the interests of employees, clients and stakeholders

Records management offers tangible benefits to organisations, from economic good practice in reducing storage costs of documents, to enabling legislative requirements to be met. An unmanaged record system makes the performance of duties more difficult, costs organisations time, money and resources, and makes them vulnerable to security breaches, prosecution and embarrassment. In an unmanaged records environment, up to 10% of staff time is spent looking for information.

The dangers of corrupted records management have been illustrated in recent years through scandals such as those at Enron in the USA, which involved the destruction of vital records. Poor records management, with the unintentional loss of documents, has caused embarrassment to organisations from government departments to small businesses.

The importance of records can be put in context by events in South Africa where records of the proceedings of the Truth and Reconciliation Commission's hearing against President Botha about his actions during the period of apartheid have been destroyed, and therefore details of this historically important event lost forever in their original form.

The principles of good records management
The guiding principle of records management is to ensure that information is available when and where it is needed, in an organised and efficient manner, and in a well maintained

environment. Organisations must ensure that their records are:

Authentic
It must be possible to prove that records are what they purport to be and who created them, by keeping a record of their management through time. Where information is later added to an existing document within a record, the added information must be signed and dated. With electronic records, changes and additions must be identifiable through audit trails.

Accurate
Records must accurately reflect the transactions that they document.

Accessible
Records must be readily available when needed.

Complete
Records must be sufficient in content, context and structure to reconstruct the relevant activities and transactions that they document.

Comprehensive
Records must document the complete range of an organisation's business.

Compliant
Records must comply with any record keeping requirements resulting from legislation, audit rules and other relevant regulations.

Effective
Records must be maintained for specific purposes and the information contained in them must meet those purposes. Records will be identified and linked to the business process to which they are related.

Secure
Records must be securely maintained to prevent unauthorised access, alteration, damage or removal. They must be stored in a secure environment, the degree of security reflecting the sensitivity and importance of the contents. Where records are migrated across changes in technology, the evidence preserved must remain authentic and accurate.

The definition of "document" and "record"
In records management it is important to be clear about the difference between a document and a record.

A document is any piece of written information in any form, produced or received by an organisation or person. It can include databases, website, email messages, word and excel files, letters, and memos. Some of these documents will be ephemeral or of very short-term value and should never end up in a records management system (such as invitations to lunch).

Some documents will need to be kept as evidence of business transactions, routine activities or as a result of legal obligations, such as policy documents. These should be placed into an official filing system and at this point, they become official records. In other words, all records start off as documents, but not all documents will ultimately become records.

Appendix I

Local authorities: Challenges to locating records

The following summarises responses from local authorities about the challenges they faced when searching for information to inform the review's work:

1. There were "difficulties of establishing the information required" due to the questionnaire's time period, which covers the "lifespan of four local authorities".

2. One local authority stated that '..the archive for [x] City Council can find no record of files relating to the Children's Officer for the former Corporation of [x]. Information relating to Social Work matters transferred to [y] Regional Council, when that body started its work. [y] Regional Council did not have an archive service for Social Work files (other than individual case files) and there was no centralised storage of information. When [y] Regional Council was abolished in 1996, no information which could be classed as centralised filing was transferred to [x] City Council, merely the personal case records of the service users for whom [x] City Council undertook responsibility. Any information that was retained from [y] Regional Council should, therefore, be in the [z] Council archive, although investigations have proved that this appears not to be the case.'

3. One local authority need to work '...on this (questionnaire) with colleagues in [x] City to jointly pull together as much information as we could."

4. The local authorities' reorganisation in 1996 means that one local authority doesn't have any information the review is requesting. '[The regional authority]... was divided up and children's files, for example, went to the district where the children lived...they aren't sure what happened to all the other files with the reorganisation. [s] Council may have retained a number of files that are archived in the office (as per structures and system) – for the old [t] Region. All the local authorities will have the same problem identifying whether the info exists and, if it does, where it's located.

5. One local authority stated they inherited policy and procedures, in 1996, which they have amended and altered to suit their smaller local authority. ... didn't think they kept any information about old policies and procedures as they made changes.

6. While expectations existed for record-keeping, often those expectations weren't met and there is nothing at all that exists in relation to residential establishments.

7. There's a voluntary agency in the local authority area that provided residential services to young people... they were approached by adults making claims of past residential historical abuse but no records exist or were found pertaining to the place where they lived.

8. One local authority used council minutes as a source of information about the opening and closure of Children's homes. The minutes also record the placement of children by the Education Department... it would appear that the care element at local authority level was not looked at all.

9. One local authority noted there were difficulties retrieving information from the archives. 'I would also make the initial comment that [q] City Archives transferred to [r] Archives and to [p] Archives all historical local government records which vested in them in April 1996. As lead authority it retains the signed copies of minutes from [o] Regional Council. It holds on deposit, for preservation, historical records of the [q]

Orphan Institution, of which the successor body is the [n] Trust, and I will consult with the [n] Trust about any composite return that that Trust will send to you. [q] City Archives hold on deposit, for preservation, fragmentary records of the former two List D schools in [q]. As both the two institutions were wound up with no successor bodies and as the depositing agents... no longer have an office in [q], the ownership of these records is unclear. What is clear is that neither these two institutions nor their records actually vest into [q] City Council.'

10. Prior to reorganisation, the local authorities had a different structure, making it difficult to respond to the periods 1950-1969 and 1979-1985...for [b] it may not be possible to tell where the records are, possibly the [t] (old regional) archives but is using the [c] archivist to assist...as to inspection records, doesn't know where they are.

11. One local authority stated they don't know where the other reports are located... maybe the [t] (old regional) archives... other reports should be located i.e. maybe... some other organisation.

12. One local authority stated they wouldn't hold historical individual files in the social work dept, if they are 'dead' (files) the 'degree of sophistication' of the local archivists will determine as to what happens to them.

13. One local authority stated have no records in the archives... (our contact) is not aware of any case files held by Social Work, but will check that there aren't any which were transferred at reorganisation but have since been overlooked.

14. One local authority made reference to three major administration changes; the first administration operated 1950-1975, the second between 1975-1995 and the current between 1995-Present. 'There is nothing in our council's archives relating to children's homes/units in the current [d] Area...Any records for these establishments may be held in the former[t](old regional) archives, alternatively it is possible these establishments were run by church or voluntary organisations who may have records.'

15. '...the retention of detailed records in regard to policy and procedures was patchy for the period you are interested in and also with the change in Local Authority boundaries different decisions would have been made about the culling of records.' ... individual files from the 1930's onwards are held in their archive but states '...the further back you go the records are likely to be less detailed' When asked if there are any management records for children's residential establishments which remain open and pre-date 1996, the response was 'not to my knowledge.'

16. '...for the period 1950-1969...it does not appear that other records pertaining to these establishments have been retained and I cannot, therefore, provide the detailed information that you are looking for in sections 2, 3 and 4 of your questionnaire. It is, therefore, difficult to confirm what management and other records or systems would have been in place during the period... For the period 1970-1985, there are formal records of Council Committees. However, as above, it does not appear that other records pertaining to sections 2, 3 and 4 of your questionnaire have been retained... For the period 1986-1995...as with the other records time periods noted above, it does not appear that other general management records pertaining to sections 2, 3 and 4 of your questionnaire

have been retained...There are some general records held within our archives section that may provide some information on the areas mentioned in your questionnaire, however, these are not archived in a format that would be easily accessed.'

17. '...social work did not have a broad record retention policy until recently so many management records, for example, may have been held for 10 years after the residential home closure and then destroyed...there was no legal requirement to keep them.'

18. One local authority stated they were trying to find information but there are few records from the earlier years...It is easier to locate info from 1974 onwards...legal advisors for the councils' are asking how councils are supposed to find information to respond to our questionnaire...can't find out what happened to the records when the district became a regional council...the council does not have an archive system...a lot of records were destroyed recently 'due to the 75 year cut-off'...

19. One local authority stated that '...it will take some time to gather the information [because] this local authority did not exist before 1996 and within the timescale, to which you refer...'

20. One local authority stated '...records relating to this period have been largely destroyed although some individual client files of children who lived in the Children's Homes still exist. However, anecdotal evidence gathered from present and past staff connected with the Home, allows me to confirm that no former resident has come back to us as an adult to make a claim of historical abuse.'

21. One local authority stated '...we have very limited material that can help you apart from having children's personnel records. There is some ancillary material relating to children such as Log Books, Register of Guardians, etc. which I have included on the questionnaire. We are currently investigating archived material and if we are successful in locating material of interest we will contact you again...the transfer of records at the time of handover from [f Regional Council] to [g Council] was very patchy.'

22. One local authority stated that '...even the identification of resources available from 1950 onwards would require a major investigation of archived material, with the likelihood that even if this was done the information would not necessarily be accurate.'

Appendix J

Former resident submission

A **former resident** of a children's home submitted these **recommendations** to the Historical Abuse Systemic Review:

1. "Files for children in care need to be placed in a high security control bank, to be accessed only on the authority of former in care children. A board should be set up of qualified people with experience in child welfare with a Board chairperson to give the final authority if police or social services require access. The Board could be set up with a minimum of bureaucratic red tape but with a set of absolute criteria which has to be met before access is allowed."

2. "People today working with children in care should never be allowed background knowledge of the child; children's files have been the breakdown of the child care system. These are very sensitive documents and should be treated as such."

3. "Workers and supervisors need to be trained to understand that a 'child in care's records' is often the only connection that the child has to memories of family members and when files are lost or tampered with, so too are the memories and history of that child. Also at times whilst the child is in care they should be kept up to date when serious circumstances arise within their family."

4. "Where at all possible several weeks should be allowed before release so that trained professional can go over the child's records with him/her in a compassionate manner so that the child is aware of why he/she was placed in care, what the family circumstances were at that time. Where parents and siblings will be at the time of release and whether there will be a welcome for a child into an extended family. If not, why not, if the professional knows, the professional should be aware of all facts of that child's life and help the child be prepared for every facet of the new life. Time must be allowed for children to absorb details that if learned later in life could be devastating."

5. "Weeks before a child leaves care, a professional should cover everything in the child's record, such as things in the child's background the child should be familiar with. It should be emphasised that the child was no way at fault for being placed in care. If a child gets upset about information in their records, they need to understand that getting upset is a normal reaction to information about one's background and family. Preparing a child in a compassionate manner to deal with emotional issues is probably the best thing a child in care specialist can do."

Appendix K

Survivor organisation submission

The following **recommendations about records** were submitted to the review by **a survivor's organisation**, representing the views of adults abused as children in residential establishments:

1. "That care organisations...respect that we are all adults now and can make informed choices for ourselves such as (we do not considerate or regard it appropriate for current [care organisation] employees to sit with you when you receive your file as they currently do in [a care organisation]. Many former children of [a care organisation] have raised concerns regards this current [care organisation's] practice."

2. "Clients should be given a choice about who they wish to help and support them. It's not for the organisation or the institution to decide, we are now adults with capacity and can make informed choices."

3. "Independent advocacy is required if there is any dispute raised with regards the record by any former child."

4. "Former children who have had convictions upheld against ex-employees in the Courts. These children's records/files are of particular sensitive nature and should be dealt with

another independent organisation all together not the organisation where the former resident was abused."

5. "All records are protected in law and as such should be treated as such and stored, retained and accessible for former residents appropriately out with the care organisation to prevent contamination or tampering of records."

6. "All Historical records are dealt with by an Independent regulator who is governed under the full auspices of the Law."

7. "All access by any individual without exception is signed for and permission and consent sought from former children prior to facilitating access, except where it is required by law. Permission, access and consent should be at the heart of any policy concerning former children."

8. "Policies and procedures concerning Children's Confidential Files which are protected in law are enshrined in law and legislation enacted to re-enforce this position. **(If necessary introduce legislation about what should be retained for the future)** Organisations are independently regulated and audited accordingly if they retain control over historical records."

9. "The law as it currently stands allows for a note to be put on a file/record where there is a dispute concerning its accuracy under the Data Protection Act 1998."

10. "All organisations and institutions must facilitate this as part of the purposes for all former children or their legal representative if anyone wishes such a note placed in their record/file as permitted in law under the Data Protection Act 1998. This is especially so in the cases of ex-employees convicted of abusing that child. It is the only true and accurate record pertaining to that child, organisation and ex-employee."

11. "All children in-care are given a copy [of their file] when they leave an institution when they become eligible at 18 years old. And that this is signed for and that any support and help is provided such as counselling at this point also."

12. "No ex-employees are permitted to have access to records or files in any official or non-official capacity such as Archivist or any other such position voluntary or non-voluntary at any time once they have terminated their employment with the institution or care organisation. This will prevent possible interference, contamination and tampering of records and files."

Appendix 4

Recommendation 6

Appendix 4

Recommendation 6

To establish a national records working group to address issues specific to children's historical residential services records. This working group should consist of all relevant stakeholders and may include – but should not be restricted to – former residents, archivists, records managers, social historians, information technology specialists and persons representing social services, education, health and law. This working group should be led by an independent person, or group, with knowledge of records legislation. The terms of reference might include:

- leading an initiative to ensure that all significant historical records associated with children's residential services are identified, catalogued and preserved;
- identifying records associated with children's residential services, including public and privately held records, for placement on a records retention and disposal schedule;
- developing standards and guidance specific to records associated with children's residential services;
- identifying what records associated with children's residential services may be considered sensitive and developing guidelines on the management of such records;
- developing a model 'access to records' policy that recognise the particular needs of former residents;
- developing and instituting processes for regular evaluation and monitoring of record management practices for records identified as significant for protecting children and monitoring their safety, promoting children's well-being and contributing to their sense of identity;
- developing standards and guidance to protect the integrity of records, particularly those children's residential services records that may be required for evidence in future inquiries, court proceedings, or both of these;
- developing records transfer standards and guidance for records generated within children's residential establishments; and
- advising government and administering authorities on matters affecting children's residential services records preservation, such as electronic record-keeping.

Appendix 5

References

Appendix 5

References

Abrams, L (1998) *The Orphan Country: Children of Scotland's Broken Homes from 1845 to the Present Day* Edinburgh: John Donald

Anthony J. (1958) in 'Other People's Children' in Todd R.J.N. (1968) *Children in Care*, London and Harlow: Longmans, Green & Co.

Archard, D (1993) *Rights and Childhood* London: Routledge

Asquith, S (1983) *Children and Justice: Decision making in Children's Hearings and Juvenile Courts Edinburgh*: Edinburgh University Press

Asquith, S (ed) (1993) *Protecting Children: Cleveland to Orkney: More Lessons to Learn?* Edinburgh: Children in Scotland

Asquith, S (ed) (1995) *The Kilbrandon Report – Children and Young Persons, Scotland* (Cmnd 2306)

Australian Senate; *Forgotten Australians*; Commonwealth of Australia; August 2004

Ball, C (1998) Regulating child care: from the Children Act 1948 to the present day *Child and Family Social Work*, 1998. 3 pp163-171

Berridge, D. and Brodie, I. (1998) Children's Homes Revisited, London: Jessica Kingsley.

Berry, J. (1975) *Daily Experience in Residential Life*, London: Routledge and Keegan Paul.

Bibby, P. (ed.) 1996 *Organised Abuse The Current Debate*, Aldershot: Arena.

Black, A. and Williams, C. (2002) *Fife Council Independent Enquiry Established By The Chief Executive Following The Conviction of David Logan Murphy For The Sexual Abuse Of Children*, Kirklady : Fife Council.

Bone, TR; *School Inspection in Scotland 1840-1966*; University of London Press 1968

Bowlby, J. (1951) *Maternal Care and Mental Health*, Geneva: World Health Organisation.

Clelland, Alison and Sutherland, Elaine; from the Stair Memorial Encyclopedia *The Laws of Scotland: Child and Family Law*

Clough, R. (1982) *Residential Work*, Basingstoke and London: Macmillan.

Colton, M, Vanstone, M and Walby, C (2002) Victimization, Care and Justice: Reflections on the Experiences of Victims/Survivors Involved in Large-scale Historical Investigations of Child Sexual Abuse in Residential Institutions. *British Journal of Social Work* 32, 541-551

Colton, M. (2002). Factors associated with abuse in residential child care institutions, *Children & Society*, 16(1), 33-44.

Corby, B., Doig, A. & Roberts, V. (2001) *Public Inquiries into Abuse of Children in Residential Care*, London : Jessica Kinglsey.

Creighton, S. J. (1992) *Child Abuse Trends in England and Wales 1988 – 90*, London : NSPCC.

Crimmens, D. and Milligan, I. (2005). Residential Child Care : Becoming a Postive Choice. In Crimmens, D and Milligan, I. (eds.) (2005) *Facing forward: Residential child care in the 21st Century* (pp. 19 28). Lyme Regis: Russell House Publishing.

Cunningham, H (2006) *The Invention of Childhood* London: BBC Books

Davis, L. F. (1980) 'Sex and the residential setting' in Residential Care, A Reader in Current Theory and Practice (ed.) Walton, R.G. & Elliott, D. (1980), Oxford : Pergamon.

Directors of Social Work in Scotland (1992) *Child Protection – Policy, Practice and Procedure*, Edinburgh: HMSO.

Doran, C. and Brannan, C. (1996) Institutional abuse, in Bibby, P. (ed) *Organised Abuse: The Current Debate*, Aldershot: Arena, pp. 155-166.

Dunford, John E; Her *Majesty's Inspectorate of Schools Since 1944: Standard Bearers of Turbulent Priests?*; Woburn Press 1998

Durkin, R. (1982a) Institutional child abuse from a family systems perspective: a working paper, *Child & Youth Services*, Vol 4 Nos 1-2, pp.109-113

Foucault, M. (1979). *Discipline and punish: The birth of the prison*. Harmondsworth: Penguin.

Foley, P (2001) The Development of Child Health and Welfare Services in England (1900-1948) in P Foley, J, Roche and S, Tucker (eds) *Children in Society: Contemporary Theory, Policy and Practice* Basingstoke: Palgrave

Franklin, B (1986) *Children's Rights* Oxford: Blackwell

Frost, N. and Stein, M. (1989) *The Politics of Child Welfare: Inequality, Power and Change* Hemel Hempstead: Harvestor Wheatsheaf.

Frost, N., Mills, S. & Stein, M. (1999) *Understanding Residential Child Care*, Aldershot: Ashgate.

Fox Harding, L (1997) *Perspectives in Child Care Policy* London: Longman

Gallagher, B. (2000) 'The Extent and Nature of Known Cases of Institutional Child Sexual Abuse' in BJSW (2000) 30, 795-817.

Gil, D. G. (1970) *Violence Against Children: Physical Child Abuse in the United States*, Cambridge : Harvard University Press.

Gil, E. and Baxter, K. (1979) Abuse of children in institutions, *Child Abuse & Neglect*, Vol 3, pp. 693-698

Gil, E. (1982) Institutional abuse of children in out-of-home care, *Child & Youth Services*, Vol 4 Nos 1-2, pp. 7-13. (USA)

Gill, A. (1998) *Orphans of the Empire: the shocking story of child migration to Australia*, Sydney: Random House.

Goffman, E. (1961) *Asylum; Essays on the Social Situation of Mental Patients and Other Inmates*, New York : Doubleday.

Hendrick, H. (1997) *Children, Childhood and English Society* 1880-1990 Cambridge: Cambridge University Press.

Hendrick, H. (2003) *Child Welfare: Historical dimensions, contemporary debate*, Bristol: The Policy Press.

Henry, R. (1965) 'The Man in Residential Care' in *Annual Review of the Residential Child Care Association, Change and the Child in Care*, Harpenden : National Children's Home.

Heywood, J (1959) *Children in Care: the development of the service for the deprived child* London: Routledge and Kegan Paul

Hill, M; Murray, K and Tisdall, K (1998) Children and their Families. In English, J (ed) *Social Services in Scotland* Edinburgh: Mercat Press

Hughes, W.H. (1986) *Report of the Inquiry into Children's Homes and Hostels*, Belfast: HMSO

Holman, R (1988) *Putting Families First: Prevention and Child Care* Basingstoke: Macmillan Education

Holman, B. (1996) The Corporate Parent, Manchester Children's Department 1948-1971, London : National Institute of Social Work.

House of Commons Social Services Committee (1984). *Children in care, Government response to the Second Report from the Social Services Committee*, Session 1983-4. London: HMSO.

Kahan, B. (2000) "Residential Child Care After Waterhouse", Accessed at http://www.childrenuk.co.uk/chukmar/mar2000/bkspeech.htm on 19 October, 2007.

Kendrick, A. and Fraser, A. (1992) *The review of residential child care in Scotland: a literature review', in The Review of Residential Child Care in Scotland: The Three Supporting Research Studies*, Central Research Unit Papers, Edinburgh: Scottish Office.

Kendrick, A. (1997) 'Safeguarding Children Living Away from Home from Abuse: A Literature Review' in Kent, R. (1997) *Children's Safeguards Review*, Edinburgh : HMSO.

Kent, R. (1997) *Children's Safeguards Review*, Edinburgh : HMSO.

Levy, A. and Kahan, B. (1991) *The Pindown Experience and the Protection of Children: The Report of the Staffordshire Child Care Inquiry*, Stafford: Staffordshire County Council.

Kirkwood, A. (1993) *The Leicestershire Inquiry 1992*, Leicester, Leicestershire County Council.

Lockyer A and Stone F (1998) *Juvenile Justice in Scotland: Twenty-five years of the Welfare Approach* Edinburgh: T & T Clark

Lothian and Borders Police, The City of Edinburgh Council, West Lothian Council, East Lothian Council, Midlothian Council, Scottish Borders Council (2001) *Joint Police/Social Work Protocol on the Management and Conduct of Enquiries into Allegations of Historic Abuse*, Edinburgh: The City of Edinburgh Council.

Magnusson, A. (1984) *The Village: A History of Quarrier's*, Bridge of Weir : Quarrier's Homes.

Marshall, K., Jamieson, C. & Finlayson, A (1999) *Edinburgh's Children : The Report of the Edinburgh Inquiry into Abuse and Protection of Children in Care*, City of Edinburgh Council.

Mayall, B (2006) Values and Assumptions Underpinning Policy for Children and Young People in England. *Children's Geographies*, Vol. 4, No. 1, 9-17, April 2006

McNair, Henry S (1968) *A Survey of Children in Residential Schools for the Maludjusted in Scotland*; Published for Moray House College of Education by Oliver & Boyd

Milligan, I. (2006) in Mainey, A., Milligan, I., Campbell, A., Colton, M., Roberts, S. & Crimmens, D. 'The Context of residential care in the United Kingdom.' in Mainey, A. & Crimmens, D. (eds) (2006), *Fit for the future: residential child care in the United Kingdom*, 6-22, London: National Children's Bureau.

Murphy, J (1992) British Social Services: *The Scottish Dimension*, Edinburgh: Scottish Academic Press

Murray, K (1983) Children's Hearings. English, J and F.M. Martin (eds) 2nd edn. *Social Services in Scotland*

Murray, K and Hill, M (1991) The recent history of Scottish child welfare, *Children & Society* (1991) 5:3, 266-281

Newson. J and Newson, E (1965) *Patterns of Infant Care in an Urban Community* Harmondsworth: Penguin

Newson, J. & Newson, E (1989) *The extent of parental physical punishment in the UK*. London: Approach

Packman, J (1981) 2nd ed *The Child's Generation: Child Care Policy in Britain*, 2nd edn. Oxford, Basil Blackwell Ltd

Page, R. and Clark, G.A. (eds) (1977) *Who Cares? Young People in Care Speak Out*, London: National Children's Bureau.

Parton, N (1979) The Natural History of Child Abuse: A Study in Social Problem Definition *British Journal of Social Work* 1979 9: 431-451

Parton, N (1985) *The Politics of Child Abuse* Basingstoke: Macmillan Education

Parton, N (2006) *Safeguarding childhood*, Palgrave Macmillan: Basingstoke

Siskind, A.B. (1986) Issues in Institutional Child Sexual Abuse: The Abused, the Abuser and the System, *Residential Treatment for Children & Youth*, 4, 9-30.

Skinner, A. (1992) *Another Kind of Home: A Review of*

Residential Child Care, Edinburgh: The Scottish Office.

Smout, T.C (1987) *A Century of the Scottish People* 1830-1950 London: Fontana

Stanely N. (1999) 'The institutional abuse of children' in Stanley, N, Manthorpe J & Penhale B (eds) (1999) *Institutional Abuse: Perspectives Across the life course*, London : Routledge.

Stein, M (2006) Missing years of abuse in children's homes. *Child and Family Social Work 2006*, 11, pp 11-21

Stevenson, O (1998) 'It was more difficult than we thought: a reflection on 50 years of child welfare practice'. *Child and Family Social Work*, 1998, pp 153-161

Stewart, J (2001) 'The Most Precious Asset of a Nation is Its Children': The Clyde Committee on Homeless Children in Scotland', *Scottish Economic and Social History*, 21, 1

Stewart, J and Welshman, J (2006) The evacuation of Children in wartime Scotland: Culture, Behaviour and Poverty, *Journal of Scottish Historical Studies*, 26.1+2, 2006, 100-120

Triseliotis J. (1988) 'Residential Care From a Historical and Research Perspective' in Wilkinson J.E. & O'Hara G. *Our Children: Residential and Community Care*, London : National Children's Bureau Scottish Group.

Sullivan, J. and Beech, A. (2002) Professional Perpetrators: Sex Offenders who Use their Employment to Target and Sexually Abuse the Children with Whom They Work. *Child Abuse Review*. Vol. 11, pp. 153-167.

Utting, W. (1991) *Children in the Public Care: A Review of Residential Child Care*, London: HMSO.

Waterhouse, R. (2000) *Report of the Tribunal of Enquiry into the abuse of children in care in the former county council areas of Gwynedd and Clwyd since 1974,* London : HMSO.

Wills, D.W. (1971) Spare the Child, *The Story of an Experimental Approved School,* Harmondsworth : Penguin.

White, K. (1973), *Residential Child Care Past and Present*, MPhil Thesis, University of Edinburgh

Appendix 6

Glossary